"Readers fulfill at least the following roles: (1) introduce a prolific thinker to new audiences in one place; (2) cover the gamut of such a thinker's oeuvre in ways that enable comparative and analytical perspective on the parts in relationship to the whole and vice-versa; and (3) provide a vista for the evolution of an important and influential set of ideas vis-à-vis the shifting contexts being navigated. *God and Gravity* meets these objectives, in particular situating Philip Clayton's three-decades-plus engagement with the science-and-theology conversation against what manifests gradually as a triadic backdrop that includes the emerging church grappling with developments in the theological academy and the field of philosophy of science. Those new to the intersection of these three spheres seeking orientation will benefit from this volume even as it serves as a handy reference for seasoned scholars and theologians wishing to engage Clayton's achievements."

—**Amos Yong**, Fuller Theological Seminary, Pasadena, CA

"This new edited collection is without a doubt the most comprehensive and in-depth look into the fascinating work and mind of its author's endeavor to situate primal and important questions about religion and science, evolution, the human mind, ecology, and their theological treatments in search for responding and responsible visions of panentheism in the current context of the pressing issues of and for the future of humanity."

—**Roland Faber**, Claremont School of Theology, Claremont, CA

God and Gravity

God and Gravity

A Philip Clayton Reader on Science and Theology

PHILIP CLAYTON

Edited by
BRADFORD McCALL

CASCADE *Books* • Eugene, Oregon

GOD AND GRAVITY
A Philip Clayton Reader on Science and Theology

Copyright © 2018 Philip Clayton. All rights reserved. Except for brief quotations in critical publications or reviews, no part of this book may be reproduced in any manner without prior written permission from the publisher. Write: Permissions, Wipf and Stock Publishers, 199 W. 8th Ave., Suite 3, Eugene, OR 97401.

Cascade Books
An Imprint of Wipf and Stock Publishers
199 W. 8th Ave., Suite 3
Eugene, OR 97401

www.wipfandstock.com

PAPERBACK ISBN: 978-1-5326-4956-1
HARDCOVER ISBN: 978-1-5326-4957-8
EBOOK ISBN: 978-1-5326-4958-5

Cataloguing-in-Publication data:

Names: Clayton, Philip, 1956–, author. | McCall, Bradford, editor

Title: God and gravity : a Philip Clayton reader on science and theology / Philip Clayton; edited by Bradford McCall.

Description: Eugene, OR: Cascade Books, 2018 | Includes bibliographical references and index.

Identifiers: ISBN 978-1-5326-4956-1 (paperback) | ISBN 978-1-5326-4957-8 (hardcover) | ISBN 978-1-5326-4958-5 (ebook)

Subjects: LCSH: Religion and science | Philosophy and religion | Panentheism | Emergence (Philosophy) | Philosophical theology

Classification: BL240.3 C54 2018 (paperback) | BL240.3 (ebook)

Manufactured in the U.S.A. 08/22/18

Contents

Preface | vii
Editorial Introduction | ix
Practicing Dialogical Theology: An Intellectual Autobiography | xxxiv
Acknowledgements | xlv

PART I. Science & Religion

1 Explanation in Science and Religion | 3
2 Systematic Theology and Postmodernism | 9
3 What Theologians Can and Cannot Learn from Scientific Cosmology | 16
4 On Religion: A Speech to Its Scientifically Cultured Despisers | 25
5 The Basic Question: Science or Religion, or Science and Religion? | 33
6 Science and the World's Religions | 37
7 The Future of Science and Religion | 48

PART II. Science, Faith, & God

8 The Context for Modern Thought about God | 59
9 The Personality of God and the Limits of Philosophy | 67
10 Biology and Purpose: Altruism, Morality, and Human Nature in Evolutionary Perspectives | 74
11 Reason for Doubt | 82
12 The Ultimate Reality | 89
13 Doubt and Belief | 96

PART III. Panentheistic Reflections on Science & Theology

14 Spinoza's One and the Birth of Panentheism | 103
15 Rethinking the Relation of God and the World: Panentheism and the Contribution of Philosophy | 110
16 Panentheism in Metaphysical and Scientific Perspective | 118
17 Panentheism Today: A Constructive Systematic Evaluation | 126

18 Panentheisms East and West | 133
19 "Open Panentheism" and Creation as Kenosis | 138

PART IV. Science & Emergence
20 The Rise and Fall of Reductionism; The Concept of Emergence; The Pre-history of the Emergence Concept; Weak and Strong Emergence | 147
21 Defining Emergence | 156
22 Eight Characteristics of Emergence | 164
23 Emergence in Biology; Emergence in Evolution; Toward an Emergentist Philosophy of Biology | 167
24 Conceptual Foundations of Emergence Theory | 176
25 Emergence from Quantum Physics to Religion | 189
26 Why Emergence Matters: A New Paradigm for Relating the Sciences | 196
27 Theological Reflections on Emergence: From Emergent Nature to the Emerging Church | 204

PART V. Science, Spirit, & Divine Action
28 Scientific Causality, Divine Causality | 215
29 A Panentheistic Theory of Divine Action | 223
30 Natural Law and the Problem of Divine Action: Can Contemporary Theologians Still Affirm That God (Literally) Does Anything? | 230
31 Rethinking Divine Action | 238
32 On Divine and Human Agency: Reflections of a Co-laborer | 246

PART VI. Progressive Theology
33 Things Have Changed, or "Toto, we're not in Kansas Anymore" | 261
34 Why the Answers Must Be Theological | 266
35 Postmodern Believing | 273
36 A Theology of Self-Emptying for the Church | 281
37 Toward a Progressive Theology for Christian Activism | 288
38 Introducing Organic Marxism | 295
39 The Ecology and Praxis of Organic Marxism | 301
40 The Many Faces of Integration: Liberal Faith between Church, Academy, and World | 304

Select Bibliography | 317
Books Written by Philip Clayton | 329
Books Edited by Philip Clayton | 331
Index | 333

Preface

WHEN I ENROLLED IN Regent University's Renewal Studies PhD program in 2006, I was a typical right-wing fundamentalist. Amos Yong, one of my professors at Regent, however, pushed me to become what it was that I previously despised: what I referred to at the time somewhat jokingly—yet somewhat seriously as well—as a "flaming liberal." Indeed, through his leadership, I faced my aversions to Process philosophy and liberal Christianity.

Yong orchestrated a doctoral "Science and Spirit" seminar in the summer of 2007, sponsored and funded by the Templeton Foundation. It was attended by only a handful of select students but headlined by numerous top-notch academics and a stellar reading list. One of the speakers at that conference was Philip Clayton. The preparatory reading for this seminar included Clayton's seminal text entitled *Mind & Emergence: From Quantum to Consciousness* (2004). It was my first intellectual interaction with Clayton, if I am not mistaken. Fortunately in retrospect, I went well beyond the required reading for the course. It was a tumultuous intellectual time for me, based in part on my consumption of Claytonian texts. Indeed, a whole panoply of new horizons opened up to me by feeding upon his writings. I got enamored with his *God and Contemporary Science* (1997); was enlightened by his and Peacocke's *In Whom We Live and Move and Have Our Being: Panentheistic Reflections on God's Presence in a Scientific World* (2004); and was energized by his and Paul Davies' *The Re-Emergence of Emergence: The Emergentist Hypothesis from Science to Religion* (2006). All of these made my supplementary reading list, and in short order I was a card-toting Panentheistic Emergentist.

From my current perspective and not at all intentionally as I wrote, the concepts of panentheism and emergence have formed the basis of my writings over the past decade, due in no small part to the exposure to Clayton in the summer of 2007. Yong also setup a one-on-one meeting of about thirty minutes between Clayton and me during one of the final days of the seminar. I treasured that occasion with Clayton at the time—and continue to treasure it today too—and in fact remember ruminating on my first-hand access to a mover-and-shaker within the science and religion conversation. I thought I had truly "arrived." Little did I know at that time that I would have innumerable further meetings with Clayton in the ensuing years as I study under him at Claremont School of Theology. If the ensuing decade is as profitable to me as the past decade has been, Clayton will have proverbially recreated himself. I do not say that lightly.

In Germany, a person's doctoral mentor is referred to as his *doktorvater*. If one looks at the constitutive parts of this compound German word, one will discover it is made up of two very expressive terms when individually translated: doctor and father, both of which are instructive for additional cogitation. Perhaps only a true father can have a larger impact on a man than his *doktorvater*. In determining to study under a particular person, in Lamarckian fashion, a doctoral student can greatly enhance—or even direct—his own subsequent evolution and development.

I take joy in knowing that I will forever be linked with a man who is not only an intellectual giant, but also a certifiably good person. Clayton knows that he is brilliant. But he is also *comfortable* with that fact. As such, he has a profound peace about him, which is a characteristic wanting in many academics.

Jesus the Christ once gave the command to go forth and make disciples; all teachers, in a sense, make disciples of themselves in the education of those who follow them. Perhaps those Germans have it right after all: a person's doctoral advisor becomes a supplementary father. If so, I have good genes.

Editorial Introduction

Einstein once said that science without religion is lame and religion without science is blind. Philip Clayton, a prominent philosopher in the science and religion dialogue, would entirely agree with that assessment. While not a full-bore process theologian himself, Clayton definitely exhibits strong characteristics of process philosophy thinking in his theologizing. While profiting from process theology, Clayton does not go all the way with them—especially regarding the implications of it to the Godhead. Before getting into Clayton's contributions to the theology and science dialogue, it is perhaps wise to identify and minimally explain the common typology for the relationship between science and theology, as developed and promoted by Ian Barbour in the late twentieth century (cf. *Religion in an Age of Science*). Barbour therein identifies four main positions regarding the relationship between science and religion:

1. There is *conflict* because of a performed commitment to either scientific materialism (e.g., Richard Dawkins, Carl Sagan) or biblical literalism (creationists).

   Creationists maintain that the universe is only thousands of years old, when there is overwhelming evidence of its great antiquity. On the other side, Carl Sagan said "The Cosmos is all that is or ever was or ever will be." Scientific materialists are those with a dogmatic bent toward the idea of reductionism and the notion that science can explain everything in life, be it philosophically-related information or information derived from one of the hard sciences (cf. Richard Dawkins, *The Blind Watchmaker*). Creationists are typically those who argue for a strictly literal interpretation of the book of Genesis and are known colloquially by their advocation of a literal six days of creation and the verity of the Flood (cf. Henry Morris's many monographs on *Genesis* and flood theology).

2. There should be an *independence* between the two because of a preformed commitment to either *contrasting methods* (e.g., Willem Drees; Stephen Jay Gould) or *differing languages of discourse* (Ludwig Wittgenstein; William H. Chalker recently).

The independence model appeals to many scientists and theologians because it gives them freedom to believe and think what they like in their respective fields; however, this strength of the model can also be considered its main weakness, for it compartmentalizes reality. In *Science and Faith,* William H. Chalker stipulates that any perceived conflict within the theology and science dialog is due to a fundamental misunderstanding, for science seeks *utility* in its search for knowledge, whereas theology seeks for *ultimate purposes* in its search for knowledge. According to Chalker, both science and theology have their proper realms—and the two are not to interface. As a result, there is the possibility to have theological truth, as well as scientific truth, even if the two are apparently contradictory (as the theological truth is concerned with the ultimate purpose characterized in the assertion, whereas scientific truth is concerned with the utility and actuality of the assertion).

Chalker therefore suggests that apparent conflict arises only when we discuss science in terms of *ultimate purposes* (i.e., theology's proper rubric), and/or discuss theology in terms of utility (i.e., science's proper rubric). He argues that conflict only occurs when science speaks of ultimate purposes (i.e., religion's domain), or when religion speaks of utility (i.e., science's domain). In arguing against this approach, Barbour writes, "We do not experience life as neatly divided into separate compartments; we experience it in wholeness and interconnectedness before we develop particular disciplines to study different aspects of it."[1]

3. Some *dialogue* is possible about *methodological parallels* (e.g., scientist/theologians Alister McGrath, John Polkinghorne, Christopher B. Kaiser, and theologian Hans Küng).

The dialogue model finds support from scholars who realize that scientific study is not as objective as once thought. Both science and theology involve personal judgment, and both deal with data that is "theory laden." Barbour himself favors this dialogue approach to science and theology, especially because of its multi-level approach to reality. Scientist/theologian Alister McGrath argues that any methodological parallels between science and theology should not imply that we have to make either field of study subservient to the other, but that we should expect to find similar complexities of concepts and even paradoxes in both. Nature, according to McGrath, is to be seen as an "open secret"[2] in that it is a publicly accessed entity, although it is only truly understood from the standpoint of Christian faith. As such, McGrath affirms the notion that the empirical is a legitimate means of discovering and encountering the divine. Indeed, McGrath's approach to natural theology holds that nature reinforces an existing belief in God retroactively through consonance between observation and theory.

1. Barbour, *Religion in an Age of Science,* 16.
2. McGrath, *The Open Secret.*

Similarly, scientist/theologian Christopher B. Kaiser, *Toward a Theology of Scientific Endeavour*, notes that theological discourse will be necessarily challenged and illuminated by interaction with the scientific endeavor. In view of such, the work of scientists can be seen as a stimulus rather than a threat to theological discourse. Kaiser posits that a "thick" natural science leads to a "thick" description of God, humanity, history, and nature itself. He highlights the fact that theology is embedded not only within one's life and work, but also within the scientific endeavor itself.

In arguing for an idea related to dialogue, ecumenical Catholic theologian Hans Küng, in *The Beginning of All Things,* notes that science and theology may seem to clash and be exclusive, but they are in fact *consonant* with one another. Küng avers that the confrontational model for the relationship is out of date, and he also rejects the integrationist model. Küng asserts that postmodern people in our era should attempt to see the book of nature, so to speak, and the book of God as fully complementary. Küng's depiction of the relationship rejects all absolutizing. Moreover, Küng's belief in the Bible does not trump science, for if scientific knowledge is certain and contradicts what the Bible says, that means a new interpretation of the Bible is due. Küng notes that philosophical thought today cannot simply start "from above," but instead must start "from below," informed by human experience of phenomena.

4. The *integration* position can take the form of a *theology of nature* (e.g., scientist/theologian Arthur Peacocke, theologian Wolfhart Pannenberg) or a *systematic synthesis* (e.g., process theologians Philip Clayton, John Haught and John Cobb).

    This model is sometimes called the "mutual support" model, for it highlights the idea that the perfection and variety in nature gives us evidence of God's power and handiwork. Process theologian John B. Cobb thinks the assertion of an independence and/or conflict model is a "myth." Cobb argues for a thorough integration of the two disciplines. Similarly, Lutheran theologian Wolfhart Pannenberg concludes that there is no reason for assuming a fundamental conflict between science and theology. Christian theologians should feel confident in using the science of our day to retell the story of God's creation of the world.

    In fact, since the introduction and acceptance of Big Bang cosmology, Pannenberg claims, the Christian doctrine of a creation of the world by God is much more in "consonance" with scientific cosmology than before. Moreover, he argues that the element of contingency and novelty in the course of natural processes is open to the belief in continuing creation, which may be advocated by viewing God as Spirit that permeates the world in a correlate manner to field theory. Further, with regard to science, Christian theologians should feel confident in using the science of our day to retell the story of God's creation of the world like the Old Testament accounts of the creation used the Babylonian knowledge about the natural world. Pannenberg argues that any sort of "bridge" model needs to be replaced by a model for the relation between the two pictured as "joint." He thinks that theology in this dialogue must take account of science, past revelation contextualized, and world religious perspectives, as well as not being premature to declare consonances between the two.

Clayton's Contributions

Since 1989, Clayton has been publishing material in the science and theology dialogue. In that timeframe, he has become an adherent to what I refer to as panentheistic emergentism. Indeed, it was in that year that he published *Explanation from Physics to Theology*. Seemingly, within this early text by Clayton, he is an advocate of the *dialogue* position with respect to the relationship between science and religion, evidenced by his affinity toward Ernst Mayr (a noted biologist). Therein, Clayton uses Mayr's *The Growth of Biological Thought* (1980) rather extensively. Within this text, Clayton makes note of how Mayr characterizes the concept of emergence. It seems apparent that Clayton's interactions with Mayr caused him to begin ruminating on the idea of emergence more so.

In 1997, Clayton published *God and Contemporary Science*,[3] which solidified his bona fides in theology and science. Indeed, in this book, theologian and philosopher Clayton tackles two of the most urgent questions that shape the constructive dialogue between theology, philosophy, and the natural sciences: how to conceive of God's relation to, and God's agency in, the world as understood by science. As such, Clayton's goal is to examine the doctrines of God, of God's relation to the world, and of God's activity in the world (6). How can one take scientific results seriously and still engage in theological inquiry, Clayton asks (6)? Clayton defends the theses that metaphysical and theological issues are raised by the methods and conclusions of science (7). This endeavor may require revisions to dearly held theological conclusions, but theologians must be intellectually honest with the data (8). Although evolution may be compatible with theology in terms of divine purpose, it does not follow that evolution gives credence to notions of such a purpose (8). Theology equals metaphysics, for science is the organized study of specific data. Science is law-like, predictable, quantifiable, and falsifiable. Two of the most important questions today in theology are God's relation to the world, and his mode of activity (if at all) within it (9).

Finite/infinite is a qualitative distinction, as is contingent/necessary. Finite space is contained within absolute space, much like the world is contained within God, but is not God, as per se (panentheism) (90). The Israelite understanding of humanity is radically monistic and holistic, composed of a single entity with numerous aspects (97), so that the tripartite division of body, soul, and spirit is vacuous. Since humans are *imago dei*, it is natural to assert that the Spirit works in and through the natural

---

3. Unless otherwise noted, parenthetical references refer to this text.

and material world. However, panentheism is better able, Clayton notes (119), to address the problem of divine agency in our contemporary scientific and philosophical context. The question of how to conceive of divine agency in the world is central to the book. Theologically, there are only two possibilities: either a) God does not intervene (because, as everything is perfect, there is no need to do so) or b) God does intervene directly in the world (190). Alternative a) is theologically inadequate because it leads to deism. Alternative b) is inadequate as well because it seems to suggest a divine repairman who is trying to fix all sorts of errors in the created world. Clayton then goes on to distinguish three kinds of divine intervention:

1) general conservation or sustaining (not at odds with natural science, because trans-empirical),

2) psychological interventions (miracles), and

3) physical interventions in the natural world.

The latter kind raises the toughest problem, for if we are to have a full theory, theology must give an account of "where the causal joint is at which God's action directly impacts on the world" (192). Without such a theory, theologians would fail to make sense of their own views. They would also fail in their apologetic task for on any strong naturalist reading divine agency in the world is physically impossible. Deism characterizes creation as self-sufficient, whereas immanentism characterizes creation as deficient.

In the final chapter of *God and Contemporary Science*, Clayton develops the so-called panentheist analogy between the relation of God's body and mind and that between a human person's body and mind. I think he is right in insisting that talk about divine agency must be analogous to the language of human agency. Some theists have criticized the analogy for being far too weak to bear the burden of providing "a guiding framework" for a doctrine of God (260). The analogy is not meant to found anything but to enable us to talk about the human mind as dependent on the world in a different sense than the divine mind. Since Clayton explicates the difference (by appeal to the dipolarity of the divine nature) quite well, I think the analogy holds its own. Underlying the analogy is a particular view of the body–mind relation, called weak supervenience, a view Clayton prefers to the many philosophical accounts of the body–mind relation on offer (substance dualism, epiphenomenalism, eliminative materialism, functionalism, the "dual aspect theory"). Reinforcing it with the doctrine of emergence and with the notion of "levels of emergence," the result is emergentist supervenience.

With these ideas having been thought-through for well-nigh fifteen years, Clayton published *Mind & Emergence* in 2004. Within it, he offers a cogent defense of the idea of emergence being a viable option, especially in view of the waning explanatory capacity of physicalism and dualism, its main competitors. It would be wise to now speak of physicalism and dualism shortly, in order to have the backdrop of what Clayton is arguing *against*, and thus also to have the basis of what he is arguing *for* in *Mind & Emergence*. Physicalism argues that, in the well-known words of Carl Sagan, nature is all there is, was, or will be; as such, this view is completely reductionistic, meaning that each larger entity is directly explicable to its component part(s); one could typify this thinking by the quasi-popular thought of Richard Dawkins, who says that human bodies are merely "replicators" that exist solely for the promulgation of the genes that in part compose them (*Blind Watchmaker*). Dualism, having a basis in gnostic thought and Neoplatonism, argues, briefly, that there two realities: God and not-God (physical or spiritual). In dualist thought, God, the supreme entity that is spiritual in nature, interacts at his leisure within the physical world. Clayton, as intimated earlier, denies the plausibility and explanatory capacity of both physicalism and dualism.

Before offering his own definition of emergence, Clayton first recounts the classification of emergence theories within the twentieth century: *strong* and *weak*. The *strong* emergentist position can be labeled ontological emergence, whereas the *weak* emergentist position could be aptly labeled as epistemological emergence. Strong emergentists postulate that evolution produces *ontologically* distinct levels of organ/isms which are characterized by their own distinct regularities and causal forces. In opposition, weak emergentists maintain that as new patterns emerge the causal processes remain those that are *fundamental* to known physics. A property of an organ/ism is *weakly* emergent if it is reducible to its intrinsic qualities, so that *weakly* emergent properties are "novel" only at the level of description (*epistemologically*). This contrasts with *strongly* emergent organ/isms in which the cause is *neither* reducible to any intrinsic causal capacity of the parts *nor* to any relation between the component parts.

Clayton notes that in the 1990s *strong* emergence theories resurfaced with great vigor through the rediscovered writings of Michael Polanyi. Whereas I agree with Clayton's critique of Polanyi in that Polanyi *went too far* in reference to finalistic causes in biology, I would like to suggest that instead of the organ/isms being *guided* by the potentialities that are open to it, that they are instead *lured* by the potentialities that are open to it; this concept of *lure* instead of guide would entail the Spirit to be ever-before the evolutionary advancement of organs/isms, *wooing* them toward their eschatological fulfillment in Christ.[4] Perhaps God (the Spirit) "only exercise[d] a continual creative pull towards conscious life while being unable to determine with certainty that life would emerge."[5]

Clayton contends that emergence is the view that evolution in the natural world is marked by the natural production of entities through occurrences that are novel, unpredictable, and non-reducible to what conditions underlie them. The component parts are necessary for the emergence of the property, as the emergent property is

---

4. These statements are reminiscent of Whitehead, who posits that the divine lure is at work since the moment of creation.

5. Cf. Ford, *The Lure of God*.

dependent upon it; however, it is not reducible to it. Clayton delineates eight characteristics of this *strong* emergence, of which I will adapt five for my own purposes *now* and in the *future*: 1) monism, 2) hierarchical complexity, 3) multivariate paths of emergence, 4) recognizable patterns across levels of emergence, and 5) downward causation.

Clayton demonstrates his further thinking about science and theology in other texts, especially with reference to how God could interact with a world that science describes—quite accurately—as autonomous and self-causative. It was during this timeframe that Clayton edited a volume with Arthur Peacocke, entitled *In Whom We Live, Move, and Have Our Being*. This text presents the philosophical case for the notion of panentheism—in short, the notion that God contains the world (and by extension everything in the world) but that he is also greater than the world at the same time (think of concentric circles: the smaller is contained within the larger, yet the smaller is entirely complete in and of itself). The panentheistic position developed therein allows for the relationality of the Godhead to the world, as the world is entirely contained *within* God. Moreover, as a result of this panentheistic relationship, God could perhaps influence the development of evolution in non-interventitive ways. One could argue that with the relationship of the world and God clarified, Clayton could then better approach the topic that had interested him for the previous decade: emergence.

Modern advances in scientific study reveal a vastly more complicated world than the reductionist program of the late nineteenth and twentieth centuries ever envisioned. In the book entitled *The Re-Emergence of Emergence*, Philip Clayton and Paul Davies contend that emergence is a viable option in contrast to the waning explanatory power of *physicalism* and *dualism*, its competitors. No longer can one seek to explain all things as being merely reducible to their physical entities or microphysical causes (i.e., *physicalism*), as *physicalism* is inconsistent with standard research theories and practices within biology. Although substance dualism was probably the dominant metaphysical view in Western history from Aristotle to Kant, one cannot continue to seek to explain all things as being composed of bipartite construction of physical components and spiritual components. Emergence is, in brief, the view that novel and unpredictable occurrences are naturally produced in nature, and that said novel structures, organs, and organisms are not reducible to their component parts.

It seems that panentheism and emergence are the opposite sides of the same proverbial coin, so to speak, regarding Clayton's metaphysics and cosmology. Panentheism attributes all regularity within the world, according to Clayton, to divine intention. It corrects the popular caricature of God as a detached, remotely interested entity; it does this by radicalizing the immanence of God within nature. Clayton argues that his panentheistic perspective allows for him to assert that God energizes and sustains the world from *within*.

While I have above employed the fourfold typology of Barbour in delineating Clayton's thoughts because it is better known, I will note that a typology based on

Editorial Introduction

Mikael Stenmark's work may better locate Clayton's position. Indeed, in his book *How to Relate Science and Religion*,[6] Stenmark denigrates the positions of scientific and religious expansionists, as well scientific and religious restrictionists in dialogue directly with the biological sciences. In a counter proposal, Stenmark avers a construction of the theology and science dialogue that he titles a "multidimensional model." Said multidimensional model entails four different levels, consisting of 1) a social dimension, 2) a teleological dimension, 3) an epistemic dimension, and 4) a theoretical dimension (xvi–xviii).

Stenmark notes that both science and religion are *social* practices, and that therefore we should attempt to understand the socially pertinent structure of each. In fact, Stenmark challenges the popular notion that whereas theology is based upon prior authority, science is based upon strict empirical evidence. In so doing, he establishes the notion that both science and religion rely upon prior authority in nearly equitable terms (cf. 19–20). Moreover, Stenmark acknowledges that both science and religion are *teleologically* governed by the goals of its practitioners in that science attempts to be predictive, whereas theology attempts to be existential (29). Science, then, attempts to understand the *causes* of things, whereas theology attempts to understand the *meanings* of things. However, both theology and science aim at *truth* (31). I affirm that the goals of both science and religion are practical and epistemic (cf. his discussion on 33–35). In addition, I contend that the goals and practices of science and religion are of different kinds (36). Stenmark contends that the goals of science and academic theology are similar in that they both attempt to address collective epistemic goals, personal epistemic goals, collective practical goals, and personal practical goals (43–44). Disagreement about the goals of both religion and science leads to problems about how to achieve these goals as well. So then, teleological distortion leads to methodological distortion, which in turn leads to epistemic distortion.

Third, Stenmark notes that both science and religion have *epistemic* objectives, and that these epistemic objectives need to be analyzed in order to appropriately engage in discourse between the two. Epistemology, in relation to theology and science, is the attempt to understand how belief originates and is regulated within the two disciplines, and what, if any, value said discovery has in relation to humanity's other concerns (cf. 52). Although science is generally considered the paradigm of rationality, both science and religion are descriptive and normative. It is unfortunate that religion has been caricatured as being inferior to science regarding its internal cohesion, comprehensiveness, fruitfulness, and explanatory power. Whereas science (and more so scientism) adheres to a strict empirically-based evidentialism, it is posited that religion does not. In contrast, many untested hypotheses (though they are called "theories") in science, particularly evolutionary biology, are based upon little, if any, hard evidence, and are the conjecture of human minds instead (cf. 57). However, if one would follow this line of thinking to its logical conclusion, Stenmark notes, people

---

6. Parenthetical notations below refer to this book unless otherwise noted.

would be proverbially frozen in fear, for people do not have the time to analyze every single presupposition with which they act in everyday life (cf. 92–93).

Moreover, Stenmark acknowledges that contrary to scientism, and in affirmation of Philip Clayton, the Inference to the Best Explanation (IBE) often adds credence to religious postulations over and above scientific ones (cf. 61). In a tragic observation, Stenmark states that [contrary to popular perception] "scientists seem never to reject a theory no matter how many anomalies there are unless they have a better theory to put in its place" (68). Must religious believers treat their belief in God as a hypothesis? Stenmark emphatically states no, "because for many of them this belief is directly experientially grounded" (78). So then, religious rationality resembles everyday rationality more than scientific rationality does (cf. 103). Indeed, one is logically founded to continue to believe that which they do until there is a specific and special reason to no longer do so (104). Moreover, we should "require stronger reasons for giving up something we believe which has greater depth of concern in our belief-world than for giving up something which plays a more peripheral role" (106). It must be noted that theological/religious rationality is a different breed of animal than is scientific rationality, for the former is an "agent-rationality," whereas the latter is a "spectator-rationality" (111).

A belief in religion is rational insomuch as it is justified and has explanatory power. So then, religion exhibits a rationality that overlaps with and is informed by scientific rationality (114). There are, according to Stenmark, several different reasons for conflict concerning the relation between rationality in science and rationality in religion/theology: 1) There are conflicting concepts of rationality, 2) there are different epistemic norms for religion/theology and science, 3) there are different ideas of the applicability of those epistemic norms in reference to rationality, and 4) there are different types of evidence accepted between religion/theology and science (116–17).

The fourth dimension of the multidimensional model posited by Stenmark concerns the subject matter of both science and religion, and therefore is referred to as the *theoretical* dimension. Stenmark asks if theology/religion and the natural sciences have the same, overlapping (i.e., "similar"), or completely different subject matters (137)? It appears apparent that Clayton—and I as well!—would support the notion that theology/religion and the natural sciences have overlapping subject matters.

Whereas evolutionary biology alone cannot establish that the universe and humans are not here for a reason, evolutionary theory in conjunction with an extra-scientific or a philosophical claim can undermine religious belief (163). Viewed in this way, Stenmark notes that God could have conscious, sentient, free, and self-aware beings in mind when he created the cosmos (through the kenosis of the Spirit *into* creation, I might add). This development of such species was God's goal, Stenmark states, and not necessarily the human species as per se. It seems to be compatible with theism, Stenmark posits in view of this analogy, that our existence is due to chance (166). With this assertion by Stenmark, I am immediately drawn (much like him) to what has been referred to as Molinism, or the middle-knowledge theory of divine foreknowledge.

Stenmark's overall contention throughout said book is that everything one can learn in one area of life from another area of life that can improve cognitive discourse could—and should—be taken into consideration by rational people. Thus, there should not be an a priori exclusion of epistemologies or methodologies between science and religion. In contrast, there should be an explicit overlap between the two (xvii). He concludes that there are in actuality five different perspectives of the relationship between science and theology, which I will modify to seven: 1) the monistic conflict view; 2) the monistic harmony view; 3) the integrationist contact view; 4) the contact dialogue view; 5) the independence view; 6) the complete scientific expansionist view; and 7) the complete religious expansionist view (cf. 259). Clayton would be a sort of ideological expansionist, for he defends a modified form of process theology, thus making him posit an overlapping of the domains of theology and science, in what I have above dubbed the integrationist contact view. Of these seven categories, I would affirm the integrationist contact view (or overlapping) and posit that Clayton would affirm it as well. Clayton would agree with Sweet and Feist (*Religion & the Challenges of Science*), who contend that science maturates religious belief; moreover, the dialogue between science and religion should be one marked by an open-ended compatibility wherein the theological positions therein advocated are open to be revisited, revised, or even reformulated entirely, which is infinitely stronger than Barbour's "dialogue" position.

Preliminary conclusions

In the contemporary dialogue between theology and the natural sciences it has become clear that the pursuit of truth in either discipline requires the candid acknowledgment of one's cultural context and, as far as possible, the identification of one's presuppositions. From a postmodern perspective, I argue that a mutual integration position would be the most fruitful for the relation between science and theology. Within *An Abrahamic Theology for Science*, for example, Kenneth Vaux advocates an Abrahamic theology as the dynamic paradigm for science and technology and argues for its continuing importance for both a pertinent and humane science. Vaux demonstrates a historical correlation between an Abrahamic theological tradition (monotheism) and the rise of science. Vaux's thesis is simple: that theology has grounded, founded, prompted, and promoted science in the past years.

Richard Feist and William Sweet, in *Religion and the Challenges of Science*, seek to answer the question of whether science poses a challenge to religion and religious belief. More specifically, one will find in Sweet and Feist's book the suggestion that religion and science do not offer conflicting truth claims per se, and that science can contribute to a *maturity* of belief to religion. However, this proto-compatibility, as it were, can only be attained by adhering to what Sweet refers to as an "open-ended compatibility," wherein both the claims of science and religion are open to be revisited, revised, and reinterpreted. Clayton would seemingly agree with this position of Feist and Sweet. Similarly, in *The Big Questions in Science and Religion*, Neoplatonist theologian Keith Ward seeks to answer the question of whether religious beliefs can survive in the scientific age. Is there something in religious beliefs of great importance, even if the way they are expressed will have to change given new scientific context? Ward assumes that the scientific account of reality is essentially correct, much like Clayton himself, though subject to revision. Ward notes that virtually all of science has had to be rethought in the twenty-first century, which has carried with it important implications for philosophy and religion. Religious beliefs, Ward asserts, cannot remain pre-modern in a (*post*)modern society, or they will fail to answer the questions of the day, a posit that Clayton would undeniably also aver. The question is then raised, "can theological beliefs survive at all in a scientific age?" Ward contends that they can survive, and in fact thrive, as long as they are modified, a contention with which Clayton would agree.

Overview of this Reader's contents

With the space that remains in this introductory chapter, I would like to give a brief overview of this Reader's contents. I will categorize the entailments of this brief overview with reference to the book's general parts, while indicating the reading number of the topic under discussion. Part I, which is entitled "Science and Religion," is composed of seven distinct readings. We encounter Clayton's first public title—*Explanation from Physics to Theology: An Essay in Rationality and Religion*—and we see that among the various functions of religious belief is explanation. Following standard usage, Clayton uses the term explanans for the account that does the explaining and explanandum for the thing to be explained. He begins reading #1 with the general hypothesis that explanations are answers to why-questions. If someone is asked to explain an action that she has performed, she will tell why she performed it, listing as explanans her reasons, her intentions, or the external forces that constrained her. Or, in order to explain the fact or explanandum, someone will give an account of why he did so, referring to various laws if applicable. Clayton offers herein four central necessary conditions that serve to guide the discussion: 1) external reference; 2) truth; 3) validity; and 4) rationality.

In reading #2, we find Clayton's "Systematic Theology and Postmodernism," as found within *God and Contemporary Science*. In this reading, Clayton explores the postmodern shift in systematic theology. He notes, in part, that the scandal of particularity is past. Why? Because the lofty aspirations of metaphysical reason are now *passe*. So then, the claims of reason to universal validity and its claim to be able to derive important truths from reason alone are now under severe challenge. Diversity is now the name of the game; multiple perspectives are the bottom line; every person and cultural group has his, her, or its particular perspective; and we rejoice in the differences between them all. There is no longer a scandal of particularity in a postmodern age because it is precisely particularity that is being celebrated by postmodern thought. Theology now faces opportunities it has not known in previous centuries. But along with these new opportunities, we must rethink, and re-present, what it *means* to make religious truth claims. For there *is* one particular move that is stigmatized in this contemporary climate: to claim that one's particularity has universal significance.

Reading #3 also comes from *God and Contemporary Science*, entitled "Creation and Cosmology: What Theologians Can and Cannot Learn from Scientific Cosmology." The writings of many recent cosmologists give rise to the strong impression that science is now being used as a metaphor for conveying religious beliefs about spirituality and the rightful place of humanity within the cosmos. At one extreme we find a sort of natural theology: thinkers who argue that science leads to theology. Others hold that contemporary physics supports one particular religious viewpoint. Unfortunately, they disagree as to what it is. The next group of thinkers maintains that science by itself amounts to a sort of religious perspective. Others hold that science supports *multiple* religious perspectives. More metaphysically skeptical are those who find spirituality in or implied by science and its results while resisting making any truth claims on *this* basis. More skeptical still are the advocates of science and theology as two distinct activities that have nothing to do with each other. Finally, others hold that theology is a pure construct, and naturalism represents the best truth we have about the world.

Reading #4 comes from *In Quest of Freedom: The Emergence of Spirit*, and is entitled "On Religion: A Speech to Its Scientifically Cultured Despisers." How do we respond to the despisers today? What do we say? Inwardness precedes the external world and trumps all other concerns; imagination reveals reason's foibles; passion is a prerequisite; and feeling is the vehicle to the deepest insights. All of these faculties and experiences together point toward the interconnection, or the *unity*, of all things. This cannot be a theology of measured restraint, but rather only through one of joyful exuberance. However, when one limits the scope of religion, one loses it altogether. We want to anatomize religion, to give it a specific location—above all, to subsume it under some specific category (to make it psychological, or historical, or anthropological, or ethical, or aesthetic, or metaphysical). But such boundary-drawing is self-refuting. Indeed, to claim to know that there *is* no metaphysical knowledge is itself to make a metaphysical claim. However, religion cannot compete with science on the level of knowledge claims.

The fifth reading comes from *Religion and Science: The Basics*, and is entitled "The Basic Question: Science or Religion, or Science and Religion." Should we talk about "science *and* religion," or should it be "science *versus* religion"? At first blush, theism and naturalism appear to be incompatible positions. Naturalists affirm that all that exists is the universe (or multiverse) and the objects within it, whereas theists claim that something transcends the universe. Naturalists generally use science as their primary standard for what humans know, whereas theists defend other ways of knowing as well, such as intuition or religious experience. Instead of black and white connections, we find a world of complex interconnections, of similarities and differences, of shared partnerships and sometimes conflicting projects.

Reading #6, "Science and the World's Religions," is also found within *Religion and Science* and seeks to bring to light the very different kinds of concern regarding science that are raised across the world's religious traditions. Whereas most readers in the West will implicitly have Christianity in mind when they begin reading a text on religion and science, there is a particular group of recurring topics that tends to set the agenda for debates about Christianity and science: an initial creation "out of nothing" by God; the purpose or directionality to evolution; human uniqueness and the existence of the soul; the question of miracles; the bodily resurrection of Jesus Christ; the possibility of divine revelation; and the Christian concern with signs of the "eschaton." It turns out that radically different concerns arise when religions other than Christianity enter into dialogue with science. Clayton begins with Judaism, in order to show how vastly different from Christianity are the concerns of historical Jewish thought and of contemporary Jewish thinkers. He then moves on to Islam and two of the major Eastern traditions: Hinduism and Buddhism.

Reading #7 focuses upon "The Future of Science and Religion," and is similarly found within *Religion and Science: The Basics*. Contrary to the reports of its impending demise, there has been a resurgence of religious commitment around the world. Religion, then, it appears, is not going away. It as obvious that science is not going away either. That means we have to find some way to deal with the relationship between these two great cultural forces. What are the possible outcomes? It could be that religion is just evil, so that, no matter how long it stays around, it should be opposed. Or perhaps modern science is just wrong. The religions (or major movements within them) may evolve in directions that become increasingly hostile to science. On a more positive level, one can also imagine establishing a (more or less) permanent truce between these two systems of thought. On the other hand, maybe the boundaries won't turn out to be so sharp after all. This essay explores all of these possible outcomes, but determines that as we delve more deeply into the issues, we find more and more reasons to wonder whether matters can really be reduced to a single either/or decision.

The first reading of Part II, reading #8, is entitled "The Context for Modern Thought about God," and it is found within *The Problem of God in Modern Thought*. The context for treating the question of God today must be skepticism. Propositional language about God can no longer pass as unproblematic. The history of reflection in this area is littered with skeletons, or it is immensely difficult to discern which are the skeletons and which the living, progressing models. Even *theologians* today have grown squeamish of the "God's eye point of view," and there are many reasons that the very idea of such a point of view is confused. There is no guarantee that theology pursued in the twenty-first century will finally converge on the results or the methods of traditional theology. Perhaps this theology pursued "from below" will diverge further and further from the traditional language of a transcendent being; perhaps it will come to be subsumed by metaphysics in some sense; or perhaps new and interesting analogies between the theological and metaphysical projects will emerge. Time will tell.

The ninth reading, "The Personality of God and the Limits of Philosophy," is likewise found within *The Problem of God in Modern Thought*. The final corollary of the move from (Spinozistic) infinite object to subject, in addition to freedom, is the personality of God—in however a minimal or attenuated sense. There are two clear conditions that the doctrine of God must satisfy:

1) God as our infinite source cannot be less than we are; God must at least have abilities comparable to ours, even though, as greater, they will be different; and

2) there must be a free decision to create.

Freedom is the quality of a being with a certain degree of self-awareness and with the attribute of will. God must be conceived as a subject with this degree of self-awareness and will, and thus we speak of God not as "it" but as person. Clayton points out that, arguably, the question of divine agency is one of the least well-articulated challenges facing theism today. Clayton suggests a correction of theological method away from the use of theistic language as merely fictitious and more in the direction of criticizable systematic proposals.

Reading #10 is found within Philip Clayton and Jeffrey Schloss, *Evolution and Ethics: Human Morality in Biological and Religious Perspective* and covers "Biology and Purpose: Altruism, Morality, and Human Nature in Evolutionary Perspectives." Herein, we find that those who pursue the more moderate approach to morality argue that the adequacy of strictly biological explanations of human behavior renders religious explanations unnecessary. A second strategy sometimes pursued is to "functionalize" the treatment of human behavior and human moral beliefs, so that no place remains for the kind of truth claims that religious believers typically make. In cases of genuine conflict, the disagreements are more often philosophical than directly scientific or religious based on human nature, its embodiedness, its temporality, its contingency, its sense of self, the inner world, self-deception, sociality, culture, or freedom. In the end, Clayton suggests that the picture yielded by combining biological and religious perspectives on human morality is richer than the picture produced by either one of these perspectives alone.

Reading #11—"Reason for Doubt"—is the first of three readings in succession to come from Philip Clayton and Steven Knapp's, *The Predicament of Belief: Science, Philosophy, and Faith*. It notes that at the same time that we recognize the depth and power of the ancient traditions, our explorations of these questions today must take place in light of new challenges. Contemporary grounds for doubting the traditional answers are serious enough that one may well wonder whether the questions can be answered at all and, indeed, whether it is even still meaningful to pose them, at least in the manner in which they were formulated by the great traditions of faith and reflection. In responding to these worries, we take as our starting point the claims embodied in one traditional way of answering questions about what is ultimately the case, the one known as "Christian." All three of the "Abrahamic" traditions are often said to fit that description. One of them, however—the Christian one—is unusual in the amount of weight it places on a single, brief episode, about which it makes perhaps the most extraordinary claims of any of these three traditions. Modernity (not to mention postmodernity!) is often taken to have changed the nature of human thought and human culture so radically that ancient beliefs are no longer viable, simply because they belong to a pre-modern era. But Clayton believes these worries are mistaken, and this reading explains why.

The reading entitled "The Ultimate Reality," as found within Clayton and Knapp's, *The Predicament of Belief,* constitutes reading #12. To many contemporary ears, the talk of the "ultimate reality" can sound suspiciously metaphysical. After all, we live in an age dominated by science and empirical methods for acquiring knowledge. Haven't scientifically testable theories about the world now replaced metaphysical speculations of this sort, rendering them therefore obsolete? Metaphysical reflections are indeed suspect when they compete head-to-head with scientific explanations of matters that lend themselves to scientific investigation. Still, Clayton contends that it is a mistake to think that science therefore becomes the authority for *all* questions. Even within "normal" science, new questions arise at the borders of each domain of inquiry. The success of natural science is not the only reason, however, that some reject altogether the idea of asking questions about the nature of the "ultimate reality," which this reading makes explicit.

The thirteenth reading is entitled "Doubt and Belief," and is likewise found within Clayton and Knapp, *The Predicament of Belief.* How do we assess our beliefs in life? The goal of doing so is to develop a position that might be embraced by those who want their most important beliefs to be rational—to be based, that is, on what they have reason to think is actually true. To say that reasons can be better or worse is to imply, however, that there is a basis for comparing them. And since that basis cannot be the direct observation of reality itself, what can it be? Unfortunately, there is no way to check if one's beliefs are likely to be true by comparing them directly with the reality they are tracking. There is no way of stepping outside one's beliefs to see which ones correspond to the way things really are. The best an agent can do is to make sure, insofar as possible, that her reasons for holding a belief are better than the reasons she might have for rejecting it.

The fourteenth reading begins Part III, which concerns "Panentheistic Reflections on Science & Theology." It is entitled, "Spinoza's One and the Birth of Panentheism."

Editorial Introduction

In this reading, we follow what Clayton believes to be the most productive strand in the tapestry of modern thought about God. But first we must deal with the *other* conclusion that is often drawn from Kantian criticisms: the postmodern attack on transcendence, with its claim that God-language should henceforth be given a *purely immanent* interpretation. In an important two-volume work on "Spinoza and other heretics," Yirmiyahu Yovel has proclaimed the adventures of immanence, as well as the thrills of the denial of transcendence. Are the "adventures of immanence" the correct response to the Kantian problem of God? Clayton's thesis in this reading is that as we turn to Spinoza's followers, we will discover that pantheism, when worked out systematically in Western philosophy, has invariably turned into *panentheism*—the view that the world is within God although God is also more than the world.

Reading #15 comes from *God and Contemporary Science*, and is titled "Rethinking the Relation of God and the World: Panentheism and the Contribution of Philosophy." It turns out that "classical Western theism or pantheism" is *not* the only choice. One sign of the inadequacy of this dichotomy is that pantheism was never seriously entertained within the orbit of Christian or para-Christian reflection. In Porphyrus, in Johannes of Eriugena, in Eckhardt, Cusa, Bruno, and many others, the actual "heretical" assertion was that finite things are fully within God; the world as a whole was never made identical to all there was of God. As the church struggled over the question of which of these views to label heretical the debate was indeed carried out in terms of whether the positions were pantheistic or not. But this was to turn a complex conceptual struggle into a matter of superficial labels, to attempt to dismiss a sophisticated theological position by means of the fallacy of "guilt by association." In this reading, Clayton hopes to show that panentheism dissolves the dichotomy that structured so many of the theological debates on this topic.

The sixteenth reading is entitled "Panentheism in Metaphysical and Scientific Perspective," and it is found within the booked edited by Clayton and Arthur Peacocke, *In Whom We Live and Move and Have Our Being: Panentheistic Reflections on God's Presence in a Scientific World*. In recent years, scholars have advanced a variety of reasons that might lead one to adopt panentheism. One might hold that classical philosophical theism (CPT) or "supernaturalistic" theism or traditional theism is no longer viable, without being convinced that atheism is the most compelling answer. One might be convinced that panentheism is more compatible than traditional theism with particular results in physics or biology, or with common features shared across the scientific disciplines, such as the structure of emergence. What's more, one may be convinced of the preferability of a metaphysical position (e.g., process philosophy), and panentheism either lies closer to, or is actually entailed by, that metaphysical position. Additionally, one might hold that panentheism can do a better job at preserving certain religious beliefs than classical theism. In the process of searching for a mediating metaphysic between Western and Eastern religious philosophical systems, one might come to believe that panentheism provides the most convincing available answer. Further, one might find panentheism religiously more viable or more attractive than the alternatives. Some have argued, for instance, that traditional Christian theism is burdened by unanswerable objections such as the problem of evil, whereas panentheistic theologies are able to avoid these objections. Or, finally, one might be convinced that classical theism has unacceptable ethical or political implications, while panentheism does not have these implications.

Reading #17 is comprised of an essay entitled, "Panentheism Today: A Constructive Systematic Evaluation," as found within Clayton and Arthur Peacocke, eds., *In Whom We Live and Move and Have Our Being.* In this reading, we find Clayton pondering whether there is such a thing as a generic panentheism. Clayton explores in what sense the contributions to Clayton and Peacocke's book may represent variations on a single theme. He supposes one might try to formulate the various positions as varieties of panentheism; would it work? Can common principles be stated, such that the label "panentheism" really expresses a common intersection set among them? He suggests beginning with this experiment, using adjectival labels to distinguish among the positions of the individual essays within *In Whom We Live and Move and Have Our Being*:

1) Participatory panentheism, or perhaps "Logoi panentheism" (described by A. Louth).

2) "Divine energies" panentheism (K. Ware).

3) Ecclesial or communal panentheism (A. Nesteruk).

4) Eschatological panentheism (or perhaps soteriological panentheism?) (e.g., J. Polkinghorne, as described by several authors).

5) Sapiential panentheism (C. Deane-Drummond).

6) Emergentist panentheism (A. Peacocke, P. Clayton).

7) Sacramental panentheism (A. Peacocke, C. Knight).

9) Trinitarian panentheism (D. Edwards et al.).

10) Pansacramental naturalistic panentheism (C. Knight).

11) Process or dipolar panentheism (D. Griffin et al.).

12) "Body of God" panentheism (Ramanuja, via K. Ward).

13) Neo-Panentheism (H. Morowitz).

14) Pansyntheism (R. Page).

Reading #18 comes from the academic journal named *Sophia* (49 [2010]), and is entitled, "Panentheisms East and West." The great process philosopher Charles Hartshorne, who was largely responsible for the twentieth-century renaissance of panentheistic thought in the West, formulated a classic definition of this concept, using the five letters E, T, C, K, and W to stand for five features attributed to the Ultimate by many panentheists: eternal, temporal, conscious, knowing the world, and world-inclusive. The Infinite One must be *eternal*, for it was never created and depends on nothing outside itself in order to exist. Next, the One is *temporal* in the sense that it contains within itself all finite things. Third, the One is *conscious* because it contains us and we are conscious. Clayton himself actually prefer the more cautious formulation that the One cannot be *less than* what we mean by conscious, but its quality of consciousness must be infinitely more than, infinitely greater than, any consciousness we can conceive. The fourth attribute is knowledge: consciousness entails knowing, the two attributes cannot be separated; so the One being who is conscious must also be a being who is knowing—knowing the world. A final attribute or argument is that, if the parts of the One possess the characteristic of knowing, and the One cannot be less than its parts, then it must possess that quality as well; it must be *world*-inclusive.

The nineteenth reading furthers this thinking upon panentheism. It is comprised of an essay entitled, "'Open Panentheism' and Creation as Kenosis," and it is found within *Adventures in the Spirit: God, World, Divine Action*. In contrast to many process theologians, Clayton is compelled to defend the doctrine of creation *ex nihilo*—the belief that there has not always been a world, and hence that the world is not co-eternal with God. Instead, on this view both the creation of the universe and the details concerning *how* it was created involved free divine decisions. The combination of these two different sources gives rise to an intriguing mediating position, which he calls *open panentheism*. This theology has a deep affinity with the work of Clark Pinnock and other "open theists" or "free will theists," though it draws more fully on process resources than most of these theologians do. Open theism is closely linked to process theism in a number of respects. Both conceive of God as involved more deeply in the temporal flow of history than classical theism was willing to countenance; both acknowledge certain limitations on what God can do and know (though, as we will see, for rather different reasons); and both think more rigorously than most classical theists did about what is entailed in the use of agency language to describe God and divine action. *Open panentheism* seeks to build further on these foundations. It recognizes that deeper ties bind process thinkers and open theists than is often acknowledged.

Part IV begins our readings about "Science & Emergence." Particularly, to start us off, there is reading #20, wherein we find an explication of emergence from Clayton's *Mind & Emergence: From Quantum to Consciousness*. It is widely but falsely held that there are only two major ways to interpret the world: in a physicalist or in a dualist fashion. It is the thesis of this book that the days of this forced dilemma are past. The discussion of emergence makes no sense unless one conducts it against the backdrop of reductionism. Emergence theories presuppose that the project of explanatory reduction—explaining all phenomena in the natural world in terms of the objects and laws of physics—is finally impossible. In a classic definition el-Hani and Pereira identify four features generally associated with the concept of emergence:

1. *Ontological physicalism*
2. *Property emergence*
3. *The irreducibility of the emergence*
4. *Downward causation*

Though it is widely conceded that George Henry Lewes first introduced the term "emergence," precursors to the concept can nonetheless be traced back in the history of Western philosophy at least as far as Aristotle. Indeed, Aristotle's biological research led him to posit a principle of growth within organisms that was responsible for the qualities or form that would later emerge.

Reading #21 is comprised of a reading from *Mind & Emergence: From Quantum to Consciousness*, identified as "Defining Emergence." Emergence is no monolithic term. Within the genus of interpretations of the natural world that it includes we have been able to identify two major competing species, commonly referred to as strong and weak emergence. The cumulative argument, I will suggest, favors strong emergence. That is, when the whole spectrum of emergent phenomena has been canvassed—from emergent phenomena in physics, through the study of organisms in their struggle to survive and thrive, and on to the phenomena of brain and mind—it is the perspective that best does justice to the entire range of phenomena. But the battle is hotly contested. In a sense, emergence theory is "that which is produced by a combination of causes, but cannot be regarded as the sum of their individual effects." In fact, however, one can locate at least five distinct levels on which the term is applied. As one moves along the continuum between the levels, one observes a transition from very specific scientific domains to increasingly integrative, and hence increasingly philosophical, concepts.

Reading #22 is the shortest of all the readings. It recounts "Eight Characteristics of Emergence," as found within *Mind & Emergence: From Quantum to Consciousness*. For example, there is monism, hierarchical complexity, a temporal or emergence monism, the idea that there is no monolithic law of emergence, the contention that patterns emerge across levels of emergence, the presence of downward causation, an emergentist pluralism, and ultimately the contention that mind is emergent.

The twenty-third reading comes from *Mind & Emergence*. It covers, broadly, the concept of emergence in its transition to biology from the chemical components. Biological processes in general are the result of systems that create and maintain order (stasis) through massive energy input from their environment. As one moves up the ladder of complexity, macrostructures and macromechanisms emerge. In the formation of new structures, one might say, scale matters—or, better put, changes in scale matter. In short, "emergence in evolution" suggests that, within the set of theories that we group under the heading of evolutionary biology, particular features can be discovered that are aptly described as "emergent." A successful dialogue between biology and philosophy requires that one begin with the biology; only when the facts are on the table can one reflect on their philosophical significance. Still, biology raises conceptual or philosophical questions that are not utterly without interest to biologists.

Reading #24 comes from *The Re-Emergence of Emergence: The Emergentist Hypothesis from Science to Religion*, edited by Clayton and Paul Davies. It is entitled, "Conceptual Foundations of Emergence Theory." It notes that without a doubt, far more philosophers in the second half of the twentieth century advocated for a position closer to Samuel Alexander's than to C. D. Broad's or C. Lloyd Morgan's. Yet these are precisely the goals that weak emergence theorists such as Samuel Alexander sought to achieve. Clayton thinks it to be important to acknowledge in advance that weak emergence is the starting position for most natural scientists. Many of us may start with intuitions that are in conflict with weak emergence. But when one engages the dialogue from the standpoint of contemporary natural science, one enters a playing field on which the physicalists and weak emergentists have the upper hand.

The twenty-fifth reading comes also from Clayton and Davies, eds. *The Re-Emergence of Emergence*, and is entitled, "Emergence from Quantum Physics to Religion." Viewed as a claim about the nature of reality, emergentism represents a species of monism, which Clayton calls *emergentist monism*. Monism rejects multiple kinds of substance, as in Descartes' theory of "thinking stuff" and "extended stuff" (*res cogitans* and *res extensa*), arguing instead that all objects and phenomena in the universe arise out of one basic matter-energy "stuff." Yet a physics-based monism cannot be the last word, since it's equally obvious that the universe produces more and more complex levels of organization. *Emergentist* monism emphasizes continuity through process, the fundamental ontological affinity between all existing things. Clayton contends that emergence theory tends to undercut dogmatic knowledge claims about the nature of God. If emergence is right, our epistemic situation is constantly changing, in so far as we are products of a pervasive process of biological and cultural evolution. Acknowledging this fact should make one far more suspicious of any knowledge claims that imply, however tacitly, that the knower stands above the march of history and has direct and immediate access to timeless truths

Reading #26—"Why Emergence Matters: A New Paradigm for Relating the Sciences"—comes from *Adventures in the Spirit: God, World, Divine Action*. Clayton herein admits that it is one thing to speculate about emergence as part of a metaphysical theory, and something else to claim scientific support for the framework of emergence. Although Clayton believes such claims are justified, they bring with them unique challenges. The quest to explain phenomena in terms of reconstructible, testable causal systems is so basic to the project of science that we could almost use it as *the* defining characteristic of science. The phenomenon of emergence makes this project more difficult, but it does not eliminate it. If it had turned out to be possible to explain higher-order phenomena in terms of lower-order laws across the scientific disciplines, then science would be in the position fully to achieve the goal in terms of which it is defined.

Our twenty-seventh reading similarly comes from *Adventures in the Spirit: God, World, Divine Action*, and is coined "Theological Reflections on Emergence: From Emergent Nature to the Emerging Church." There is a core set of topics that a Christian theology is expected to address: Christology, pneumatology, ecclesiology, eschatology, and so forth. But the scaffolding—the organizing framework that one uses to respond to these questions—is not given once and for all; theology is "always reformed, always reforming." What would a systematic theology look like if developed out of the context of emergent thinking? How would one be inclined to respond to the traditional *loci* using the framework of emerging systems?

Reading #28 is the first one in Part V, which broadly covers, "Science, Spirit, & Divine Action." Indeed, this reading comes from Clayton, *God and Contemporary Science*, and is entitled, "Scientific Causality, Divine Causality." The present-day crisis in the notion of divine action has resulted as much as anything from a shift in the notion of causation. In pre-mechanistic science, which was dominated by the influence of Aristotle, a component of divine causal action or teleology was included in every action. Thomas Aquinas insisted that every event involved not only the efficient cause (what we would now speak of as the cause of an occurrence), but also the formal and material causes, or the influence of the matter and the form on the outcome. As a fourth type of causality, Thomas stressed the role of "final causes," that is, the overall purposes of God, which act as one of the causal forces in every event. Some contemporary theologians have attempted to preserve something like this "final" type of causality. Clayton adds his voice to this discussion in this reading.

Reading #29 also comes from Clayton, *God and Contemporary Science*, with this being labeled "A Panentheistic Theory of Divine Action." Therein, Clayton notes that no contemporary theologian has come closer to the panentheistic theory of divine action defended by Clayton himself than Arthur Peacocke; and of those who hold similar positions, none possesses a superior knowledge of the scientific developments. But like Philip Hefner's well-known theory of humanity as God's "created co-creator," Peacocke stresses that there is an ongoing creativity within creation itself: in fact, because we have to see God's action as being in the processes themselves, as they are revealed by the physical and biological sciences, this means we must stress more than ever before God's immanence in the world. The most adequate way to think of this immanence is to understand the emergence of new forms primitive life, higher organisms, and human self-consciousness as a result of God's immanent creative action in the world.

The thirtieth reading draws from Clayton's *Adventures in the Spirit: God, World, and Divine Action*, and similarly concerns divine action. Physical science, it appears, leaves no place for divine action. To do science is generally to presuppose that the universe is a closed physical system, that interactions are regular and lawlike, that all causal histories can be traced, and that anomalies will ultimately have physical explanations. Unfortunately, the traditional way of asserting that God acts in the world conflicts with all four of these conditions; it presupposes that the universe is open, that God acts from time to time according to particular purposes, that the ultimate source and explanation of these actions is the divine will, and that no earthly account would ever suffice to explain God's intentions. The problem of divine agency is therefore one of the most pressing challenges theists face in an age of science. How can one attribute events to the causal activity of God if science is based on the assumption that any given event is part of a closed system of natural causes?

Reading #31 draws from Clayton's *Mind & Emergence: From Quantum to Consciousness*, and seeks to "rethink" divine action. Theism is doubly hard to conceive in the contemporary context, for first, in the face of science's strong push towards immanent explanations one must make the case that language about a transcendent being or dimension is meaningful. Although Clayton argues that the rejection of transcendence is unnecessary, clearly the move to transcendent mind is one that many resist. Once this move is made, a second challenge arises: the task of making some sense of the idea of divine causal activity in the world. The model that Clayton herein employs—an influence at the level of integrated persons, which in turn influences specific mental, affective, and physical processes—avoids the implausibilities of the competing models of divine action.

Reading #32 explores "On Divine and Human Agency: Reflections of a Co-laborer," and is found within the concluding (editorial summation) chapter of Arthur Peacocke's *All That Is: A Naturalistic Faith for the Twenty-First Century*, which is edited by Clayton. Clayton herein relays that a set of brilliantly interconnected insights underlies Arthur Peacocke's work. The core motivation for his naturalism is the recognition that science stands in tension with many traditional views of divine action. Thus, if one accepts a picture of the world consistent with the best of scientific practice, then one cannot imagine that God regularly intervenes in the natural order in a miraculous way. Peacocke insists, however, that preserving the integrity of the natural order is not inconsistent with Christian faith. The world can still be created by God and sustained in its existence at every moment by the divine will for the world can be located within God, as panentheists maintain, such that God is "in, with, and under" all things—present to them in the most intimate way possible. The result is a notion of divine influence strong enough to undergird many, if not most, of the traditional Christian doctrines.

The thirty-third reading begins Part VI, which roughly concerns Clayton's "Progressive Theology." "Things Have Changed, or 'Toto, we're not in Kansas Anymore,'" is the first of five consecutive readings that come from Clayton, *Transforming Christian Theology: For Church and Society*. Over the last half-century, all of us have watched the geography of the American church undergo a radical transformation. It's almost as if there has been a major earthquake—or, more accurately, a series of major earthquakes—realigning the entire landscape in which we live. Thus, Herberg could write in 1955 that, "Almost everybody in the United States today locates himself in one of the three great religious communities. Asked to identify themselves in terms of religious 'preferences,' 95 per cent of the American people, according to a recent public opinion survey, declared themselves to be either Protestants, Catholics, or Jews." Such is no longer the case. What it means to be a church today, and what it will mean over the coming two to three decades, is affected just as strongly by the explosion of new technologies and the radically new forms of social networking that they create.

The thirty-fourth reading is labeled, "Why the Answers Must be Theological." Herein, Clayton remarks that every Christian has a theology. For that matter, so does every Jew or Muslim or Hindu. A theology, in the broadest sense, just means what you believe about God (*theos*). Tragically, theology somehow got turned into a professional sport—a move that produced many of the negative tendencies that we already know from professional sports in America (except for the high salaries). In fact, the invention of "theologians" as the professional authorities on Christian belief may turn out to be one of the really damaging things that has occurred in the history of the church. This invention doesn't get as much press as the invention of clergy—which has tended to undercut the "priesthood of all believers"—but it equals it in importance. The quickest way to understand why the dichotomy between professional theologians and the rest of us won't work is to talk about worldviews. Clayton then relates the customary components of the Wesleyan Quadrilateral—scripture, tradition, experience, and reason—to what he refers to as "world-life views."

Reading #35 is entitled, "Postmodern Believing," and is the third reading from within Clayton, *Transforming Christian Theology*. Herein, he relays that scientism, the return to the pre-modern, and the rampant rise of fundamentalism are all the last gasps of later modernity. What's encouraging is that they set the stage for some much-needed new ways of believing. Postmodern believing is not less deep and powerful than modern believing. But it encourages some very different (and, Clayton thinks, refreshing) attitudes toward certainty and doubt. He notes that it is marked by the presence of doubt, which is neither to be condemned or avoided, for it heralds a return to a thinking faith. This, in short, is the lesson of postmodern Jesus-discipleship: *belong, behave, believe*. It's not as neat and pretty as the account we were taught when we were young: "get your beliefs right, then get your life in order, and then you can join us." But then again, human existence is rarely as black and white as we were taught when we were young.

Reading #36 is "A Theology of Self-Emptying for the Church." The kenosis of the Christ, as spoken of within Philippians chapter 2 is, from a Christian perspective, *the* central narrative in God's relationship with the world God created. The particular contribution of Christian voices within the dialogue of world religions is to talk about this narrative. In this notion of self-emptying, we encounter what is for Clayton the central Christian teaching about Jesus' "mind," about God's self-revelation—and indeed about God's own eternal nature. When Clayton ask what it means for to try to love as God

XXXI

loves, the answer must always begin with self-emptying. What Christ emptied himself of was having the *highest conceivable* glory, the glory of equality with God's eternal nature. If a theology and the lifestyle that goes with it are to be Christ-like, they will be pervaded by this self-emptying. As radical as it sounds, Clayton suggests that we need to apply the attitude of self-emptying *even to our own Christian theologies.*

Reading #37 is the last one to come from *Transforming Christian Theology,* and pursues a "Progressive Theology for Christian Activism." There are two different senses of the word *progressive*. The broader sense of the term—changing, improving, making things better—should be uncontroversial. How could a theology not seek to be progressive in this sense? Our theological understanding is always evolving under the guidance of the Holy Spirit and in response to new events in human history. Progressive theologies express our ongoing attempt to interpret scripture, our attempt to say what it means here and now—in *this* world, reacting to *these* new ideas, in conversation with *these* people, in dialogue with *this or that* world religion or philosophy. As such, these theologies are never the absolute revelation of God, for they always include a human dimension—the perspective of their authors. But progressive theologies have a concrete side as well. In actual practice they always imply specific social, political, and even moral positions. Progressive theologies in this sense tend to emphasize social justice issues as strongly as they emphasize questions of individual responsibility and morality.

Reading #38 is the first of two concerning "organic Marxism," as found within Philip Clayton and Justin Heinzekehr, *Organic Marxism: An Alternative to Capitalism and Ecological Catastrophe.* It stipulates that in practice, most of global economics now functions according to the principles of the so-called free market economy—with disastrous consequences for the planet and much of its population. The domination of capitalist principles has been so thorough that Francis Fukuyama proclaimed "the end of history" in 1992, arguing that humanity has finally attained its highest and ultimate form of government: Western-style capital-based democracy. Nothing less than a shift in the global economic paradigm will allow human nations, cultures, and civilizations to survive in anything like the forms in which we have known them heretofore. However, Marxism is not a universal predictive science. Marxists do not need to insist only on state ownership, state-run businesses, and the abolition of all market forces. Further, Marxism was never meant to be a purely theoretical dispute among university professors. Finally, a vibrant, living Marxism cannot be "one size fits all."

Reading #39 concerns "The Ecology and Praxis of Organic Marxism," as found within Clayton and Heinzekehr, *Organic Marxism.* At the heart of the Manifesto on organic Marxism stand three central claims: capitalist justice is not just; the "free market" is not free; and the costs of global climate disruption will be most severe among the poor. Justice is conceived very differently in capitalist and Marxist theory. Marx writes, *"From each according to his ability, to each according to his need."* Adam Smith, the founder of the concept of capitalism, believed that markets are the most rational and moral way to regulate human interactions. According to *laissez-faire* capitalism, governments are required not to intervene in the markets in any way. Smith even used the metaphor of God: markets are so good at rewarding the virtuous and punishing the lazy that it is *as if* an "invisible hand" were guiding capitalist society. Unless we intervene, however, climate change will wreak untold suffering on the world's poorest citizens and on a third to a half of animal species.

Our final reading, the fortieth, captures the thrust of this entire Reader. Indeed, it analyzes "Liberal Faith between Church, Academy, and World," and is found within Clayton, *Adventures in the Spirit*. Just as pursuing differences and concerns in personal relationships often leads to growth and intimacy, so wrestling with the tough challenges of our age leads to a stronger and more enduring form of faith. Among all the theological traditions, liberal theology after Schleiermacher inherited the sixteenth-century motto, *Ecclesia reformata, semper reformanda!* (the church reformed and always reforming) and moved the call to continually new forms of integration into its very self-definition. In this closing chapter, Clayton wishes to reclaim that great integrative project—with its wide-ranging conceptual, ethical, political, and personal dimensions—as the core commitment of a new liberal theology for our day.

That's it. When we get to this point, our introductory (and I pray that it is merely introductory!) exploration of the thought and theology of Philip Clayton has come to an end. I hope that you use this Reader as a springboard to closer reading directly of this powerful and potent Christian philosopher and theologian.

Bibliography

Barbour, Ian. *Religion in an Age of Science: The Gifford Lectures, vol. 1*. New York: HarperCollins, 1990.

Chalker, William H. *Science and Faith: Understanding Meaning, Method, and Truth*. Louisville: Westminster John Knox Press, 2006.

Dawkins, Richard. *The Blind Watchmaker*. London: Penguin, 2006.

Feist, Richard, and William Sweet. *Religion & the Challenges of Science*. London: Routledge, 2007.

Ford, Lewis. *The Lure of God: A Biblical Background for Process Theism*. Augsburg Fortress, 1978.

Kaiser, Christopher B. *Toward a Theology of Scientific Endeavour: The Descent of Science*. London: Routledge, 2007.

Küng, Hans. *The Beginning of All Things: Science and Religion*. Grand Rapids: Eerdmans, 2007.

Mayr, Ernst. *The Growth of Biological Thought: Diversity, Evolution, and Inheritance*. Cambridge: Belknap, 1980.

Stenmark, Michael. *How to Relate Science and Religion: A Multidimensional Model*. Grand Rapids: Eerdmans, 2004.

Vaux, Kenneth. *An Abrahamic Theology for Science*. Eugene, OR: Wipf & Stock, 2007.

Ward, Keith. *The Big Questions in Science and Religion*. West Conshohocken, PA: Templeton, 2008.

Practicing Dialogical Theology
An Intellectual Autobiography

PHILIP CLAYTON

Introduction

TECHNICALLY, ONE SHOULD NOT write an intellectual autobiography until one is dead, though I admit that solution raises problems of its own. Even if it is your own life you are describing (and perhaps *especially* then), the best that can be done is to compose a (more or less) coherent narrative, and hopefully one that is also (mostly) true. Heidegger is right: the way that each person construes the "meaning of [her] being" is to "run forward" toward her own death (*das Vorlaufen zum Tode*) and then, reflecting backwards from that moment of possible completion, to construct an authentic identity in the present. Theology is equally about telling the story from the end backwards, as Wolfhart Pannenberg always emphasized; the meaning of the whole of history can only be conceived, if at all, from the standpoint of its final culmination, the eschaton.

From Fundamentalism to Fallibilism

It could hardly be said that I was inculcated with religion from a young age. My father was not only an atheist but an evangelical atheist, one who was sharply critical of religion and sought to free as many people from it as possible. At fourteen I became a Christian in a dramatic conversion at a religious summer camp. When I came home with excitement to tell my parents, I'm sure my father thought it was some form of teenage rebellion. If so, it was far more effective than I could ever have dreamed up. Sitting at the breakfast table, I told my parents the story of the universe as I had come to (vaguely) understand it over my first few hours as a Christian:

> *See, God created the heavens and the earth, and a bunch of animals and man. And then God took a rib out of Adam to make Eve, and if the woman doesn't submit to the man she'll lose the rib again. Anyway, God had to find someplace to put them, so He created a garden, but they ate an apple off the Evil Tree and were ashamed of being naked, so God kicked them out and put big angels and fire at the gate. Anyway, lots of bad things happened after that, like God making babies hurt, and flooding the world, and turning homosexuals into pillars of salt, and Israel becoming a prostitute to the nations. Fortunately, God finally sent Jesus to die for us and take away all our sins and make us sanctimonious. Because I'm saved now, I'm not condemned for my sins any longer, but you still are. Someday Jesus will come back, and he's going to be angry, especially at people like you. And there will be a big hell where all the non-Christians go.*

My father was too shocked to say a word, but I do remember my mother crying softly into her breakfast cereal.

High school years moved me even further to the right theologically. I chose a college that, at that time, held to the doctrine of plenary inspiration, which meant that God had dictated scripture, which meant that the Ur-text could not contain any mistakes about any matters scientific or historical or otherwise. (The school, Westmont College, no longer espouses this view.) To make things worse, by the time I arrived at Westmont I had decided that, if the Bible is the decisive revelation of God's eternal nature, then it must contain *all* truth, so we don't really need to read any other books in the search for truth—a great mindset for entering college!

My five years as a fundamentalist had a first challenge and a final collapse. Every verse of the Bible had to be true, so 1 Corinthians 11:10 also had to be true: "Therefore the woman ought to have a symbol of authority on her head, because of the angels." It puzzled me what a woman's head covering would have to do with angels. So I went to my youth minister for guidance. He thought for a moment and then announced that the head covering is for the sake of the angels because it keeps them from feeling sexual lust for the women while they're in church. Of course I trusted my youth minister, but as a hormone-charged male adolescent I *knew* that this one didn't make sense: the angels see the women all the time, in bikinis and taking showers, but they can't handle observing the women's hair in church? That one I just couldn't affirm. But if there's even one verse that isn't right—here's the slippery slope—then the Bible can't be inerrant in every respect. (I'm sure someone will now email me to tell me there's a completely compelling interpretation of this verse.)

The second moment was even more troubling. I had become a Pentecostal Christian, the kind that speaks in tongues and believes that God gives direct, literal prophecy to people. To be "charismatic" you needed a second baptism, the so-called Baptism in the Spirit, so that you could live the fullness of the Christian life. We had scripture verses that, we believed, proved that Pentecostalism is the true form of Christianity. At Westmont College my Greek and exegesis professor, Dr. Moises Silva, challenged our interpretation of those verses. Thus began a kind of shuttle diplomacy: driving from Greek class to the Assemblies of God church across town, gathering the pastor's answers to the newest challenge, driving back to school, trying them out on Dr. Silva in the next exegesis class, and then repeating the cycle. Long story short, Dr. Silva won and the Pentecostal minister lost. Strike Two.

The final departure from fundamentalism came during my Junior year. We were sitting in rapt attention as our favorite philosophy professor, Dr. Stan Obitts, was lecturing on Leibniz and Christian apologetics. The energy in the room grew and grew; we were approaching eternal verities. Suddenly he brought the discussion to a halt with his hands, like a symphony conductor, held us for a long dramatic pause, and then announced decisively, "*These* are the questions!" In that instant, as quickly as a snap of the fingers, I got it: in the end, it really is more about the questions than the answers! I am certain that Dr. Obitts, of blessed memory, would never have agreed with my conclusion. But it stuck. From that day onward, I knew, I would devote myself first to the *questions* as my highest passion. Where answers emerged, I would hold them hypothetically, seeking out criticisms more than confirmations, and modifying my beliefs accordingly.

If You Want to Be a Great Theologian, Study Science

The trajectory to my first professorship was shaped by that moment in Dr. Obitts' classroom. Since Christianity makes truth claims, it needs an apologetic, in the sense of 1 Peter 3:15, "Always be prepared to make a defense (*apologia*) to any one who calls you to account for the hope that is in you." Three of us therefore resolved to write Senior Honors theses on faith and reason. Knowing that science is the most rigorous form of knowledge humans have achieved, I worked to show that contemporary science supports Christian truth claims. The conclusions reached by my two friends represent, even today, the two major options to my theological right and left. Kevin Vanhoozer argued for the trustworthiness of the God revealed in scripture, the God of Abraham, Isaac, and Jacob; Dustin Anderson, a skeptic, argued that all arguments (including his own) fail to demonstrate their conclusions; no position can be shown to be more true than any other. Kevin became a famous systematic theologian, and Dustin became a farmer in Sweden. It's somehow fitting that the last three decades of scholarship at the intersection of science and theology still locate me somewhere near the midpoint between these two positions.

To my Assemblies of God pastor, each of the career moves that followed pushed me further down the slippery slope. He warned me to avoid Fuller Seminary because its liberal doctrine of scripture would destroy my faith. Unfortunately, I not only enrolled there but immediately fell in with the bad crowd. On Tuesday evenings, while some of my Westmont friends enjoyed punch and Bible study at a home, I was in a pub with the other Fuller heretics drinking beer and quoting Nietzsche, or in the classroom confronting poor old Professor Dan Fuller as he worked to derive a Christian theodicy from the text of the Book of Job.

By this time I was fully enmeshed in the theology–science debate. Intense discussions with Thomas F. Torrance tempted me toward his Barthian *Theological Science*. But four years of studying under Wolfhart Pannenberg in Munich drew me away from Barth and toward a God revealed not only through scripture and theology, but also through nature, secular ("universal") history, philosophy, and of course the sciences. No surprise, then, that the choice at Yale would be to do doctoral work in two departments and three areas: philosophy, philosophy of science, and theology. Focusing the dissertation on "rationality and religion" (the subtitle of *Explanation from Physics to Theology*) deepened my knowledge of the sciences and the philosophy of science; it also sent me for a number of years in the direction of what Kevin Vanhoozer and John Cooper called "the God of the philosophers." Moving to the Philosophy department at Williams College, and later returning home to teach philosophy at Sonoma State University, were natural next steps along this particular trajectory.

Life at the Intersection of Philosophy, Science, and Theology

During my research fellowship at the University of Cambridge, John Polkinghorne once arranged an invitation to dinner at the Triangle Club. At the end of a sumptuous meal in the mahogany room, I was asked to lay out a problem and a proposed solution, with crisp arguments and flawless presentation (no notes allowed!). The only condition was that it needed to include three different fields: philosophy, science, and theology. During the lengthy discussion and critique that followed, the dozen or so brilliant Cambridge professors challenged the adequacy of my argument from all three disciplinary perspectives; failure of any one of them meant failure of them all.

I have held myself to this same three-fold standard across the decades of my career. The collection that follows provides a cross-section of the results, nicely organized by Bradford McCall, so they do not need to be re-presented here.

The question of why these particular themes arose and how they fit together deserves a quick comment. The strength, and the curse, of a systematic thinker is the drive to make one's ideas connect over one's entire opus. These include methodological principles, conclusions about God or science, "meta" principles like the theory of knowledge that one uses, the influence of particular thinkers, and even intuitions and experience. It may however be helpful to reconstruct the progression, to bring to the surface the sometimes-hidden story behind it.

First, though, I happily acknowledge the hundreds of hours of discussions and the literally thousands of pages of correspondence with Steven Knapp, which have influenced my positions on virtually all the themes that follow. Every assumption and conclusion needs to be highly nuanced and its weaknesses acknowledged. For the sake of time and clarity, however, let me present them in the form of nine brief theses, knowing that the chapters that follow will add the necessary qualifications:

- All knowledge claims are fallible. They are thus best held as hypotheses, which remain open to criticism and revision. Satisfying allies in one's own discourse community is not a high enough standard. Charles Sanders Peirce was right: one should seek feedback from the relevant communities of inquiry—experts in the fields that one covers who do not already agree with one's own position.

- The natural sciences offer the most rigorously tested theories that humanity has yet produced. Theological and philosophical attempts to refute empirical conclusions within a scientific domain are never more likely than the science they attempt to refute.

- However, science also shows that the world is indeterministic at the bottom. As the universe increases in complexity, first through cosmic evolution and later through biological evolution, the emergent structures and functions and their behaviors manifest openness and unpredictability. In the case of extremely complex systems, such as human social constructs, the unpredictability increases exponentially. The world that we experience is contingent; it could have been otherwise.

- Theologically, one does need to be able to show that the natural order is not a deterministic system, since otherwise no opening would exist for real, constructive relations of persons with persons. Language of divine Spirit would be equally interventionist and miraculous. But reflection on quantum physics undercuts determinism in the necessary way, making it possible to speak of intentions as a form of natural causation.

- It is thus false that physics—or genetics or neurology or Marxist economics—can offer explanations for all that we experience and observe, even in principle. Emergent organisms, E. coli or porcupines or your neighbor, are agents in their own right; their behaviors can be explained only in frameworks that include their own irreducible forms of causality ("strong emergence"). This conclusion applies also to questions such as ethics, the meaning of history, spirituality, and (it would seem) theology as well.

- If there is a God, God has intentionally created this open-ended cosmos—a universe that allows agents to evolve and act in increasingly (but never fully) unconstrained ways. Answering the problem of evil requires real contingency and ontological openness. If God controls the process or can intervene to set aside natural law, evil and suffering cannot be reconciled with the existence of God.

- Creation is best understood as located *within* the Divine, although God is also more than the world (panentheism). Process theologies offer powerful descriptions of internal relatedness, divine lure, and free response. But one can draw on these resources without affirming panpsychism or a necessary creation.

- One can do constructive Christian theology while learning deeply from comparative philosophy and theology. One does not need to be a relativist or reductionist about religious beliefs, and yet Hindus are not "anonymous Christians." Nothing about science or comparative philosophy forbids one to construct a Christology, ecclesiology, or eschatology.

- There is no reason not to develop theories of ultimate reality, metaphysical accounts of science, or systematic theologies. But as one's beliefs become more comprehensive and less testable, one's degree of certainty decreases. At the limit, the mystics are right. "Whereof one cannot speak, thereof one must be silent" (Wittgenstein).

Return to Theology

Somewhat to my surprise, the intense preoccupation with philosophy and science eventually made it possible for me to find my own theological voice again. Like the prodigal son, I had spent some years "in a distant land" doing prolegomena (the foundations *for* theology) and talking *about* theology. Taking up theology again does not mean that one's commitment to dialogue with science, philosophy, contemporary culture, and other religions ends; it means that one can now do constructive Christian thought *in and through* these diverse dialogues—and not only after all the pieces have been tied together, all questions answered, all critiques laid to rest. Perhaps the owl of Minerva (philosophy) only starts its flight with the falling of the dusk (Hegel), but if the eagle of theology cannot be in the air at dawn and throughout the day, it might as well never fly.

I owe the return to a Korean doctoral student at Claremont School of Theology. Interviewing the Koreans who were forced to become "comfort women" (read: sex slaves) for the Japanese during World War II, she was overwhelmed by the private suffering they had endured through their entire subsequent lives, especially since they were not able to speak about the horrible events for fear of shaming themselves or their families. And yet, the young scholar added, these women had powerfully experienced the presence of the Holy Spirit, which helped to sustain them.

Finally I got it. For years my colleagues and I had been looking for the causal mechanisms that could show the possibility of divine action in the world. But that, it turned out, was a category mistake. Emergent complexity means that we should not expect to be able to link quantum events to human subjective and spiritual consciousness. Surely, then, the starting point for our talk of God's activity must be at the level where we actually live. In John, the Spirit is called the "Paraclete" (*paraklētos*, John 14:16), the one who is "called in aid," the one who comes alongside. Listening to my

Korean student, I realized that an account of divine action should center on God's presence to suffering and move outward from there. How to relate "God with us" to the causal nexus of the natural world remains an important question, but it does not need to be where theology starts.

The new approach also opened new doors for conceiving God's presence to and influence on persons. Arthur Peacocke had long pushed me in this direction. Most unforgettable were the walks out of the very small farming village in southern Poland where Pope John Paul II had grown up. At sunset, after long days of work on the Divine Action Project, we would stroll out into the fields, debating personhood and divine action as we walked between the haystacks. Arthur wanted me to give up the insistence on a traditional causal account, beginning instead with the influence of God on the world as a whole and, similarly, on the person qua person. The understanding of God and persons that grew out of these conversations was eventually published as chapter 4 of *In Quest of Freedom* (which, incidentally, out of all the books was the one that I most enjoyed writing). In the years that followed, I have devoted less time to apologetics and more to reflecting theologically in ways that are enriched by science. Although one sees this shift in parts of *Adventures in the Spirit*, it was in writing *The Predicament of Belief* with Steve Knapp, and even more in the final chapters of *Confronting the Predicament of Belief*, that it comes to full expression.

Looking back, I can see that my movement through the theological traditions was part of the same progression. I began with Reformed theology (Calvinism), with its push toward theological determinism, affirming a God who is in causal control of history. Later, the four years in Munich brought with them the "solas" of Lutheran theology (*sola Scriptura*, *sola fide*, etc.), and the doctrine of "two kingdoms." But Luther's methods and conclusions seemed to diverge from the drive for full integration that fueled my work—though I have to admit that many Lutheran theologians, above all my *Doktorvater* Wolfhart Pannenberg, have been brilliantly systematic. Later I found myself at home in the Radical Reformation tradition and, in particular, in the radical Quaker practices of worship and activism. Friends' emphasis on "that of God in each one" grounds Quaker presentism—seeking "leading" in each moment and responding with non-violent actions aimed at bringing about peace and social justice, at whatever cost to oneself and one's community.

Most recently I've found these conclusions supplemented by the theology of John Wesley. When he writes, Wesley wraps himself in the language of the New Testament. His is not a systematic theology; it's a practical theology, suffused with the ethos of proclamation and response, testimony, and the love of God. Above all, it's a theology of "grace upon grace." Like John Cobb, I am drawn to the radical Wesley, with his personal *and* social sanctification, his call to poverty, his readiness to challenge existing social structures. Radical Wesleyanism does not require scriptural literalism, but it does provide a basis for a systemic critique of contemporary society and for activist forms of Christian faith. It's best summarized by what Albert Outler would later call the Wesleyan Quadrilateral, with its four sides of scripture, reason, tradition, and experience. A theology that succeeds in integrating all four is balanced, relevant, and powerful. This final phase in my four-step theological progression makes it possible now to return to constructive work in theology proper, including pieces on Christology, Spirit, providence, and spiritual healing.

Theology in Dialogue with Church and World

The journey also led me into the emerging church. The journey started with a student named Tripp Fuller, who would live tweet my systematic theology lectures to an audience (I later found out) of some 10,000 followers. Soon we were organizing conferences with names like "Theology after Google" and doing programs on Tripp's blog site, HomebrewedChristianity.com (check it out). Friends like Tony Jones, Doug Pagitt, Brian McLaren, Nadia Bolz-Weber, and Monica A. Coleman destroyed any chance that I would be perceived as a respectable theologian. I owe the popular book *Transforming Christian Theology* to this search for church-beyond-church and to the mantra that I learned from Phyllis Tickle, of blessed memory. For Phyllis, Christian life is not about determining one's beliefs, deriving one's behavior from them, and then belonging to a church. It moves in the other direction: *belong, behave, believe*—be unconditionally accepted by a community, learn how to behave in that community, and then sort out your beliefs as you are able (or not!). Interestingly, the Sermon on the Mount is equally central for Quaker, Wesleyan, and emerging church practice.

 The word "radical" appears often enough in my career to raise problems. Already the *Explanation* book, my first, defended the idea of "secular believers"; religion–science work led to a hypothetical theology; Steve Knapp and I developed the "not even once" principle and other theological heresies in *The Predicament of Belief*; and my inaugural lecture at Claremont, "The Many Faces of Integration: A New Vision for Liberal Theology between Church, Academy, and World," brought the ire of the seminary's president at that time, though it also catapulted me into the closing pages of Gary Dorrien's monumental history of American liberal theology. It's an inflammatory combination: the Radical Reformation, iconoclastic Quakerism, the radical Wesley, and radical forms of Christian community and practice beyond the sacred–secular divide.

 Publishing a book with the title *Organic Marxism* is apparently seen as the most radical. My co-author and I have attempted to explain that the book was written for Chinese readers in order to advocate a postmodern, ecological philosophy, grounded in the ancient Chinese traditions, one that can serve as the foundation for a strong environmental movement in China. Mar*xism* will not be helpful in North America, I think, but an "ecological socialism for the common good" could be. One can hope that my two recent books on American socialism (both religious and secular) will help to set the record straight.

Did Theology Die?

I've heard it said that theology became impossible sometime after Barth but the theologians failed to notice. Actually, it didn't die; it bifurcated and the two sides lost contact with each other, like the two sides of Congress divided by an aisle that no one crosses. The one side affirms that theology can no longer be done in the traditional sense, the other that pursuing theology in the traditional sense is the only way to save it. With an evangelical background and a Wesleyan identity, I had hoped to do some bridging. It hasn't happened. I consider this Great Divide to be the greatest tragedy for theology over the last 150 years.

It's not just the dialogue with science and contemporary culture that separates us, nor how we read philosophy, nor our doctrine of scripture, nor how much we care about the sexual habits of our clergy. No less important is the way that we interact across religious boundaries. Can Christianity learn from other religions, or must it first emphasize the differences? Surveys show a rapid growth of hybrid religious identities and decreasing interest in traditional religion. In a fluid and intersectional world, perhaps all theology becomes in some sense comparative theology.

I don't think I really understood panentheism until Loriliai Biernacki and I did *Panentheism across the World's Traditions*, nor divine immanence until Andrew Davis and I hosted the interreligious project, *How I Found God in Everyone and Everywhere: Memoirs of Spiritual Return*. Comparative theology, done well, avoids both the fall into relativism and the simple rejection of the religious other. It works in the space where comparisons and mutual learning take place without claiming a standpoint above them all, a "view from nowhere" (Nagel). With its rapid increase in breadth and sophistication, comparative theological work is becoming a basic part of the training of seminarians and the next generation of theologians.

Conclusion

In the *Histories,* Herodotus records the words of Solon the Wise to the immensely wealthy and powerful Croesus, "In truth, I count no man happy until his death . . . ." I am convinced that an open-ended, transformative theology-in-dialogue is the most appropriate form of religious reflection (and action) for today's world. But then again, as the fallibilist must always add, I could be mistaken.

Dialogue can be opened up or cut off, a boon for some and pure discomfort for others. It presents unexpected perspectives, invites one to see differently, challenges assumptions, increases complexity, undercuts prejudice. Theology, once the queen of the sciences, has been asked to leave her throne and come into the streets, to show what she has to offer on the open market. It's time to accept that challenge.

I am excited to expand the dialogue into new areas: how science, ethics, environmental action (and others) participate in the quest for ultimacy or God. How ecological civilization can bring hope in what may look like a spiraling collapse of natural systems. New books wait to be written: *Christology and Contingency*. *Emergent Ecclesiology*. A *Global Handbook of Religions and Sciences*. *The Space between the Atoms*. *This Sacred Planet*.

Sometimes I hear the reprimand: "But it's not theology." I disagree. In a monologue (literally, "speaking alone") the speaker defines his terms and lays down his parameters. A religious community too can monologue at the surrounding world. In dialogues, by contrast, we converse with *(dia-logos)* those around us. The theology I started with, the one I quoted at the beginning, is not the one I hold now. The journey continues, and I cannot predict its outcome. There is risk involved. I wouldn't change it for the world.

Claremont, California
June 1, 2018

Acknowledgements

AT THE OUTSET I wish to thank Bradford McCall, the editor of this volume. From first conception to final product, he has led the project with a firm hand. I am proud of the outcome and grateful to Bradford for his vision and the ability to bring it to fruition.

I also want to sincerely thank the staff at Cascade Books for their encouragement of the project from the very beginning and for the professional editing and production of this volume.

Finally, I express my sincere gratitude to the various presses that have allowed us to excerpt material from the books that I have published with them. Publishing houses today work on a very slim margin, and each one could well have declined our request in fear that this volume would decrease their own sales. The fact that they were nonetheless willing to grant permission for these passages to be published is not to be taken for granted. So please buy the books!

PART I

Science & Religion

1

Explanation in Science and Religion[1]

FOR BELIEVERS, RELIGIOUS BELIEFS help to explain the world and their place within it. Of course, religious beliefs do a number of other things as well. They can also function as redescriptions of the rites and practices of believing communities, as expressions in the language of faith of psychological and sociological needs and influences, or even as attempts to answer philosophical (ethical, aesthetic, literary) questions in religious terms. In addition, religious beliefs reflect a general sense of meaningfulness on the part of the believer, an existential attitude underlying particular dogmas that can be formulated and discussed. In this last sense, actual beliefs may be subordinated under a (possibly ineffable) picture, mood, or blik, a sense of fit or meaning, which relativizes their function as explanations of the world or events within it.

Still, among the various functions of religious belief is explanation. Ideally, one would begin a comparison of explanations in scientific and religious contexts with a complete definition of explanation. But if a definition were specific enough to be helpful, it would be specific enough to beg some of the questions along our way. Indeed, it would be question-begging in an even more onerous way, for one of the more interesting issues implied by this book's title is whether there even is a single concept of explanation that runs from physics to theology. We will find that the bulk of our task lies in specifying how one can even speak of explanation in the singular when referring to a broad spectrum of disciplines. The two concepts that I treat in greatest detail, coherence and criticizability, provide at best a few necessary conditions and thus only the beginnings of a unitary theory of explanation.

Following standard usage, I use the term explanans for the account that does the explaining and explanandum for the thing to be explained. I begin with the general hypothesis that explanations are answers to why-questions. If one is asked to explain an action that she has performed, she will tell why she performed it, listing as explanans

---

[1]. "Explanation in Science and Religion," as found within Clayton, *Explanation from Physics to Theology*, 1–17. Reprinted with the kind permission of Yale University Press.

her reasons, her intentions, or the external forces that constrained her. Or, in order to explain the fact or explanandum that two magnets move together in a certain manner, one will give an account of why they did so, referring to the laws of magnetic attraction and the way that these particular magnets were aligned. It is sometimes argued that explanations need only answer how-questions, that is, that one can provide no more than a description of a series of events in order to explain the explanandum. In order not to beg this question, we must construe the term why-questions in a rather broad sense, such that their answers may be given by relatively unembellished descriptions of states of affairs. Theories of explanation in particular disciplines will then have as their goal to specify the standards for agreeing that an explanandum is explained by its explanans in their field: must the explanandum be construed as the effect of certain causes? as the action that resulted from certain reasons (as in Aristotle's practical syllogism)? or merely as the thing that a certain description describes?

In general, then, an explanation makes some area of experience comprehensible to a number of individuals, either by presenting it in terms of its components or details (analysis), or by placing it into a broader context within which its meaning or significance becomes clear (synthesis). Unless one denies that the explanatory moment has any place among the variety of functions served by religious belief, it is important for the study of religion to carry out a careful analysis of religious belief as explanation.

Religious beliefs function to make sense of the world for the believer. They tell why something within the world—or why the world as a whole—is. They provide a framework within which, ideally, life as a whole can be viewed. Prima facie, we may expect to find some connections between explanations in religion and other areas of human belief and practice. Obviously, it is in the various sciences that we find the human explanatory project in its most fully developed and reflected form....

The parallels with the sciences are both intriguing and fruitful for the understanding of religion. However significant the parallels, religious explanations have unique aspects as well: they may be all-encompassing and deeply personal; they arise from vague and elusive questions concerning the meaning of an individual's life or human mortality; as religious answers they function to provide a context of significance and security, to "make life meaningful." In most cases, at least in the Western tradition, religious explanations involve positing the existence of a transcendent being or beings, who may be accessible (knowable) only to the believer or obedient follower. Both the scope and content of this sort of explanation separate it from explanations in other areas. Our task must include assessing the discontinuities as well as the continuities between religious and other types of explanation....

Types of Religious Explanation

In developing an initial list of types of religious explanation, a number of approaches can be used. If one took explanations to be no more than redescriptions of the world as the believer sees it, one could merely redescribe the descriptions. The goal would be to avoid any categories or "external" terms whatsoever, to portray only how specific beliefs and practices vary among religious traditions. (But, as I argue below, does not any redescription or comparison tacitly impose some framework on one's data?) Or, if religious explanations could be divided into a limited number of formal models, we could analyze these formal types, subsuming actual instances under them. (But theologians have encountered formidable difficulties in producing such formal models.)

By contrast, I will concentrate on the type and scope of the justification that is claimed for religious explanations. In doing so, I assume that the problems of explanation and rationality are integrally linked. Justification involves the nature and adequacy of the warrants that are given for particular explanations. A religious community may formulate beliefs of extremely broad scope that are believed to be true of or for all humanity; it may also view these beliefs as in principle intelligible to all persons; and yet it may still hold that the reasons for the beliefs are accessible to (carry weight for) the members of the community alone. It is my thesis that a rough spectrum of epistemic positions emerges, lying between absolute, universal, or objective justification claims and purely private justifications. Below, I focus on the categories of private, communal, and intersubjective explanations. If we are to draw any nontrivial science/religion comparisons in the final chapters, I must defend the intersubjective approach as at least one viable form of epistemic justification in religion.

The typology should begin with the private explanations, since a number of the options, whatever they may be in addition to being private, also make appeal to private justification. This category covers religious explanations that are held to be warranted solely by the fact that they make subjective sense of experience for the believer. It allows us to speak of the explanatory potential of religious traditions that are utterly unconcerned with the justification question. Tribal religions are often cited as examples of this category, insofar as they lack a consciousness of choice or multiple options and have not developed a tradition of rational defense or apologetics. Where religious belief and practice are pursued as a means to individual salvation or release, as in many of the Eastern traditions, the justification of religious explanations reduces to the personal efficacy of specific spiritual disciplines for achieving the desired spiritual state. One thinks of traditions within Buddhism in which the doctrines of the endless wheel of becoming (*bhavacakra*), impermanence (*anicca*), and no-self (*anatta*) explain primarily in the sense of defining a spiritual problem and the path that the believer can follow to escape from a life of suffering. Where the justification of a religious explanation is rooted in its personal disclosure value alone, I will speak of private explanations.

An especially clear example of private explanations is provided by the emphasis on the individual in recent Western religious thought, especially during the last two centuries. Paradigmatic is Kierkegaard, who held that "truth is subjectivity," and for whom the utter paradox of the Christ event transcended the fruit-lessness of philosophy by leading to "an objective uncertainty held fast in an appropriation-process of the most passionate inwardness," an "infinite passion of the individual's inwardness." But the believer who claims that her sense of the presence of God in scripture is sufficient reason for her faith fits the same model. Whatever broader epistemic warrants may be found for religious beliefs or traditions, this sense of fitting relevant aspects of one's life into a subjectively perceived coherent structure or whole remains a central component of religious explanation.

The second variety of explanation is similar to private explanation in limiting the horizon of its justificatory task. In this category, the limitation in epistemic scope is not to the individual but to a circumscribed community of believers or language users. Under this model, reason-giving (for instance, appeals to the Qur'an) is taken as authoritative for the entire linguistic community but is not assumed to carry weight for others unless they join the community of believers. This epistemic view, which has exercised a strong influence on the philosophy of religion through the influence of the later Wittgenstein, can be categorized as relying on communal explanations, since the standards for adequate explanations are set by the particular believing and practicing religious community. Since we are considering modes of justification rather than the scope of explanations, communal explanations need not be broader in content than private explanations or more circumscribed than transcommunal ones.

Not all religious explanations can be subsumed under the private or communal types. Especially within the Christian tradition, many thinkers have maintained that religious beliefs can be given a justification that transcends the boundaries of the individual religious community. Historical movements such as the apologetic tradition, natural theology, and perhaps even the quest for a systematic theology as such, have earned an important place for the notion of transcommunal justifications within the Christian tradition. When expressed in systematic form, Christian beliefs are often held to offer a reasonable or rational explanation of the world or of particular areas of human experience, one which the believer takes to have more than merely communal validity.

Explanations of this type need not be foundational in structure; they may involve appeal to broad (inter-systematic) coherence rather than to indubitable premises or intuitions upon which beliefs are grounded. Though I wish to preserve a role for private and communal explanations in religion, the central task of this book is to explore the possible nature, scope, and structure of transcommunal explanations. Because they claim to be valid intersubjectively or, in principle, without restriction, I label them intersubjective explanations. A more accurate label would be pansubjective, since these explanations often claim validity for (virtually) all knowing subjects. (Communal explanations are also, strictly speaking, intersubjective, in that they are accepted as valid among a specified group of persons.) Nevertheless, to avoid the neologism I will consistently use the term intersubjective with the broader sense of pansubjective. In epistemological contexts, intersubjective explanations are explanations whose warrant is not limited in principle to a specified individual or group of individuals.

Intersubjective explanation is at this point a term more suggestive than precise, especially since a theory of explanation only gradually emerges in the coming chapters. Intuitively, one can imagine a whole gamut of positions regarding the strength of the epistemic claims that might be made on behalf of intersubjective explanations. Presumably the strongest version of intersubjectivism is the attempt to prove one's religious beliefs, to give them deductive warrant. Natural theology often proceeded in this way, especially in its preoccupation with the proofs for the existence of God. However, the deductivist model as a standard for religious explanation rightly finds few advocates in contemporary philosophy of religion; even the theistic proofs are today more often taken merely to predispose one toward belief or to offer a retrospective justification.

In that it works toward a decision between these options, this book can be taken as a contribution to the epistemology of natural theology. As such, however, it stands in strong opposition to older, deductivist models. My thesis is that recent reflection on rationality, informed by work in contemporary philosophy of science, has effectively overcome the traditional dichotomy between rationalism and fideism in the faith/reason debate, thus requiring a complete rethinking of what a natural theology would entail. More specifically, I defend the quest for intersubjective explanations in the Western religious traditions by exploring their similarities to and differences from the various models of explanation that have been advocated in the natural and human sciences. Such explanations can claim to be intersubjectively or pansubjectively accessible even when they draw their content and form from a given religious community or tradition rather than from any outside discipline . . . .

Nevertheless, four central necessary conditions serve to guide the discussion.

1) *External reference*. To the extent that a religious explanation is alleged to be intersubjectively valid, it must be regarded as referring beyond the parameters of the believer's or community's experience. When Judeo-Christian believers speak of God, for instance, they do not intend to make a statement only about their own experience but about an actually existing entity as well. The intersubjectivist takes the objectivity, or subject-independence, of the referent—and the representational theory of language often linked to it—as providing prima facie reason for attempting to formulate religious explanations in an intersubjectively assessable manner.

2) *Truth*. Closely linked (and perhaps equivalent) to external reference is the claim that sound religious explanations must themselves be true and not merely, for example, enlightening to a given individual. The intersubjectivist argues that the ideal of truth is relevant to explanatory warrants as well. The concept of truth

implies something about what is in fact the case, whether or not I know or believe it to be so. Likewise, a theory of rational explanation must include the distinction between adequate and inadequate justifications; explanations must "get the world right" if they are to be adequate. Epistemologists have traditionally conveyed this requirement with their definition of knowledge as "justified true belief." If anything, the link must be stronger for religion: it is easy to imagine a practicing scientist who views her theories instrumentally or as "useful fictions," less easy to imagine a religious believer who does so. Of course, the fact that the question of truth is indispensable to religious belief does not yet resolve the debate concerning which of the various theories of truth is most adequate. Conversely, depending on which theory of truth one advocates, the relationship between the various necessary conditions presented here may be altered.

3) *Validity*. To avoid the murky waters of the contemporary truth-theory discussion, I often speak neutrally of the validity claims that various explanations make. In light of the goal of intersubjectivity, we can grant religious explanations to be intersubjectively valid when they are accessible to rational criticism by any person who wishes to examine the reasons for and against them. They are not merely arbitrary reflections of the contents of the individual's consciousness and his will to believe. To speak of reason-giving in an intersubjective context is not a return to objectivism: we may still discover significant influences on the knowledge process from personal, societal, and historical perspectives. Yet it is to say that, when intersubjective validity claims are made by believers, a certain burden of proof rests with them to defend these claims.

4) *Rationality*. It is clear from the appeal to validity that an intersubjective explanans will claim to explain its explanandum in a rational manner. Obviously there are vast differences between explanations with regard to the objects being explained and the methods used for explaining them. Moreover, there are differences between explanations formulated in one's day-to-day experience and those developed within an academic discipline. My seat-of-the-pants explanations of my neighbor's behavior are not very likely to coincide with the explanation that a psychologist would give. Likewise, the believer may go about explaining events in the world in a rather different manner than would the theologians of his tradition . . . .

2

Systematic Theology and Postmodernism[1]

The Postmodern Shift

ONCE UPON A TIME theology faced the "scandal of particularity." In New Testament times the scandal of particularity meant that the Greeks speculated about general principles of the universe (what could be broader than Aristotle's speculation on "the theory of being *qua* being"?) whereas Christians preached Christ crucified. . . . The scandal was back in the modern period, after a hiatus of several centuries in which Christian thought had dominated in the West without seeming scandalous—for was it not obvious to everyone that God exists and that he is revealed only in the history of the Christian religion (and represented only by Rome)? Our early modern predecessors broke with the obviousness of the Middle Ages. For them it was *again* the general principles of reason that caused the scandal. This tradition dominated modern thought in the West for 150 crucial years, and much more of modern philosophy owes its existence, its questions, and its fundamental intuitions to this line of thought than is usually acknowledged.

Ontotheology seems to have met its match at the hands of Kant. Kant was the one who (again, according to the received view at least) destroyed the ontological proof of the existence of God, the one who strew antinomies where once the evidences of the hand of God had been. Kant notwithstanding, most of the nineteenth century was still motivated by the perceived need to overcome the *pre-Kantian* modern tradition. Ontotheology represented for that tradition the highest claims of human reason: knowledge of the infinitely perfect being (*infinita perfectio*) who exists out of his own necessity; conclusive proofs of this being's existence; human nature as based on (and mirroring) this being; and all knowledge of the world as having its source in him. No wonder, in the face of such ambitious claims made on behalf of human reason, that

---

1. "Systematic Theology and Postmodernism," as found within Clayton, *God and Contemporary Science*, 1–9. Reprinted with the kind permission of Eerdmans.

Christian identifications of God as Trinity and of Jesus as the way to (knowledge of) the Father would represent a scandal for the Enlightenment!

But now the scandal is past—so, at any rate, my thesis. Why? Because the lofty aspirations of metaphysical reason are now *passe*. The claims of reason to universal validity and its claim to be able to derive important truths in an a priori fashion, "from reason alone," are now under severe challenge. Actually, the preceding sentence might be taken as a thumbnail sketch of what is widely called "postmodernism," that apparently dominant movement that is receiving so much attention in Western culture today. Diversity is now the name of the game; multiple perspectives are the bottom line; every person and cultural group has his, her, or its particular perspective; and we rejoice—at least in theory—in the differences between them all. There is no longer a scandal of particularity in a postmodern age because *it is precisely particularity that is being celebrated by postmodern thought.*

However, theologians have not yet caught onto this change of climate, it appears. By and large, they continue to march forward under the umbrella of *protecting* themselves and their traditions against the universal demands of reason, apparently not seeing that the sun is actually shining on particularity. (Liberal theologians seem to have recognized the new context, less so conservative theologians, who are generally those who aim to "conserve" as much as possible of the historical tradition of Christianity.) Most traditional theologians continue to write as though their readers will find it scandalous that they begin with the biblical documents, documents with a highly specific history, a series of culturally influenced ethical claims, a savior who lived at one particular time and place, and a set of highly specific claims about God.

This defensiveness is a grave mistake. Precisely what postmodern readers *can* accept about Christianity (as also about Judaism and other religious traditions) is the fact that it has its own particular set of sacred scriptures and its specific cultural location. For, they will retort, does not *every* religion in the world have the same specificity? Postmodernism or "multiculturalism," seen as a worldview, accepts and rejoices in such specificity. . . .

Thus, I suggest—to a degree that would have been unpredictable to most of *us* only fifteen years earlier—the doors have opened again for Christian theology. The long battle for Christian particularity, the context that forced Karl Barth to his famous "Nein!" some seventy years ago, is over. Christian theology has *not* lost out to the universalizing and homogenizing forces of philosophy and natural theology, as theologians throughout the modern era feared it would.

Unsurprisingly, the meaning and implications of the term *postmodernism* are hotly debated today—as one might expect of the label for a broad (all-encompassing?) cultural movement. For example, Nancey Murphy distinguishes vehemently between "Anglo-American" post-modernism and "Continental" (mostly French) postmodernism. As a result, I suspect (following Wenzel van Huyssteen) that the term *post-foundationalism* would be significantly less misleading than *postmodernism*. Van Huyssteen's

Essays on Postfoundationalist Theology provide a clear portrait of a theology that proceeds in critical dialogue with the sciences and philosophy—yet without the sense that theology's truth has to be derived at the outset from more general foundations!

Whatever the label, the shift has unfortunately caught most theologians by surprise. They continue to fight for exactly what is now being offered to them free of charge. If we believe that old-style *Fundmentaltheologie*—prolegomena understood as apologetics—is no longer credible in the current context, we must begin in a very different way, naming our particularity right at the outset and without apology. What follows, then, is an extended reflection on the very particular Hebrew and Greek texts out of which Christianity arose, on a specific man, Jesus, around whose person and teaching Christianity revolves, and on the symbols and concepts that have created and informed the almost two millennia of Christian thought.

Can Theology Still Make Universal Claims?

I wish in no way to deprecate this new development called postmodernism nor to undervalue its significance. Theology now faces opportunities it has not known for centuries. But along with these new opportunities comes a new task: to rethink, and to re-present, what it *means* to make religious truth claims. For there *is* one particular move that is stigmatized in the contemporary climate: to claim that one's particularity has universal significance. Christian thinkers have tended in recent years to move in one of two directions: either to formulate their truth claims in a more and more vehement fashion, refusing to give any ground and "damn the consequences," belittling "secular humanists" and "the secular mindset" and anything that would challenge the tradition (the fundamentalist orientation), or to cease to make any specifically Christian truth claims at all, proclaiming themselves satisfied to represent one particularity alongside the others (the liberal response). . . . Better, it seems, to address the methodological issues by making some sort of progress on the questions themselves; to paraphrase the scholastic saying, the best proof of the possibility of something is actually doing it.

There is a related task, however, which *is* basic to the present project. Let us grant that Christianity does in fact make some truth claims, that is, claims that can in principle conflict with truth claims made in other contexts. The task then becomes not only to relate Christianity to other religious traditions, but also to the (in the public's mind, and perhaps rightly) major source of knowledge about the world: science. For, at the same time that cultural and religious particularity have received new credence, the authority of scientific conclusions as an overarching framework of knowledge has never been so great. This is no coincidence, of course; it is yet one more manifestation of the old fact/value distinction that emerges in the earliest texts of modern thought. According to this view, there can be multiple ethnic and religious perspectives, and one can glory in this fact, precisely *because* they are all merely systems of values, myths, stories, interpretations. Because if none of these stories and none of their claims represent facts about the world, it is said, there is no reason that one cannot be a pluralist in all matters ethical and religious. The pluralism of cultures is not disturbing, one continues, because we *do* at *least* have a common understanding of how the world works: that provided by science. In short: one account of the world, many interpretations of that world; one physical world, many "meaninged" worlds. If Christian theology is going to resist the widespread application of the fact/value dichotomy, it will have to carry the discussion beyond a "self-explication of our particularity," and beyond inter-religious dialogue as well, to the level of a *fundamental discussion of the nature, status, and truth claims of both theology and science.*

The appeal to postmodern sensibilities—or to faith!—must not be allowed to make *theology's* task today easier than it really is. Though not necessarily antithetical to religion, the scientific mindset often stands in sharp contrast to the religious mindset. Pick any issue of a popular science journal such as *Scientific American* or *Physics Today* and thumb through its pages. The articles are about empirical phenomena observable in the physical universe around us. Most of the articles describe a concrete discovery that researchers have made about this world or a pattern emerging out of a group of such discoveries. Each discovery is described in rigorous terms; it is reconstructed with the *help* of a theoretical framework that explains large segments of the empirical world; and it includes a full accounting of the physical states or events that caused the observed phenomena. Even when the proposed explanation is a speculative one—indeed, especially then—the author takes pains to show the conditions for checking her explanatory hypothesis empirically. She inevitably presupposes that explanations are strongest when they account for the widest possible range of empirical data with greater adequacy than any of their competitors.

Of course, a scientist is a person too. She has prejudices, she may hold religious beliefs, and she may wish or hope that certain results will turn out to be true and others false. Sometimes she may even be less than fully objective in her judgments about whether or not new evidence counts against or in favor of her own hypothesis. Yet when she is in the lab, it is her business to pay close attention to the data, to the viable explanations, and to the theories and hypotheses that best predict observed phenomena. If her theory predicts or explains less well than those of her competitors, the scientific establishment will eventually leave it behind. And if she falsifies her data, makes a computational mistake, or puts forward empirical claims that are untrue, the odds are that her mistake will eventually be uncovered.

Scientists' concern with empirical data does not rule out any interest in broader explanations of the universe and humanity's place in it—explanations that may be, say, philosophical or religious in nature. Indeed, in so far as the book you are holding is located primarily within the discipline of theology, you have a right to expect that it will look carefully at a variety of explanations that go beyond what can be inferred, strictly speaking, from empirical data. Our goal will be to examine the doctrines of God, of

God's relation to the world, and of God's activity in the world. I will be presenting multiple positions, criticizing some of them, and offering a constructive systematic theology of my own.

But how is *this* possible, one might well ask. How can one take scientific results with the utmost seriousness, as I suggest we must, and still engage in constructive theological inquiry? The question is a serious one; it will occupy us in detail in the pages that follow. Imagine that one is convinced (as I am) of the importance of taking empirical inquiry seriously *and* of the importance of reflecting on broader theological and metaphysical questions. Even then, it is crucial not to deceive oneself about the sorts of answers that are most congenial to the scientist *qua* scientist—lest one pretend to satisfy science when actually ignoring it. Let us take one example: the study of "mind." Surely the phenomenon of thought—the individual experience of intentions, desires, ideas, volitions, and the like—is more widespread than the experience of God (at least as classically understood). Yet note what the scientist *qua* scientist would most hope to discover about mind. As a scientist, she would be most successful, by all accounts, if she were able to define "mind" exhaustively in terms of empirically observable phenomena that admitted of clear patterns and were fully quantifiable. She would be even more pleased *qua* scientist if she could then find a full explanation of this clearly defined set of phenomena, where by "full explanation" she would mean one that predicted them in terms of observable changes in the physical world (e.g., changes in brain states).

The goal I have just described is often called "explanatory reductionism" or "methodological naturalism." Of course, the success of the reductionist program would not be good news for ordinary or "folk psychology"—nor for theology, at least as the discipline has been traditionally understood! But there is no doubt that it would be good news for science as such. Bad news for science, by contrast, would be the discovery that mental phenomena are irreducible, that they obey (say) supernatural laws of their own, that their explanatory principles are inaccessible in principle to empirical study, or that they seem to be expressions of some kind of thing (say, the soul) that lies entirely outside of the physical world altogether. Clearly, there is some tension between the mindset of science and the goals of theology, at least at this methodological level.

Much of this book is about reasons to think that explanatory reductionism is, ultimately at least, inadequate. I will defend the theses that metaphysical and theological issues are raised by the methods and conclusions of the sciences; that theology and science share some basic principles of rational inquiry in common; that physical determinism and explanatory reductionism have (so far) been unsuccessful, and perhaps that they *must* be so in principle; that the world around us evidences sets of emergent properties that we call "life" and "mind" which exercise a causality of their own; and that the entire complex of data and experiences available to us are ultimately better explained in theological language than in the language of materialism and physicalism alone. Nonetheless, one must not make the task sound easier than the data actually allow. Theology may of course be pursued in abstraction from the results and methods of the sciences. But if we do choose to attempt a theology of nature "in light of contemporary science," then we must not pretend the task is more simple than it really is. As we will find, the task requires an openness to scientific results and to the various directions in which they point; it necessitates that one wrestle with tendencies that run counter to traditional theological answers; it demands an openness to revising certain dearly held theological conclusions; and, at the points at which one may wish to break with the (apparent) implications of the scientific results, it mandates that one either find reasons *inherent within the sciences themselves* for making that break, or that one supply reasons that might be held to be convincing in other fields (history, the human sciences, ethics, or philosophy) which point in the direction of the theological conclusions one wishes to defend.

The bottom line is that theologians must be intellectually honest with the data and conflicts that their discipline faces when it wishes to take contemporary science into account. It may be that the study of biological evolution is compatible with the notion of an overall purpose behind the universe; but it does not follow that the data of evolution *prove or give evidence for* the existence of such a purpose. It may be that Big Bang cosmology is compatible with the Christian doctrine of creation; still, the two are not identical. It may be, finally, that we are able to show that life is an emergent property out of physical matter, or even that consciousness is a real emergent in sufficiently complex biological organisms such as the higher primates; but such results would at best only suggest but would not prove that a spiritual dimension arises within consciousness at a particular stage....

A word should be said about the human sciences. As I attempted to show in an earlier work, the human sciences represent a crucial *tertium quid* between the "hard" empirical sciences and theology or metaphysics. Science (in the sense of the Latin and German words for science, *scientia* and *Wissenschaft*, which mean the organized study of a specific domain of data) requires that one take the human being and its behaviors and actions as a specific object of study and devote disciplines such as psychology, sociology, and anthropology to it. But if "organized study" were a *sufficient* condition for a science, then T. F. Torrance would have been right to claim that theology is as fully scientific as physics. What such easy equations do not mention are the specific strengths that characterize the empirical or "hard" sciences—lawlike ("nomological") explanations, prediction, quantification, rigorous falsifications—which are not shared by any other area of organized inquiry. Social scientific explanations that play well in Western culture (say, Freudian psychoanalysis) may seem absurd to non-Western men and women, and what passes as a compelling metaphysical position in one culture may not seem at all compelling in another. Yet the explanatory power of, say, quantum mechanics is equally as strong in *all* cultures, and the leading figures of science are drawn from throughout the world. The fact is that the natural sciences have the tools to overcome differences of opinion in a way that is not matched by any other set of human disciplines. This is why I maintain that the debate with the natural sciences has a particular urgency for those who make theological truth claims. . . .

3

What Theologians Can and Cannot Learn from Scientific Cosmology[1]

Creation and Cosmology

WHAT DOES IT LOOK like to do theology with one eye to the results of actual scientific inquiry? . . . When volumes and volumes have been written in a field, a single chapter cannot cover the entire gamut from primary scientific data to sophisticated theories. But it *is* possible in brief span to present a representative sample of the *sorts of ways* in which scientific cosmology can contribute to theological conclusions, on the one hand, and on the other, of the ways scientific work stands in need of an interpretive framework of the sort that theology (and other metaphysical theories) offers. . . .

Non-Theistic Non-Materialism

One quick way to see "how close and yet how far" scientific cosmology can come to supporting belief in God as Creator is to examine interpretations that come near to classical theism (or panentheism) yet diverge from it at the last minute. One good example of this phenomenon is Robert Wesson's *Cosmos and Metacosmos,* which comes about as close as one can come to theism without actually asserting it. His reflection begins with Big Bang cosmology, the theory that the material universe or "cosmos" began from a point about 15 billion years ago. According to him, it was generated from a matrix, which he labels the "Metacosmos."[2] The universe as we observe it now is so utterly improbable that, Wesson argues, it appears as though it must have been

---

1. "Creation and Cosmology: What Theologians Can and Cannot Learn from Scientific Cosmology," as found within Clayton, *God and Contemporary Science,* 127–61. Reprinted with the kind permission of Eerdmans.

2. Wessen, *Cosmos and Metacosmos,* 8ff.

designed for the development of intelligence. Yet one should not draw any theistic conclusions from the appearance of teleology, as for example advocates of the teleological proof have done.... Instead, all one can say is that the "Metacosmos" must contain *something* parallel to creativity, intelligence, and purpose, albeit on a higher level than anything we know.... Wesson's initial skepticism, his caution about drawing robust theological inferences directly from the cosmos, has much to be said for it. Wesson thinks there is reason to conclude that the universe points to *something outside itself*, and yet he is extremely cautious about developing a detailed metaphysics on the basis of physics....

Using Science to Convey Insights about the Spiritual Nature of the Cosmos

The writings of many recent cosmologists give rise to the strong impression that science is being used as a vehicle (or metaphor?) for conveying religious beliefs about spirituality and the rightful place of humanity within the cosmos. Angela Tilby's *Science and the Soul* is one good example of this category. Indeed, she makes no bones about it: "What interests me . . . is the way in which contemporary science is acting as a catalyst to the transformation of religious ideas, particularly in spirituality."[3] Such approaches should help warn theologians of the dangers of "deriving" a doctrine of the God/world relation directly from science.... Unfortunately, though, Tilby does not really allow too wide a dialogue to develop with regard to theological positions. Her treatment of the types of theological imagery associated with major developments in science through the centuries does not take a position in defense of a particular theological program but remains purely descriptive: she *describes* how biblical imagery has changed in response to scientific developments.... Tilby's pluralism and her ability never to be dogmatic about theological positions are admirable, yet they are won at the cost of not taking any particular position within theology at all....

Science Usurps the Role of Theology

The career of the physicist Frank Tipler serves as an interesting example of another model for relating science and theology. As Tipler worked on the "origins" question in physical cosmology, he discovered that the role of the human observer might be much more significant than physics had assumed. The fundamental values of the universe are slanted towards the eventual emergence of higher life forms in such an improbable manner; it is as if the emergence of life were a necessary feature of the universe. Together with John Barrow, Tipler wrote the now-classic *The Anthropic Cosmological Principle*. The book helped bring home to a broad readership that the values of a large

---

3. Tilby, *Science and the Soul*, 2.

number of fundamental physical constants lie within an extremely narrow range—the only range that would allow for the emergence of life. The observation of the a priori improbability that all of these values would line up in precisely *this* manner so as to allow for intelligent life is today called the *weak anthropic principle*. . . . Barrow and Tipler's *strong anthropic principle* is a rather harder pill to swallow. Based on work by John Wheeler and others, it involves the assertion that the universe *had* to bring forth life, in order (among other things) to resolve the quantum probability functions into a given macro-physical state. Under one interpretation of quantum theory, a photon of light travelling for millions of light years through the universe is strictly speaking only a probability function until the moment that it strikes your eye at night; at that moment it is retroactively resolved, back through those millions of years, into this particular photon. According to Barrow and Tipler's argument, the arising of life had the same sort of necessity to it: there would not have been an actual universe without the eventual emergence of an observer who would retroactively resolve the quantum states into the macrophysical universe that we know. . . . I suggest that this sort of linear approach and final control by physics represents a straitjacket on theological reflection that is artificially tight. . . .

Science Itself Challenges Reductionism and Supports Theistic Design

Another group of thinkers draws major inferences for theology directly from scientific cosmology, albeit without, like Tipler, trying to make the science itself do the work formerly assigned to theologians. One of the best known is Paul Davies, who has argued over a number of years that physical reductionism is counterindicated by an adequate understanding of current scientific cosmology. Because of Davies' prominence, and because he offers something like a science-based teleological proof, he may serve as a paradigm example of this group of thinkers.

Paul Davies first attracted the attention of theologians with his *God and the New Physics* in 1983. This book was in some ways the theist's response to an earlier batch of books that had emphasized parallels between contemporary physics and the Eastern religions, particularly Buddhism and Taoism. In a very accessible manner Davies was able to show that recent developments in physics and cosmology have reduced the distance between theistic belief and physics. Instead of trying to make physics itself religious, he contented himself with points of contact, with relative probabilities, and with metaphors allowable in the contemporary context that are congenial to theism. . . .

Theology Has the Interpretive Authority over Science

It is tempting for the theologian to set down the conditions on science in advance. "Here is what we know about nature, here is how it must be," she specifies in advance, "now let the scientists go out and learn what they may. If they come up with other conclusions, however, we will reject their findings, since we will know that they have made atheistic or naturalistic assumptions that are unacceptable to us." Such positions represent a popular paradigm for the science/theology relationship.

Ted Peters is a theologian at the Graduate Theological Union in Berkeley who has been one of the major voices in the science/theology dialogue. Not only has he reflected theologically on major scientific developments, but he has also been involved in a firsthand way with actual projects, for instance serving as principal investigator on the ethics side of the human genome project. Both as editor of *Cosmos as Creation* and as the author of an influential typology of positions in theology and science, he has helped to make clear the dangers and opportunities for theology in its discussion with science. . . . In "On Creating the Cosmos," Peters argues that enough progress has been made to relax the separation between the neutral language of science, which is concerned with "how" questions, and the language of theology, which raises "why" questions.[4] Peters advocates an active search for "hypothetical consonances"—harmonies between these disciplines.[5] . . .

Faith "Discovers" Belief in the Creator as the Best Answer

Some make a stronger claim on behalf of theism: the claim that faith in the "making of heaven and earth" by a Creator is the metaphysical foundation that (alone) can ground both science and philosophy. Consider, for example, the argument in *Cosmos and Creator* by Stanley Jakti. Jakti maintains that there is no incompatibility between science and religion when they are mediated by faith in a Creator God; rather, on this basis (and only on it) one realizes that both are legitimate and that the future progress of humanity requires both.

Like many religious "compatibilists," however, Jakti ends up challenging science. He urges, for example, a greater skepticism about scientific knowledge claims in order to correct for the overemphasis on science in our day: "Thinking when done by scientists is not necessarily the source of truth, scientific or otherwise. More likely than not, it is suggestive of presuppositions whose truth rests with the scientist's philosophy and not with his science." Because of the role of philosophical assumptions in allegedly pure scientific arguments, we should be much more cautious about appeals to scientific and mathematical "proof" as the standard for knowledge.[6] . . .

---

4. Peters, "On Creating the Cosmos," 275.
5. Peters, "On Creating the Cosmos," 274.
6. Jakti, *Cosmos and Creator*, 102f.

PART I: Science & Religion

Holism without Transcendence

The early reactions to relativity theory and quantum mechanics by physicists were more philosophical than religious. In now classic works, Sir Arthur Eddington, Werner Heisenberg, Carl von Weizsäcker, and others began to analyze the philosophical implications of the new physics for which they were responsible. It is a tradition that has continued down to the present day. Among these works, David Bohm's was one of the first to have a clearly religious ring to it.

First Bohm challenged the determinism that had dominated modern physics since Newton. With the developments in quantum physics, he saw, chance now had to be admitted as a key component in even our best physical theories. . . . Bohm next realized that the ontology of independently existing objects—or even that of individual particles, the core concept of Newtonian physics—needed re-examination. Mechanistic philosophies of this sort, he argued, are arbitrary and unsupportable. The number of things we take there to be depends, *inter alia,* upon the purposes for which theories are constructed and how we measure the world (this claim has been further substantiated by recent work in mereology, the set-theoretical calculus of parts and wholes developed by Lezniewski). What "really" exists, then, is a differentiated whole; any parts that we divide out must therefore be viewed as interdependent. Bohm thus stressed the innate tension between "autonomy" and "reciprocal relationship" in the concept of a thing. . . . At the conclusion of this work, Bohm makes clear the theological stakes of his interpretation of the implications of quantum theory: "In conclusion, a consistent conception of what we mean by the absolute side of nature can be obtained if we start by considering *the infinite totality of matter* in *the process of becoming* as the basic reality." In the physical world, "relativity is absolute"; as a result, "the essential character of scientific research is, then, that it moves towards the absolute by studying the relative, in its inexhaustible multiplicity and diversity."[7] . . .

The Desirability of Maintaining a Mystical (Panentheistic) Response to the World

A number of thinkers begin from the assumption that (something like) Kant's critique of metaphysics has made it impossible to do theology, that is to formulate beliefs about the nature of a transcendent being. At the same time, a worldview formed by science alone would be barren and devoid of meaning; and, they argue, many scientists *do* retain some sort of spiritual response to the world. Could there be some way to preserve the *function* that religion has traditionally fulfilled—providing a "sacred canopy," a framework that protects one from the sense of *anomie* and chaos in the physical world—without getting into the metaphysical morasses that belief in God seems to entail?

---

7. Bohm, *Causality and Chance in Modern Physcis*, 146.

Edward Harrison serves as a good example of this (widespread) approach. Harrison approaches cosmology with a strong dose of Kantianism. He holds that the Universe (that is, the universe in itself) is fundamentally unknowable, and that all interpretations that we put upon the Universe are founded in particular social/cultural contexts. Harrison endorses "learned ignorance" as the rational alternative to positive articulations of metaphysical knowledge. What remains when we are hard-headed enough to dispense with all metaphysics? Only a pantheistic/mystical appreciation of the Universe, supplying meaning in an otherwise barren universe. . . . Harrison argues that humans cheapen their existence by moving away from religious belief. Such a move is more an expression of prejudice based on the success of science than a response to argument. Moreover, the consequences of atheism are negative, since atheism goes against our very nature. . . . What kind of religious worldview, then, would serve the function Harrison advocates? Significantly, when he describes the kind of religious belief he thinks is needed, he comes closest to pantheism. . . .

Sophisticated (Religiously Tinged) Naturalism

As an example of sophisticated (religiously tinged) naturalism we can turn to one of the most sophisticated scholars in the discipline of religion/science writing today, Willem Drees. Drees begins with the premise that all elements of reality are constituted by the same kinds of matter (ontological naturalism). "Higher" or more complex phenomena, such as religion and morality, are thus to be viewed as natural phenomena; they may have their own concepts and explanations, but should in no way be considered as supernatural: "The challenge is to accommodate religious positions not merely to contemporary physics, but also to insights gained through evolutionary biology and the neurosciences as well as the social sciences."[8] At the same time, Drees insists that he is not eliminating or reducing the importance of religion: "Religious traditions are phenomena which differ from physical characteristics in that they embody an awareness of a reality which is different from the reality of our daily lives."[9] . . . Drees and I may be on opposite sides of the religious fence, since the present book is a defense of theology in the face of the naturalism that thinkers like Drees take as given in "the age of science." But I must nonetheless underscore his model of the discussion between science and theology. Drees sees that it is not possible to move directly from physical conclusions to theological ones—whether positive *or* negative—for there are "methodological problems arising in the transfer of ideas from one . . . system of language and thought to another."[10] This was a central thesis of my *Explanation from Physics to Theology*: the move to theological explanations must include, among other things, the concern with contexts of human meaning basic to the social sciences.

8. Drees, *Religion, Science, and Naturalism*, xii.
9. Ibid.
10. Ibid.

Drees (often) realizes that many of the meetings and negotiations between science and theology concern questions that are fundamentally philosophical in nature. What he has not seen quite as clearly is that many of these questions are trans-physical and therefore not decidable based on scientific results alone. . . .

Implications of the Discussion

We have discovered a continuum in the positions on the science/theology dialogue about cosmology.

1. At one extreme we find a sort of natural theology: thinkers like Jastrow argue that science leads to theology.

2. Others hold that science (contemporary physics) supports one particular religious viewpoint. Unfortunately, they disagree as to what it is. The natural theologians argue, for example, that the best answer is some form of theism. Some of their opponents find a closer connection with Eastern metaphysics, others with generic spirituality, and yet others with metaphysical views that are thoroughly non- or even anti-religious.

3. The next group of thinkers maintains that science by itself amounts to a sort of religious perspective. Thus, Tipler in *The Physics of Immortality* finds within physics alone sufficient reason to expect a sort of immortality for intelligent agents, without (he thinks) needing to move beyond physical theory to a religious perspective.

4. Others hold that science supports *multiple* religious perspectives. Paul Davies, for example, finds arrows in the direction of a religious interpretation of the universe, though he would insist that these indications underdetermine the choice between particular religious traditions.

5. More (metaphysically) skeptical are those who find spirituality in or implied by science and its results while resisting making any truth claims on *this* basis (Harrison, Tilby).

6. More skeptical still are the advocates of science and theology as two distinct activities that have nothing to do with each other.

7. Finally, others hold that theology is a pure construct, and naturalism represents the best truth we have about the world. . . .

What I have tried to convey is at least an initial sense of what science does and does not provide. Only when these parameters are in place can a clear picture be given of what it is that theology adds to the natural scientific knowledge of the universe. The net result is an interweaving of scientific and theological components into a rich account of what is involved in the creation and sustenance of the world by God. I summarize this theology in eight theses:

1. God's time is not our time because, assuming God pre-existed the world (a belief I take to be required by any version of theism), he *could not* have existed in anything like the (physical) time that characterizes the physical universe. Conceiving God as an agent requires that this pre-universe existence not be understood as a state of timeless eternity in the sense of Augustine. Yet clearly the passage of time in the divine life must be marked in a manner very different from the one we know. . . .

2. God created the universe in a singularity of matter/energy, a point infinitely small and infinitely dense. Physical space and time were not created separately or prior to the "moment," as Newton thought, but rather emerged along with the creation of the world itself. The universe does not expand into empty (physical) space, but space itself expands as the universe unfolds. Nonetheless, the universe begins and ends within the divine being, outside of which there is truly nothing.

3. The universe evidenced lawlike behavior (mathematical regularities) from the very beginning, although the laws that controlled the expansion in the very first instants were very unlike the laws we now observe in the universe. *That* the fledgling universe was lawlike and exhibited regularities of motion is, theologically speaking, an expression of the regular and rational nature of God. . . .

4. From the beginning, this universe was such that it was possible, if not inevitable (this, I think, we do not know), that life would someday emerge. Further, it was possible though not inevitable (this also, I think, is unknown), once life emerged on our planet, that it would someday evolve into intelligent life forms—the sort that could be reading and comprehending a sentence like the present one. . . .

5. The net result of these regularities (3–4 above) is that the universe appears to the physical scientist—at least to the one who takes *her own existence as inquirer* as one of the data to be explained—as though it were designed *in order that* humanity (and perhaps other intelligent life forms) could one day emerge. . . . Theologically, one can only conclude that the appearance of order in the universe is precisely what we would expect in a universe designed by God for life to emerge and prosper.

6. In theological terms, one will wish to say much more about the God/world relation than can be said on the basis of the evidence deduced so far. Above all, the theologian will wish to affirm, "Behold, it was (is) good," because the nature of the One who created it *is* to be good, and indeed to set the standards for goodness. The Christian proclamation is that everything that has occurred—including the very costly "means" of evolution, which involved incredible suffering—somehow works together for good (Rom 8:28). . . .

7. Theology also makes assertions about the place of humanity in the cosmos that cannot be derived from science. Specifically, it asserts that humanity has a moral

nature, that it is made specifically in the image of God, and that God has special purposes with humanity....

8. Finally, theology makes certain claims about the future of the universe that cannot be derived from anything we currently know through science (though, again, eschatology presupposes some knowledge of the physical cosmos and its probable future). In particular, Christian theology turns on the promise that God will someday complete the work that he has begun, drawing all things into the divine presence and perfecting the work he began at creation....

Perhaps surprisingly, then, our conclusion has been that *it is not the particular conclusions in physical cosmology that are most helpful to theologians.* ... Instead, *the single greatest positive result of current discussions in cosmology lies in the fact that scientific results plead for metaphysical, and ultimately theological, treatment and interpretation.*

4

On Religion

A Speech to Its Scientifically Cultured Despisers[1]

The Theme of Freedom

The goal of this chapter is to suggest—in what will certainly be complete heresy to some—that naturalism as a whole may not be sufficient for comprehending human persons and their agency. Such a radical thesis demands a different style of argumentation, one unlike any of the other chapters in this book. I have elsewhere made a philosophical case for this thesis.[2] Here, however, breaking from the standard mode of objective, academic presentation, I will not only analyze dispassionately but also advocate with passion, hoping thereby to break through the rather significant academic prejudice against all things religious. The goal of this unusual approach is to defend a perspective, indeed a world, that is widely considered to be an embarrassment within the Academy: religion. (That I do not thereby defend all doctrines that pass as religious, much less all actions that claim that name for themselves, should go without saying.) . . .

Critics tell me that it is too dangerous to publish a passionate defense of the religious or spiritual perspective: what if scientists conclude that the book as a whole is anti-scientific, or philosophers that it is anti-rational, or religious thinkers that it is anti-religious? I am told that adopting the language and style of Schleiermacher's famous *On Religion: Speeches to Its Cultured Despisers* from 1799 will confuse readers,

---

1. "On Religion: A Speech to Its Scientifically Cultured Despisers," as found within Clayton, edited by Parker and Schmidt, *In Quest of Freedom*, 112–32. Reprinted with the kind permission of Vandenhoeck & Ruprecht.

2. See Clayton, *Mind & Emergence*, chapter 5.

that they will miss the point and read poetic sentences as philosophical or theological assertions, confusing the language with expository passages elsewhere in the book. . . .

The goal of these pages is thus not so much to analyze as to evoke—to let the flowing tones of religion sound in a manner too seldom heard in scholarly publications like the present one. Rather than raising up conceptual requirements for "the essence of religion" and then looking to see whether or not the actual religious life satisfies them, I shall attempt to paint the world as religion sees it. After all, what purpose does it serve to regale my readers with a scholastic treatise on "theology in an age of science"? What profit would that bring? "For the letter killeth, but the spirit giveth life" (2 Cor 3:6). Or, in Schleiermacher's words, "I wish to lead you to the innermost depths from which religion first addresses the mind."[3]

To the Scientific Despisers of Religion

"I, for my part, am a stranger to the life and thought of this present generation," writes Friedrich Schleiermacher in the *Soliloquies*. "I am a prophet-citizen of a later world, drawn thither by a vital imagination and strong faith." Indeed, to imagination and faith "belong my every word and deed."[4] He continues a little later, "For I live always in the light of my entire being. My only purpose is ever to become more fully what I am; each of my acts is but a special phase in the unfolding of this single will."[5]

Are we today afraid to wed "a strong faith" with "a vital imagination"? Or do today's cultured despisers of religion secretly harbor the belief that religious persons should be like scientists, taking the measure of an object lying outside of them so that all can agree on its mass, energy, and velocity? Admittedly, an objectified theology is the safer course for one to steer, for if we can indeed establish the objective dimensions of the divine—whether in its nature or in its self-revelation—we will have protected ourselves from the ever-whispering fears of Feuerbach and Freud: *that all God-talk is a projection of inner wishes and constructions.* . . .

The academics among my readers will seek to label and categorize my call, assigning it to an "-ism." Already I imagine them mouthing the word "Romanticism," in an attempt to hold this message at arm's length. If the approach be Romantic, does that prove it wrong? At its heart, Romanticism turns on the role of the individual and the irreducibility of her experience. It arose as a movement of protest against the dominance of reason in the Enlightenment; do we not today need a similar rebellion against the dominance of scientific reason and its drive to become the arbiter of all truth? . . .

---

3. Unless otherwise noted, Clayton uses the translation by Crouter of Schleiermacher, *On Religion*, 10.

4. Schleiermacher, *Soliloquies*, 62.

5. Ibid, 71.

Let the message to today's cultured despisers of religion be as clear as possible: Schleiermacher's early vision of religion—call it Romantic if you wish—is one powerful means for meeting the demands placed on theology today: to connect with Nature as she is threatened by environmental crisis; to find in Nature more than the "dead mechanism" of reductionist science; from Nature's ecological interconnectedness to learn about the interpenetration of all things; and, through all this, to rediscover a sense of the divine as all-encompassing infinite Source, in Whom all finite things live and move and have their being.[6]

Consider that renaissance of interest in spirituality that has burst on the scene in recent years in Europe and America. . . . This growing interest in spirituality deserves our attention even if some of its manifestations lack sufficient depth and philosophical acuity. After all, before one can "lie directly on the bosom of the infinite world,"[7] one must have learned something of that inner self-cultivation that the religious traditions have fostered through their core spiritual practices. For without cultivating one's individuality and inner life there can be little understanding of God. . . . Not only inner listening is necessary for religious understanding, however. According to Schleiermacher, one must also have tasted romantic love, which he says also helps prepare the soul to understand its heavenly destiny. . . .

How then do we respond to the despisers? What do we say? Inwardness precedes the external world and trumps all other concerns; imagination reveals reason's foibles; passion is a prerequisite; and feeling is the vehicle to the deepest insights. All these faculties and experiences together point toward the interconnection, indeed the *unity*, of all things. This cannot be a theology of measured restraint, but rather one of joyful exuberance. It is not a theology for ripe old age: "Of what avail is it to economize and conserve action," writes Schleiermacher, "if you must weaken its inner content, and if finally you have nothing left anyway? Rather spend your life in a few years with brilliant prodigality, so that you may enjoy the sense of your strength, and be able to survey what you have amounted to."[8] No dogma should ever serve as a resting point, distracting from this passionate search: "What I aspire to know and to make my own is infinite, and only in an infinite series of attempts can I completely fashion my own being."[9]

Dangers in the "science of religion"

A certain style of treating religion—let's call it the reductionist study of religion—stands sharply opposed to this study. It may come as a surprise to see any religion scholars included among the "cultured despisers" of religion. "Are we not the ones

---

6. See Clayton and Peacocke, eds. *In Whom We Live, Move, and Have Our Being.*
7. See Schleiermacher, *On Religion: Speeches*, 43.
8. Schleiermacher, *Soliloquies*, 91.
9. Ibid, 96f.

who survey its territory, clearly lay out its boundaries, laying bare to all its essence?" they will retort. Yet a certain genre of books in the study of religion—one thinks of examples such as *Religion Explained* (Pascal Boyer) or *Darwin's Cathedral* (David Sloan Wilson)—is especially distant from the religious dimensions we have been describing. In the end, this genre may do more damage than even the well-known atheists and opponents of religion—more damage than the Steven Weinbergs and Peter Atkinses, the Jacques Monods and the Richard Dawkinses.

Even a style of scholarship that is less overtly hostile can still do damage. When an inept critic attacks his object in an unsophisticated or superficial manner, he raises the suspicion that no *deeper* criticisms are possible, making himself in the end an ally of the defenders of faith. But when we scholars of religion make a mediocre case for our object, we "damn with faint praise." When we dissect and lay out religion's various parts with the objective eye of an anatomist, we may provide knowledge of its structure and its functions. But we show forth its beauty about as effectively as the entomologist who tacks up the dead butterfly in his display case.

Much better to allow religion to spread its wings and move freely in its natural habitat. Not that seeking to *understand* religious phenomena is misguided; still, always our goal must be (as Marx insisted in another context) not *merely* to understand. Religion is a life that needs to be felt, experienced, and lived in order to be comprehended. It is no more accessible to purely dispassionate reason than the heart of an intimate relationship is to the surgeon's scalpel. Religion is lived from the inside out or not at all.

Criticism based on natural science

Scholars of religion, in their drive to dissect, are capable of doing damage to religion, sometimes by intention and sometimes merely by failing to bring it to life. (Of course, their depth interpretations and phenomenological redescriptions can also do great good.) But it is science—or, more carefully, a certain attitude often thought to be "scientific"—that may have done the most to deaden our ears to the music of religion. Lest this attitude be confused with science as such, let me refer to it as *scientism* rather than science. Richard Dawkins' outlandish thought (in *The God Delusion*) that biology as such would disprove the existence of God offers one of the most painful recent examples of scientism.[10] If we wish to regain our hearing for religion's inner life, we must understand how and why this scientistic mindset contrasts so sharply with the actual phenomenon of religion.

To the scientistic critics of religion I reply: How deep is your preoccupation with science, and how you hold it up as a standard for all else! If any claim is made about

---

10. Dawkins, *The God Delusion*. But even the less inflammatory sounding *Consilience* by Wilson makes the case that all actual knowledge is scientific knowledge; religion as such has no epistemic function but only emotional and aesthetic functions.

what is true or real, you proclaim that it must fall under the provenance of the sciences, since taken together they mark the boundaries of all things knowable. When we argue that some reflection should also be devoted to the nature of the world as a whole, as in the previous chapter, you write off the very possibility as meaningless. And when we suggest that religion is not about the purely objective—whether it be objects in the world or attitudes and opinions that can be objectivized—but concerns primarily the experience of the subject, her feelings, and her sense of absolute dependence, you dismiss our approach as merely subjective romanticizing and hence of no interest to hard-minded seekers after truth like yourselves.

Consider this: if religion does not in some way recede from the scientist's analysis, then there is no such thing as religion. Religion is only of interest, and there is only such a thing as "religion–science discussion," if religion is *another kind of thing* from scientific analysis. Yet if it is, one can't merely acknowledge these differences by the by and still approach "the religious object"—that very phrase should make us wince!—with the very same tools that one uses in the sciences. If religion is a living, breathing reality, then it needs to be held in one's hands as gingerly as one holds the baby robin fallen from its nest. If you do not feel its small fluttering heart and its warmth against your fingers, you have not known this creature.

Science represents the most efficient and effective means for knowing the natural world ever devised by humans. It provides the paradigm of knowledge—at least knowledge in the sense of truth claims for which reasons can be given, testing can occur, and false theories can be recognized. But objective testability and confirmability also come at a price; they require a very deliberate narrowing of the horizon. . . .

One soon learns, however, that the gods of testability and replicability are harsher masters than one might have expected; and scientists will be the first to tell you how heavy is their yoke. For example, their standards necessarily make one conservative about inherited science. Any theory *may* be overturned, of course; that's the principle of open-ended inquiry. But in practice one needs extremely strong reasons to show that a new proposal is more worthy of scientific acceptance than the existing theories, with their weight of theoretical and observational evidence garnered over decades (or centuries) and their established role in the training and habits of scientists.[11] . . .

In short: let us not be shy about affirming the strengths of the scientific mindset. There is no point in a Rousseauvian longing to return to the age of innocence before science, for truly there is no turning back. But we should also not be shy about challenging "Dawkinsian" over-extensions of the authority of science into philosophy, religion, and other non-empirical realms where the controls that make great science possible are missing. The power of scientific prediction and preciseness comes at a price; these virtues do not automatically transfer to every field about which the scientist himself may have strongly held opinions. Only when we recognize these limitations on the applicability of scientific method will we remember to raise our eyes

---

11. See Kuhn, *The Essential Tension*.

above the horizon of the mundane and to recognize the unique beauty and attraction of religion, its *mysterium tremendum et facinans*, its fascinating but also frightening mystery. . . .

What is a religious vision?

When one limits the scope of religion, one loses it altogether. This conclusion displeases many today. We want to anatomize religion, to give it a specific location—above all, to subsume it under some specific category, to make it psychological, or historical, or anthropological, or ethical, or aesthetic, or metaphysical. Fundamentalists, who might otherwise seem paradigmatically religious, are often guilty of limiting the scope of religion, seeking to domesticate it, to give it clear parameters, to make it this and not that, to formulate its truths and exclude falsehoods. Arguably, the response of E. O. Wilson in *Consilience* is the scientific equivalent of religious fundamentalism; it is the black-and-white drive to say that if religion is not a science then it cannot represent knowledge at all.

When the drive to anatomize breaks down, the scientifically cultured despisers of religion become the most vehement of all. "If religion cannot be this or that specific thing, then it must be nothing at all." Religion finds herself being told that if she will not subsume herself under some *specific* discipline or field, then she is forbidden to have anything to do with any of them. For example, if religion is not captured by the doctrines and creeds of a specific faith tradition, then it is "antinomian" or "apophatic." Or, as John Hick tells us, it is the Real which, being captured by no specific proposition, in fact eludes them all.[12] If religious belief and practice cannot be captured by a particular system of ethics, then religion is anti-ethical, immoral, infantile.

Metaphysicians (or metaphysically minded theologians) can be among the harshest of all the critics of the religious vision. If religion will not tie herself to a specific set of metaphysical or theological propositions, she is nothing more than vague enthusiasm or generic spirituality.[13] Is it really possible to guard the purity of the field of metaphysics (or, for that matter, theology), and the distinctiveness of religious phenomena, in this way? Clearly Hegel is not the only thinker who seeks to construe religious representation as the penultimate stage of a journey that culminates with philosophical system. Over and over again in the history of the West (though, interestingly, much less in the East), the "dream of a final theory" acts as a sort of magnet, taking up the diverse pieces of religious intuition and orienting them all toward a single pole.[14] When the hold of this dream is broken and its one-time advocates

---

12. Hick, *An Interpretation of Religion*.

13. This criticism has been raised by such diverse figures as Marion (*God without Being*) and Lindbeck (*The Nature of Doctrine*), albeit in radically different ways.

14. See Weinberg, *Dreams of a Final Theory*. Of course, Weinberg is referring to a final *scientific* theory only.

awaken to the fragmentation and diversity of religious phenomena, they frequently become the most hostile toward the metaphysical dimension and all its questions. Metaphysical language is "meaningless," they now tell us; it diverts attention from what is truly important; and, above all, no part of it may be treated as knowledge in any way.

But isn't such boundary-drawing self-refuting? To claim to know that there *is* no metaphysical knowledge is itself to make a metaphysical claim. If one is uncertain about metaphysical knowledge claims, shouldn't one become an agnostic, admitting uncertainty as to whether or such claims can pass as knowledge. It is as impossible to avoid treading on metaphysical soil altogether as it is absurd to insist that all who touch on metaphysical matters must be bound by exactly the same rules.

Despite all that Kant got right, one recognizes in him an archetype of this response. Finding certain metaphysical systems to be underdetermined by human experience as a whole (as, e.g., in the antinomies), he boldly declares that not an ounce of knowledge can be derived from the entire weight of metaphysical speculation. Out goes the baby with the bathwater. The truth is that we are continually confronted with hints and questions of significance that belong to no particular scientific discipline and yet will not let us go. We draw these hints and pieces together into always incomplete metaphysical proposals or hypotheses—what Anders Nygren called *Sinnentwürfe*, "meaning-sketches."[15] Inevitably we start to live according to these metaphysical visions, despite their fragmentary and incomplete nature. Always we seek to add more pieces and to fit them together more coherently, in the hope of achieving a *Weltanschauung* that is tied down to experience, a vision comprehensive enough to address the world as a whole. When we think and live according to these meaning-sketches, how can we fail to call them "religious"? If one is truthful, naturalists and humanists are no less engaged in such (broadly speaking) religious activities than are theists.

That the results of this quest are always fragmentary and incomplete does not mean that they are without value. Indeed, the quest to assemble metaphysical pieces together becomes all the more important when one discards the belief in perfect philosophical systems. The nonscientific pieces are invaluable; they would be lost or abandoned if they are not preserved in meaning-sketches and beliefs that are both metaphysical and religious. Above all, I've suggested, the inherence of the finite within the infinite may be the piece that is most indispensable for fitting all the rest together.

Conclusion

The role of this particular chapter in the book has been to show that science represents a very particular interest. Religion cannot compete with it on the level of knowledge claims. After all, knowledge in the strictest sense is possible only when one specifies

---

15. Nygren, *Meaning and Method*.

some domain of inquiry, rules of evidence, a reference group, and methods of inquiry. Yet if religion is the intuition or experience of the infinite within the finite, then by definition it cannot construct the sort of neat boundaries that make for testable knowledge claims in other fields.

In these few pages I have sought to show that at least some metaphysical proposals can remain in harmony with the music of religious intuition, despite clear differences of emphasis and phrasing. I stressed panentheism, although other examples could have been adduced as well. I have also sought, if only for a few moments, to break free of a scholarly genre of writing about religion, so that you might hear, however faintly, the melody of the religious voice and feel its tug, if only for an instant. . . .

Those who are drawn, as I am, by the harmony of this interpretation of religion may begin to grasp how that indefinable thing or experience that people like to call Romanticism has come to play, not least through Schleiermacher's work, a rather greater role in the development of liberal theology than is often acknowledged. What response is appropriate to this insight, and how might one reflect, and live, in response?

This, at any rate, is the space where religion lives and moves and has its being. Rising up from the ground of human experience like spring water issuing forth from the earth, it flows over all domains of human experience. It motivates our deepest ethical commitments; it flows through our most intimate personal and emotional connections; and it motivates our highest speculations about the nature of reality. Religion comes to us through experience and intuition, through hints and "intimations" of transcendence (Peter Berger), and through that fundamental drive to make sense of our total experience.[16] . . .

---

16. Clayton, *Explanation From Physics*, chapter 5.

5

The Basic Question
Science *or* Religion, or Science *and* Religion[1]

The Debate That No One Can Avoid

It is hard to imagine any institutions in human culture and existence today with deeper roots than religion and science. Religion is so basic to human history that the human species has been called *homo religiosus*, the religious animal. Indeed, some scholars even connect the origins of our species, *Homo sapiens sapiens*, to the first archeological signs of religious rituals and practices. A huge proportion of the world's population today is identified with at least one of the major religious traditions of the world.

It is equally impossible to imagine humanity without science. By 1900, about three centuries after the dawn of modern science, it was clear that this new means of studying the natural world and organizing our beliefs about it was transforming humanity more than perhaps any other development in the history of our species. By the end of World War II, when much of Europe had been reduced to rubble and Hiroshima to an atomic fall-out zone, science had changed the face of the planet for ever. Today there is virtually no aspect of human existence that does not depend in some way upon scientific results and technological inventions. From immunizations to heart surgery, from fertilizer to genetically modified crops, from our cell phones to our computers, from roads to airplanes, from the bananas on our table to our "cash" in the bank, existence without science has become inconceivable.

As we will see in the following pages, the impact of science is not only limited to its products. The scientific mindset has transformed humanity's views of what

---

1. "The Basic Question: Science or Religion, or Science and Religion," as found within Clayton, *Religion and Science*, 1–14. Reprinted with the kind permission of Routledge.

knowledge is, how it is obtained, and how knowledge claims are evaluated. Even people whose central moral and religious beliefs are not determined by science are still impacted by the growth of science, since *others* will judge their knowledge claims in light of their agreement with or divergence from scientific results.

Science and religion: compatibility or conflict? Should we talk about "science *and* religion," or should it be "science *versus* religion"? By the time you finish this book, you will have a good sense of the whole range of answers that have been given to this question and the best arguments that are being made on both sides. This should give you enough information to make up your own mind and to defend your own positions in each of the major areas of the debate.

Certainly the dominant message in our culture today is that science and religion stand in deep tension. Nowhere is this message clearer than in the debate between naturalism and theism. *Naturalism* is the view that all that exists are natural objects within the universe—the combinations of physical mass and energy that make up planets and stars, oceans and mountains, microbes and humans. In normal usage, naturalism usually implies the claim that real knowledge of these natural objects comes through, or is at least controlled by, the results of scientific inquiry. Cognate terms are *materialism* and *physicalism*. The former has traditionally meant "all is matter"; the latter technically means reducible to the laws, particles, and forms of energy that physicists study.

Theism is the belief in the existence of God, an ultimate reality that transcends the universe as a whole. Passing over a few exceptions, Jews, Christians, Muslims, and Hindus are theists. When the term is used broadly, it includes pantheists, panentheists ("the world is in God"), and polytheists—hence most of the native African religions and the world's indigenous or tribal religions. Typically God is described as a personal being, often with the qualities of omniscience (all-knowing), omnipotence (all-powerful), and omnibenevolence (all-good). Based on the sacred scriptures of their particular tradition (the Bible, the Qur'an, the Upanishads), theists often ascribe other qualities to God, such as consciousness, love, justice, and righteousness.

Theists usually defend specific ways of knowing, distinct from science, through which humans are able to know something of God and God's nature. Traditionally, they have believed that God created the world, providentially guides it, and reveals God's self in it. This means that God does things in the world ("divine action"), carrying out actions that are either consistent with natural law or that involve setting natural regularities aside (miracles).

At first blush, theism and naturalism appear to be incompatible positions. Naturalists affirm that all that exists is the universe (or multiverse) and the objects within it, whereas theists claim that something transcends the universe. Naturalists generally use science as their primary standard for what humans know, whereas theists defend other ways of knowing as well, such as intuition or religious experience.

So let us explore. Are the two positions incompatible? Or, when one probes deeper, can one detect any deeper compatibilities? The best way to find out is to arrange a debate between a knowledgeable representative from each side and then to see what emerges. As you know, good debates between naturalists and theists in real life are hard to find; they often deteriorate into name-calling and shouting matches. . . .

Taking Stock

What can we learn from this debate? First, it breaks at least one widespread stereotype: the tendency to associate all naturalists with science and all theists with an anti-scientific attitude. This is the first assumption many make in any discussion of science and religion; it is also one that is widely popularized in the media and in large-market books. Many people tend to identify science with an ultimate or "metaphysical" naturalism; they then associate belief in God with an anti-scientific attitude.

Yet our short debate has already shown that such easy identifications are too simplistic. Our theist, at any rate, was interested in the results of science. He accepted evolution and incorporated it as part of his understanding of life on earth and of human beings. He grounded his arguments for the existence of God in data about the origin of the universe and its laws (cosmology). His understanding of God and the created world drew significantly from scientific results. Clearly, he saw science and religion as compatible, though not identical.

Nor did the naturalist fit the stereotype of a scientific naturalist, just as many scientists don't fit the stereotype either. She was not inherently antagonistic to religion or to broader metaphysical positions. Of course, she did greatly value empirical data and would not endorse any position that made the doing of science impossible. She also tended to be skeptical about metaphysical claims and did not herself believe in the existence of God or a higher power. But she manifested a sort of healthy agnosticism about such questions, rather than a virulent hostility toward them. She might even have said, "Whatever religious or spiritual beliefs I end up affirming, I am concerned that they should not be in conflict with empirical results, for I want to learn as much as possible from scientific inquiry."

Even this brief debate provides some sense of the range of possible positions. As we will soon see, the range only increases as we consider the vast differences between the world's major religious traditions. Some theists are deeply antagonistic toward all science, and some scientists are hostile toward all religion. We will look at the reasons that these two groups give for their views in the next chapter. But sometimes the roles are reversed. Many theists build the core ideas of their theism out of science. If this is true for theists, it holds all the more for non-theistic traditions such as Buddhism. . . . Likewise, devotion to the practice of science need not make one anti-religious. Many scientists have pursued the practice of science out of deeply religious ends.

PART I: SCIENCE & RELIGION

It will be our goal in the following chapters to explore the intricacy of the questions and the main answers that are being given to them today—to take this opening debate deeper, as it were. Instead of black and white connections, we will find a world of complex interconnections, of similarities and differences, of shared partnerships and sometimes conflicting projects. Readers will be encouraged to take their own positions on the various debates and to construct the best arguments they are able to construct. Sometimes you will resonate strongly with one or more of the existing positions in a given debate. At other times you may find yourself formulating and defending positions that no one has ever advanced before. Like all philosophical topics, this one admits of many different possible responses, which—ideally—will lead to ever deeper and more adequate answers.

6

Science and the World's Religions[1]

IN THE NEWSPAPERS AND textbooks one usually reads about "religion" and science. Advocates defend religion; its opponents attack it. Both sides tend to assume that there is an essence, a single viewpoint, "religion," which either is or is not compatible with science. But *is* there such a thing as "religion"?

The goal of this chapter is to bring to light the very different kinds of concerns that are raised across the world's religious traditions. The order of presentation is particularly important here. Most readers in the West will implicitly have Christianity in mind when they begin reading a text on religion and science. A particular group of recurring topics tends to set the agenda for debates about Christianity and science: an initial creation "out of nothing" by God; the purpose or directionality to evolution; human uniqueness and the existence of the soul; the question of miracles; the bodily resurrection of Jesus Christ; the possibility of divine revelation; and the Christian concern with signs of the "eschaton" (the second coming of Christ, which is said to bring about the transition from this order to the next). . . .

But what about religions other than Christianity? It turns out that radically different concerns arise when other religions enter into dialogue with science. In many cases, the relationships with science that emerge are not nearly as conflicted as the ones we have observed so far. This helps explain the frustration that members of other traditions frequently voice about Western books on religion and science. . . . Let us spend some time, then, with each tradition separately. We commence with Judaism, in order to show how vastly different from Christianity are the concerns of historical Jewish thought and of contemporary Jewish thinkers. We then move on to Islam and two of the major Eastern traditions.

---

1. "Science and the World's Religions," as found within Clayton, *Religion and Science*, 43–65. Reprinted with the kind permission of Routledge.

PART I: SCIENCE & RELIGION

Judaism

Those who are aware of the way in which the discussion between Christians and science has gone will be immediately struck by the vastly different world of Jewish thought and observance. The Christian questions—at least those that are covered in the media today—often involve sharp oppositions: how can miracles occur? How can a man be raised from the dead? How can the Bible be inerrant in its historical and (implicit) scientific claims? How can God create the world in six days? How can God guide all of history toward his intended goals? How is one to understand the second coming of Christ, the judgment, and the establishing of a "new heaven and a new earth"?

With a few exceptions, to which we will return, the Jewish discussion with science has been very different. For centuries most rabbinical commentators have not worried about the exact historical details about how the text of the Torah arose, nor have they worried whether it is exactly correct on all scientific and historical details. Because obedience of the Law is central to Jewish identity, interpreting the legal requirements was viewed as more urgent, since the primary task of the rabbis was to guide Jews in their religious observance.

Specific events in the history of the Jewish people further influenced Jewish thinking. The second destruction of the temple in 70 CE led Jewish scholars to interpret specific predictions and prophecies in the Hebrew Bible more metaphorically and less historically. God's calling to his chosen people was obviously broader than maintaining the temple cult, which is what a literal reading of the Torah would have led one to expect. Moreover, the concerns of a people in diaspora, with no homeland and often fighting for survival in the face of persecution, were more pressing and more concrete. The Shoah (or Holocaust) in the twentieth century raised very fundamental questions about God's presence and care for Jews, questions that could not be answered by a literal reading of the Tanakh (the Jewish Bible) alone.

Now add to all these factors the incredible influence of Maimonides (1135–1204) and the tradition of "negative theology"—a tradition extended into the Jewish mystical or "Kabbalistic" tradition. The net result was a very different understanding of those theological debates that don't directly bear on observance. Among Jewish commentators, one finds a widespread willingness to treat many claims in the Hebrew Bible as metaphorical or figurative: the six days of creation, concrete historical claims, divine miracles, and details that might otherwise resemble scientific claims. There are even passages in rabbinical commentary (*midrash*) that suggest that rabbis should be guided by the best (i.e., most reasonable) interpretation of the Torah even over what might appear to be a direct sign from God. It doesn't take much reflection to realize that this attitude will produce a very different sort of religion-science debate than one finds in the books by the best-known Christian thinkers. . . .

These factors, though presented here only in the briefest outline, help explain some of the distinctively Jewish emphases in the religion-science debate. Consider these three. First, Jewish thinkers have generally been welcoming of, rather than resistant to, new scientific breakthroughs in fundamental physics, cosmology, origins-of-life research, evolutionary biology, and ecology. Overall, one encounters little anxiety or defensiveness about science in general or about new scientific theories. When Jewish authors relate scientific theories to the Tanakh, the Jewish Bible, they tend to write comfortably about how the results are consistent with Jewish identity. Analogies are drawn with teachings in the Torah and *midrash*, and writers tend to draw positive parallels for Jewish thought, identity, and practice. In reading these works, you generally don't detect the worry that Jews face a bunch of dangerous conceptual conflicts that must be overcome.

Second, ethical and political questions often move to the forefront; they tend to be far more important than the question of how Jewish beliefs could be true in light of science. For most Jewish scholars and educated readers, the more interesting questions lie elsewhere: How are humans different from other animals? What is distinctive about human existence? Are humans basically selfish rather than altruistic? Are we primarily individualistic or social? When are genetic interventions allowed, and when are they wrong? Could scientists someday build a robot that would be indistinguishable from biological persons?

When scientific results seem to show why Jewish observance is healthy or rational or functional, they naturally receive more positive attention; results that seem to undercut Jewish practices are reviewed with concern (and sometimes dismissiveness). Jewish authors have written some of the best analyses of the ethics of scientific research and practice, and their subtle and complex analyses often set the standard for other authors. Finally, another tradition of Jewish writing offers more mystical readings of the scientific results. Where this tradition predominates, science is generally used as a means for emphasizing the spiritual connection humans can have with the universe and with its Creator. . . .

There is one final feature about Judaism and science that distinguishes it from Christianity-science dialogues: the capacity to disagree with grace. Rabbis have always disagreed about virtually every topic they have written about, so Jewish scholars don't expect a convergence of opinion. Early in my career I remember watching three Jewish scholars dispute over science-religion topics and thinking, "They'll never talk to each other again after this battle!" Yet when the Friday afternoon session ended, the three scholars donned their coats and prepared to walk to the synagogue together for the opening of *Shabbat*. Christians have much to learn from this capacity to disagree gracefully.

PART I: Science & Religion

Islam

Islam was one of the first traditions to engage "natural philosophy," the predecessor to modern science. Muslim philosophers first translated Aristotle's writings into Arabic, which led to their translation into Latin and their growing influence in the West. But until recently the dialogue between Islam and modern science seemed to be a far lower priority.

In the past few years, however, the discussion has begun to receive intense attention. It is far more multifaceted than most readers realize. Some thinkers mirror the oppositional language of the more conservative wings of the Christianity–science debate; others call for a smooth integration of Islam and contemporary science; and others describe Islam as the "bridge" between the Western theistic traditions and the more mystical traditions of the East.

Seyyed Hossein Nasr speaks for many Muslims, both in the Arab world and in the West, when he challenges the identification of all science with Western science and calls for a distinctively "Islamic science." Materialism, naturalism, and reductionism—in short, a worldview hostile to God—have come to dominate contemporary science. Looking back to the medieval writings on nature by Jewish, Muslim, and Christian authors, these authors argue that it is not necessary for science to be anti-religious. Thus, Muslims (and, by implication, other theists) should develop and practice forms of science that do without these assumptions....

Reductionism and materialism are not intrinsic features of science; they are unfortunate by-products of decoupling the pursuit of knowledge from the search for wisdom. We should look first for signs (*ayat*) of the Creator's hand in the world around us. Once we have the correct metaphysics in place, it is unproblematic to develop specific scientific theories and technologies. But if we do not first acknowledge God, they argue, science will end up working in opposition to the Creator of all things—and thereby fall eventually into falsehood.

Defenders of Islamic science focus on a close reading of the Qur'an as a guide for knowing when science has drawn correct conclusions and when it errs (or goes beyond the evidence) and begins to manifest materialist and anti-theological prejudices. Like the secular "cultural critics," these authors call for a recognition of political biases—in particular, Western imperialist interests—in the allegedly neutral scientific theories. Western science promotes Western interests. When these are recognized, they argue, it becomes possible to develop forms of science that can promote the insights of Islam.

What kinds of questions interest Islamic writers and readers? Distinctive themes include the dependence of all knowledge and truth on God; the order in nature as reflecting God's creative activity; the need to begin with an initial divine creation in order to account for the world as we see it; the uniqueness of human beings in comparison to the animals; questions about what is the essence of humanity; the purposiveness of creation; the teleology or directedness of evolution, and hence the general preference for Intelligent Design over Darwinian biology. Authors describe the essence of human beings as moral and religious beings, looking to both science and revelation to understand what are our moral and religious obligations. One frequently reads lists of signs (*ayā*) that the universe is meant to run according to principles of justice, along with discussions of what those principles are. Muslim authors sometimes explore evidence that God is directing the entire process toward some particular outcome, including signs of divine judgment. History-based (and sometimes science-based) arguments are offered for the uniqueness of Islam and its superiority to other religions. Similar to the Jewish case, Muslim authors also look for scientific evidence that Islamic law (*sharia*) is conducive to human health and happiness.

Some Muslim authors hold that it is sufficient to study the Qur'an, Hadīth (the words and deeds of the prophet Mohammed), and Sharia. But many thinkers also emphasize the study of philosophy as an important means for expanding beyond narrow views of science. If metaphysical language is dismissed as meaningless, how can one possibly recognize the role of the Creator? . . .

Muslims believe almost universally that the Qur'an was dictated by Allah through his prophet Mohammed, so that the Arabic text thus expresses a direct communication by God. Many equate being a Muslim with regarding the Qur'an as the literal words of God. Nevertheless, there are an increasing number of Muslim thinkers who argue for the necessity of developing a Muslim hermeneutic, that is, principles for interpreting the Qur'anic texts in light of science and philosophy.

An important new book by Nidhal Guessoum, *Islam's Quantum Question: Reconciling Muslim Tradition and Modern Science*, argues for the possibility that there can be multiple readings and interpretations of some of the Qur'an's passages. Sometimes the best interpretation is not literal but allegorical. The principles for allegorical interpretation can be traced back to the great medieval Islamic philosopher Ibn Rushd (Averroes). When there appears to be a contradiction, "the (religious) Text must be allegorically understood and subjected to interpretation by those whom the Qur'an calls 'rooted in knowledge.'" Reclaiming these classic Islamic ideas would greatly reduce the tension between Islam and contemporary science. . . .

We close with two interesting features of the recent Islam–science discussion. One dimension involves the growing environmental movement among Muslims, including a rich use of the Islamic tradition to foster ecological awareness and concern. The other stems from the long Muslim tradition of mysticism and negative theology, which influences many Muslim responses to science. Sufi mystics have traditionally emphasized the unknowability of God, holding that one can only experience God through nature, other human beings, and mystical experience. Sufi authors beautifully and poetically evoke the divine in and through nature, encouraging spiritual rather than literal interpretations of contemporary science and its conclusions. One can trace this emphasis on God in and through all things all the way back to the thirteenth-century mystic Ibn 'Arabī. . . .

Clearly these more mystical Islamic voices offer a path to a less conflictual relationship with contemporary science than one sees in thinkers like Nasr. They also evidence important connections with some of the Eastern traditions, to which we now turn.

Hinduism

Hindu thinkers have been at the forefront of religion–science discussion in several respects. One contribution has been to emphasize common features that run across the world's traditions. Gandhi famously praised Jesus as an important spiritual teacher and identified with some core Christian positions. (He is reported to have said, "I like your Christ, I do not like your Christians. Your Christians are so unlike your Christ.") Many Hindu thinkers like to cite the text from the Gospel of John, "The kingdom of God is within you." . . . This Hindu emphasis tends to raise attention above the specific doctrinal (historical, philosophical) claims defended by the different religions and to concentrate attention instead on what they share in common. When one moves to this level, many of the specific conflicts with science decrease in importance. . . .

This more philosophical form of Hinduism leads to a very different sort of religion–science discussion. It accounts for the more mystical approach of many Hindu writers. The world can be accepted in its various forms of manifestation, and it can be studied by scientists without any conflict, but Hindu thinkers will generally insist that, ultimately, all these phenomena are manifestations of one single ultimate reality. All living things are contained within Brahman and express its nature in one way or another. Regularities in physical movement—what scientists call natural laws—are manifestations of the will and the habits of Brahman. Understood in this way, Hindu belief does not seem to come into significant conflict with the sciences.

It does, however, lead to a particular focus: the study of consciousness. Brahman exists in an eternal and unchanging state of existence, consciousness, and bliss (*satchidananda*, or *Sat-cit-a ñanda*). According to the great mystical philosopher Sankara, whose writings are at the center of the "non-dual" (*advaita*) tradition in Hinduism, these are the only three qualities that Brahman possesses; it is otherwise wholly without attributes (*nirguna Brahman*). As a result, we can know ultimate reality only through blissful awareness, which means only through our own meditation and consciousness. This has led Hindu thinkers to study the evolution and functioning of consciousness with the same sort of intensity that Buddhist thinkers have (as we will see in a moment).

Since there is only the one Brahman and all things are part of it, Hindu scholars have usually resisted any ultimate dualism of mind and body. This has made them interested in studying the ways in which mind–body connections work in human existence. They have generally been integrationists and interactionists, advocating a holistic approach to the human person. (We return to traditional Indian medicine shortly.) But there is also a deeper reason for the focus on consciousness, one that can lead to some conflict with contemporary science. The Upanishads also affirm that there is an eternal principle in each living thing, a soul or Ātman. It is this Ātman that is reincarnated again and again through the cycle of birth and rebirth (*samsara*). Hindu practice and thought exists for the ultimate purpose of liberation from this cycle (*nirvana*). Thus many Hindu scholars hope that the empirical study of consciousness will shed some light on the nature of this ultimate metaphysical principle, Ātman. This focus on an eternal soul has led to some conflict with Western scientists and their approaches to the study of the human person.

The conservative wing in the Hinduism–science discussion exhibits certain parallels with the conservatives in the Christian and Muslim traditions. Perhaps its most extreme form is manifested in those thinkers who maintain that all the major scientific discoveries of the modern period are already present in the Vedas, the original Hindu scriptures. This school defends the superiority of Hinduism over other traditions, highlighting science that supports core tenets of Hindu thought and challenging scientific results that appear to be opposed to them.

Mainstream Hindu thought does not make these claims. In some religions devotees are unlikely to be practicing scientists, but one often encounters Hindu practitioners who are physicists, engineers, neuroscientists, or doctors. As a Hindu physicist once told me, "Scratch a scientist in India, and you are likely to find a deeply devout spiritual person." They experience no tension between their science and their spiritual practices: keeping an altar in the home, bringing offerings to temples, and practicing the traditional ceremonies. Hindu belief and practice are likely to affect their ethical judgments, their beliefs about what is morally right and wrong, and their political stances on the burning issues in Indian politics today....

Writings on Hinduism and modern science have been dominated by a very different set of concerns than one finds in the Abrahamic faiths. In first place comes the study of the nature and efficacy of consciousness. In quantum physics, in evolutionary biology and ecosystem studies, in medicine and all aspects of human studies, Hindu scholars have sought to show that consciousness plays an indispensable role in the functioning of the universe. Purely materialistic explanations cannot be sufficient....

Still, Hindu scholars across the sciences are less known for these proofs and more for their emphasis on the mystical dimension of reality. The mathematical order and lawfulness of the physical universe, they argue, can and should prompt a deep spiritual response. Authors frequently encourage readers to discern the Ātman in plants and animals throughout the biosphere. Physiology, neurology, and medicine need to be pursued not "mechanically" but with an awareness of the spiritual dimensions of human existence. Above all else, Hindus emphasize the oneness of all reality in, or as, Brahman. They encourage meditation and spiritual reflection on science, with the goal of realizing the ultimately mental nature of all existing things as manifestations of a single reality and experiencing the connection of all existing things.

PART I: Science & Religion

Buddhism

Buddhism is widely regarded as the easiest religion to synthesize with contemporary science. One could argue whether this reflects a permanent feature of Buddhism or whether it signals how much Buddhist belief and practice has successfully adapted to the modern scientific world, at least in the West. Still, the outcome is the same in either case: Buddhist belief and practice today has become the poster child for successfully integrating religion and science.

Especially in comparison with Christianity and Islam, Buddhism—or at least Western Buddhism—seems to have slid into the scientific age with surprisingly little friction, conflict, or disharmony. Buddhist thinkers and practitioners frequently emphasize that this religion (if they still consider it to be a religion) focuses on meditation; it is primarily a way of seeing the world and a mode of existing in the world. They admit that Tibetan Buddhists and Japanese PureLand Buddhists (to name just two examples) held and continue to hold a wide variety of very specific religious and metaphysical beliefs. But the spokespersons for Buddhism in the West today tend to place the focus on meditative practices rather than demanding strict adherence to traditional beliefs. (Scholars dispute whether this approach reflects the core of the Buddhist stance or rather a smart and creative move on the part of its best-known teachers.) Thus, for example, the Dalai Lama has famously proclaimed that, if contemporary science conflicts with any tenets of Tibetan Buddhism, he will side with science and against the tradition.

In some ways, this "minimalist" Buddhist approach is not unlike the mystical Hindu approach that we encountered above, but its metaphysical sparseness is probably unmatched across the world's traditions. The "minimalist" Buddhist practitioner engages in a variety of meditative practices. She holds certain values about living with and treating other living things. At most, she will espouse some very general metaphysical beliefs (though she may not think of them as metaphysical at all!), such as the belief that all things are interrelated or interdependent, or that all that exists is "interbeing." She may or may not affirm the traditional doctrine of reincarnation....

Indeed, the Buddhist worldview is the opposite of reductionism, since it affirms the full and irreducible value of every manifestation of life in the universe, of every life form, no matter what its evolutionary history or level of complexity. Moreover, it places great value on the phenomenon of consciousness or awareness, which—at least in the forms in which human beings experience it—is an extreme latecomer in the field of evolution.

This difference leads us to one of the really distinct features of the science-and-Buddhism dialogue: the focus on consciousness. Buddhist scholars are very strongly motivated to engage in the study of consciousness, its origins, and its effects. They do not have any compulsion to link consciousness with some immaterial soul that carries and produces it. As a result, they are extremely interested in studying the natural emergence of consciousness, its evolution, its manifestations in humans and other animals, its contents, and its effects. *That* in turn inclines Buddhists to be allies with scientists across the whole range of sciences that bear on consciousness: the human sciences, of course, but also cognitive science, neuroscience, evolutionary psychology, genetics, and the classical Darwinian accounts of evolutionary history. If one is only interested in how consciousness arises and what its dynamics are, one need not fear or resist results of any of these disciplines, for all shed light on that question.

The other Buddhist focus is on the *contents* of consciousness. The technical name for this study is "phenomenology"; it involves the study of phenomena as they are presented to conscious awareness and as we immediately experience them. Buddhist focus on lived experience has actually helped to produce a new area of cooperation between scientists and Buddhists that many take to be a model for science–religion work to come. Known as the study of the "neural correlates of consciousness," this approach focuses on the correlations between perceived conscious states and brain activity....

What makes these results particularly interesting is that the scientific data produced *could not have be acquired without reference to the mental or conscious state that the subject was in*. This scientific research studies human beings in their full or "emergent" form; it depends on the conscious awareness and intentions that the subjects themselves produce and experience. Rather than "reducing" consciousness, the experimenters were *presupposing* consciousness. Put differently, the scientific knowledge was acquired, in part, by means of the religious beliefs and practices of the subject, rather than by asking the researcher to view religious beliefs as mistaken or at least irrelevant.

Scientists may welcome this sort of experimental method because it provides data on how mental experiences and brain states are correlated. For their part, Buddhist thinkers are enthusiastic about scientific evidence that shows that the discipline of meditation can actually alter one's perception of the world. Some scholars suggest that religion–science discussions should concentrate on partnerships of this kind where there can be satisfaction on both sides, rather than on those areas where religious belief and scientific results stand in dramatic tension....

Of course, the Buddhism-and-science dialogue also has its critics. Some argue that the pro-scientific statements are actually nothing more than good propaganda. Buddhism is, after all, a religious system, and it includes a large number of "superstitious" beliefs that clash with the scientific mindset. Other critics argue that the focus on the subjective contents of consciousness cannot be scientific, because it is not objectively testable and verifiable. It is fine for Buddhist subjects to participate in scientific experiments as long as the terms of the collaboration are set by the laboratory researchers. But the critics warn against allowing meditative practices (and the convictions they produce) to bypass scientific testing and pass for knowledge of reality. Belief in reincarnation, for example, is basic to all the traditions of Buddhist doctrine and is presupposed in most Buddhist rituals. Yet reincarnation actually presupposes something essential about a person that can continue from life to life. This belief, the critics note, cannot be consistent with any naturalist understanding of the world, and actually flies in the face of what we know about the dependence of "mind" on states of the brain and body.

Conclusions and Further Questions to Explore

At the beginning of this chapter I noted that critics frequently allege that religion, *by its very nature*, stands in tension with science. To speak in such generalities, I suggested, does not do justice to the incredible diversity between religious traditions and interests.

Some amazing cultural upheavals are taking place as each of the world's major religious traditions encounters modern science and begins to interact with it. In every case there is change. Some traditions immediately go into battle mode, placing themselves for decades or even centuries in an oppositional stance to most of what contemporary science stands for. They criticize specific results (especially those that conflict with their own traditional beliefs); they challenge the assumptions that underlie science, such as materialism and naturalism; they interpret science as a worldview and then contrast it to their own beliefs about ultimate reality. These traditions will often offer their own competing form of science in its place, as in Islamic science or various forms of Native American science. Other religions are torn for decades or centuries between "modernist" and "traditionalist" schools; one thinks of the intense debate over Modernism that rocked the Catholic Church in the late nineteenth century and continues into the present. Still other traditions such as Buddhism seem to slide effortlessly into the scientific age with little friction or conflict or disharmony.

Studying the various traditions in their distinctness should not obscure common themes across the traditions. Intelligent Design has adherents in Christianity, Islam, and even among some Jews and Hindus. Likewise, "progressive" or liberal approaches across the traditions share important features in common. Orthodox Jews and conservative Christians sometimes share a common interest in using science to defend the accuracy of the Hebrew Bible, and Muslims have similar interests for the Qur'an. Hindus and Buddhists are interested in evidence from the neurosciences that meditation can change brain states and, in particular, that the neurological responses of advanced meditators are different from the brains of ordinary people.

Certainly the diversity we have encountered in this chapter undercuts the claim that all religions are simply hostile to science. . . . Our exploration suggests one final possibility: that the religions, when one abstracts from their specific beliefs and traditions, may together point toward a more general feature of human existence that we might call "human spirituality." . . . In this regard, it is interesting to read the comments on spirituality by some of the most vocal science-based opponents of religion, such as Richard Dawkins and Daniel Dennett. Both individuals have commented in public that they know something of spiritual experience; both are happy to call themselves "spiritual but not religious." If the most vocal opponents of religion are willing to countenance the spiritual dimension of human existence, how could anyone argue that spirituality (in this sense) and science are intrinsically incompatible? And if they *aren't* incompatible, couldn't one work with the various religious traditions to identify those features of each tradition that focus on this spiritual dimension, which means the features that could be most easily synthesized with the sciences? In such a project, Buddhists will clearly play a leading role, but it could well be that this project could be extended to many other traditions as well.

7

The Future of Science and Religion[1]

Summarizing the Options

THERE WAS A TIME when it seemed that religion might just disappear. Throughout the modern period secularism continued to grow. It appeared that the religions of humankind would be superseded by science and left behind as historical artifacts, like Egyptian temples, the Greek gods, and many Christian churches in Northern Europe today. Certainly the hope of a world without religion continues to motivate some thinkers. Richard Dawkins' "Beyond Belief" movement and advertising campaigns in Britain and Canada have precisely this outcome as their goal.

And yet at present the outcome they strive for appears unlikely. If anything, there has been a resurgence of religious commitment around the world. Any decline in religion in Europe and North America has been more than compensated for by the rapid growth of Pentecostal and charismatic movements in churches around the world. Even non-religious thinkers, such as Jürgen Habermas, one of Germany's leading philosophers, now speak of moving—contrary to their and others' expectations—into a post-secular society.

Religion, then, it appears, is not going away. I take it as obvious that science is not going away either (if only because most people love their electronic toys too much). That means we have to find some way to deal with the relationship between these two great cultural forces. What are the possible outcomes? I consider five; perhaps you will be able to formulate others.

1) It could be that religion is just evil, so that, no matter how long it stays around, it should be opposed. On this view, religion is like racism or sexism or abusing children: no matter how inevitable it is, we should oppose it whenever and

---

1. "The Future of Science and Religion," as found within Clayton, *Religion and Science*, 152–71. Reprinted with the kind permission of Routledge.

wherever it arises. Something like this seems to be the position of Christopher Hitchens, who titles his book *God Is Not Great: How Religion Poisons Everything*.

2) Or perhaps modern science is just wrong. Perhaps one of the religions actually has the true answer, not only about God or the religious ultimate, but also about how the natural world functions. (It seems clear that not *all* the religions can be right, since they say different things about the ultimate nature of reality.)

3) The religions (or major movements within them) may evolve in directions that become increasingly hostile to science. The scenario might look something like this. Suppose the liberal, progressive, or "mainline" groups within Judaism, Christianity, and the other traditions continue to develop an openness to scientific methods and conclusions, as they are currently doing. But imagine that the result—say, an integration of Christianity and modern science—fails to provide that sense of meaningfulness and significance that is the primary function of religion. Imagine that too many people become disillusioned with liberal religion—either because it's too distant from the traditions as traditionally taught and practiced, or because it is not distinct enough from the surrounding secular culture, or because in other ways it fails to hold people's religious interest. . . .

If this happens, liberal religion wouldn't just disappear, but it *would* become increasingly marginalized. Modernist or progressive religious people would either move on to some sort of generic spirituality, one decreasingly linked to the historical religions, or they would give up on religious concerns altogether. Both responses actually amount to the same thing; after all, "spiritual but not religious" means, in practice, post-religious. . . .

Such a shift would leave the conservative and anti-scientific positions as the only significant religious voices in Western society. That outcome would certainly produce a sustained, bitter, warfare-to-the-death between science and religion. Conservative religious people would increasingly pull their children out of public schools where standard science is taught, either home-schooling them or placing them in religious schools, yeshivas, and madrasahs. Such people would vote against public funding for basic science research. . . . In response, the rhetoric of scientifically interested people toward religion would become increasingly harsh, and the number of religious people in the sciences would presumably decline.

4) On a more positive level, one can also imagine establishing a (more or less) permanent truce between these two systems of thought. Imagine that scientists and philosophers of science came to agree that religion is concerned about a separate realm altogether. Let us say they were able to precisely specify the domains in which scientific knowledge can be gained, happily leaving the remaining realms to art, literature, philosophy, and religion. One could even imagine that the chief spokespersons for science in our society would in this case even have positive

things to say about the arts and humanities, including religious studies—as long as they remained distinct from the sciences and did not make claims to scientific knowledge.

Then imagine that religious thinkers and practitioners accepted a similar distinction, though in their case for religious reasons. . . . Attempts to include religious beliefs about creation in science textbooks or science classes would immediately disappear. Religious persons might begin to say, "You know, my belief in God increases my interest in studying the natural world, and that's why I'm becoming an evolutionary biologist or neuroscientist." Non-religious scientists would be free to pursue their philosophical interests as well—outside of the lab, of course. . . .

A religious consensus would gradually emerge that passages in the various scriptures and commentaries—passages that many believers today interpret as scientific and historical claims—are actually better interpreted metaphorically or theologically. Phrases such as "Hindu science" or "Islamic science" would cease to be used. Presumably theologians would find their own ways to interpret scientific activity from the standpoint of their religious tradition and texts. But these interpretations would always be offered in such a way that the science itself was left untouched.

Similarly, scientists would become very clear about whether they were reporting actual scientific results, possible scientific results, philosophical interpretations of those results, or religious debates about what those results do or do not imply for the various world religions. Of course, maintaining the truce would require some discipline on the parts of both parties, but it certainly seems possible in principle.

(5) On the other hand, maybe the boundaries won't turn out to be so sharp after all. Let us also assume that, as the years go by, only a small number of religious extremists will want to stand in opposition to well-attested scientific results. Imagine that religiously interested thinkers and scientists increasingly become partners in exploring the intriguing borderlands between their fields. . . .

One need not assume that all religious believers would converge upon a single system of belief (though I suppose one cannot rule out this outcome). But one can imagine that people could come to hold a variety of religious interpretations of the world in ways that are compatible with and respectful of the spirit of science. We return below to a few of the positive results that would accrue from this sort of integration. . . .

Debates will continue as to which of the five options above is actually the best or most likely outcome. Progress is more likely if the participants have some training in questions of religion and science and understand the various options. The author hopes that those who have worked through this book and its questions will now be in a better position to engage in such debates—whichever positions they finally decide to defend.

Making the Case for Partnerships

In closing, let us consider a completely different approach to the question about the future of science and religion. Let us assume for the moment that religion *can* serve some positive functions in society. Indeed, many people are able to agree when religion is performing a positive role, even if they don't agree about the truth claims of the religions in question. If so, a society might be motivated to encourage constructive partnerships with and between the various religions—and to convince religious people themselves also to develop such partnerships. And if that's true, the urgent question becomes: what two-way partnerships might be possible, in principle, between religion and science? Consider (and evaluate) these four:

Values from science, values from religion

It is hard to deny that science teaches and exemplifies some particular values. During World War II the famous philosopher of science Karl Popper argued that science stands on the side of "the open society" and hence against totalitarianism, Marxism, and (his third nemesis) psychoanalysis. Similarly, Jacob Bronowski derived a number of specific values from the practice of science, including dissent, respect, freedom, tolerance, independence, reason, and justice. The well-known new atheist Sam Harris writes in a similar vein when he argues in *The Moral Landscape* that science provides all the values that one needs . . .

All this suggests a natural form of partnership. Science provides data about the world, and a correct understanding of the world represents the indispensable starting point for any reliable decision-making. Universal principles of fairness and justice then provide a first (and certainly indispensable) context for decision-making. No specific culture or religion should trump the basic requirement that persons are always ends in themselves and never merely a means for someone else's happiness or success.

The religious traditions and the scientific method

Religions are often associated more with blind belief than with reasoned reflection, but there are aspects in the various traditions that encourage the pursuit of rational discussion and the scientific study of the world. Fostering these connections would be essential for any partnerships with science. . . .

The same shared texts of the Hebrew Bible emphasize that God can be known in and through the natural order, which provides yet another theological basis for studying and knowing the world. Each religion nuances that mandate somewhat differently. The Jewish tradition has emphasized the tasks of studying and gaining knowledge. The call to study began with the Torah and commentary, but it gradually generalized to a major emphasis on studying the world in all its features. In the medieval period, Islamic philosophers played a major role in the development of the new "natural philosophy," which eventually gave birth to modern science. There are many Qur'anic texts that stress the order and regularities in the natural world and call Muslims to appreciate and understand that world....

Throughout the modern scientific period, religious authors have written theologies that support the pursuit of science and the scientific method—contributions that have often gone unnoticed by scientists and the broader public. In an age when scientific conclusions and the value of science itself are being challenged in many cultures, the religious supporters of science represent important allies. By seeking them out and forming collaborations for the public understanding of science, scientists could do much to deepen the reception of their work within these religious communities.

Compassion and justice

The simplest thing that we associate with religion may also be, in the end, its most valuable contribution. Critics of religion point out the hypocrisy of people who say they serve the God of peace, unity, and love while at the same time they treat their opponents, members of other religions, and even their co-religionists in such unloving ways. Note that the criticism itself acknowledges how deeply rooted is the call to compassion in most of the religious traditions....

Non-religious people will rightly respond that it is not the task of the religious traditions alone to exercise compassion or call for justice. One does not have to believe in God to think that it is good to act in a loving manner toward one's fellow citizens or the people in one's neighborhood. This is surely true; religions don't have a corner on the compassion market. Still, non-religious groups that work to mitigate suffering or to bring about more equitable treatment for the disadvantaged will welcome religious groups who wish to become their allies in this endeavor. Surely such involvement is a step up from religious groups that seem only interested in protecting their own rights or debating the sexual habits of their clergy.

The environmental crisis

We close with perhaps the most important example of all. There is overwhelmingly strong scientific evidence that human activities, such as the release of greenhouse gases, are fundamentally changing weather patterns on this planet. People in Europe and North America are only beginning to notice the shifts, but the effects are already striking the global South. Unfortunately, given the nature of the systems in question (for example, the way in which glaciers and ice sheets melt), the impact will be felt gradually at first and then more and more dramatically. Current models suggest that the effects of a continuing increase in greenhouse gas emissions, especially if it moves toward 600 parts per million, will have catastrophic effects on the global environment. The models suggest that the effects of these changes could last as long as 1,000 years.

Scientists have voiced immense frustration that governments and citizens are not responding rationally to the urgency of these data. By and large, the data are being ignored. Worse, members of the public (and some religious groups) have been inclined to challenge the science, offering counter-arguments that are uninformed or, in some cases, patently false. Scientists often ask, "What more can we do to motivate people to pay more attention to the scientific evidence and to act in ways that will avoid, or at least mitigate, the disaster?" . . . Only scientific models can work out the precise consequences for the planet of different levels of greenhouse gases being released into the atmosphere.

By contrast, scientists are, frankly, not particularly good at motivating ordinary citizens to change their lifestyles. Science can explain empirical relationships and causes, but reciting the facts often leaves people cold (as those who work with data know only too well!). Yet science's weakness is precisely religion's strength. For centuries, religions have played crucial roles in influencing their followers' beliefs about right and wrong and in motivating them to live differently in the world. That is what religions do. . . .

Recall that the importance of the natural world and humanity's responsibility to care for it lies right at the heart of many of the world's traditions. The three Abrahamic faiths go back, as we saw, to the Book of Genesis, which calls believers to cultivate and care for the earth. For Jews, Christians, and Muslims, nature is not a lifeless or mechanical thing, a mere compilation of "matter in motion," but a creation of God and therefore a thing of great value. As a result, believers in God have every motivation to protect it from destruction, especially destruction at their own hands. . . .

The Eastern religious traditions are, if anything, even more oriented to treat the surrounding world as a thing of value. Earlier we studied the call to compassion in Buddhism. In this tradition there can be no temptation to treat the surrounding world as a mere means to human ends, since Buddhists do not single out human beings as intrinsically more valuable than other animals. The central Buddhist call is a call to compassion for *all living things*. A Buddhist environmental ethic is thus central to the entire Buddhist lifeway.

Buddhists have also warmly embraced environmental science and ecology. They argue that it is consistent with the Buddhist teaching of the interdependence of all living things, and that focusing on the welfare of ecosystems—and all the living beings within them—mirrors core Buddhist convictions and practices. Earlier I mentioned the movement known as Engaged Buddhism, which practices ecological activism based on traditional Buddhist principles. For example, Buddhist monks in Thailand have gone into forests that were marked for logging and have conducted the ceremonies of blessing there, placing the mark of blessing on the trees. No Buddhist logger, or anyone who respects the sanctity of the Buddhist practices, could cut down such trees in good conscience, since this is the mark normally placed on a person when she is blessed by the monks. Activist efforts such as these are fascinating, because they bring the resources of environmental studies and the concern with ecosystems together with very traditional Buddhist beliefs and practices.

We also observed that Hindus and Jains recognize a soul in all living things. The process of reincarnation for them not only includes human beings but the *Ātman* or *jiva* of all living things. Thus, caring for the earth and preserving the environments on which other living things depend remains at the center of these traditions. This holds even more for the African, Native American, and other indigenous religious traditions. Tribal peoples knew themselves to exist in an intimate balance of receiving and giving with the animals and environment around them. Much more than in contemporary culture, they knew their precarious dependence on the weather and how devastating climate abnormalities such as droughts and floods could be for their peoples. . . .

Although all the partnerships envisioned in this section are important, the one considered above may be the most urgent of all. Even if all the other collaborations fall through, even if religions and sciences continue to clash over beliefs and worldviews, a successful partnership in staving off a centuries-long climate catastrophe would be enough to make the entire effort worthwhile. . . . In most of the topics that we examined, we found these two groups locked in their battle to the death, arguing for diametrically opposed positions on each topic.

As we delved more deeply into the issues, however, we found more and more reasons to wonder whether matters can really be reduced to a single either/or decision. The range of religious beliefs and attitudes turned out to be much broader than one might have expected. Not only are the different religious traditions concerned about very different sorts of issues, but their attitudes toward scientific knowledge vary just as widely. Nor is science a single monolithic theory. The different sciences study vastly different sorts of phenomena, from quarks to kangaroos to consciousness, with each bringing its own set of theories, methods, and types of data. These differences are a part of the story, alongside the common features of scientific method shared across the natural sciences.

Perhaps the fundamental choice the reader has to make is the choice between the incompatibilists and the compatibilists. If one sides with the incompatibility of science and religion, one needs only decide which of the two opposing sides to join. Subsequent decisions become rather simpler. Whenever a new topic comes up—stem cell research or the origins of life or medical ethics—one only needs to know which answer supports his side and undercuts the other side. All the rest are details. . . .

But the challenge of science and religion also has something to offer those who are less drawn to the speculative questions. One can be a skeptic about the truth questions and yet an enthusiastic supporter of their practical importance. People who are more practically oriented may still believe that the sorts of partnerships outlined in this chapter are potentially of great significance for humanity and this planet.

Especially with regard to the global climate crisis, one should acknowledge the "opportunity cost" of failing to work together. Those who follow science and take its conclusions seriously know that there are potentially catastrophic consequences for not changing current human patterns of consumption. We are amazed to find people willing to set aside the consensus of scientific opinion or to ignore it (it is not clear which of these two is worse) and to continue current practices at the personal, communal, and national level. One does not have to be religious to welcome any positive role that the world's religious traditions can play in helping to resolve this global crisis. It would be tragic if unnecessary feuding between the scientific and religious establishments meant that the chance was lost for them to work together as powerful allies to affect human policies. That is one opportunity cost we cannot afford to pay.

PART II

Science, Faith, & God

8

The Context for Modern Thought about God[1]

Introduction: Skepticism and Metaphysics

NOT TO PUT TOO fine a point on it: the context for treating the question of God today must be skepticism. Propositional language about God can no longer pass as unproblematic. The history of reflection in this area is littered with skeletons—or better: it is immensely difficult to discern which are the skeletons and which the living, progressing models. Past thinkers may appear overly bound by the philosophical fashions of their day and by the world as they constructed it; yet we have no reason to believe ourselves *more free* of such forces than they. Even *theologians* today have grown squeamish of the "God's eye point of view," and many reasons have been advanced for worrying that the very idea of such a point of view is confused.[2]

The concept of God refers to a reality that is in some essential sense transcendent of, and thus not locatable within, experience. In our day, I shall argue, this concept presents itself more as a problem than as a solution.[3] God is not at home in any of today's disciplines outside of theology—and even there the professionals voice misgivings. Whatever its accessibility in the context of religious faith (and there are also reasons to wonder about this accessibility, especially among an academic public), the concept of God has inherited a variety of unresolved intellectual difficulties. Arguably, the status of God-language has never fully recovered since the collapse of the Scholastic doctrine of analogy. It is a concept that is construed in mutually exclusive

---

1. "The Context for Modern Thought about God," as found within Clayton, *The Problem of God in Modern Thought*, 3–49. Reprinted with the kind permission of Eerdmans.

2. Putnam, *Reason, Truth, and History*, 49ff.

3. Kaufman, *The Problem of God*, 7. The literature on the changed context for the use of God-language, and on the contemporary problem of God, is immense. See, e.g., Gilkey, *Naming the Whirlwind*; Tracy, *Blessed Rage for Order*; MacQuarrie, *Thinking about God*; Schwarz, *The Search for God*; Flew, *God: A Critical Inquiry*; Armstrong, *The History of God*.

fashions. As long as we do not know whether God-talk has a solid basis in human experience—and, if so, *where* in human experience—the relationship between theism and the various sciences, both in content and in method, remains problematic.

Since the theme of this book is the concept of God, the *problems* associated with this concept will thus serve as its backdrop. At the outset, atheism must be taken as a full and live possibility.[4] Perhaps naturalism is right; we may be the doomed inhabitants of a dying universe. . . .

Such a naturalistic scenario, whether its tone is negative (as in the Nietzsche quotation) or more optimistic, must be treated as a live option by any contemporary theory of God. It is thus methodologically unacceptable to immediately assume the impossibility of atheism. . . . But of course we *can* believe this. It's fully possible that there is no general meaning to be had, only the meanings that we create. Indeed, don't religious skeptics from Hume to Kai Nielsen offer ample evidence that it's possible to orient oneself toward the atheist conclusion? It is therefore overquick to assume that "in our explicitly religious turning toward God in prayer, and in metaphysical reflection, we merely bring to our conscious attention what we had always implicitly known about ourselves at the very base of our personal existence."[5]

A crucial way in which the philosophical tradition has expressed this general skepticism concerns the question whether language about God can be "constitutive," that is, can refer to an object and express actual positive content about it. The distinction between constitutive and nonconstitutive goes back to Kant, for whom concepts without empirical content—and thus especially the concept of God—could only be "empty" as knowledge claims (A51/B75).[6] But one need not be a Kantian to approach theistic language with a certain degree of doubt; the lines of argument leading toward skepticism about the rationality of God-talk are legion. As examples I will trace only two here: the difficulties with "metaphysical explanations" in general, and the problems stemming from the historicity of knowledge.

1. Evidence and Rational Explanations

If language about God is to be constitutive, it must evidence some explanatory value vis-à-vis human experience. But, to put the issue in general terms, it isn't clear how explanations that refer to God *could* be rational explanations. Many specific versions of this criticism have been formulated: theistic explanations are literally meaningless (A. J. Ayer); they are untestable and thus vacuous (Anthony Flew); they are unfalsifiable and therefore must be sharply bordered off from scientific language (Karl Popper); the

---

4. For a vibrant example of contemporary intellectual atheism see the work of Nielsen, e.g., his collection of essays *God, Scepticism and Modernity*.

5. Nielsen, *God, Scepticism and Modernity*, 63.

6. References to Kant's *Critique of Pure Reason* are given in the text in this form, "A" referring to the first and "B" to the second edition of Kant's first Critique.

series of causes in a theistic explanation cannot be reconstructed and hence natural explanations should be preferred over supernatural explanations (the presumption in favor of naturalism).

The difficulties with such efforts at sharply demarcating science from metaphysics have been widely discussed and need not be rehearsed here.[7] It seems, at least, that it's no longer possible to rule out reflection on first principles using dichotomies such as scientific vs. mythical, falsifiable vs. falsification-immune, or meaningful vs. meaningless. Science is just not as neat as we once thought.[8] Still, one does need to focus on the differences that still remain, especially where they help reveal the epistemological challenges—the challenges about its status as knowledge—that theology faces. One way to grasp these remaining difficulties is in terms of a distinction that Bernard Williams' draws: scientists are required to provide a theory of error—a newer theory must be able to say why and where its predecessor went wrong—whereas philosophers working in ethics or metaphysics cannot and need not do so.[9] So the question becomes, Can metaphysics provide a theory of error? Does it possess procedures for testing its claims—or at least for separating out those areas that are rationally undecidable? Can one specify procedures for the critical treatment of theological truth claims?

The following chapters claim to make some progress in addressing these questions. Nonetheless, it does seem unlikely that the explanatory claims of theology could ever achieve the same rational status as the knowledge claims advanced within more concrete and precise disciplines.[10] And it will be hard to claim truth for selected theological theories if the community of scholars is unable to say of *any* theory in the field that it is false. Ironically, the oft-heralded eternality of metaphysical debates is at the same time their chief weakness. For example, it's often viewed as a strength if a contemporary thinker can trace her position back to Parmenides or Heraclitus, Plotinus or Aquinas. Unfortunately, though, such practices give the impression that in this field absolutely nothing has been resolved since the beginning of its history. If we are to rescue the possibility of progress on the question of God, we will have to provide a clear notion of what constitutes progress and which criteria signal its presence

I open this book with a chapter on method, written against the backdrop of pluralism and skepticism, out of deference to the difficulty of these worries. For those of us who do not want to abandon all explanations containing the term "God," the task is clear: we must specify a way of treating theological questions that justifies their claim to be rational explanations—for instance by showing how such explanations are necessary for specific dimensions of human experience. This means showing how

---

7. Among many other examples see Clayton, "Religious Truth and Scientific Truth."

8. See e.g., Laudan, *Progress and its Problems*.

9. Williams, *Ethics and the Limits of Philosophy*, chapter 8. Williams' immediate reference is to ethics; still, the epistemic worries he raises about moral theories apply directly to traditional metaphysics as well.

10. As argued in Clayton, *Explanation from Physics*.

metaphysical claims are to be evaluated critically. Should we fail at this effort, then we will have to acknowledge that decision procedures are absent in metaphysics. Presumably this would leave an irreducible pluralism of gods—or no god(s) at all.

2. Historicity

A second major challenge to the present project involves historical skepticism—limitations allegedly placed on one's knowledge (or on one's knowing that she knows) because of one's particular position within the history of thought.

The hermeneutic shift

The pervasiveness of interpretative issues in the study of history *may* not ultimately be a block to knowledge, for history *could* of course lead to a final unity of perspectives. Nonetheless, the plurality of perspectives or "conceptual schemes" does present problems for interpreting past metaphysical positions; it also raises questions about the possible timeboundness of our own reflection about the nature of God. Advocates of the hermeneutic shift have argued convincingly that there are disparities between our "horizon" and the horizons of our those whose texts we study; criticism and appropriation always require that one achieve a fusion of disparate horizons.[11] Now admittedly, exorbitant claims are sometimes made about how hermeneutics, the "science of interpretation," will change everything. One occasionally reads, for example, that no distinction can any longer be drawn between theory and observation, between fact and value, between knowledge and interpretation, between interpreting and appropriating a text—even between reading and writing a text! I have argued elsewhere that hermeneutics does not force one into complete skepticism of this sort.[12] Nonetheless, the discussion of hermeneutics does suggest certain limits on any reconstruction of the theories of past thinkers. On the one hand, one must be constantly on the watch for the "otherness" of the historical texts and authors she interprets. Although it may sometimes be possible to criticize or appropriate an author's position and arguments directly, at other times a radically different set of assumptions may separate that world from ours. Only by carefully reconstructing the author's own intellectual and social context can we understand the meaning of her concepts, that is, what *she* meant by them. As a byproduct, such reconstructions often bring home the huge distance between the present and (say) the thought-world of the sixteenth and seventeenth centuries, a distance that one doesn't automatically perceive merely by reading the texts of that time.

---

11. Important works include Gadamer, *Truth and Method*, and Ricoeur, *Conflict of Interpretations*.
12. See *Explanation From Physics to Theology*, chap. 3.

On the other hand, contemporary theologians need to be equally aware of the links between their metaphysical assertions and *their own* historical or cultural context. We are initially much less likely, for example, to give credence to theories of timeless being, or to definitive theories of the Absolute—in fact, to definitive theories of anything! Footprints of our Zeitgeist rest on titles such as *Reason, Truth, and History* or *On the Plurality of Worlds* or *The History of God* or *God: A Biography*.[13] Are these prejudices justified? To the extent that we recognize the objects of our study to be timebound, we must suspect our own conclusions to be so as well. . . .

3. First Implications for Metaphysics

General skeptical worries associated with the hermeneutic shift, and specific difficulties involved in knowing the sort of being that God would be, have transformed the manner in which one must approach theism today. We've already seen how the changes affect the study of the history of modern thought, how they demand a movement toward hermeneutically sensitive methods of study. Typically, they result in the call to recognize the ineliminable role of *context* in all intellectual inquiry.

Yet there's one discipline that is still claimed to rise above the fray: theology's philosophical sibling, metaphysics. Throughout its history, metaphysics has been concerned with timeless truths. Perhaps the challenge of contextualization would be relatively unproblematic for historians, or even political theorists, for whom timeless truths are not the issue. But how can *metaphysical* reflection do justice to this changed epistemological climate and still remain metaphysics? Can there be a metaphysical reflection on God whose claims remain preliminary and hypothetical, whose method builds in a sensitivity to context? Is "pluralistic metaphysics" a viable shift within this discipline or a *contradictio in adjecto*?

Ultimately, I will argue, metaphysical reflection must remain by its nature dissatisfied with multiple outcomes; the driving force in this discipline is always to unify, to select the *best* theory from among competing alternatives. Still, there are cases where a clear rational decision cannot yet be made between the competitors. In such cases, claims for the finality and certainty of one's own position can only appear as absurd and unwarranted.[14]

Our own epistemic position is characterized by the lack of ultimacy—no less when it's the Ultimate that's under discussion! This fact calls for a certain continuing attitude of humility toward one's own constructive theological proposals. But it also

13. By Hilary Putnam, David Lewis, Karen Armstrong, and Jack Miles respectively.

14. Consider, for example, the dismissive opening words of Thomas Morris's collection of essays, "it is hard to see how anyone whose personal faith is rooted in the Judeo-Christian religious tradition, and who is aware of the metaphilosophical facts of the matter, could be tempted in the slightest to buy into any such impoverished philosophical perspective [such as Hume, Kant, or positivism], vetoing as it would effective human reflection on ultimate matters" (Morris., ed., *Divine and Human Action*, 4). Clearly, analytic philosophers are not immune from absolutist claims.

suggests handling the great texts of the past in a different manner as well. No longer can they appear as necessary, canonical moments in a perfectly unfolding story. This gives us a new task: not just to interpret authors' intentions but also to rationally reconstruct their work in light of the narrative as we now see it.

4. Non-constitutive Approaches to Metaphysics

Since Kant a number of thinkers have responded to skeptical considerations such as the ones adduced above by denying that statements about God serve an explanatory or epistemic role at all; language, they say, is being used in other than a constitutive sense in this realm. Some of these critics interpret God-language in a noncognitive sense, so that it has cognitive force only when eliminated or translated (call these *eliminative views*), whereas others would continue to theorize in something like the traditional mode while interpreting its status differently (*revisionist views*)....

Conclusion: The Prospects for a "Theology from Below"

There is no guarantee that theology pursued in the manner I've been suggesting will finally converge on the results or the methods of traditional theology—or, for that matter, on traditional metaphysical language about God. There are three logically possible options: perhaps theology pursued "from below" will diverge further and further from the traditional language of a transcendent being; perhaps it will come to be subsumed by metaphysics in some sense; or perhaps new and interesting analogies between the theological and metaphysical projects will emerge.

Theology without transcendence

Perhaps it will turn out that the boundaries of subjectivity can't be broken. If one starts from below, from human experience, perhaps one will always remain within its sphere. On this view, whenever theistic language is employed, it will always refer exclusively to human, or at least thisworldly, realities.[15] It may be, for example, that the God-idea serves various positive functions—in ethics, in epistemology, or for religious persons. But note that the idea "God" might serve a variety of useful functions without picking out any being or state of affairs whatsoever. Indeed, its usefulness as an idea is compatible with the complete unknowability of God—and indeed with the non-existence of God as well!

Nothing in this opening methodology chapter can prove in advance that transcendence will survive the critical objections raised against it. Perhaps the cleft between

15. Those who advocate this view are fond of citing as example the concept of "world" in Heidegger's *Being and Time*, insofar as it clearly remains (for the early Heidegger at least) an existential feature of Dasein, stemming out of (and in this sense relativized to) human experience.

human thinkers and the concept of the Absolute is unbridgeable; perhaps our fate as would-be knowers is to grasp the infinite only as a projection out of the finite reality that we experience. If this is the case, philosophies of immanence will eventually have to be substituted for traditional theism, emphasizing even more its fictional status—as in Feuerbach's critique of religion or A. J. Ayer's critique of metaphysics. Could it be that in the end theology is fated to consist of nothing more than aesthetic preferences and bourgeois sensibilities?[16]

Theology qua metaphysics

Perhaps, by contrast, exercises in philosophical theology like the present one will uncover a powerful version of philosophical theism, one that answers the major objections as well as incorporating and explaining the major assertions of traditional theology. In this case, the reduction of theology to the human dimension would be circumvented, but at the cost of making theology a special case of metaphysics.

I must admit to a certain degree of skepticism about this happening, though I suppose it remains possible in principle. Imagine the following scenario: a conceptual structure (a philosophical theory) is developed that provides the first principles of scientific rationality *and* persuasive interpretations of the major theories in the sciences and theology. Imagine, for example, that all of these things come to be understood as moments in the self-unfolding of the Absolute. In this case, the theory of the Absolute would subsume all the steps taken to reach it. One would then have to say that exploratory studies of the problem of God in modern thought—and theology in general, for that matter—were a sort of prolegomena on the way to a fully adequate theory of God. They would be merely "phenomenology" in Hegel's sense: arguments that only *appear* to climb their way upwards from below but are really guided (unbeknownst to them) by the end that they anticipate. If this were to occur, no cleft would remain and all other items of knowledge would be sublated (*aufgehoben*) into the true philosophy, to which efforts like the present one would be mere propaedeutics. It could happen, I suppose, but in the meantime I recommend the attitude perfected by the fine people of Missouri: "show me."

Theology and metaphysics as parts of a common project

There is a possibility between these first two options, however, which I hold as the most likely of the three. Examining concepts such as infinity or perfection or "the unity of all that is" may point toward (something like) traditional metaphysics as its

---

16. Of course, transcendence and immanence are not exclusive options. Several of the more recent versions of theism suggest new ways to mediate between them. Perhaps the most important initiative in this regard is panentheism. For further references to the literature on panentheism see Clayton, *God and Contemporary Science*.

PART II: Science, Faith, & God

ideal, without ever being able to *demonstrate* that these ideas are actually components of true theories. Put differently: metaphysical concepts may prove useful, even indispensable, in various disciplines; they may summarize important areas of experience; they may even act as vital components of theories in various areas (from cosmology to theories of human nature).

One of the disciplines in which they have proved most useful is theology. It is a basic premise of this book that theologians can make use of metaphysical concepts and theories (as metaphysicians can make use of contributions from theology) without the subsumption of the one discipline by the other. Those who know the histories of the two disciplines know that they have been closely associated from the beginning (often by those who are most eager to assert their total independence). If the analogies between them can be recognized and the common ground tilled together, apart from the foolish struggle for hierarchy and dominance, then the potential for cross-fertilization can be maximized. But I will only convince readers to turn their swords into plowshares if I can demonstrate the mutually beneficial nature of the dialogue in actual practice.

And with this challenge it is time to turn from epistemology to the questions themselves. For eventually one must set aside the "what if . . . ?" and "what would be the status of . . . ?" questions and begin to look at the best constructive responses to the problem of God that have been made over the last several hundred years. Perhaps we will be able to make some progress, and perhaps we will bog down in hopelessly confused concepts and marshlands of implausible assumptions. Which of these will be the outcome is not something that can be settled a priori, and certainly not by the ruminations of methodologists! Only by wrestling with the major authors of the modern period and with the actual arguments they advance can we hope to reach some informed conclusions. It's time to start.

9

The Personality of God and the Limits of Philosophy[1]

Divine Personality

IF, AS SCHELLING SUGGESTS, freedom is the highest principle in God, it is what is unlimited (or infinite) in God. Hence, will is crucial, since the concept of will connotes actions not dictated by the nature or properties of an entity. Now, we associate will exclusively with persons. Personality, therefore, is the final step in our reflection on God as infinite. The final corollary of the move from (Spinozistic) infinite object to subject, in addition to freedom, is the personality of God—in however a minimal or attenuated sense.

Schelling argues that "personality consists . . . in the connection of an autonomous being with a basis which is independent of it, in such a way namely that these two completely interpenetrate one another and are but one being" (7:394f.).[2] He claims it follows that God is the highest personality. But this will only work, he realizes, if one avoids both pure realism (Spinoza) and pure idealism (Fichte), that is, if one says neither that the whole is beyond subjectivity (for this would imply that subjectivity is only an illusion) or that all just is subject. The most attractive alternative to these two extremes is panentheism, since "God's personality can only be based upon the nexus between him and nature" (7:395).

Schelling's own way of making the argument is to view the divine will in two parts, incorporating Spinoza's realism as the divine "will of the basis" and Fichte's idealism as the will of love (7:397). With its intricate detail and host of questionable assumptions introduced as alleged necessities of personal development, the position

---

1. "The Personality of God and the Limits of Philosophy," as found within Clayton, *The Problem of God in Modern Thought*, 501–8. Reprinted with the kind permissionof Eerdmans.

2 All Schelling quotations are from Schelling, *Schellings sämmtliche Werke*, vol. 7.

remains unconvincing, and I will not pause to give it a full exposition here.[3] Instead, let's remain with the basic idea of the position: there can be freedom in God—or, what amounts to the same thing, God can be conceived as person—only if panentheism is the case. For there are good reasons to follow Schelling in espousing his central principle: "All existence must be conditioned in order that it may be actual, that is, personal, existence. God's existence, too, could not be personal if it were not conditioned, except that he has the conditioning factor within himself and not outside himself" (7:399). Division, he adds, is the condition of God's own existence qua personal (7:403).

Thus, there are two clear conditions that the doctrine of God must satisfy: 1) God as our infinite source cannot be less than we are; God must at least have abilities comparable to ours, even though, as greater, they will be different; and 2) there must be a free decision to create. But freedom is the quality of a being with a certain degree of self-awareness and with the attribute of will. Because God must be conceived as a subject with this degree of self-awareness and will, we speak of God not as "it" but as person.

Schelling only did justice to the personhood of God in his later philosophy. Earlier (e.g., in the Bruno) his thought is dominated by his fascination with the undifferentiated One in which all distinctions, even the finite/infinite distinction, are resolved. Only later—after he had worked through the stages we've covered here—did he see that the specificity of personhood language could properly apply to God.

But personhood is bought with a price. If creation is the result of a free creation by a personal being, then no theory will be able to proceed forward step by step from the structures of possibility that we have been exploring to deduce the world as we know it. Metaphysics, as the study of what must have been the case to give rise to the world as it actually is, will have to give way to empirical science, the a posteriori exploration of what actually is. Nor should it be otherwise: the most embarrassing moments for both philosophy and science occurred when philosophers like Descartes and Hegel (especially in the latter's philosophy of nature) attempted to deduce philosophically what only empirical experimentation could establish.

This contrast has been nicely formulated by Schelling in his distinction between negative and positive philosophy. The main idea behind the distinction (writes Brown) is that "actual existence or real being cannot simply be inferred from the structures of thought itself."[4]

---

3. For an exposition of Schelling's position see Brown, *The Later Philosophy of Schelling*, 133–40 and the therein cited works. The union of principles required for divine life cannot be within the actual being of God as existent, Schelling argues, but only in the distinction between the ground and the existence; and the dynamics of this process cannot be spelled out with necessity. The concept of "primal ground" (7:406) should thus be retained, along with that of the "groundless" (7:407).

4. Brown, *Late Philosophy of Schelling*, 249. He writes, "Concepts can represent either the possible structures of real being, or an a posteriori analysis of real being. But concepts cannot account for the actual existence of being."

Since contingent (finite) being is the product of God's will and not a necessary byproduct of his nature, finite being cannot be conceptually derived from God's being. Philosophical theology can show the preferability of a free God over, for instance, a (Spinozistic) blind force of nature. But having done this, it too must turn to the record of the development of the world and humankind for actual empirical guidance. Thus, Schelling shifted in his final years to a philosophy of "mythology," examining the history of religion as the record of revelation in human history. Likewise, the theologian will have to turn, finally, from philosophical theology to the history of religions, to potential sources of revelation such as religious experience, and to the systematization of the resultant beliefs.[5] I would even suggest that something like the doctrine of the Trinity belongs within this sort of "positive" examination, functioning not as an a priori condition of the possibility of any revelation at all but as the most adequate expression of the nature of God, at least as revealed in the Christian tradition. (What reasons there are, if any, to think that the Christian tradition is the most adequate record of divine revelation is clearly not part of our project here.)[6] The fact that beliefs of this sort are not grounded in metaphysical deductions does not bar them from having any rational content or intersubjective justification. They now become religious hypotheses, concrete proposals regarding what God's will may be in human (and world) history and what the outcome of the process of revelation might be.

We can now, at the conclusion rather than the beginning of this section, consider the connection between Schelling's theory of personhood and his philosophy of spirit (Geist). A strong case has been made that the theory of Geist is the overarching framework that ties together the various stages of Schelling's career. The same general understanding of Geist shines through the various stages of his intellectual development: transcendentalism, objective idealism, and the positive philosophy.

Many of the German commentators select only the first period as philosophically significant; others, like Erna Stamm, search for a necessary progression through Schelling's three stages of affirmation, negation, and reaffirmation/synthesis. I think both approaches stand in need of correction. The middle period (objective idealism), I have argued, is closest to correct because it best does justice to the logic of the infinite incorporating the finite within itself. Yet, as Stamm shows, it is not as though Schelling succeeds at this synthesis by obscuring the distinction between spirit and nature; instead, as we have seen, he develops an evolutionary theory of spirit as emerging from a source that is better comprehended as spirit than as pure object.

Divine Agency

Arguably, the question of divine agency is one of the least well articulated challenges facing theism today. To avoid deism, theists must say that God can be, and is, active

---

5. See Pannenberg, "The Reality of God," in his *Systematic Theology*, vol. 1, chap. 3.
6. Ibid.

in the world subsequent to creation. Yet there are serious problems with maintaining that God continues to intervene directly into the natural order. For example, it would seem to threaten the integrity of this order, disrupting the regularity and predictability of the natural world that is necessary for free and reasonable human action. It also threatens to make a mockery of scientific method, since if there were regular miraculous divine interventions one could never know, for a given natural occurrence, whether it even had a natural cause. Finally, divine interventions seem to break the law of the conservation of energy—unless God could act by introducing information into the natural order without any influx of energy.[7]

On the one hand, if the finite and infinite are defined as incompatible, as having nothing to do with one another, then clearly an infinite being could not act within a finite creation. But in that case neither could the absolute have a personal side, nor be a being (much less a personal one), nor be related to any finite thing or person. In short, there could be no God as the Western traditions have understood this being. On the other hand, surely one cannot define the finite and infinite as identical.

The dilemma cannot be easily solved, but panentheism does seem to soften it in comparison to classical philosophical theism. Refusing the separation of world and God does bring the two closer and thus minimizes the difficulties with divine action.[8] The action is now not "into" a realm that is "outside" of God; it is easier to speak of God's causal action when that action takes place *within* God. For panentheists, divine agency is a matter of causal sequences that are internal to God, just as, on the ordinary view of human will and action, minds have the capacity to act on bodies to bring about particular goals. Yet, in other sense, God remains different from the world—indeed, absolutely different, since he has an infinite nature whereas the world's is finite. The greater the difference between God and world—be it spatial, essential, or temporal vs. atemporal—the more difficult it is to develop a coherent theory of divine action.

I can see only one possible answer to this dilemma: a dialectic between the infinity and the finiteness of God. We have already discovered a dialectical relation between the absolute as ground and the personal God as consequent. A similar relationship of difference-in-sameness characterized God's relation to the world, understood neither as external to God (for what could be external to infinity?) nor as identical to God (since the essential features of the absolute such as eternity and necessary existence certainly cannot be predicated of us as finite individuals!). The same paradigm provides the framework for understanding divine agency—not surprisingly, since the causality question is always a subset of the ontology question. In one sense, all interactions within the world include a divine cause as a component, since the world remains

---

7. The suggestion has been made by Polkinghorne in *Science and Providence*, 18–35, and is made in Arthur Peacocke's *Theology in an Age of Science*. I have pursued non-interventionist models of divine action in *God and Contemporary Science*.

8. I have developed this argument in more detail in "In Defense of Christian Panentheism," 201–8. Four critiques of this defense of panentheism and my response to these critics appeared in *Dialog* 38 (Summer 1999).

a part of its infinite source. In another sense, insofar as God is also different from the world, those "lures"[9] that stem from God-as-transcendent represent an influx from something that is also distinguished from the world. Of course, if divine influence were not limited in frequency and scope, humans would lose all ability to distinguish the natural order from its divine source; thus the influence must remain somewhat isolated and limited in scope.

It is clear that, given the resources of panentheism, a theory of divine agency no longer confronts the problem of absolute differentness. Further, the position sketched here, which links God as a being to the world and yet also to the infinity of God's nature, does offer possibilities for reconciliation that are not open to more traditional positions. I pursue the details of this position in a separate work.[10]

Conclusion

We began this chapter with Schelling's most famous disciple in twentieth-century theology, Paul Tillich, moving backwards from his "God above God" to Schelling's much more sophisticated theory of God as infinite ground and God as personal subject. I believe I have shown that there is no reason to treat this philosophical theology as merely mystical or negative theology, and no reason to follow Tillich in reducing it to its existential implications. For Tillich, perhaps, there were rhetorical reasons to do so. Tillich wrote from an apologetic interest, hoping to rekindle theological appetite in readers who were dissatisfied with theism but who still recognized areas of ultimate concern. "The God above God" thus had for him a negative function, as an attack on inadequate notions of God found in classical philosophical theism that are artificially abstracted from the world. Yet, we found, the insight into the two poles of God can also be given a positive expression of the sort that we discovered in Schelling's theology of freedom and in panentheism. Rhetoric aside, one who presents a more adequate theory of God is still a theist; she corrects previous, flawed views, rather than becoming a meta-theist or something of this sort. It's just that the most defensible understanding of theism is one that moves beyond the dichotomy between God and world.[11]

I have therefore suggested a correction of theological method away from the use of theistic language as merely fictitious and more in the direction of criticizable systematic proposals. The oppositions that fuel theological debates should lead not to a "premetaphysical" (and therefore symbolic) theory of divine reality expressed in terms of human existential reality, but to a theory of God that is both regulative and

---

9. See Ford, *The Lure of God*.
10. See Clayton, *God and Contemporary Science*, esp. chapter 8.
11. Indeed, Tillich admits as much in his Systematics: "In this respect God is neither alongside things nor even 'above' them; he is nearer to them than they are to themselves. He is their creative ground, here and now, always and everywhere" (*Systematic Theology* 2:7).

constitutive. Indeed, only this sort of theory would constitute a true correlation of metaphysical reflection with "the question implied in man's finitude" (Tillich).

In what terms would the details of this proposal be worked out? In his later years, Schelling called it the philosophy of mythology. More recent philosophy of language suggests a different route: construing theological proposals as hypotheses to be tested on the basis of their conceptual (and sometimes empirical) adequacy and their ability to make sense of present human experience. (See Clayton, *Explanation from Physics to Theology: An Essay in Rationality and Religion*.)

By these means one can perhaps move far beyond the minimal ontological and metaphysical conditions for philosophical theology defended in this book. The more concrete theories we attain—detailed theories of divine agency or of God's trinitarian life, say—may not play the same sort of foundational philosophical role as does the idea of God as ground and consequent, yet this does not make them mere fictions or mere symbols used to convey only human existential truths. Even as metaphors or models, they may still serve as hypotheses that are plausibly true—and they may also fail to do so.[12] In sum, Schelling did not make a category mistake when he distinguished between his groundwork in metaphysics and biblical language about God. But nor should we give up on the possibility of a rational evaluation of constructive theological proposals such as his.

Remember that the epistemic limits that we encountered above themselves stemmed from a conceptual argument, namely the argument for a panentheism based on the concept of freedom. Under this view, the divine life is not the result of a necessary development (Entäußerung) of some a priori structure into an existing world, as in Hegel's philosophy; rather, only a pure act of freedom can accomplish the transition from the infinite nature of the divine to reality.[13] Consequently, no system of thought could know or predict the self-revelation of God a priori (or at least couldn't know if it had). Reason's job—as "positive philosophy"—is only to recognize what has already come to be through the pure freedom of divine decision. Even if one understood God only as the triune structure or *potentia universalis*, Schelling realized, one would already have "presupposed [God to have] a relationship to the world, and indeed, with one that would be essential to him" (11:293). . . . In this case God's transcendence would remain unthought. Instead, Schelling suggested, God is "subject in the truest sense of the word," "that which is absolutely prior" (see 13:159). Where Hegel offers a necessary externalization, a dialectical unity of being and thought, Schelling lays greater stress on the negative moment: reason "sets" being "as an absolute outside-of-itself" (13:163). . . .

---

12. Recent philosophy of science has moved in this direction. The shift, and its implications for theology, are clearly spelled out in Barbour, *Myths, Models and Paradigms*. For a detailed account of the evaluation of theological statements as metaphors, see Soskice, *Metaphor and Religious Language*.

13. This is the main theme of Heidegger's masterful treatment of Schelling's Freiheitschrift (note 48 in the original text).

The Personality of God and the Limits of Philosophy

Schelling saw correctly that reason must be in some sense *verlassen*, left behind: "The great, final and fundamental crisis lies in the fact that God, the one who is found at the end, has been ejected from the Idea, and thus that the 'science of reason' itself is thereby rejected or left behind."[14] . . . Here, finally, is Schelling's exhortation to constructive philosophical theology: to grant that the metaphysical project is unavoidable; to take on the rigorous demands of this sort of reflection; to hold one's results, however tentatively, as true; and at the same time to acknowledge that the object after which one is searching partially recedes beyond even one's most perceptive conceptual grasp. One cannot help but notice that in this final point, Schelling is again true to his Spinozistic heritage—this time to the Spinoza of the closing pages of the *Ethics*:

> Insofar as our Mind knows itself and the Body under a species of eternity, it necessarily has knowledge of God, and knows that it is in God and is conceived through God. . . . The Mind's intellectual Love of God is part of the infinite Love by which God loves himself.[15]

---

14. Bucheim, "Die reine Abscheidung Gottes," 95–106.
15. Spinoza, *Ethics*, trans. Curley, Book V, P30, P36.

10

Biology and Purpose
Altruism, Morality, and Human Nature in Evolutionary Perspectives[1]

Agreements Stated and Unstated

I CLOSE WITH A theological reflection on evolution, morality, and purpose. . . . We learn most about strategies of opposition by considering those who find incompatibilities between science and religion or, in our case, between the neo-Darwinian understanding of evolution and the values that follow from belief in God. Let's call them "incompatibilists." Consider first those incompatibilists who resolve the conflict in favor of science and against theism. Here, too, there is a spectrum of responses, depending on whether one thinks that biology should disincline one toward theism or, more radically, that biology renders belief in God completely without rational justification. (None of the authors in this volume explicitly takes this latter position; elsewhere, Richard Dawkins is perhaps its most famous spokesperson; see, for example, Dawkins 1987 and 1998.)

Those who pursue the more moderate approach do not argue for a logical incompatibility between biological and religious explanations. Instead, they find more subtle ways in which the biological data can be used to undercut religious explanations. Two in particular deserve mention. One strategy is to argue that the adequacy of strictly biological explanations of human behavior renders religious explanations unnecessary. After all, if one has a perfectly good scientific account of some set of behaviors or beliefs, why would one need to introduce religious entities or causes in the first place?

---

1. "Biology and Purpose: Altruism, Morality, and Human Nature in Evolutionary Perspectives," as found within Clayton and Jeffrey Schloss, *Evolution and Ethics*, 318-36. Reprinted with the kind permission of Eerdmans.

In an updated version of Laplace's famous retort, the biologist might simply respond, "I have no need of that hypothesis."

A second strategy sometimes pursued is to "functionalize" the treatment of human behavior and human moral beliefs, so that no place remains for the kind of truth claims that religious believers typically make. If the only question that remains to be asked is, "What social or biological functions are served by this particular religious belief or behavior?" one never gets to the question of whether it is really true.

Both strategies can be found in the writings of David Sloan Wilson, whose position in *Darwin's Cathedral* (2002) is frequently cited in these pages. At times Wilson makes use of the first strategy: as the power of explanations in evolutionary psychology increases, the need for any other kind of explanation, and in particular the need for explanations in terms of divine agency, is decreased. But he also employs the second strategy: once the social-biological functions of Calvin's religious beliefs have been detailed, the beliefs have been fully explained. For example, no grounds remain for raising the question of whether some of the beliefs might actually be true of metaphysical entities or realities such as God.

Analogous strategies are employed by the "incompatibilists" who resolve the conflict in favor of religious belief and against science. Some authors argue for a strong incompatibility: religious explanations are necessarily in tension with biological explanations. The tensions between biology and Christianity are, they maintain, as great as Dawkins thinks they are; it's just that the reasons for accepting Christianity are stronger than the reasons for accepting the biological explanations. Incompatibilists of both types appear to work with the assumption that religion–science comparisons involve a "zero sum" game: the greater the adequacy of theological explanations, the more suspect scientific explanations become, and vice versa. To the extent that scientists are able to account for species development or behavior in biological terms, to that same extent religious accounts of the world will be undercut. No one explicitly argues this position in this text. But it would be interesting to explore to what extent certain of the authors implicitly make this assumption.

Another type of argument used by religious incompatibilists, which is related but not identical to the previous one, seeks to point out limitations or flaws in biological accounts of behavior. There is a suspicion—possibly justified—that biological accounts of morality tend to undercut theological accounts (or perhaps that they do so intrinsically). The goal of Christian thinkers, it is then assumed, should be to reveal all the ways in which biological accounts of behavior are inadequate. This may involve either demonstrations that the biological explanations are not really adequate to the data or, if they are, that the biologist has illicitly extrapolated beyond the theory's sphere of validity, drawing conclusions beyond the domains in which the theory is actually valid. Thus, for example, Holmes Rolston III argues that theories of altruism that are based on the genetic transmission of behaviors, and in particular the constraints on altruism that arise in these contexts, no longer hold when altruistic values are culturally or religiously transmitted. (Joseph Poulshock's essay points in the same direction.) Similarly, John Hare argues that descriptive accounts of moral behavior cannot pass as genuine positions in moral philosophy.

Strategies of Mediation

In the last paragraphs we have concentrated on areas of disagreement, of alleged incompatibility. One should note, however, that many of the authors in this text are compatibilists, at least concerning large areas of the "ethics and evolution" debate. For compatibilists, scientific and religious theories can contribute together to a fuller understanding of the phenomena of human moral beliefs and behaviors. In the remainder of this reflection we explore a broadly compatibilist strategy.

Suppose that one takes as her goal to develop the most adequate possible explanation of ethical beliefs and practices using the terms and theoretical resources of both biology and theology. On this view, which is also my own, one does not worry, at least initially, about theoretical over-determination, that is, that by using several different theoretical frameworks one might come up with more than one adequate explanation of some set of data. The goal of this approach is to produce the most powerful explanations that one can possibly produce, and there is nothing wrong with working on multiple fronts at the same time. Such an approach, which is utilized by many of the writers in this book, does indeed present one at some point with the task of integrating competing theoretical explanations. The integration, on this view, must be achieved using the terms of a third discipline, so that there is no question of the reduction of one explanatory system to the other. It turns out—and I think this is the moral regarding many of the questions in this volume (more on this below)—that much more of both sets of disciplines can be retained than one might have expected. Much of biology can be right in explaining human behaviors, and much of religious language can be retained for formulating matters of ethics, morality, and ultimate purpose. When one encounters areas of conflict, it is often possible to detect where one or the other theory has overstepped its bounds, extrapolating further from the data than is warranted or making assumptions that are not necessary to the field in question. In the cases of genuine conflict, the disagreements are more often philosophical than directly scientific or religious. In this case, the philosophical alternatives must be clearly formulated and reasons for or against a particular interpretation developed. One may not achieve agreement among all the discussion partners, but one will at least have identified where the (philosophical) issues lie. . . .

On Human Nature

We turn now to the synthetic questions that arise naturally within the topic of "evolution, ethics, and purpose." It seems appropriate, given such a task, to draw on the discipline of philosophical theology. (One could also say "theistic metaphysics," except for the frightening sound of the term!) Or, to say the same thing in different terms, these pages seek to employ the more constructive tools of the science–religion debate in a quest to formulate some areas of common ground and potential agreement that seem to arise out of the previous chapters. Whatever one calls it, the goal of this closing exercise is to take the best results of science and (in this case) some of the core beliefs from theology, and to see whether one can think the two fields together into a unified account. Call it the compatibilist hypothesis.

Such an account will necessarily weave together facts and values—not arbitrarily, one hopes, but under the control of the scientific studies and guided by insights from the theistic religious traditions. As a Leitfaden or red thread, I suggest using the experience of being a human person to guide the reflection. The guiding question is, What are the core phenomena of human experience, as informed by both science and faith? . . .

Embodiedness

As humans, we are essentially located in a body. An animal body. This body has very high genetic similarity to the bodies of other higher primates. Phenotypically, we thus have deep similarities: our visual apparatus is similar to the chimps (thus presumably our visual experience is similar); our stomach sensors are similar (thus presumably our experience of hunger is similar); our sexual arousal hormones and sexual organs are similar (thus presumably our experience of sexual arousal is similar); our process of birth and nursing is similar (thus presumably some of the experiences of mother and baby are similar).

Bodies have a history. Your genome is a record of the evolutionary history that brought about homo sapiens. . . . As a nonreductionist, I argue that the drives to reason cannot be fully understood without including the experience and the rules of reasoning (cultural and logical rules). But the full truth about reasoning is not stated until we also acknowledge that reasoning would not occur apart from the precise neocortical functioning on which it depends. What we reason and how we reason is deeply influenced by the brain and central nervous system that we have. Thus, the neocortex is linked to drives of its own: to understand, to resolve cognitive ambiguities, to obtain new and novel data, to vary existing ideas and concepts. Thus, even our higher-order drives—including our drives for novelty and creativity—bear the marks of our genetic origins and evolution.

Temporality

Each of the bodily systems so far described has a history, a context of evolutionary origin. In this sense, time is basic to human being. We are products of our phylogenesis, of how our species came to be. Indeed, each particular individual is a product of the unique facts of her particular ontogenesis, of the history of her body, her brain, and her psyche from her conception onward.

We are a conjunction of histories: of biological history, of cultural history, of the unique history of our body and psyche. Human nature can no more be understood in abstraction from the history of emergence of our species than your friends and family can understand you in abstraction from your personal history, which has formed you to be the particular individual you are.

Contingency

We need constant inputs from the environment: air, water, food, warmth, and shelter. Remove the required inputs and we die: without air, in minutes; without water, in days; without food, in weeks. We also have vast and complicated psychological and social needs, to which I return below. Needs of this "higher-order" type are more difficult to specify: what is a need and what is merely a want, a desideratum for the organism to thrive and experience fulfillment? Still, the human need for love, even if more amorphous than our need for food or water, is no less a driving force in our make-up....

"Weltoffenheit"

The famous philosophical anthropologist Arnold Gehlen defined human nature in terms of the *Weltoffenheit* or "openness to the world" of the human animal.[2] We don't have a given environment but are open to arbitrarily many data from our surrounding world. Much less of human behavior is determined by instinct than is the case with any other animal on the planet. Instincts influence some of our behavior, but they do not determine human choices. In comparison to other animals, humans are "biologically unspecialized"; we construct our own environment to a much greater degree than our animal cousins. Since our behavioral repertoire is much broader than that of even the other great apes, our need for behavioral selection principles is much greater. The existence of codes of behavior is thus a virtual mandate; without them, social existence would be impossible for this species....

Sense of self

Here, then, is the crux: we are an animal who has an inner sense of self. We form an internalized representation of "the other"; we have, as one says, a theory of mind. This fact gives to the human animal an inner complexity that corresponds to the

---

2. Gehlen, *Man: His Nature and Place in the World*.

unique complexity of our central nervous system, without being identical to it. It is this complex brain and nervous system that causes our inner complexity—even though, I maintain, the world of subjective awareness is neither equivalent to, nor reducible to, the physical structures of the brain. . . .

The Inner World

As part of this capacity, we can anticipate an experience that has not yet occurred, trying out actions or words in our head until we light upon what we think is the most adequate one. (I rewrote the previous paragraph three times before moving on to this one, each time imagining you reading it and struggling to find the most effective way to communicate my thoughts so that you would understand them.)

Yet there are downsides to this inner complexity, since it's not always easy to live with an inner world that constantly re-creates the outer world within oneself. Animals suffer—we can recognize it in the eyes of the sheep or cow being slaughtered. But this is, as some authors have dismissively dubbed it, "dumb" suffering. In most cases, the animal suffers the actual pain inflicted on it, but not more. We alone, it appears, are capable of "magnifying our suffering far beyond the original stimulus itself." We are experts at "adding insult to injury," at recalling the circumstances of our pain and experiencing the pain all over again. . . .

Self-deception

Inner complexity has another downside: self-deception. In any competitive situation, it is to others' advantage to be able to discern the contents of their opponents' "inner world," so that they can better anticipate what actions their competitors are likely to take. Clearly this is true in relationships between predators and prey, but it is also true of the less radical competitions that occur within in-group relations. . . .

Sociality

Humans are inherently social. A deeply communal animal, we learn largely by imitation . . . . Even the inner states that make up our experience in the world are deeply influenced by the environment and can be manipulated by the persons around us. . . .

Culture

Physics and chemistry describe the structure of the physical world around us, and biology describes the living worlds of our body and our ecosystem. But this interpersonal world that we inhabit is only partially grasped by describing the biology of the agents who inhabit it. The world of sociality is also the world of culture. . . .

PART II: SCIENCE, FAITH, & GOD

Morality

Of course, values are expressed whenever there is an end that an organism selects and strives for. But are we not also moral in a stronger sense? Thanks to neurological structures such as mirror neurons, we experience within our bodies what we see happening to others around us. We smile when another smiles with happiness; we cringe when another experiences pain. (If you're not sure about this, try watching skateboarding videos with the teenager in your household.) Most importantly, our large neocortex allows us to have a sense of self: we know that the one hurt by our actions experiences the unpleasantness of pain as we ourselves do. . . .

Freedom

There are numerous ways in which humans are not free. Drugs can change behavior. Social or cultural reinforcement can make behaviors more probable. The repetition of a behavior can increase the future probability of its recurrence; hence habits can change behaviors.

But individuals can also initiate behaviors based on factors idiosyncratic to themselves. . . . Contemporary philosophy offers two main options for defining freedom. The first is "libertarian" or counterfactual freedom: free agents might have acted otherwise, even if all the causal influences on them were identical. The second is "compatibilist" freedom. Perhaps every one of our "choices" is itself the product of a chain of internal or external causes. As long as the individual does not will not to perform the behavior she engages in (a desire which itself is the product of causes), then the action counts as free. "Compatibilist" freedom is fully compatible with scientific explanations, since the causal lines remain unbroken and each action is causally determined. . . .

The experience of agents in the world, as we have seen, is the experience of reasoning, of recognizing others as persons similar to ourselves, of experiencing moral oughts and living in light of them. The understanding of freedom that corresponds to such phenomena is agential freedom—freedom for which the agent's own choice is the sufficient cause for at least some of her actions. To act freely is to act on the basis of purposes—to exercise the sort of intentional, teleological action . . . . I believe this emergent capacity is both a product of evolution and a sign of the image of God in humanity. . . .

Altruism or love

With altruism we reach the crucial question for religious ethics. I will suggest that one cannot develop an adequate account of altruism, morality, or human nature without the strong notion of agent-based freedom just discussed.

Darwin first suggested in 1871 that altruistic behaviors on the part of individuals might be compatible with evolutionary biology. Advances in understanding since the sixties have provided many of the details of the answer. Enough has been said in this volume about the evolutionary dimension of natural or reciprocal altruism that further comments would be redundant. Universal altruism is a different matter, however. It involves the decision to act apart from, or against, any considerations of survival advantage for self, friends, or kin. I follow the definition put forward by Thomas Oord (in this volume) "to love is to act intentionally, in sympathetic response to others (including God), to increase overall well-being." ...

Altruism and human nature

To advocate an ethics of universal love immediately raises the question of human nature. How great is the contradiction, if contradiction there is, between our genetically pre-given drives and these high moral aspirations? Certain religious traditions, such as Reformed Christianity, emphasize a strong sense of sin and the need for redemption: the love ethic could be achieved only with divine help. Others place less emphasis on fallenness and hence are more optimistic about the human capacity for culture-transcending moral behavior. In either case, the altruistic struggle is intimately linked to the freedom question: will one act in a manner different from one's selfish (or nationalist) inclinations? ...

Conclusion

Developments in biological theory such as evolutionary psychology have shown that evolution and ethics are not unrelated. At the same time, the treatments in this volume have also shown that the evolution–ethics axis does not exclude religious belief and religious explanations. In the end, the religious level nicely supplements the biological contribution in comprehending human morality.

Numerous theorists have warned that the understanding of human flourishing would be truncated if we fail to provide a comprehensive theory of human nature. This brief closing exploration has shown that a complete anthropology can include both biology and freedom. To include freedom, I have argued, is to include morality, that is, to include both the ideal and the possibility of altruistic action in the strong sense of universal altruism. Finally, the entire complex can be conceived against the backdrop of divine purpose—an overall creative intent by God in history to accomplish certain goals. The synthesis of biology, morality, and theology is not mandated by the empirical evidence (how could it be?), though it is supported by arguments such as the one sketched in these pages. In the end, I suggest, the picture yielded by combining biological and religious perspectives on human morality is richer than the picture produced by either one of these perspectives alone.

11

Reason for Doubt[1]

The Modern Predicament

OVER THE COURSE OF human history, countless answers to these questions—call them, for short, *questions of ultimacy*—have been offered. In fact, whatever their differences may be in other respects, one of the features shared by all human societies of any duration has been their tendency to formulate questions of ultimacy and to attempt to answer them. Claims, theories, beliefs about what is ultimately the case and what they mean for human existence are among the salient artifacts of all human cultures.

At the same time that we recognize the depth and power of the ancient traditions, however, our explorations of these questions today must take place in light of new challenges. Contemporary grounds for doubting the traditional answers are serious enough that one may well wonder whether the questions can be answered at all and, indeed, whether it is even still meaningful to pose them, at least in the manner in which they were formulated by the great traditions of religious faith and reflection.

In responding to these worries, one has to start somewhere, and we take as our starting point the claims embodied in one traditional way of answering questions about what is ultimately the case, the one broadly known as "Christian." . . . Many books have been written about the "modern predicament" and the threat it poses to the traditional ways of conceiving and responding to the questions of ultimacy—and most of all to those religious beliefs that depend on claims about miraculous events said to have happened in the very distant past. All three of the "Abrahamic" traditions (so called because they all give a major founding role to a single ancient patriarch) are often said to fit that description. One of them, however—the Christian one—is unusual in the amount of weight it places on a single, relatively brief episode, about which it makes perhaps the most extraordinary claims of any of these three traditions.

---

1. "Reason for Doubt," as found within Clayton and Steven Knapp, *The Predicament of Belief: Science, Philosophy, and Faith*, 1–22. Reprinted with the kind permission of Oxford University Press.

Modernity (not to mention postmodernity!) is often taken to have changed the nature of human thought and human culture so radically that ancient beliefs are no longer viable, simply because they belong to a pre-modern era. Responding to this charge, numerous books written to defend Christianity against the various threats posed by modernity argue that things have not changed as much as might appear. Others argue that the changes are real but illegitimate and so should be rejected by those who hold to the true faith. Still others suggest that the changes are vast and legitimate but do not affect the core beliefs on which the religion depends; or, finally, that we can save the core beliefs by reinterpreting them, giving them a modern or postmodern interpretation that will enable them to thrive in this no-longer-new intellectual environment.

A great deal of excellent thought and eloquent writing has gone into the project of extricating Christianity from the modern predicament by means of one or more of these strategies. We do not wish to minimize that effort or those achievements, let alone to claim that our approach is a radical departure from those of our predecessors. We have learned from these defenders of traditional Christian belief (as well as of defenders of other faiths and of religion more generally) and draw frequently on their arguments in what follows. But we do diverge in important ways from those who maintain that the threat to Christian belief and commitment emanates merely from a cultural change in the way human beings understand themselves and what surrounds them. We belong to a growing body of people who are committed, or at least strongly drawn, to the ancient claims but who are also deeply struck by evidence and arguments that point in the opposite direction. We respect those for whom the traditional Christian claims seem to need no defense or who believe that the objections can be easily answered by the various forms of Christian apologetics. But it seems to us, as it does to many others, scholars and laypeople alike, that there are strong and sometimes compelling reasons for doubting whether some of the traditional Christian claims are actually true. Many of these reasons would not have arisen without the changes that are part of modernity—for instance, the rise of modern natural science. Others are themselves quite ancient and would likely have emerged (or reemerged) in the course of human reflection, with or without the aid of science or other peculiarly modern developments. What is new in their case is not the reasons themselves so much as the freedom and safety in which they can now be discussed, thanks to the rise of modern ideas like tolerance and freedom of conscience that were either absent or suppressed until the last three centuries (and that are still resisted, sometimes violently, in many parts of the world). . . .

Starting as far back as the seventeenth century, there has been a widening gap between, on one side, discourse about the ultimate nature of the universe and the truth or falsity of religious claims in general and, on the other side, discourse about the highly specific claims that emerge from the testimony and experience of particular religious traditions. The former is generally perceived as rational, dispassionate, and, increasingly, the purview of academic specialists; the latter as personal and passionate, more a matter of autobiography than of inquiry. Some even doubt that the claims of a particular tradition should be regarded as truth claims at all, interpreting them instead as vehicles of ethical and emotional engagement. . . .

For reasons that will emerge over the course of the succeeding chapters, we remain committed to the core Christian hypothesis, despite all the sources of doubt. But we must emphasize from the start that there are many ways of defending such a commitment that are, in our view, problematic. For instance, some make the argument that faith should step in wherever reason fails. Others appeal to religious feeling or religious "experience" as something that is both more elusive and more fundamental than anything one can reason about. Still others appeal to the richness of Christian "symbols" as sufficient to motivate Christian practice, despite the multiple ways in which such symbols can be understood. Another response is that of Christian agnostics, who are content to act on Christian claims while eschewing both the possibility and the need to determine if any of those claims is actually true.

Our approach is different from all these responses, and that for at least one major reason. What all such approaches have in common is their tendency, intentional or not, to *immunize* Christian claims from the criticisms of non-Christians. (In fact, they are often used to immunize beliefs from criticism by other Christians as well, such as those who think that one of the most important of all Christian values is fidelity to the truth and who therefore worry—rightly, in our view—about the dangers of being misled by delusion or error.) To put it bluntly (again, without impugning motives), many of the typical responses amount to what might be called *immunization strategies.*

For those who reject such strategies and yet still want to know whether the Christian understanding of ultimate reality is viable, there is only one alternative, and that is *to understand the reasons for doubt as fully and clearly as possible*: to look those reasons, so to speak, directly in the eye. Only then can one decide whether or not there are countervailing reasons that rightly override the reasons for doubt. And only after these reasons have been presented can one determine how much doubt appropriately remains, and what to do in response. Some critics will object that we have not gone nearly far enough in our response to the predicament of Christian belief today, whereas others will complain that we have gone far too far. It is good to keep in mind, however, that those who seriously engage the arguments share at least that much common ground, in contrast to the kinds of strategies mentioned in the preceding paragraph.

This, at any rate, is the task we undertake in the following pages. But first, it is important to state what many take to be the main reasons for doubting that the core Christian understanding of ultimacy can emerge intact from its modern predicament.

Reasons for Doubting Christianity

Science

For reasons not hard to understand, the rise of experimental science presents a reason—perhaps the single most important one—for doubting Christian clams. Over the course of roughly the last three centuries, the modern era has been deeply influenced by scientific methods, results, and ways of thinking.... In fact, the progress of science today depends on the willingness of scientists to assume that whatever needs explaining will yield, sooner or later, to naturalistic explanations—which, again, means explanations given in terms of regular cause-and-effect relations among things in this world, without any influence or interference from anything beyond this world. That essential working assumption to which all scientists must subscribe (at least as long as they are working as scientists) is sometimes called the *presumption of naturalism*.... It is important to recognize that the presumption of naturalism is methodological not metaphysical, because otherwise the presumption would be arbitrary, a matter of (nonreligious) faith or dogma....

Evil

The best known, and surely the most troubling and painful, problem for the credibility of Christian claims is the one traditionally known as the problem of evil. Stated in its simplest terms, this is the problem of reconciling the hypothesis of a good and powerful God with the existence of bad things that such a God, if this being really existed, would be expected to stop or prevent.... This reason for doubt is no less serious, intellectually, than the other reasons. But it also has an emotional force that other objections to Christian claims—and indeed to theistic claims more generally—cannot match.... The problem of evil is not unrelated to another question, one that goes to the heart of supposing that the ultimate reality is the kind of being that (or who) would or could take any sort of interest in the welfare of human beings. Even if we have reason to think that there is a mind-like or (in some sense) a personal being at the beginning and end of all reality, why should we suppose that what matters to such a being—so much vaster and more powerful than anything we can concretely understand or imagine—is anything even remotely resembling what matters to us?

Religious plurality

In many ways, this is the most obvious, and one of the most ancient, of all reasons for doubting the claims of Christianity: other traditions make equally strong claims about the nature and purposes of the ultimate reality, and their adherents are at least as strongly committed to them as Christians are to theirs. The challenge of religious plurality does not lie simply in the fact that there are many religions. Instead, it lies in the fact that there are many religions that command the allegiance of vast portions of humanity; that give rise to truly impressive personalities (prophets, saints, gurus, as well as believers of ordinary station but impressive moral and spiritual strength); and that provide the basis for extraordinary achievements in the arts, in individual moral behavior, and in social reform.... There are several reasons why the existence of multiple religions, each possessing the cultural and moral power just mentioned, creates a problem for the credibility of Christian claims. First, there is the obvious question: if other people believe other things with equal conviction and, as far as we can tell, with equally good spiritual and moral effects, what makes anyone think that her religion is preferable to theirs?... The unresolved tragedy of Christian relations with Judaism brings home, as strongly as anything does, the difficulty of claiming the superiority of Christian affirmations over those of its religious alternatives.

The state of the historical evidence

... The records we have of the way that rabbi [Jesus] was remembered and understood by his followers do not show any obvious signs that supernatural care was taken to ensure their clarity. According to most experts, none of the records that has come down to us was directly produced by anyone who actually knew the rabbi, Jesus of Nazareth, during his earthly life.... To summarize the various parts of this complex reason for doubting Christian claims: (1) it is hard enough to believe that not only the history but the cosmic destiny of humankind turned on the life and death of a single human being. But now add to that difficulty the facts (2) that this claim is embodied in a set of ancient writings that, in the earliest versions we possess, were produced decades after the events in question; (3) that those writings were created and then selected and preserved not by neutral scholars but by communities with a profound interest in how the events were to be remembered and interpreted; (4) that long-suppressed but recently discovered texts of equal or nearly equal antiquity (the so-called gnostic gospels) present a very different picture of this person and his teachings from what we find in the canonical Gospels; and finally (5) that there are significant differences even among the canonical Gospels themselves, suggesting that each was shaped by the selective memory of a particular community and/or the preconceptions of it author or authors. Taken separately or together, these considerations are surely sufficient to raise doubts about the reliability of the historical testimony on which Christian claims about Jesus are founded.

The claim of resurrection

There is one traditional Christian claim that requires particular attention, because it is so well known among nonbelievers and believers alike, so central to a nearly universal understanding of what Christianity is, and by its very nature so immediately and enormously dubious. This is the claim that, three days after his execution, Jesus of Nazareth rose from death, appeared to his disciples, and then "ascended to heaven." This alleged event, more than anything else, is traditionally regarded as warranting the claims mentioned earlier that Jesus in some sense embodied the authority and indeed the personal presence of the ultimate reality itself. . . . Part of what sets this claim apart is the fact that, more fully and dramatically than any other feature of Christian testimony, it seems vulnerable to every one of the sources of doubt we have considered so far. . . .

Why Not Be Agnostic?

These all seem to us powerful reasons for doubt, although our readers will certainly differ in their assessment of which are the stronger and weaker among them. . . . Faced with the seriousness of the objections, one wants to know: can—and, more important, *should*—the doubts they foster be overcome? Should a commitment to the viability of Christian claims be maintained in spite of them? In the rest of this book, we will lay out a case for a positive answer to that question. We will argue that it makes sense even for non-Christians to regard belief in at least some Christian claims—those that Christianity shares with other theistic religions—as rationally preferable to their rejection; that it is intellectually better, consequently, to affirm those claims than to deny them; better also than to refuse to affirm them. And we will also argue that it makes sense for those who find themselves engaging ultimate reality in and through their participation in the Christian tradition to have a similar attitude toward certain claims that are particular to that tradition and are not shared by others. Here again, we think it is better for those so situated to affirm the claims than to deny them. Better—but not beyond all shadow of doubt. Because we judge the reasons to affirm Christian claims, even for those who find themselves "inside" the tradition, to be only somewhat stronger than the reasons not to affirm them, we regard our position as a kind of *Christian minimalism*. . . .

A minimalist thinks the reasons for affirming Christian claims are stronger than the reasons for denying them; but she may hold that the balance is only slightly in favor of the Christian claims. She is thus unable to say that she knows with certainty that these claims are true. What practical difference does it make whether one affirms something as only somewhat more probable than the alternatives, in contrast to simply not knowing *what* to believe? After all, it is perfectly possible that her reasons for affirming Christian claims, like her reasons for doubting them, will shift over time, so that those reasons will seem to her weaker or stronger, better or worse, in the future. And yet how can she not remain open to new evidence and new arguments that she encounters over the course of her life? . . . One could solve that problem by deciding to believe at some point in time and then paying no attention to evidence and arguments against one's belief in the future—the fideist option that we criticized earlier. Or one could solve it by resolving to be a Christian agnostic, that is, by remaining committed to Christian practices but concluding that there is just no way, even in principle, to tell whether Christian claims are likely to be true, or even plausible.

. . . We do agree with many commentators today that it is difficult to make the case for Christian belief—difficult, that is, to make a case that is, or even *should* be, convincing to those who do not already participate in the experience of Christian faith and practice. What separates us from Christian agnostics is, first, our unwillingness to decide in advance that no progress in assessing Christian claims can be made and, second, our conviction that pursuing the question of what is really the case, what is really true, is not just an intellectual game but an urgent religious responsibility. . . . Here one first glimpses what will be one of the most important claims made in this book. That claim is that the strength of one's practical commitment may and very often does exceed the certainty of one's belief. Against the agnostic we will be making the case that it is permissible actually to believe, even in cases where the "objective" evidence is very close to neutral. . . . One limitation must be acknowledged from the outset: the case that we will make for Christian minimalism will have a different status for those whose beliefs have been shaped by the tradition and those whose beliefs have not. Some of our conclusions have, we think, a claim on the attention of all rational agents who are concerned about ultimacy. Others will be fully credible only to those whose experience of ultimacy has taken place within, and been interpreted by, the context of Christian belief and practice. Our hope is to be able to present at least some of these intra-Christian claims in such a way that those who stand outside the tradition will regard them as justified for people who have experienced ultimacy in these ways. In other words, we hope they will at least be able to make the counterfactual judgment: "*Had I had the experiences in question*, I would be justified in holding these beliefs."

. . . In short, a crucial result of our inquiry will be the realization that not all the claims we end up affirming will turn out to have the same degree of rational justification. As important as it is to test the rationality of one's beliefs, in the religious lives of most (if not all) believers there are some beliefs that go beyond what one can fully explain or justify, even to one's own satisfaction! . . . Just as the strength of one's commitment can exceed the degree of certainty of one's beliefs, what one finds oneself believing can go beyond what one can defend in terms of publicly compelling reasons. Indeed, as one proceeds from general questions that cut across religious boundaries into the richer but far more specific territory of a particular tradition, it becomes more and more difficult to formulate the grounds for belief in ways that lend themselves to rational assessment. . . . That is one reason why this book cannot be read as a manual of Christian apologetics. We do not regard ourselves as offering "knock-down arguments" against, or for, the claims of Christian orthodoxy.

12

The Ultimate Reality[1]

CHRISTIAN CLAIMS, AS WE understand them, presuppose a certain hypothesis about what is ultimately the case. In the opening chapter, we stated that hypothesis as "the belief or wager that behind or beyond all things, at the beginning of everything we see and know, there exists an ultimate reality that in some sense intended us (or beings like us) to be here and—again in *some* sense—desires our flourishing." Because it is capable of something like intention and something like desire, this ultimate reality—call it the UR for short—must be conceived, on this hypothesis, as having properties at least similar to those of a person. . . . As Christian minimalists, however, we come at the questions in a rather different way. Our approach is not to canvass all the possible responses that could be offered but to seek out the most plausible version of Christian theism that is still consistent with what we take to be the tradition's core commitments. . . .

Why Even *Ask* about the Ultimate?

To contemporary ears, all talk of the "ultimate reality" can sound suspiciously metaphysical. After all, despite some powerful rearguard action by certain antiscientific communities, we live in an age dominated by science and empirical methods for acquiring knowledge. Haven't scientifically testable theories about the world now replaced metaphysical speculations of this sort, rendering them obsolete?

Metaphysical reflections are indeed suspect, in our view, when they compete head-to-head with scientific explanations of matters that lend themselves to scientific investigation. . . . Still, it's a mistake to think that science therefore becomes the authority for *all* questions. Even within "normal" science, new questions arise at the borders of each domain of inquiry. . . . The success of natural science is not the only

---

1. "The Ultimate Reality," as found within Clayton and Knapp, *The Predicament of Belief*, 23–43. Reprinted with the kind permission of Oxford University Press.

reason, however, that some reject altogether the idea of asking questions about the nature of the UR....

We have just defended the reasonableness, indeed unavoidability, of asking metaphysical questions—questions, that is, about the nature of the UR that underlies or "grounds" all that we know and experience—and at least attempting to answer them. Indeed, we have suggested that any attempt to block the consideration of metaphysical questions must itself take the form of a metaphysical argument; it becomes the very thing it seeks to discourage. Of course, one can always refuse to take an interest in such questions, but one cannot invalidate them on the basis of reasoned argument.

One of the questions that has preoccupied humanity across centuries and cultures is whether UR is in any sense conscious or mindlike. Many have affirmed that UR is personal, that is, that it shares certain important qualities that we associate with ourselves as persons. But is this claim still plausible? What reasons are there for thinking of UR as a *person*, or indeed as anything *like* a person? Whatever grounds all things is of course also the ground of us, who are personal beings. But this does not automatically mean that it must itself be personal, any more than the ground of colored things must be colored or the ground of heavy things must be heavy....

How, then, can the emergence of any phenomenon—including the emergence of persons—serve as evidence that the source of all reality must itself be (in some sense) personal? We no longer suppose, with the ancients, that like arises out of like, and therefore, for instance, that mind can only emerge out of mind. Theories of evolutionary emergence offer an increasingly precise way of explaining how unlike arises out of unlike (life from nonlife, and mental properties from nonmental neuronal structures). Thus they would seem to defeat any simple effort to argue backwards from the emergence of persons to an ultimately personal source.

Given the successes of the evolutionary sciences, then, one does not need a theory of the UR in order to explain scientifically how beings like us could have evolved in a universe initially characterized by physical forces only. This helps to clarify, once again, the difference between scientific and metaphysical explanation. Science, aided by theories of evolutionary emergence, can in principle explain the causal mechanisms by means of which physical and biological processes gave rise to life and eventually to beings like us. But it would seem that science cannot even in principle answer the larger question—the *metaphysical* question—of why the most fundamental processes should exist in the first place. One can dismiss this question as meaningless (a strategy mentioned earlier), but one cannot answer it by scientific means....

For example, the very fact that the initial conditions of the universe were what they were, and therefore that there exists a universe in which intelligent life could evolve, seems to demand an explanation that goes beyond the processes of evolution itself. And the best available explanation, in the eyes of many who have reflected on this question, is that our universe was created, on purpose, with that possibility "in mind." If so, whatever the UR is, it must be capable of purposive action.

There is, however, a standard and oft-repeated skeptical response to this argument. Note that the argument proceeds from the conditions necessary for life to the conclusion that the UR must be capable of intentional action and therefore must be (something like) a person. Many physical cosmologists today answer that, for all we know, ours is only one of a great many of universes—perhaps an infinite number—each with its own initial conditions and its own natural laws. If that's the case, then it is not surprising that at least one of those universes would be such that it meets the conditions necessary to sustain the emergence of life and, eventually, of mind. . . .

The multiverse objections to theism deserve a serious hearing, even if there are reasons for asking whether the multiverse theory could ever be a testable scientific hypothesis, or for that matter even a coherent postulation. But suppose one grants the reasonableness of thinking that our universe is only one of the countless universes that actually exist. Does that assumption really lay to rest the question of why there should exist a natural order capable of supporting the evolution of life and mind? . . . All multiverse theories implicitly accept the possibility of making assertions that are true of the entire (presumably infinite) ensemble of existing universes. . . .

These reflections show that someone who wants to characterize the UR in strictly physical terms faces a serious dilemma. If she accepts the notion that there is only one universe, she is confronted by striking evidence of fine-tuning that at least seems to suggest that our universe was intentionally framed with initial conditions that would be conducive (in the long run) to the emergence of intelligent life. If, on the other hand, she rejects the fine-tuning argument and affirms the theory that ours is only one of innumerable universes, she then finds herself subscribing to a framework of universe-transcending laws, which in turn implies the existence of a mindlike realm that precedes or transcends the infinite succession of physical universes. Either way, she ends up with an interpretation of the UR that conceives it as mindlike. In one case, the UR might be an intentional agent who purposely created the only universe that exists; in the other case, it might be a mindlike realm of principles or laws on which the many universes within the multiverse depend for their very existence.

From Mind to Agency

In the foregoing sections, we have laid out a case for the view that everything we know and experience has its ultimate source in a reality that is more like mind than matter. Even if there are multiple universes in addition to the only one we can observe, we have reason to suppose that there is a set of ordering principles or laws that underlies them all, and we have reason to suppose that those laws must have their source in (something like) a mind.

That conclusion, however, is only part of the hypothesis we set out to defend at the beginning of this chapter. The full hypothesis was not just that the UR had (something like) mental properties. It included the idea that the UR was not just a kind of mind but also a kind of *agent*, capable of forming something akin to what we call intentions and acting in accordance with them. In particular, the hypothesis included the notion that the UR was such that it was capable of having beings like us (benevolently) in mind; that it desired their existence and, indeed, their flourishing, and acted to bring about the existence of at least one universe in which it would be possible for them to exist and to flourish. Only in that case, after all, would it make sense for us to regard the UR as a personal (or, at least, *not less than personal*) being with whom we might interact in the ways suggested in the previous chapter. And only if *that* makes sense will it be plausible to suppose that the UR may have become involved in human history in anything like the way suggested by the most important claims of Christian theism, no matter how minimalistically those claims are to be understood.

Why should we suppose, then, that the UR is more than mind*like* and is, in fact, a kind of agent—that is, a mind that is capable of performing purposeful actions, which it must be if we are to regard the creation of the universe (or multiverse) in anything like Christian terms? This question is fairly easy to answer if we accept the claim that there is only one physical universe: the fine-tuning evident in the initial conditions of our universe (if it's the only one), when combined with the mindlike nature of UR, strongly suggests that this universe was endowed on purpose with conditions ultimately conducive to the emergence of intelligent life. . . . But even if one accepts the multiverse theory—which was designed, at least in part, precisely to avoid the implications of fine-tuning—it remains more plausible to affirm than to deny the reality of a mindlike source of the regularities that hold across the vast array of universes and that (according to multiverse advocates) explain the relationships among them.

Suppose the UR is mindlike but also that there are, or may be, multiple universes. What then? Perhaps the multiverse arises from the UR by a kind of necessity; perhaps the mindlike reality that is the source of all that exists is simply such that it necessarily (automatically, involuntarily) produces that which is other than itself. An interesting speculation, but what reason do we have, or *could* we have, to think that this speculation was actually true?

Perhaps, however, the multiverse just happens to "emanate" from its mindlike source, not by necessity but by some process or mechanism of which we have and *can* have no idea. Again, that is an intriguing notion; indeed, it's one with a substantial pedigree in the history of Platonic and Neoplatonic thought. But to accept it would be to leave the relation between the physical universe and its mindlike source entirely unexplained. It would leave us with two distinct realities, of two radically different kinds—the physical universe and the mindlike UR; it would tell us that these very different kinds of reality must have something to do with each other; but it would offer us no prospect of ever understanding what that "something" might be. . . .

And there *is* another option: namely, to understand the emergence of the universe or multiverse from its mindlike source on the model of the production of a physical effect by a mental cause—or in short, on the model of an intentional action.

Unlike the first two options, this one does provide us with an explanation of the relation between the mindlike UR and the multiverse: that the former reality is a kind of agent, and that this agent intentionally brought about the existence of the latter reality.

With that step, we arrive at the conclusion that the universe we see around us—or the multiverse to which that universe belongs—is best understood as the product of a mindlike and agentlike UR that purposely brought about its existence. We believe that this is the most justified position, the one that can best stand up to objections by those who are experts both in the relevant sciences and in the metaphysical debates concerning these topics.

What are those objections? They tend to fall into two broad categories. Those in the first category charge that one cannot speak of the UR as mind or mindlike without falling into an illicit projection of human experience and categories onto the ultimate. . . . A second set of objections maintains that it is impossible in principle to decide between personal and impersonal understandings of the UR. Because some religions (and philosophies) attribute personal or mental properties to the UR whereas others affirm a UR that transcends all such attributes, it is argued, the best solution is to conceive the UR as beyond the personal–impersonal distinction altogether. . . .

Note also that attributing mindlike or personlike qualities to the UR does not require one to deny that it has any other types of qualities. In fact, philosophers have shown a number of ways in which impersonal qualities might exist alongside mindlike aspects. Although the discussions are rather technical, it is not hard to see how both kinds of qualities, rather than cancelling each other out, actually play complementary roles when one attempts to speak of the UR. Examples include the distinction between the "primordial ground" and the emerging personal aspects of God drawn by the nineteenth-century idealist philosopher Schelling, later echoed by the theologian Paul Tillich, and the distinction between the primordial and consequent "poles" of God in the work of the process philosopher Alfred North Whitehead. Similar examples can be found across the religious and philosophical traditions, providing further ways to model this understanding of the UR. . . . The notion of agency we have so far applied to the UR is an extremely limited one; it's a notion of agency that falls far short of what people usually have in mind when they refer to the UR as "God." We have not yet said anything that would suggest that the UR is the *summum bonum* (the "highest good"); that the UR has benevolent intentions toward beings outside itself, let alone that it is "omnibenevolent"; or that the UR exercises a "providential" care for the world or its inhabitants. Indeed, we haven't shown that the UR has any moral or ethical qualities whatsoever. We still need to ask whether what matters to the UR has anything to do with what matters to us. . . .

Creation and the Love of Others

... But even if we stipulate that the UR is both a mind and a purposeful agent, we still have to ask why one should take the further and—for our overall hypothesis—crucial step of supposing that the UR has any interest in the things that interest *us*, or in any way cares about the things *we* care about.

At least since Hume's *Dialogues Concerning Natural Religion* (1779), philosophers have been keenly aware of how difficult it is to argue for the goodness of God from the natural world as we find it. Given a universe that is as morally ambiguous as the one we inhabit, it has seemed manifestly implausible to claim that we inhabit the "best of all possible worlds," as Leibniz notoriously put it. We therefore propose to approach the question differently. We begin by asking what conclusions about the moral nature of the UR follow from the assumption that the UR has intentionally brought about the existence of a universe in which it was possible for rational and moral agents—that is, for persons—to evolve. . . .

An obvious reply is that we are not aware of any ulterior motive on the UR's part, and therefore we should assume that the UR created a universe in which we would exist simply for our sake—that is, out of *love* for us—and not in the service of some other purpose. But consider a perfectly plausible ulterior motive for the UR to bring about the existence of sentient beings other than itself: in order to expand its own experience to include theirs. Why not suppose that the UR created the universe (or multiverse) only with the goal of introducing genuine novelty into its own experience, say out of a sort of cosmic boredom? Perhaps that is the only reason the UR wanted to create finite agents with enough autonomy that they would not simply be projections of its own will. In short, there seems to be at least one plausible reason, other than love of others, for a divine being to want to limit its power in order to bring about the existence of creatures like us. . . .

Earlier we introduced the theological term *kenosis*, for the self-limiting mode of action the UR must undertake in order to permit the development of beings other than, and independent of, itself. We can now add another Greek term, *agape*, naming a kind of love: specifically, the kind of selfless love that, in contrast to the kind denoted by the term *eros*, focuses on the well-being of the loved one rather than on the needs of the self. Once again, we have been led to ascribe this disposition to the UR by reflecting on the reason an infinite being might wish to bring about the existence of beings other than itself.

The Divine Lure

Our reflections on the UR's intentions have been restricted so far to what can be inferred from the sheer fact of creation. But there is another, very different source of insight that, in our view, sheds significant light on this question.

What we have in mind is closely related to the intriguing exploration by the sociologist Peter Berger of what he has called "signals of transcendence," that is, human experiences that seem to point in the direction of an ultimate and ultimately benevolent reality, even if they fall short of counting as sufficient evidence that such a reality actually obtains. Perhaps the most important such signal, for present purposes, is the experience of being guided by what is traditionally known as *conscience*. . . .

If the UR is indeed a personal (or, as we would prefer to say, a not-*less*-than-personal) agent, and if that agent is indeed motivated by the kinds of values and intentions (or something like values and intentions) that we have been describing, then we are not very far removed at this point from the vision of ultimate reality embodied in the Abrahamic traditions. Those traditions all yield, after all, a vision of the UR as an infinite agent who is not less than personal and who has performed at least one self-limiting act of creation motivated by *agape*, that is, by a love of others from whom one needs nothing in return. . . .

Nevertheless, it is impossible not to notice how close the concept of the UR at which we have arrived stands to what the theistic traditions have meant by the notion of God. Theists conceive ultimate reality as an infinite personal reality, a reality that has no intrinsic need of the others whom it freely and lovingly creates. We seem then to have arrived at, or close to, a theistic view of UR. Indeed, this theism or almost-theism might also be said to have a "christological tinge," insofar as it conceives the UR as intrinsically involving the compassionate and self-giving relation to others that is associated, in Christian thought, with the character and actions of a particular human being.

13

Doubt and Belief[1]

How Do We Assess Our Beliefs?

Our aim in this book has been to explore a certain account of what is ultimately the case, an account that many continue to find compelling, at least in its general outlines if not in all its traditional details. In the process, we have considered the most powerful reasons for doubting the claims this account entails. Although the objections sometimes required modifications, they also made it possible to develop (what we hope are) more adequate answers. The goal, at any rate, was to develop a position that might be embraced by those who want their most important beliefs to be rational, that is, to be based, as far as possible, on what they have reason to think is actually true.

Implicit in that project has been a certain conception of what it means to be a rational agent, a person who cares about whether she *should* hold the beliefs she is inclined to hold. This is not to suggest that human beings are entirely, or even largely, rational in their approach to their own beliefs. Some will care more than others about whether they possess reasons to believe that others—or even they themselves—should regard as good. But even those who *do* want their beliefs to be based on good reasons will find themselves relying on some beliefs they can't rationally justify. No one—not the greatest philosopher nor the most rigorous scientist—is capable of citing a rational basis for every belief she holds. Nor is there a single standard of rationality to which all one's beliefs might be held. As we will show in a moment, there are varying degrees of rational justification, and the degree of one's justification for holding any particular belief changes over time with the state of debate on the subject in question and with one's relation to the relevant communities of inquiry. In the paragraphs that follow, we will distinguish as many as six different levels or degrees of justification.

---

1. "Doubt and Belief," as found within Clayton and Knapp, *The Predicament of Belief*, 111–35. Reprinted with the kind permission of Oxford University Press.

That said, our theory of rational agency is, at bottom, a simple one. Its fundamental premise is that what it means to be a rational agent is to want the beliefs on which one relies to be beliefs that, as far as one knows, are likely to be true, and indeed are *more* likely to be true than the alternatives. Unfortunately, however, there is no way to check if one's beliefs are likely to be true by comparing them directly with the reality one hopes they are tracking. The reason is obvious: the results of any checking one might do themselves take the form, necessarily, of beliefs that would have to be checked in turn. So, once again, there is no way of stepping outside one's beliefs to see which ones correspond to the way things really are. The best an agent can do is to make sure, insofar as possible, that her reasons for holding a belief are better than the reasons she might have for rejecting it.

To say that reasons can be better or worse is to imply, however, that there is a basis for comparing them. And since that basis cannot be the direct observation of reality itself, what can it be? Our answer is that, in any given sphere of inquiry, a belief counts as rationally justified if it is held for a reason or reasons that the relevant community of experts (henceforth RCE) either regards as good, or would regard as good if that community had the right amount and kind of information.

In the best case, most RCE members will simply agree that the agent's belief is the right one to hold. If I want to know the date on which a famous person died, I look it up in a well-known encyclopedia, which I have reason to regard as a reliable distillation of expert opinion on the fact in question; the belief I acquire as a result of this procedure is one I regard as fully justified. In cases where there is a clear consensus of expert opinion, it is hard to imagine a belief that I would feel more strongly justified in holding.

But it would be absurd to insist that a belief is only rationally justified if the experts happen to share one's reasons for holding it. . . . The history of science is replete with instances in which a new hypothesis conflicts with received opinion and is therefore mistakenly ruled out of court. (One thinks, for instance, of the long-resisted hypothesis that peptic ulcers were caused by a certain bacterium, *Heliobacter pylori*, a hypothesis that contradicted the RCE's certainty that peptic ulcers were caused by stress.)

In cases like the ones just described, the agent has what we will call a *theory of error* for the RCE's failure to endorse her reasons for belief. This need not be a theory of error in the technical sense in which philosophers use the phrase, which generally requires demonstrating how a set of data is being misinterpreted and why, if it were correctly interpreted, it would necessarily lead to the correct conclusion. . . . Although matters of religious belief are not quite as clear-cut, one is sometimes able to produce a strong argument for a belief *as well as* to show why the RCE's widespread rejection of the belief is mistaken. In such cases, it would be better from the agent's own point of view if the experts agreed with her, but it would seem absurd to suggest that her belief was rendered irrational by their failure to do so.

Suppose, however, the agent *lacks* a theory of error for the RCE's disagreement with her. Suppose she does not regard the RCE as making some kind of identifiable mistake but instead regards the RCE's attitude as perfectly reasonable, given the RCE's point of view. We might say that, in that case, the agent regards the claim in question as *irreducibly controversial*, a matter about which reasonable people can and do appropriately disagree.

What factors make a claim irreducibly controversial? They may include the dependence of belief in that claim on particular kinds of experience. Imagine, for example, that an agent or group of agents has had specific experiences that are not shared by the RCE. Although religious experiences are the classic example, they are not the only kind of experience that might qualify; nor are experiences the only types of factors that can lead people to hold beliefs the RCE does not have sufficient reason to endorse. I might believe that a particular suspect is guilty of a crime because I sense something strange in his behavior after the crime occurs, even though I do not expect the RCE to view my "evidence" as sufficient. In many cases, decisions on irreducibly controversial topics are extremely complex, relying on the differential assessment of multiple intuitions, assumptions, data, and inferences. Can an agent who holds a belief about a matter *that she herself regards as irreducibly controversial* still be justified in holding the belief in question?

We submit that she can, and that there are degrees of justification in the case of beliefs about irreducibly controversial matters just as in the case of ordinary beliefs that can be confirmed or disconfirmed by "checking the facts." Even if the RCE does not endorse the agent's belief or her reasons for holding it, the RCE may nevertheless agree that the agent's reasons are good reasons *for her*—good reasons, that is, for someone who has had the kinds of experiences the agent has had, or who has other reasons, not universally shared or accessible, that incline her to hold a particular set of beliefs.

Alternatively, the RCE may decide that the agent's reasons for belief are not the kind of reasons one could rationally cite as justifying the belief in question. They may be so vague, complex, or uncertain that the agent herself cannot see any way of subjecting them to public discussion, including even a discussion of whether such reasons might be good reasons for someone in her particular situation.

What we are gradually unfolding here is a typology of degrees of rational justification an agent may regard herself as having for relying on—that is, guiding her thoughts and actions by—a certain claim or proposition....

Imagine the case of a person (say, Joan) who understands all the reasons for doubting her own belief in the uniqueness of Jesus' relationship with God but nevertheless finds herself inescapably drawn to that belief. What reasons might she give, even to herself, for this apparently stubborn disposition? Or rather, what reasons might she have for regarding her belief as rationally permissible, and not just as an irrational compulsion she might be better off suppressing? It seems to us that she might credibly settle on the following four:

First, Joan seems to encounter, in and through the New Testament documents, an individual she can't adequately capture under the headings of powerful prophet, good rabbi, or moral exemplar. She fully understands the ways in which, according to scholars, the Gospels have been composed from multiple, sometimes conflicting sources, and the narratives have been shaped by literary techniques. Yet she can't shake off the conviction that she here encounters something other than a brilliant literary fiction. She seems to catch glimpses in these documents of one who is powerfully permeated by the presence of God, one in whom "the fullness of God was pleased to dwell." . . .

Joan's sense of these texts as authentic witnesses to the self-manifestation of God is enhanced, second, by what she herself experiences outside the context of reading and reflecting on the New Testament accounts. She knows that subjective religious experiences—whether they occur during prayer or on some life-changing occasion such as witnessing the death of a loved one—are fallible and that every person filters them through her own interpretive framework. Still, she cannot deny that *what* she experiences, in those moments that are to her most revelatory of the UR itself, seems to be the same God to whose presence and nature Jesus testified. . . .

Third, Joan is well aware that Christians have not held identical beliefs through the entire history of Christianity. She knows that Christian faith is *semper reformata, semper reformans,* as the Reformation thinkers said: "always reformed, always reforming." Yet somehow, across all the centuries, she perceives a basic continuity of Christian belief and experience. However diverse their cultural and historical settings, participants in this tradition continually return to the biblical texts; they believe that in Jesus God was somehow powerfully manifest; they repeat a core message, a proclamation they have called the "kerygma" or gospel; and they share a hope for a future in which God plays a role. . . .

A fourth argument is more philosophical in nature. It hearkens back to the intuitions about values and the UR that have repeatedly played a role in earlier chapters. When one conceives God as sharply distinct from the world, the task of conceiving God's possible involvement in the Jesus event—or any other revelatory event, for that matter—becomes proportionately more difficult. Yet throughout this book we have made the case for a participatory relationship of human and divine action, not just in moments of transformative divine action or human holiness, but as a defining feature of the created order. On this participatory and panentheistic account, human values like justice and love both respond to and help shape the influence of divine values that are communicated to finite beings through what we have called the divine "lure."

But there is one final step. Let's suppose that Joan cannot help but notice an extraordinary fit between (on one hand) her intuitions concerning the ultimate value of compassion and (on the other hand) the sayings and actions attributed to Jesus in the New Testament narratives, . . . a compelling account can be given of the relationship between divine compassion and Jesus' kenotic actions. There we described the self-giving love of Jesus as responding to and embodying the self-giving love of God. The link between the two, on this account, was more than circumstantial; Jesus' perfect obedience to God's will actually became identical with the divine compassion or love. . . .

Joan is right to find some additional support for her belief in this convergence. And yet how can she know that no other human being ever manifested perfect self-giving love as fully as Jesus did? She *believes* that Jesus uniquely manifested divine grace and compassion; she has some reasons for her belief; and yet she cannot actually *demonstrate* this conclusion even to her own satisfaction. . . .

But now suppose that, in addition to her belief in the uniqueness of Jesus' relation to the divine Spirit, Joan finds herself drawn to the traditional belief that, after his death on the cross, Jesus' body was miraculously restored to life in a newly powerful and immortal form, left his tomb, and appeared to his disciples. . . . On that assumption, Joan cannot claim to have reasons for the belief in a physical resurrection that we have just described—at least not reasons that render that belief rationally permissible, let alone rationally indicated, from the point of view of the relevant communities of inquiry. If she remains attached to it nonetheless, she presumably regards it as something she *hopes* may yet turn out to be true, even though she lacks sufficient reason at present to believe it. Or perhaps she can no longer even *hope* that it may turn out to be true, in which case it becomes for her at best an inspiring fiction. In other words, it falls to . . . cases in which the agent either hopes the claim is true (but does not regard it as rationally permissible when judged against her other beliefs and the standards of any relevant communities of inquiry) or is content to use it as a metaphorical way of expressing what she does, in fact, believe about Jesus. . . .

In the previous sections, we developed a scale of degrees or levels of rational justification. We then indicated where the various arguments and conclusions presented in earlier chapters seemed to fall along that scale. In the process, we have in effect been sketching the boundaries of a Christian theological position that stands somewhere between the most liberal end of the spectrum, where one holds only those beliefs about Jesus that might be endorsed by any moderately theistic observer, and the most conservative or orthodox end, where one affirms without qualification the boldest Christian claims about the physical resurrection of Jesus and his unity ("hypostatic union") with God. On the position at which we have arrived, believers can give strong reasons for affirming that Jesus manifested the grace and compassion of the UR during his life and continued to do so after his death, as God acted in such a way as to make "the mind of Christ Jesus" present to the disciples and their followers.

At the end of the last section, we went on to consider the status of an additional claim, namely that Jesus rose bodily from his tomb and appeared to his disciples and their followers.

PART III

Panentheistic Reflections on Science & Theology

14

Spinoza's One and the Birth of Panentheism[1]

WE HAVE FOLLOWED THE major strands of modern thought about God from Descartes' infinitely perfect being to Leibniz's Architect of the best of all possible worlds. After Leibniz, however, we ran into the brick wall of Kant's critique of metaphysics. The last two chapters were devoted to the task of understanding how devastating is the possibility raised by Kant—that God-language reveals much about how human reason functions but nothing about whether there really is a God or what the divine nature is. We did find a way over the wall, but only at the cost of circumscribing theology's claims, of acknowledging how much God-talk is about the limits of *human* understanding. And yet Kantian skepticism does not have the last word, for we also found that some God-language has to be taken not only regulatively (as describing the limits on what we can know) but also metaphysically—as offering models for thinking the divine nature. It may be a humbled theology that beckons us . . . , but it is a viable theology nonetheless.

It may seem strange to begin Part II [of *The Problem of God in Modern Thought*] with a movement *back* in time to Spinoza, a thinker who preceded both Leibniz and Kant. The reasons to do so are compelling. Spinoza offers a greatly circumscribed view of the divine, a view fully compatible not only with the science of his day but also with the science of our own. His stress on immanence rather than transcendence avoids some of the pitfalls for theology that Kant discovered. Most importantly, Spinoza's approach to the God-question is designed to avoid the reliance on theories of perfection (both medieval and Cartesian) that we have found to be conceptually inadequate.

In this and the following chapters, then, we follow what I believe to be the most productive strand in the tapestry of modern thought about God. We will see how other strands came to and were woven in with Spinoza's initial insight, leading finally to the rich theories of the self-revealing God in the early nineteenth century.

---

1. "Spinoza's One and the Birth of Panentheism," as found within Clayton, *The Problem of God in Modern Thought*, 387–401. Reprinted with the kind permission of Eerdmans.

PART III: PANENTHEISTIC REFLECTIONS ON SCIENCE & THEOLOGY

But first we must deal with the *other* conclusion that is often drawn from the Kantian criticisms: the postmodern attack on transcendence, with its claim that God-language should henceforth be given a *purely immanent* interpretation.

Yovel's Spinoza

In an important two-volume work on "Spinoza and other heretics," Yirmiyahu Yovel has proclaimed the adventures of immanence, the thrills of the denial of transcendence.[2] The book has attracted significant attention.[3] Yovel hasn't, strictly speaking, provided a history of Spinozism since, as he notes, he's more interested in a particular theme, immanence, with a particular twist. The modern father of immanence, Spinoza,

> rejected both the dualistic transcendence of the Christians and the denaturized, transcendence-ridden this-worldliness of his fellow Jews. A "Marrano of reason," he shed all historical religions (though not all religious concerns), and offered salvation neither in Christ nor in the Law of Moses, but in his own kind of religion of reason—naturalistic, monistic, and strictly immanent.[4]

Yovel nowhere offers a precise definition of immanence; indeed, I believe his project *depends* upon stretching it well beyond the early modern context. For in fact Yovel writes out of a *contemporary* context in epistemology, which he labels neo-pragmatism and which we might associate—loosely perhaps but with surprising accuracy—with the name Richard Rorty. It would be only a slight exaggeration to say that the "adventures of immanence" encompass those modern thinkers who turn out to have been (at least under Yovel's interpretation) in some sense or another precursors of postmodernism á la Rorty.

Why then title the book *Spinoza and . . .* ? As one of the great outsiders of the tradition, and as a clear opponent to a God who is separate from and transcendent of the world, Spinoza might appear to represent the perfect starting point, the opening chapter in a narrative of the birth and blossoming of postmodernism from Spinoza to Rorty. This fact explains Yovel's choice of thinkers (Kant, Hegel, Heine, Hess, Feuerbach, Marx, Nietzsche, Freud) many of whom are only tangentially connected to Spinoza—or connected to him more by opposition than by agreement. Whatever the principle of selection, it's bound to be an exciting story, touching as it does on most of the controversial thinkers of the late eighteenth and nineteenth centuries and

---

2. Yovel, *Spinoza and Other Heretics*. Unless otherwise noted, references are to vol. 2, *The Adventures of Immanence*.

3. It was, for example, the object of an APA (Midwestern) session in April, 1991. Expanded forms of the papers appeared in *Inquiry* 35 (1992). Allison, "Spinoza and the Philosophy of Immanence," 55–67; Schacht, "Adventures of Immanence Revisited," 69–80; and Yovel, "Spinoza and Other Heretics," 81–112.

4 Yovel, *Spinoza and Other Heretics*, 2:169.

spilling over via Freud into the twentieth century. There are some omissions—Lessing, Schopenhauer (almost), and Heidegger—but these presumably provide room for follow-up articles. And the connections make for dramatic reading—linking Kant to Nietzsche, Herder to Marx, Heine to Freud, and all to their ultimate source in Spinoza.

Those of us who are unpersuaded by Yovel's case could, of course, criticize Rortyan neo-pragmatism. (Of course, Rorty has over the years proved rather impervious to frontal assaults—a distinct advantage of being a post-philosopher holding a non-position.) But I suggest an alternative route instead. Suppose we began by granting Spinoza the role of spokesperson for the philosophy of immanence. After all, he has developed a naturalistic metaphysics of the sort congenial to many of our contemporaries. On his view, if the term *God* is to play any role in philosophy at all, it must be as a tag for (some aspect of) the natural world and not as designating a supernatural, transcendent being. For Spinoza, God exists if and only if the equation *Deus siva natura* ("God, that is, nature") holds. By implication, then, all those who advocate a purely immanent account of divinity—the viewpoint that has traditionally been called *pantheism*[5]—will check in as "Spinozists" for purposes of this discussion.

Are the "adventures of immanence" the correct response to the Kantian problem of God? My thesis will be that *Spinoza's own mature doctrine, his thoroughgoing pantheism, is unsuccessful, and that no philosophically adequate form of pantheism has been developed in modern Western philosophy*. As we turn to Spinoza's followers (those who qualify as Spinozists according to the definition just given) we will discover that pantheism, when worked out systematically in Western philosophy, has invariably turned into *panentheism*—the view that the world is within God although God is also more than the world. Of course, when this occurs these views cease to be purely immanent and become immanent/transcendent philosophies. The present chapter traces this transformation—which I take to be both inevitable and desirable—in the case of Spinoza and his early followers (and critics) themselves.

How is the theological debate between pantheism, theism (or panentheism), and atheism to be adjudicated? . . . Naturally, this question can be resolved only by means of a careful analysis of competing explanatory proposals.[6] In particular, this chapter chronicles the fundamental competition between Spinozism and what I will call *minimal personalist (panen)theism* or *MPT*. I will argue that the series of criticisms and modifications of Spinoza's original position that we will encounter gradually point toward some variant of *MPT* as the most viable systematic answer. In subsequent chapters, we will observe how the core of a panentheistic metaphysic, still little more than a set of basic intuitions in the later eighteenth century, gradually took sophisticated form during the early years of the nineteenth century. . . .

5. See Levine, *Pantheism*.
6. To spell out and defend this method of analysis would require a paper as long as the present one. See chapter 7 in *The Problem of God in Modern Thought*, and Lipton, *Inference to the Best Explanation*, esp. chap. 3, "The Causal Model."

PART III: PANENTHEISTIC REFLECTIONS ON SCIENCE & THEOLOGY

If I am right about the strengths of *MPT*, the most urgent contemporary choice is between it and a non-(or post- or anti-)metaphysical position such as Rortyan immanentism. Since I take it that Rorty will be little moved by metaphysical criticisms or alternatives (and perhaps the same holds for Yovel), it is unlikely that this chapter's careful look at the history of Spinozism will be sufficient to sway the Rortyan reader.[7] Still, it's not unreasonable to hope that working through the various criticisms of Spinoza will aid most readers in forming their own rational evaluations of this influential modern thinker.

The Case against Immanence Alone

In this chapter I counterpose to the "adventures" of immanence the thesis of the modern *temptation* of immanence. The seductiveness of this temptation cannot be overestimated. Among its charms are the widespread dissatisfaction with transcendence and the attractiveness of the mystical sense of oneness or interconnection. But immanence will remain no more than a promise or temptation as long as mystical/experiential attractiveness remains a substitute for conceptual adequacy. As an antidote to the temptation I will seek to show, first, that no satisfying pantheism has been presented, and second, that panentheism need not be epistemically naive but can be formulated in a manner that takes into account the Kantian worries addressed in the last two chapters.

The case against Spinozistic immanence cannot be made by vague generalizations about seventeenth- and eighteenth-century philosophy; it requires one to work one's way analytically through the arguments of specific thinkers. In the interests of juxtaposition and context-setting, I begin with a (brief) summary of the contemporary discussion of Spinoza's doctrine of God/Nature, which provides a somewhat clearer picture of the difficulties that Spinoza resuscitators *should* have faced in their efforts. We next turn to three initial (but significant) critiques from the early years after Spinoza's death....

As we will see, Spinoza's philosophy is not adequate in its original form. In particular, we will be looking at the difficulties with Spinoza's philosophy of the one infinite substance with infinite attributes and at his inability to derive the finite from the infinite. This exposition will then serve as the backdrop for the question: if Spinoza failed to develop an adequate version of naturalistic pantheism, did his followers fare any better at this task? Were any of them able successfully to modify Spinoza's system in some way—say, by reducing its naturalistic bias, or by relying more heavily on the concept of self-consciousness? If they were, was the result a model of God that is philosophically preferable to personalist theism?

What one discovers, I believe, is that no such model was advanced in the first 110 years after Spinoza's death—that is, prior to German idealism. None of the figures

---

7. I also provided some epistemological counterarguments to Rorty's position in chapter 1 of *The Problem of God in Modern Thought*.

we will examine was able to establish the connection between the finite and the infinite without pushing outside the bounds of pantheism, that is, without reintroducing some aspect of transcendence. By contrast, in the following chapters on Fichte and Schelling we will find increasingly sophisticated formulations of the "immanence plus transcendence" view of the divine. The net effect, I will argue, is to raise panentheism to one of the most (if not *the* most) serious metaphysical options that has emerged out of the first 300 years of the modern period.

Spinoza's *Ethics*

The attractiveness of Spinoza

It's not as though Yovel was mistaken to choose Spinozism as a watershed in metaphysical thinking, for there's much here to attract the contemporary philosopher. Spinoza's one substance does provide the unifying perspective required of a metaphysical theory. What is most fundamental in Spinoza's great work, the *Ethics*, is Absolute Substance, which he calls God-or-Nature (*deus siva natura*). Spinoza defines the one substance as "that which is in itself and is conceived through itself" (E1 def. 3).[8] He then works to demonstrate in his first fourteen propositions that, given this definition, only one substance can exist. Human individuals, since they are not separate beings, must therefore be modes; humans are the states or "affections" of the one substance, being "in something else and conceived through something else" (E1 def. 5).

Spinoza contends that his metaphysics provides a place for real (albeit reconceived) human selves, individuated in both body and mind. Now it might seem that, if God is the only substance, human selves could not have separate existence. But selves can still be *modes* of substance: "Particular things are nothing but affections of the attributes of God; that is, modes wherein the attributes of God find expression in a definite and determinate way" (E1 P25 cor.). This dichotomy is exhaustive: everything is either substance or mode. Substances—rather, the one substance—has fully independent existence; it "requires nothing else in order to be thought." This isn't true of us: we're clearly contingent, and require other things in order to be understood. So we must in some way be expressions of substance. At best, then, we are distinctions within substance. Moreover, no individual is correctly regarded as the "cause or sufficient reason of any other: the only sufficient cause can be God or Nature."[9]

Against classical theism, then, Spinoza argues that everything is in God (P15). It follows that God is not a transient but the immanent cause of modes (P19) God's causes do not pass over to the modes like the motion of billiard balls, but rather God

---

8. Parenthetical references, unless otherwise noted, are to Spinoza's *Ethics*; I usually follow the translation of Shirley (1982).

9. Mason, "Spinoza on the Causality of Individuals," 207.

as indwelling cause is *in* his effects.[10] God is the efficient cause also of their essence (P25). Therefore, Spinoza argues, "*in the same sense (eo sensu)* that God is said to be self-caused he must also be said to be the cause of all things."[11] Hence Spinoza's famous dictum: "particular things are nothing but affections of the attributes of God." . . .

From this hierarchy Spinoza draws his famous metaphysical conclusion: "If we thus continue to infinity, we shall readily conceive the whole of Nature as one individual whose parts—that is, all the constituent bodies (*omnia corpora*)—vary in infinite ways without any change in the individual as a whole." . . . Only when viewed from the top of the hierarchy, from the perspective of carrying the progression on "to infinity," is it true to say that there is only one self-existent thing, Nature, and that our identity is in some sense dependent on it. Viewed from lower points in the progression toward unity, there will appear to be many individual things. Thus, in Moreau's defense of Spinoza, the metaphor of the body is the key for combining substantial monism and modal pluralism: "the diversity of singular things . . . is a collection of single modes that are unified as the organs of one body. The universe must be considered as an individual Soul, of which the parts change without its ceasing still to persist in its form as a total Individual."[12] . . .

Conclusion

My case is now complete. We began with the agreement among contemporary philosophers that Spinoza himself was unable successfully to derive the finite from the infinite and thereby to achieve a monistic metaphysics. He suggested, correctly, that the infinite can be "modified" according to infinite modes and that finite things can be defined by a process of mutual limitation through other finite things. Still, this fails to be an *explanation* of how the infinite would come to be modified in finite ways or to take finite form—precisely the explanatory task that Spinoza would have to resolve were he to provide a philosophical alternative to theism. . . .

One does not want to be unfair to the advocates of a full-on philosophy of immanence. We have found some intriguing phrases, some intimations of immanence. But none of these thinkers formulated a real philosophy of immanence; none achieved an updating of Spinozism that dispensed entirely with transcendent claims. All three thinkers found it necessarily, for instance, to distinguish God as agent or spirit from finite things, leaving behind the strict equation *deus siva natura*. Lessing saw the need for complexity and for dialectical development within God; Jacobi pointed the way toward a Kantian transcendental reading of Spinoza; and Mendelssohn showed why the world must be thought as both within God and yet not as identical with God. Yovel may be right that the quest for a philosophy of immanence is adventuresome. Yet, at

---

10. Shirley, trans. and ed., Spinoza's *Ethics*, 25.
11 Ibid., scholium, emphasis mine.
12. Moreau, "Spinoza Est-il Monist?" 26.

least until the period after Hegel's death, it remains a poetic seduction (or a Rortyan conversation?), falling short of coherent systematic expression.

What then do we conclude? Some form of minimal personalist theism (or panentheism) may still emerge as philosophically viable, even if it leaves this discussion and enters the next saddled with several specific unresolved difficulties. Pantheism, by contrast, is faced with apparently insurmountable problems. It may still be true that the mystical yearning for immanence, or for the absolutely transcendent One (the two, interestingly, may turn out to be equivalent) finds its quintessential expression in Spinoza's philosophy. But his actual position and arguments haven't provided the sort of philosophical grounding for this intuition that can stand up to critical examination. Nor, apparently, is it to be found in any of those, so far, who followed after Spinoza and used his name.

15

Rethinking the Relation of God and the World

Panentheism and the Contribution of Philosophy[1]

THIS BOOK IS PREMISED on the assumption that there is a hermeneutical rather than a linear relationship between biblical interpretation and theological reflection. It is no more possible for one to exclude from the interpretive process what one finds scientifically and philosophically (and ethically!) credible than it is for one to read individual texts about God's creating and redeeming without being influenced in some way by one's broader theologies of creation and redemption. There is no shortcutting the hermeneutical circle. One can nonetheless shift its center of focus. . . .

From Classical Theism to Panentheism

It turns out that "classical Western theism or pantheism" is *not* the only choice. One sign of the inadequacy of this dichotomy—despite its rhetorical role within the history of theology—is that pantheism was never seriously entertained within the orbit of Christian or para-Christian reflection. Always—in Porphyrus, in Johannes of Eriugena, in Eckhardt, Cusa, Bruno, and many others—the actual "heretical" assertion was that finite things are full God; the world as a whole was never made identical to all there was of God. Admittedly, as the church struggled over the question of which of these views to label heretical the debate was indeed carried out in terms of whether the positions were pantheistic or not. But this was to turn a complex conceptual struggle into a matter of superficial labels, to attempt to dismiss a sophisticated theological position by means of the fallacy of "guilt by association." In what follows I hope to show

---

1. "Rethinking the Relation of God and the World: Panentheism and the Contribution of Philosophy," as found within Clayton, *God and Contemporary Science*, 82–106. Reprinted with the kind permission of Eerdmans.

that panentheism dissolves the dichotomy that structured so many of the theological debates on this topic.

The Argument from Space

In *God in Creation*, Jürgen Moltmann shows convincingly why a full understanding of creation must eventually lead theologians to something like panentheism, the position that he himself advocates, and not to pantheism in the sense that the defenders of orthodoxy feared. In Moltmann's presentation, what plays the key role is closer reflection on the question of *God's relationship to space and time*. On the one hand, the Christian tradition has never reduced the world to unreality or illusion. There really are separately existing things, which means that they are spread out in real space and time. As Moltmann notes, "If space is interpreted as the dimension of God's omnipresence, pantheistic conclusions are impossible."[2] God can only be present to all parts of his creation if there really are such parts in the first place. . . .

One cannot help but note the analogy with Augustine's theory of time. Augustine allowed the entire flow of time to be encompassed within the eternal Now, which expresses God's awareness of all temporal moments at once. As God can be present to every now while still subsuming all nows within the eternal Now that transcends and encompasses finite time, so also God can be present here while still subsuming all heres within a divine space that transcends and encompasses physical space. (The analogy is strengthened by the role of "spacetime" in contemporary physics.) Thus, Moltmann can conclude, "'Absolute space' means the direct presence of God in the whole material world and in every individual thing within it."[3] The motivation of the doctrine of divine omnipresence, then, is not to pretend that all things *are* God, but to locate all things *within* the divine presence, which is the only source of all existing things. If space is an attribute of God, then God must be present at all points in space. Theologically, "if God perceives everything immediately and directly through his omnipresence, this presupposes that God's eternal, uncreated omnipresence is *the same as* the omnipresence of space."[4] If space is God's space, then the world is not "outside" him but by definition within him.

It thus seems that we must not separate the world's "space" from God's omnipresence. One might worry that pantheism will result, since space (and thus all finite things) are no longer placed outside of God. But pantheism means that *no* separation is made between God and the world, whereas I am suggesting that the separation ought to be drawn in a different way. Fear of pantheism drove theologians to use spatial difference as the "specific difference" between God and world when they should have trusted the power of more fundamental theological categories: finite versus infinite,

---

2. Moltmann, *God in Creation*, 117.
3. Ibid., 154.
4. Ibid., 155.

contingent versus necessary, imperfect versus perfect—created versus Creator. We are not God because we are different in *our fundamental nature* from God. Thus, it does not matter where we are located: within the overarching divine presence, and even (in one sense) within the divine being itself, we remain God's created product, the work of his hands.

A word should be said here about the finite/infinite distinction, since it plays a very important role in panentheism. It is never merely a quantitative distinction, as if the infinite were merely a bit more than the finite—or even *a lot* more! Like the difference between contingent and necessary, it expresses a qualitative distinction, a difference in nature or being. This point is especially crucial because finite space *might* turn out to be endlessly extended and there might be an uncountable number of objects (say, atoms) within it. Nonetheless, as Georg Cantor, the founder of the theory of transfinite sets, realized, even a mathematics of infinite sets still requires as its limit case the notion of the absolute infinite, which is qualitatively different from any infinite set. Applied to space, this means that even an endless ("infinite") space could be included within God without being identified with him. To preserve Cantor's distinction theologically, we might say that God encompasses infinite (created) space but that God *is absolute* space. This distinction makes it possible to think of God as coextensive with the world: all points of space are encompassed by God and are in this sense "within" him. Nonetheless, created space is precisely that—created, contingent. Only God himself has the ontological status to be absolute and to contain all space within himself. In short: finite space is contained within absolute space, the world is contained within God; yet the world is not identical to God. Precisely this is the core thesis of panentheism.

Admittedly, this view calls for a dialectical way of thinking that has not always been embraced within the Christian tradition. Not infrequently, the God/world question has been posed in terms of an either/or: *either* the world is separate from God and exists "outside of" him, *or* the world and God must be identified, in which case there can be no distinction between the two—and pantheism results. To think of the world as within God and at the same time as different from God is to think in terms of a both/and: there is *both* identification or inclusion *and* distinction of God and world. Of course, it would be conceptually "cleaner" if one could specify in which respects the two are identified and in which others they are separate. For instance, why not just say that the world is in God spatially and yet distinct from God as the contingent is distinct from the necessary? Such formulations are helpful—and yet none of them, in my view, completely abolishes the tension.

In order to be theologically adequate, every assertion of the independent existence of the world must be balanced by the (equally true) assertion that the world is absolutely dependent upon God at every instant for its continued existence. The world really exists, *and* the world really depends on God moment to moment for its sustenance, such that nothing would exist in the next instant without the conserving will of God. Physical matter/energy really exists, *and* physical matter/energy has no independent existence apart from God. Such dialectical thinking is fully familiar to students of contemporary environmental science, where it appears in organic form in the *symbiotic* relationship between individual organisms and their life-world of other living beings and objects. We know that ecosystems are more than the sum total of living and non-living things within them. Now imagine an ecosystem of "all that is"; it too must be more than the sum total of its parts. If you also imagine that its identity is living and conscious, and (for this is the claim of theism) that its existence also *preceded* its being filled with living things, then you will have some sense of the dialectic between God and world envisioned by panentheism. Even if the dialectic is not reducible, it remains conceptually consistent and theologically fruitful. . . .

Arguments for and Implications of Panentheism

How else can this distinction between classical Western theism and panentheism be made? What are the main reasons that point us in the direction of panentheism? The following six points present the case for panentheism, though each is actually only a shorthand sketch for what would have to be a much fuller argument.

1. The inadequacy of atheism

The theological case begins with arguments for the inadequacy of purely physicalistic or materialist accounts of the universe. Here the most important datum is perhaps the reader him- or herself. We seem to ourselves to be conscious beings, to have mental states we call feelings and thoughts which are not reducible to their physical sources, for example to neurophysiological states. . . .

Once one is convinced of the existence of a spiritual power, the crucial questions concern its relation to the world and whether it is to be understood as personal or impersonal. Although some question whether any reasons can help us to decide the latter question, I do think a reasonable case can be made for the personalist answer. As Edward Pols has noted, "The most fundamental and concrete sense of power accessible to our intelligence is power in the sense of agency."[5] If we are trying to conceive of the divine as being (or possessing) the highest sort of power of which we are aware, we will be driven to understand the divine as agent rather than as "merely" impersonal power. Kirkpatrick, citing Pols, argues that we will also need to make the next step: "power in the sense of agency necessarily means 'the power of an agent regarded as an entity.' Therefore, if ultimacy has to do with power, then only *a* being can have the requisite ultimacy because only an agent-being can exercise power."[6] If we conceive of

---

5. Pols, "Power and Agency," 295.
6. Kirkpatrick, "Understanding an Act of God," 165.

God as *an agent,* we conceive of the divine as *a* being, rather than as, say, "the Ground of Being" (Tillich). I shall speak in this way in what follows, although there are serious (and in my mind not fully resolved) metaphysical difficulties raised by speaking of the highest principle as *a* being.

2. *The inconsistency of classical Western theism*

We earlier examined the historical forces that led the Israelites from polytheism to classical theism. What we found to be the historical development in the biblical texts also makes sense conceptually: Yahweh's relation to the world will be very different if he is thought of as one among many gods (polytheism), or as so much more powerful than the others that it is *as if* no other gods existed at all (henotheism), or as the One and Only from which all else stems (radical monotheism). I made the case that the biblical texts launch one on a trajectory of belief and thought that begs to be extended beyond the classical Western account of God's separation from the world. A theology that places God "outside of" his creation has not yet fully thought through what is entailed in the move from many gods to the *ex nihilo* creation of heaven and earth by an absolutely infinite God. Now it would be a mistake to claim that *only* panentheism adequately fits the biblical data, for the biblical texts underdetermine the choice between systematic theological models. Nonetheless, I think it possible to show that panentheism captures the central biblical teachings about the God/world relationship, and at least a serious case can be made that it does a better job with this task than many models do, including some versions of classical theism.

3. *The biblical resistance to dualism*

The Israelite understanding of the human individual is radically monistic or holistic: the human being is a single entity that, although including a number of aspects, is not fundamentally divided up into separate parts. This holistic emphasis emerges already in the opening descriptions of humanity's creation. The biblical creation texts know nothing of a pre-existent soul that is combined with—much less one that is imprisoned within!—the body. Man and Woman become individually *nephesh* or "living soul," and no prior living soul is "attached" to the body. Westermann adds, "Man, created in his state as a living being, is created as a complete unity. Any understanding of man as consisting of body and soul, or of body, soul, and spirit, is excluded from the start."[7] The notion of a soul that survives the body—and consequently any clear notion of an afterlife—does not occur until the post-exilic period. When the belief does arise that the person survives death, there is no indication in the Hebrew texts that this post-mortem existence would be in anything other than an embodied state.

---

7. Westermann, *Creation,* 77–78.

The Greek dualism of mind or spirit and body, and the subsequent valuation placed upon mind over body, is thus utterly foreign to the Hebrew texts. The same is true of the New Testament the goal for which the authors long is not a disembodied state of freedom from the body, but an integrated existence of both soul and body in the direct presence of God. The New Testament speaks not of escaping *soma* (body) but overcoming *sarx* (the flesh).

The temptations toward dualism in the history of Christian theology have come primarily from the Greek notion of the priority and purity of the mind or spirit *(pneuma)* and the concurrent notion of the evilness—or at the very least, the inferiority—of the body. . . . But God need not be defined as spirit *in opposition* to the world (ontological dualism) as long as matter is not seen as evil or inferior. If we take seriously the "and it was very good" of Genesis, then it is not an evil thing for God to be closely related to the world, to "walk in the garden in the cool of the day" (Gen 3:8). Indeed, if humans are really made in the image of God, imbreathed with God-given Spirit, then it would be mare natural to conceive of God as Spirit working in and through at least some parts of the material world. For Christian theology, the world can never be divinized, *made into God,* but it *can* be included within the overarching span of God's universal presence and being. These are, of course, conclusions shared by many systematic theologians. Panentheism's difference is to stress the desirability of God's actually including the world, once the final vestiges of Greek or gnostic dualism are abandoned.

4. Divine infinity

We have found that both biblical and theological lines of argument point toward the infinite/finite contrast as a crucial conceptual means for drawing the distinction between God and his creation. Yet it turns out to be impossible to conceive of God as fully infinite if he is limited by something outside of himself. The infinite may without contradiction include within itself things that are by nature finite, but it may not stand *outside of* the finite. For if something finite exists, and if the infinite is "excluded" by the finite, then it is nor truly infinite or without limit. To put it differently, there is simply no place for finite things to "be" outside of that which is *absolutely unlimited.* Hence, an infinite God must encompass the finite world that he has created, making it in some sense "within" himself. This is the conclusion that we call panentheism. One criticism ought to be immediately addressed: that the Bible does not explicitly speak: of God as infinite. Like the doctrine of the Trinity, the doctrine of the infinity of God is an inference drawn from the biblical texts, an inference that theologians have found far more acceptable than the alternative. [For t]he Bible does emphasize the awesome power of God, . . . God's eternity, . . . omnipresence, . . . his otherness, . . . and his unknowability. Some passages [even] come very close to a doctrine of divine infinity. . . .

PART III: PANENTHEISTIC REFLECTIONS ON SCIENCE & THEOLOGY

5. The problem of divine causality

When the world is understood as ontologically "outside" God, then any actions that God takes within the world must represent interventions "from outside" into the world's order. This model of God as a sort of foreign agent intervening in an independently existing order raises numerous problems. If the creation (and its Creator) were perfect from the start, why would it have to be "fixed" in this manner? Are regularities within the world to be understood as representing a causality independent of God, one that functions all on its own? Would it not be far better theologically to view even inner-worldly causality as (in at least some sense) a manifestation of divine agency? How could these divine interventions be known at all by humans if they come from completely outside the order that we inhabit? These are not merely apologetic questions. . . . Much more, they represent the urgent task of how *even believers,* speaking from the standpoint of faith, can find any way to make sense of the idea of divine "interventions" from "outside" into the world. The issue of divine causality explains why panentheism and the theory of divine action are so closely linked in the present monograph. We will find in the ensuing pages that the action of God can be much more coherently conceived if the world bears a relationship to God analogous to the body's relationship to the mind or soul. Making sense of the analogy will force us to *think* in some detail about the relationship of the mental to the physical in humans . . . and it will also require us to think carefully about God's relationship to the world. In what follows I shall call it the *panentheistic analogy.*

If the analogy turns out to be theologically fruitful, one can already begin to anticipate what it would suggest about divine action. As an opening hypothesis, it appears to suggest that there is no *qualitative* or ontological difference between the regularity of natural law and the intentionality of special divine actions. . . . The fact that our universe exhibits the physical regularities it does could be taken as a surd, a brute fact needing no further explanation (atheism); or it could be attributed to an original act of God, by which he "set the clock in motion" and then let it run on its own (deism). Classical Western theism has held that the continuing "concurrence" of God is required to keep things ticking along. Panentheism stands closest to classical Western theism in this regard, yet it draws an even closer link between physics and theology: since God is present in each physical interaction and at each point in space, each interaction is a part of *his* being in the broadest sense, for it is "in him [that] we live and move and have our being" (Acts 17: 28). . . . Natural regularities within God's universe, then, are roughly analogous to autonomic responses within an individual's body—the things that one's body does without conscious interference or guidance. . . .

6. A closer relationship with God

Finally, panentheism conceives of an ontologically closer relationship between God and humanity than has traditionally been asserted. Theologians have of course always insisted upon the role of God as Creator, and the tradition has emphasized the necessity of a continual *sustaining* of the created order by God (the doctrine of *conservatio*). When the tradition spoke of the word of God or a sense of God within the individual human (the *sensus divinitatis*), this locution could be (and was) interpreted as the work of God in one of three different ways: as a product of the original image of God "built into" humanity at creation and thus "reflected in" our being in the present; as a sign of the presence of God as Conserver or Sustainer within the human being; or as a manifestation of direct divine agency. Panentheism, one might say, adds a fourth mode of the *sensus divinitatis,* an ontological one: we are aware of God because we are within God. God has created out of nothing other than himself all that exists in the finite world; we are composed, metaphorically speaking at least, out of God. More carefully, Schleiermacher wrote in the *Speeches,* "Everything finite exists *only* through the specification of its boundaries, which must be simultaneously cut out *(herausgeschnitten)* of the Infinite. Only in this fashion can [each thing] be infinite within these boundaries and have a form of its own."[8] . . . This way of conceiving the God/world relationship makes the relationship of Creator and created *as close as it can possibly be without dissolving the difference-in-nature between the infinite God and the finite created world,* that is without falling into pantheism.

---

8. See Schleiermacher, *Uber die Religion,* p. 53 of the 1799 edition, quoted here from the Otto Braun edition, *Philosophische Bibliothek.*

16

Panentheism in Metaphysical and Scientific Perspective[1]

IN AN ARRAY OF publications I have defended panentheism as an outcome of developments in modern philosophical theology, as a framework for speaking of divine action in the context of modern science, and as a response to specific conundrums within Christian systematic theology. Reading the chapters in this volume has made me think again, however, about the basic question: how, if at all, could one make an effective case for panentheism with a discussion partner who was skeptical about this theological program? Like several of the other authors, I am interested in the question of why one might espouse panentheism—and why one might decline to do so.

In recent years, scholars have advanced a variety of reasons that might lead one to adopt panentheism. Consider this rational reconstruction of some of the central options:

- One might hold that classical philosophical theism (CPT) or "supernaturalistic" theism or traditional theism is no longer viable, without being convinced that atheism is the most compelling answer.
- One might be convinced that panentheism is more compatible than traditional theism with particular results in physics or biology, or with common features shared across the scientific disciplines, such as the structure of emergence.
- One may be convinced of the truth or preferability of a particular metaphysical position (process philosophy, German idealism); and panentheism either lies closer to, or is actually entailed by, that metaphysical position.
- One might hold that panentheism can do a better job at preserving certain religious beliefs than classical theism can. So, for example, one might argue that viewing the world as within God allows for the development of an adequate

---

1. "Panentheism in Metaphysical and Scientific Perspective," as found within Clayton and Peacocke, eds. *In Whom We Live and Move and Have Our Being*, 73–94. Reprinted with the kind permission of Eerdmans.

theory of divine action, whereas classical theism, if it succeeded in avoiding deism, could only support an "interventionist" theory of divine action.

- In the process of searching for a mediating metaphysic between Western and Eastern religious philosophical systems, one might come to believe that panentheism provides the most convincing available answer.

- One might find panentheism religiously more viable or more attractive than the alternatives. Some have argued, for instance, that traditional Christian theism is burdened by unanswerable objections such as the problem of evil, whereas panentheistic theologies are able to avoid these objections.

- One might be convinced that classical theism has unacceptable ethical or political implications, while panentheism does not have these implications.

The recent debate, however, reveals a rather remarkable breakdown in the actual debates for and against panentheistic theologies. In order to understand what kind of a debate is involved in pro-and-con discussions concerning panentheism, a few methodological observations are in order.

First, a quick survey of the literature reveals that panentheism is advocated much more often by philosophical theologians than by systematic or biblical theologians. The term is found most frequently in authors who are wrestling with connections between theology and other disciplines: science, or metaphysics, or ethics and social-political philosophy, or the contemporary cultural context. The shared argument paradigm among these authors runs something like this: "Theology faces some serious difficulties when it enters into interdisciplinary debates, and traditional doctrinal language has not been effective in responding to these difficulties. By contrast, a panentheistic understanding of the God–world relationship is able to make connections with other academic fields. Until we find a conceptual structure that does a *better* job of addressing these problems, we are justified in turning to panentheism as a framework for making sense of God language in the face of its detractors. Even if this move involves some revisions vis-à-vis traditional formulations, it is a cost one should be willing to pay."

Second, an overview of the papers in this volume will reveal how difficult it is to express shared criteria for deciding the panentheism question: even the most rigorous argument in one category may fail to interest those whose motivation stems from another field or set of questions. Likewise, thinkers who are moved by one or another criticism *against* panentheism are sometimes unmoved by even the strongest arguments in its favor. For some, the steps that panentheism takes away from traditional Christian formulations already constitute sufficient reason to reject it.

Perhaps the best case for panentheism, then, would be a cumulative one: because there are so many difficulties (and dissatisfactions) with classical theism, and because panentheism offers a potentially attractive response to various (theological, philosophical, ethical, social-political) difficulties, the authors in this volume are drawn to it as a model. Only a multi-faceted defense of this sort could make the case that recent work on panentheism constitutes a progressive research program,[2] one that brings new resources to unresolved religious and philosophical debates. If it can be shown to open up new solutions to theology's contemporary difficulties, and if classical theism is not able to do the same, then one will have reasons for pursuing the panentheist option. . . .

A single paper, however, can only develop one or two specific arguments in any detail. In what follows, I reconstruct two of the central arguments in more detail, one stemming from developments in the modern "metaphysics of the subject" and the other from the theory of emergence as it is being developed today in the philosophy of science and the philosophy of mind. Combined with the other arguments in this book, I believe these two arguments are sufficient to advance panentheism as a very serious option within philosophical theology today.

On God and Persons

Theologians in the twentieth century were particularly drawn to person language. Rarely do recent defenses of the continuing relevance of theism in today's intellectual climate or "in light of modern science" explain the God–world relationship in terms of interacting substances, for example, as one might have done in the fourth century. And contemporary philosophers, though they have worked in detail on the problems of personhood, have made scant use of the concepts of *hypokeimenon*, *hypostasis*, and *substantia* (though some of the essays in this volume suggest that it would behoove them to do so).

Instead, when theists attempt to explain why theism should still be viewed as a live option, they most often have recourse to language about persons. God's nature, it is argued, is not less than personal, even though it is infinitely more; God is a personal agent who forms intentions and acts in the world; the divine being consists of the "persons" of Father, Son, and Spirit; and in his relations *ad extra* God is personally present to the world. Indeed, person-based arguments are sometimes even used against panentheists: panentheism must be false, it's sometimes said, because we really are persons—agents who engage in personal relationships and who initiate personal activity within the world—whereas panentheism would make us merely "parts" of some larger divine whole.

Unfortunately, however, "person" is not a self-explanatory category. It's my contention that, although the Latin term *persona* first arose in a context in which the metaphysics of substance was dominant, it has today largely lost contact with that particular context of origin. Indeed, one of the major reasons for panentheism's

---

2. See Lakatos, "The Methodology of Scientific Research Programs."

significance as a theological resource, I suggest, is that the "panentheistic analogy" provides a rigorous way of specifying what we mean when we apply person-language to God—a sort of rigor too often lacking in discussions of God and personhood. (Of course, the argument will be convincing in the end only if it is supported by both metaphysical and scientific considerations.)

In the struggle to re-establish a credible theory of personhood after the demise of substance metaphysics, modern thinkers have turned to the natural sciences; to sociobiology and evolutionary psychology; to social sciences such as psychology, sociology, economics, and cultural anthropology; to history, literature, and the arts; and, of course, to metaphysical reflection. Among the lessons that this modern "quest for the person" teaches[3] is that no simple appeal to an alleged "common-sense theory of the person" will suffice for rehabilitating the God–world relation. Contemporary deconstructive treatments of personhood alone, for example, are probably sufficient to undermine "common-sense" language about persons (esp. the personhood of God!); for additional evidence, one need only consider the radically different understandings of personhood across the world's cultures and religious traditions.

Theologians in the Western traditions have typically maintained that the closest analogy for the relationship between God and humans is the person-to-person relationship, rather than the relation of impersonal forces or deterministic causes. "God relates to us as one person relates to other persons," it is often said, even if God remains infinitely more than "just a person."

But it is one thing to use the notion of personhood as an intuitive starting point, quite another to treat the assertion "God is personal" as all the philosophical basis one needs for determining God's relation to the world. When theologians leave unexplained the sense in which God is personal, has intentions, or relates to the world in a personal fashion, their lacuna is not filled simply by turning to biblical theology for data on the God–world relationship or by providing a historical survey of the various things doctrinal theologians have said on the topic through the ages.[4]

If one were satisfied with this mode of proceeding, one might well have no motivation for developing a panentheistic theology. The trouble, however, is that the expression "relating to us as persons," especially when applied to God, expresses a desideratum—it's the place-holder for an answer rather than the answer itself. Gesturing in the direction of personhood is not enough; theology faces serious theoretical objections, and new conceptual work is necessary to answer them. . . .

From "Being as Subject" to Panentheism

Here is where panentheism enters: the metaphysical framework that was developed during the modern period from Descartes to Hegel necessitates a rethinking of the

3. See Taylor, *Sources of the Self*.
4. For a book-length appeal to the biblical data, see Collins, *The God of Miracles*.

God–world relationship. One can't merely tack the new metaphysics of subjectivity onto the old metaphysics of substance with its separate notions of God and world. . . .

Among the infinite attributes of the one whole, which Spinoza called *deus siva natura*, are thought and extension. If thought and extension cannot be separate types of substances, à la Descartes, they must be distinct aspects of the One (hence Spinoza's "dual-aspect monism"). To every mode in the world corresponds an idea; and just as the modes proceed upward in an interlocking hierarchy to the physical totality that we call nature, so also the hierarchy of "ideas of ideas" proceeds upwards to the interlocking whole that Spinoza called "God or Nature."

The trouble is, Spinoza was unable to conceptualize the principle of activity. Of course, he *asserted* that ideas were both active and passive, and he spoke of nature both as fact (*natura naturata*) and as activity (*natura naturans*). But he did not recognize that there must be a center of agency—what Kant called a "transcendental unity of apperception"—to serve as the unifying force behind any center of conscious experience. It is fascinating to observe how the commentaries of Spinoza's three most important interpreters prior to Kant (Lessing, Jacobi, and Mendelsohn) gradually pull the Spinozistic system in the direction of an active unifying principle.

Were Spinoza to have added the transcendental unity of apperception, however, he could not have maintained the strict pantheism for which he is so famous, the complete unity of God and Nature (*deus siva natura*). . . .

The Panentheistic Analogy

As it turns out, these two major strands in the history of philosophical theology—the concepts of the infinite and the perfect—tend to link with monistic and pluralistic understandings of reality respectively. In *The Problem of God in Modern Thought* I tried to show that these two separate families of concepts—infinity-based ultimate unity and perfection-based irreducible pluralism—help form the terrain on which modern theology moves. When one emphasizes the complete perfection of God, one has reason to separate all created, less-than-fully-perfect beings and objects from the divine, because the perfection of God would be compromised if he took into himself other objects before they had been sufficiently cleansed (sanctified) from their imperfection (sin). Much of the history of Calvinism exhibits the outworking of this logic. By contrast, the logic of the notion of infinity ultimately excludes anything that might be "outside" the infinite; all must be included within it.[5] The emergence of panentheism in the nineteenth century reflects this conceptual world.

As neat as this conceptual division may appear, there are theological reasons to suspect that neither of the two approaches can stand on its own. On the one hand, a strong monism leaves inadequate place for individual difference or the integrity of

---

5. I skip over a large number of subtleties and nuances that would have to be (and have been) added in a fuller treatment.

creation—precisely the criticism raised again and again of Spinoza's philosophy. On the other hand, a sharp distinction between God and world has led in the modern period to deism and to the apparent impossibility of divine action.[6]

What to do, then? When two factors are both desirable yet neither can stand alone, one looks to the possibility of combining them. Admittedly, the rules of metaphysical debate tend to push one to choose one option *or* the other in the interest of simplicity and systematicity. But must we consent to this pressure? Sometimes the conjunction supplies the better answer; sometimes the position that's more adequate to the data is the one that is *less* simple. Perhaps, among the options, the best is the one that preserves both the essential, eternal nature of God and the essentially temporal process of God's relations to others. Herein lies the continuing attraction of "dipolar theism" as it has been defended by process theologians over the last decades. Dipolar theism is the view that God consists of two natures: an "antecedent" nature, which is fixed and unchanging, and a "consequent" nature, which is fully responsive to the world and arises only in interaction with it.

What happens when we return with this result to the question of God's relation to the world? Earlier we found ourselves pulled between the monism of Spinoza's "one substance with many modes" and the separation of God and world based on the demands of divine perfection. Dipolar panentheism suggests a more dialectical answer: not unity or difference, but unity-in-difference. The world is neither indistinguishable from God nor (fully) ontologically separate from God. Univocal language breaks down here, as it often does when we try to express dialectical relations. Arguably, one of the great weaknesses of the line of thought from Whitehead to Hartshorne was to advance dipolar theism with insufficient emphasis on the dialectical nature of the relationship. A Hegelian (or Peircean) revision of process thought would retain the "two-ness" of the two poles in God but would attempt to add as a third moment the movement of relation between them. The resulting trinitarian form of process theology represents a fascinating new research program.[7]

The more abstract (metaphysical or logical) presentation of panentheism is not for everyone; some will wish for a paraphrase that uses metaphors or analogies. But what kind of metaphor could express the truth that the infinite must comprehend all finite things? Highly concrete metaphors—e.g., the world exists in the womb of God—are evocative but too specific to be of broad theoretical interest. For a truth of this generality, one would need to make use of the most general metaphors that language offers.

Herein lies the justification for the central metaphor of panentheism—the "in" metaphor—which is built into the very etymology of this position (pan*en*theism =

---

6. Many feminist theologians have argued that it has also led to a treatment of the environment as merely "instrumental," a mistake the consequences of which are palpable in the water and air and forests around us today.

7. See Bracken and Suchocki, eds., *Trinity in Process*.

all-*in*-God). "In" is a metaphor—an expression that defines or explains by identifying non-identicals—because it ascribes spatiality to God (at least in God's relation to the world) even though God as the Creator of space cannot be intrinsically spatial. Indeed, that the "in" is used metaphorically should be obvious from the fact that panentheists use it in two different directions—the world is in God, and God is in the world—whereas in mundane spatial relations this is impossible: the pie can't be in the cupboard and the cupboard in the pie at the same time! Like the tensions that are created by all living metaphors,[8] this tension drives one beyond any literal interpretation of the two-fold "in." It is not difficult to paraphrase the fundamental claim being made by the metaphor: the *inter*dependence of God and world. The world depends on God because God is its necessary and eternal source; without God's creative act it would neither have come into existence nor exist at this moment. And God depends on the world because the nature of God's actual experience depends on interactions with finite creatures like ourselves.

Thus the analogical relationship suggests itself: the body is to mind as the body/mind combination—that is, human persons—are to the divine. The world is in some sense analogous to the body of God; God is analogous to the mind that indwells the body, though God is also more than the natural world taken as a whole. Call it the Panentheistic Analogy (PA). The power of this analogy lies in the fact that mental causation, as every human agent knows it, is more than physical causation and yet still a part of the natural world. Apparently, no natural law is broken when you form the (mental) intention to raise your hand and then you cause that particular physical object in the world, your hand, to rise. The PA therefore offers the possibility of conceiving divine actions that express divine intentions and agency without breaking natural law. On the PA, there would be no *qualitative* or ontological difference between the regularity of natural law conceived as expressing the regular or repetitive operation of divine agency and the intentionality of special divine actions. . . .

Emergence and Panentheism

Much remains to be said beyond this brief sketch of emergence.[9] But time and space are short, and the links to panentheism must now be drawn. My thesis is simple: emergence provides the best available means, for those who take science seriously, to rethink (i.e., establish a new conceptual basis for) the immanence of God in the world. Where emergence seems to make God *too* immanent and not transcendent enough, there are reasons *internal to the emergence argument itself* to correct it back in the direction of transcendence.

It is widely acknowledged that during the modern period the emphasis on God's transcendence of the world merged with the growing power of naturalist explanations

---

8. See McFague, *Methaphorical Theology*; Soskice, *Metaphor and Religious Language*.
9. See Clayton and Davies, eds., *The Re-emergence of Emergence*.

to break the delicate balance between transcendence and immanence that theists had established in previous centuries. Unfortunately it turned out that, if God is transcendent and the world is fully explained by natural law, then there *is* no place for any divine involvement in the world. Naturally, theists still wanted (and want) to affirm that God is omnipresent, aware of and responding to the world. But—and this is the point that theologians continue to fail to see—the *conceptual basis* for these claims, which had undergirded divine-action claims in the patristic and medieval periods, gradually collapsed under the pressure of modern science and modern philosophy. Conservative evangelicals and fundamentalists have responded by encouraging us to ignore or contradict modern science. But that is an answer that neither I nor the other authors in this book are willing to countenance. Instead, we accept modern science and look for a new conceptual basis—or a rediscovery and renewing of older conceptual resources—for asserting the immanence of God. Like the other authors, I find panentheism to provide the most adequate means available, and particularly in the combination with emergence that we have called emergentist panentheism.

Arthur Peacocke has already nicely described the way in which emergent systems represent a sort of nested hierarchy: parts are contained within wholes, which themselves become parts within greater wholes, and so forth. . . . If the same structure could be applied to God's relation to the world, it would comprehend the world as internal to God—precisely the sort of intimate connection of God to world that the theological doctrine of immanence has traditionally offered. Indeed, the connection is closer than is often recognized. For example, note that the terms "in" or "internal" are used metaphorically by emergence theorists as well. What emergence actually offers, put in more formal but less evocative terms, is the set-inclusion relation "belongs to," "is a member of," etc. This is a relation of logical inclusion rather than (primarily) one of location. Conceptually it's much closer to the (Hegelian) case for the finite being included within the infinite, sketched above. Emergence thus represents a powerful answer to misgivings about the preposition "in."

Note that the nature of the "in" or self-inclusion relation changes as one moves up the hierarchy of complexity in nature. As long as one remains with the nested hierarchies that constitute actual objects in the world, the "in" is indeed locative: atoms are in molecules, molecules in cells, cells in organs, organs in organisms, etc. By contrast, organisms are in an ecosystem in a rather difference sense. Consider the further differences introduced by "William is in the Army," "Vermont is in the Union," "her love is in her heart," "we live in community," and "no man is an island; all persons exist in society."

17

Panentheism Today
A Constructive Systematic Evaluation[1]

ONE CANNOT FINISH READING the previous chapters without invariably finding oneself wondering, What do they share in common? Despite some clear differences and disagreements among the authors, can one discern here the makings here of a recognizable school of thought concerning "God's presence in a scientific world"? Do these essays offer a platform for new constructive reflections on the nature of God's relationship to the world?

It is the view of this book's editors and most all of its authors that panentheism does in fact represent a coherent theological program today. Many explicit agreements, and a number of underlying similarities, will already have become clear to the discerning reader. The goal of this concluding chapter is to draw attention to the family resemblances that provide this volume with its thematic unity.

The words "constructive" and "systematic" in this chapter's title need not entail "dominant" and "dismissive." The arguments given here are meant as an invitation to further dialogue, not as a technique to end it. Consider this chapter as another in this book's list of essays—albeit with the difference that, in place of the diverse sources of information employed by the preceding authors, this essay takes *their* work as its data.

In substance if not in name, panentheistic theologies play a role in many of the world's religious traditions. The Jewish kabbalistic traditions and the Muslim Sufi tradition have clearly identifiable panentheistic elements, and many (perhaps even most) of the Hindu philosophical traditions are panentheistic. As a matter of actual fact, however, all of the authors in the present volume either identify themselves as Christians or stand closer to that tradition than to any other. The following comments thus

---

1. "Panentheism Today: A Constructive Systematic Evaluation," Clayton and Peacocke, eds. *In Whom We Live and Move and Have Our Being,* 249–64. Reprinted with the kind permission of Eerdmans.

primarily reflect the Christian theological context, even though a number of them may be relevant to other religious contexts as well.

Generic Panentheism?

The first and most natural thing one wants to know is in what sense the contributions to this book represent variations on a single theme. Suppose one tried to formulate the various positions as varieties of panentheism; would it work? Can common principles be stated, such that the label "panentheism" really expresses a common intersection set among them?[2] I suggest beginning with this experiment, using adjectival labels to distinguish among the positions:

1) Participatory panentheism, or perhaps "Logoi panentheism" (described by A. Louth)
2) "Divine energies" panentheism (K. Ware)
3) Ecclesial or communal panentheism (A. Nesteruk)
4) Eschatological panentheism, or perhaps soteriological panentheism? (J. Polkinghorne, as described by several authors)
5) Sapiential panentheism (C. Deane-Drummond)
6) Emergentist panentheism (A. Peacocke, P. Clayton)
7) Sacramental panentheism (A. Peacocke, C. Knight)
9) Trinitarian panentheism (D. Edwards et al.)
10) Pansacramental naturalistic panentheism (C. Knight)
11) Process or dipolar panentheism (D. Griffin et al.)
12) "Body of God" panentheism (Ramanuja, via K. Ward)
13) Neo-Panentheism (H. Morowitz)
14) Pansyntheism (R. Page)

Let's assume for the moment that the adjectives are adequate and that the authors in question would be willing to use the term "panentheism" when modified in these ways. What precisely is the intersection set that arises out of these usages?

When they met together, several of the authors attempted to give panentheism a generic description, such that it would apply to all, or at least most, of the essays above. Consider four of the proposals:

A. Generic Panentheism according to David Griffin:

---

2. The following exercise is not meant to imply that every one of the authors would agree that "panentheism" is the best label for the position they present, though in fact most have agreed that this label is indeed appropriate to their work.

1) The world (the totality of finite things) is in some sense in God.

2) The world has a degree of independence in relation to God, whether necessarily or by grace (divine decision).

3) Besides influencing the world, God is also influenced by the world.

4) Hence, besides being unchanging in some respects, God also changes in some respect.

5) God is related to the world somewhat like the human mind is related to its body.

B. Generic Panentheism according to Niels Gregersen:

1) God contains the world, yet is also more than the world. Thus, the world is (in some sense) "in God."

2) The world is (in some sense) independent from God (or: entities in the world have some causal autonomy; or: they can be viewed in some sense as causal agents).

3) As contained "in God," the world not only derives its existence from God, but also returns to God. The world is (or: will be) united with God, while yet preserving the characteristics of being created (i.e., while remaining world). Thus, the relations between God and world are (in some sense) bilateral.

C. Generic Panentheism according to Philip Clayton:

Panentheism is located as part of a continuum that runs from classical philosophical theism to pantheism. Although the endpoints (1) and (7) lie outside panentheism, some of the other theses are not distinctive to panentheism alone.

1) God created the world as a distinct substance. It is separate from God in nature and essence, although God is present to the world (classical philosophical theism in the West).

2) God is radically immanent in the world.

3) God is bringing the world to Godself.

4) The world is in God—at least metaphorically, and perhaps also in a stronger sense.

5) God is related to the world in some sense analogous to the relationship between mind and body.

6) The world and God are co-related (contingently for some authors, necessarily for others).

7) The world and God are "non-dual" (Shankara's *Atman* is *Brahman*), or there is only one substance that can be called "nature" or "God" (Spinoza's *deus siva natura*).

D. Emphases of panentheism according to Michael Brierley:

1) The cosmos as God's body

2) Language of "in and through"

3) The cosmos as sacrament

4) Language of inextricable intertwining

5) God's dependence on the cosmos

6) The intrinsic, positive value of the cosmos

7) Divine possibility

8) Degree Christology

Clearly, there are differences among these four lists. The diversity of the lists matches the diversity of adjectives with which we began; both are reminders that panentheism expresses family resemblances between related theological programs rather than the name of a single set of theses accepted by all panentheists.

At the same time, the four attempts to formulate generic features of panentheism clearly share some common features. All speak of a location of the world "within" God, even if they vary on the degree to which the "in" is meant metaphorically (see following section). Likewise, all resist an omni-determinism by God or an obscuring of the separate identity of the world. In all cases, created beings are seen as retaining a certain degree of autonomy or independence from God. Finally, what characterizes all four accounts is a sense that the world has a deeper influence on God than was generally accepted in classical Western theology. This commonality represents one of the most important common emphases in this book.

The "in" of Panentheism

Already the etymology of the term *pan-en-theism* suggests that the little pronoun "in" linking "all" and "God" must bear the brunt of the interpretive burden. Can it hold up under the pressure?

For some authors the "in"-relation suggests a relationship of spatial inclusion: the world is located within the sphere of the divine, so to speak. Others employ the analogy with the human body: panentheism means that God is located within the world in some way analogous to the way the mind is located within the body. Yet already the conjunction of these two views reveals the difficulty: the former uses "in" to locate the world within God, whereas the second "in" would locate God within the world. How can both be true?

The unity among panentheists would be greatest if the word "in" could be given a single, distinct, sharp logical or conceptual meaning, rather than merely a locative or metaphorical sense. For example, all panentheists might accept Hegel's argument that the world must necessarily be contained within the Infinite, since it is a logical entailment of any adequate definition of the infinite (*das Unendliche*) that it not be limited by a finite (*ein Endliches*) which is set over against it.

At present, unfortunately, Hegel's argument has not won such universal acceptance. What one finds instead is a sort of family-resemblance relationship between the various usages of the word "in" by panentheists. Tom Oord of Western Nazarene University has put together a list of the various meanings of "in" that seem to be entailed by the positions presented in this volume. His list is illustrative: *The world is "in" God because:*

1) that is its literal location

2) God energizes the world

3) God experiences or prehends the world (process theology)

4) God ensouls the world

5) God plays with the world (Indic Vedantic traditions)

6) God "enfields" the world (J. Bracken)

7) God gives space to the world (J. Moltmann, drawing on the *zimzum* tradition; A. Peacocke and many of the authors in this text)

8) God encompasses or contains the world (substantive or locative notion)

9) God binds up the world by giving the divine self to the world

10) God provides the ground for emergences in, or the emergence of, the world (A. Peacocke, P. Davies, H. Morowitz, P. Clayton)

11) God befriends the world (C. Deane-Drummond)

12) all things are contained "in Christ" (from the Pauline *en Christo*)

13) God graces the world (all of the above)

In this case, as with the previous examples, one notes the diversity of approaches. Yet one recognizes in them variations on a common theme. Indeed, the variations may even be encouraging, insofar as they reflect the theological richness of the underlying notion—one concept is expressed in a more than dozen different ways while being identical to none. The chief test of the depth, and potential significance, of the shared commitment may well lie in its application. That is, critics of Christian panentheism must look to see whether these various approaches give rise to coherent, connected responses as adherents begin to apply them across the spectrum of questions traditionally addressed by Christian doctrine (e.g., Christology, pneumatology, soteriology, ecclesiology, eschatology).

Panentheist Approaches to the God–World Relation

Michael Brierley opens this volume with a thorough overview of panentheism. His tracing of its historical antecedents and his listing of major theologians and philosophers who are panentheists offers data for evaluating the background and current scope of panentheistic theologies. Likewise, the presentation of eight "common panentheistic themes" helps to locate features that many panentheists share. Of course, one might wish to dispute one or another of these theses. Thus, for example, I have resisted (v), God's dependence on the world, if it is taken to imply that God must necessarily create a (contingent) world. Two different lines of argument support this resistance. One is drawn from the Christian theological tradition, which has maintained that God's act of creation must be completely free and unconstrained. Another comes from those process traditions (e.g., Schelling, Samuel Alexander) which defend the emergence of (at least the personal side of) God. On these views, the personal God develops as the world develops; if what the world becomes is contingent, so too is God. On Brierley's side, however, are Hegel and Whitehead, who provide weighty, although not necessarily consistent, arguments for a necessary correlation of God and world.

This debate cannot be resolved here. But it is a good reminder that Brierley's eight features of panentheism should not be taken as individually necessary conditions for panentheism. Instead, his list well describes features that are generally typical of panentheistic positions. To understand the various arguments he summarizes is to get a good sense of the thought-world that generally motivates and permeates panentheistic theologies. . . . Thus, for better or worse, I have attempted to develop panentheism in a different direction. In part, the resources of process thought make it possible to conceive a greater degree of direct divine involvement. Process metaphysics preserves the regularities necessary for science without accepting that the physical order is metaphysically closed. As Griffin shows, process thought also supports a particular understanding of individual moments of experience ("actual occasions") that does not rule out a conscious influence on them by God.

But another line of argument also supports a panentheism with focally intended divine actions. Imagine that one begins with the "ladder of emergence" idea and uses it to help introduce the concept of a God who pervades and contains the natural history of emergence. Is the addition of theistic vocabulary only a sort of "coloring" of the whole, bracketed as it is between a divine origin and divine *telos*? Or does the introduction of theistic language not transform one's understanding of the entire process of natural history? To introduce the idea of a being or reality that is qualitatively distinct from the universe as a whole—infinitely greater than it, distinct from its nature as the necessary is from the contingent or the morally perfect is from the imperfect—is to reorient, rethink, and reinterpret all things.

For example, if something of God transcends the world as a whole, then the notion of pure spirit cannot be absurd, at least with regard to this element of the divine that transcends. (I assume, against Whitehead, that God is not necessarily correlated at all times with an actually existing world.) Thus, one might be inclined to say that there is within us as well an element that is pure spirit, insofar as it participates in the divine essence. *Science* can never justify such language, of course; it allows only for talk of mental properties and causes, not mental essences. But if one makes theological assertions, must these assertions not at least partially *reinterpret* the world?[3]

Our struggle is to understand what the minimal conditions are for asserting divine causal influence on the world. One could not give credit to a God who created an open-ended universe and then merely *hoped* for a final consummation that would be to his liking. God must also "draw the world unto himself" through some sort of causal activity. The tradition has called this influence providence. If one endorses the concept of providence, must one not also leave room in one's interpretation of the world for its influence? Perhaps not at the level of macrophysics, for here all the influence that is needed can be built in *ab initio* and left to run its own course.[4] But certainly by the point that minds emerge, some influence on their creativity and comprehension could be postulated—especially if, as I think, our minds are not ultimately algorithmic or law-driven.[5] Moreover, to the extent that sentient beings of all sorts—hence most of the animal kingdom—evidence an openness and a creative striving that anticipates the virtually unconstrained creativity of mind, could there not also be some space for response to actual divine influence, even of the most limited or constrained kind, here as well?

For students of the sciences, these are difficult suggestions. But they are not absurd, and some progress has been made of late in parsing them. Panentheistic theology can undergird a research program that attempts to think the theological endpoint together with the sophisticated understanding of mechanisms offered by contemporary science. The project, though difficult, is not impossible. It may be that a more cautious approach to divine action will in the end prevail. But in the meantime it seems worthwhile to search for ways to think together more fully the scientific and the theological understandings of events in the natural world.[6]

---

3. Arthur Peacocke has responded [in a personal communication], "I agree that if God transcends the world then we can use a special word about God's ontology and describe God as pure 'spirit.'"

4. There are difficulties here as well, it turns out. See the essays in Russell, Murphy and Peacocke, eds., *Chaos and Complexity*.

5. Donald Davidson calls this view of mind "anomalous monism"; see Davidson, "Thinking Causes."

6. I am grateful to Arthur Peacocke and Mary Ann Meyers for helpful criticisms of earlier drafts, and to Steven Knapp for detailed discussions of the problem of divine action, which have influenced the position, and in some cases also the formulations, in this chapter, particularly in the final section.

18

Panentheisms East and West[1]

Charles Hartshorne's Classic Definition

THE GREAT PROCESS PHILOSOPHER Charles Hartshorne, who was largely responsible for the twentieth-century renaissance of panentheistic thought in the West, formulated a classic definition of this concept. He used the five letters E, T, C, K, and W to stand for five features attributed to the Ultimate by many panentheists: eternal, temporal, conscious, knowing the world, and world-inclusive. Of course, there are panentheists who do not affirm one or another of these five attributes. Still, Hartshorne correctly realized that these are some of the most important attributes of the Ultimate that concern panentheists.

In order to see this, try to think your way into the worldview of panentheism. Even though you are a devout panentheist, you still admit that things *appear* to be separate and discrete; they appear to exist as individual substances. But ultimately, you believe, they are grounded in the One Ultimate Reality. For you, what we call "objects" are, ultimately speaking, modes or manifestations or expressions of that One. Hence their appearance as separate, independent existents is not ultimately real.

Now you begin to see why Hartshorne's five qualities are attractive to you, why they at least pose the right questions. The Infinite One must be *eternal*, you conclude, for it was never created and depends on nothing outside itself in order to exist. And the fifth property, being "*world-inclusive*," seems obvious to you as well, given Hegel's argument about the infinite.

Next, the One is *temporal* in the sense that it contains within itself all finite things. Why would this make it temporal? Well, we certainly believe that *our own existence* is temporal, for we know our past, live in a continuously changing present, and

---

1. Clayton, "Panentheisms East and West," *Sophia* 49 (2010) 183–91. Reprinted with permission.

anticipate a future that has not yet arrived. If the temporal features of our existence are not altogether illusory, then they must exist within the One Unity and hence must be attributes of it as well.

Fourth, you reason, the One is conscious because it contains us and we are conscious. On the one hand, this isn't actually a sound argument as it stands; after all, why should the One have all the properties that we have? Thus a number of panentheists actually deny that the One is conscious. On the other hand, the argument works if you are committed to the additional premise that the One cannot be (metaphysically) *less than* what its parts are. The One need not share the imperfections of its parts: it need not be able to cheat, lie, and steal; or to be dependent on another; or to die. By contrast, consciousness has seemed to many Eastern and Western thinkers to be a *positive* attribute that we must attribute to whatever is the Ultimate Reality. I prefer the more cautious formulation: the One cannot be *less than* what we mean by conscious, but its quality of consciousness must be infinitely more than, infinitely greater than, any consciousness we can conceive.

The situation is similar in the case of the final attribute, "knowing the world." One reason is that being conscious entails knowing; the two attributes cannot be separated. A second argument is that, if the parts of the One possess the characteristic of knowing, and the One cannot be less than its parts, then it must possess that quality as well. We know our world or environment; thus the One must also know its "world," that is, all that exists. . . .

Rāmānuja

There is no location-free, and hence no value-free, form of comparative philosophy. I consider Rāmānuja's work to be one of the greatest expressions of panentheistic thought across the world's traditions,[2] and I hold it up unapologetically as a model for contemporary Western panentheism. In effect, I am implicitly suggesting that Western philosophers could develop a "purer" form of panentheism if they paid closer attention to his thought. (The same holds for Sri Aurobindo, who magisterial *The Life Divine* is one of the great metaphysical and spiritual treatises of the twentieth century.) Of course, it goes without saying that Rāmānuja's views are not representative of all the Vedantic traditions, much less of the history of Indian philosophy as a whole.[3]

Rāmānuja beautifully affirms the dual status of finite individuals. It is possible to ascribe real agency and even a form of freedom to them (more on the freedom question in a moment). And yet finite agents do not have independent subsistence.

---

2. The interpretation of Rāmānuja as a panentheist is widely shared among Hindu scholars. For example, Jeaneane Fowler notes, "The ultimate transcendency of God never permits him to be merely the pantheistic whole that unites the parts: while causative, he panentheistically transcends all" (Fowler, *Perspectives of Reality*, 318).

3. This is not to say that panentheism doesn't play an important role in other Schools as well.

"*Brahman* is reality, consciousness, infinite" (*Tait. Up.* 2.1.1); hence it alone enjoys independent subsistence.[4] Thus, all conscious and nonconscious entities (*cit* and *acit*) exist only as modes of *Brahman*.[5] C. J. Bartley, in his excellent treatment of the theology of Rāmānuja, summarizes the position:

> For Rāmānuja a mode is a reality . . . which has neither essence, actuality, nor purpose independently of some other entity upon which it is existentially dependent and to which it is "adjectival." This amounts to the thesis that contingent conscious individuals are ultimately subsidiary states and constituents of *Brahman*—a way of being of *Brahman*.[6]

The world is held together by "the immanent divine presence," which gives to it both its existence and the regularities that it manifests.[7] God is not only the efficient cause of things, the way that the potter molds the clay, but is also the "substrative" cause, that of which everything is made.

Other agents can thus arise only through a sort of self-limitation on the part of *Brahman*. Thus, we can say that finite agents *are Brahman* as it conditioned by *karma*, *avidyā*, and *kamā* (desire). The brilliance of Rāmānuja's work lies in the almost perfect balance that he establishes between *Brahman* and *atman*. *Atman* is non-different in that it remains a mode rather than an independently existing thing, yet it is different because it is a mode and because, thanks to the grace of *Brahman*, it is able to exercise its own (albeit limited) form of agency. The intricacy of this conceptual balancing act is all the more remarkable when one realizes that Rāmānuja is seeking to do justice to three different requirements: the plain sense of the sacred scriptures, the demands of metaphysical reflection, and the requirements of *bhakti*, that is, the life of obedience and devotion to God.

Western panentheists, and even many classical theists, have affirmed that all finite things exist only through participation in the divine. But Rāmānuja radicalized the sense of participation, extending it beyond things to include all thought, action, and language as well. In so doing he was able to draw on the widespread Indian view that language, insofar as it is true, does not merely *stand for* its referent but also participates in the reality to which it refers. This allowed him to develop a perfect

---

4. John Carman summarizes the five defining attributes of the essential nature of *Brahman* for Rāmānuja: (1) *satya* (true being) describes *Brahman* as "possessing unconditioned being, thus distinguishing Him from nonintelligent matter, which is subject to change"; (2) *jnana* (knowledge or consciousness) describes "the state of permanently uncontracted knowledge, thus distinguishing [Him] from released souls, whose knowledge was at one time contracted"; (3) *anantatva* (infinite, free from all limits of time and space); (4) *ananda* (full of bliss); and (5) *amalatva* (purity or, literally, stainless); see John Braisted Carman, *The Theology of Rāmānuja*, chapter 7, 102.

5. Rāmānuja writes, "In short, He is the core, whether manifest or not, of all beings in whatever condition they exist. The totality of beings, mobile or immobile, cannot exist apart from God, who is the atman within themselves" (quoted in Fowler, *Perspectives of Reality*, 318).

6. Bartley, *The Theology of Rāmānuja*, 70.

7. Ibid., 85.

isomorphism for all aspects of reality: individual things have their existence only in the one true Reality; individual minds or spirits (*atman*) participate in the one *Brahman*; all true affirmations likewise participate in the One and thus express reality both ontologically and conceptually.

Rāmānuja boldly used the metaphor of mind and body to explain the relationship between *Brahman* and the world. The mind is the controller of the body; the body, although a real actor in the world, is ultimately the agent of the mind. The sole essence of the body, he argues, is to be an attribute of a self.[8] The same relationship holds between *Brahman* and its modes:[9] the world, like bodies, is *apṛthaksiddha*, that is, "incapable of independent existence" or, literally, "not separately established."[10] From a Vedic perspective there is a further advantage to this philosophy: just as *atman* is not decreased by the death of the body, but continues on through reincarnation to be paired with another body, so *Brahman* is not affected by the impermanence, change, and decay of the world but remains always in its eternal perfection.

One final point: Rāmānuja recognized that understanding finite agents as modes of *Brahman* threatens to lead to fatalism and determinism, the abolition of all human agency. This consequence would be disastrous, since it would render the moral exhortations of the scriptures vacuous and would make genuine devotion (*bhakti*) on the part of believers impossible. Here too Rāmānuja's answer is a model for the perennial Western struggles with the problem of God and freedom. The same divine self-limitation that allows finite reality to exist also creates a place for finite agency. A purely naturalistic, object-based account of reality, one without the concepts of *atman* and *Brahman*, is not sufficient to support genuinely free agency.[11] By contrast, the only way that free agency *can* exist is if finite agents are sustained by an ultimate consciousness in which they participate. The Divine gives (and sustains) the capacity for action.[12] In Rāmānuja, as in some Western theologians, one finds hints that finite agents are only truly free when they choose to act in accordance with the divine purposes;[13] all other action produces karma and thus binds the agent more fully to the world of materiality and illusion. But *atman* itself is not ultimately illusory, since its very agency has been given by God.

8. Bartley, *The Theology of Rāmānuja*, 83n29.

9. "*Brahman*, because it is embodied by the conscious and non-conscious entities that are its modes, is always referred to by every denotative expression (naming term)" (Bartley, *The Theology of Rāmānuja*, 83n31).

10. Bartley, *The Theology of Rāmānuja*, 84.

11. I have made this argument in *In Quest of Freedom*.

12. Rāmānuja writes, "The Supreme Self has provided all conscious beings in common with all the assistance needed . . . either to perform or to abstain from actions. In order to accomplish this, he who is their ontic ground enters them, exercises control in that he guides and permits them to act and exists in them as the principle to whom they are ancillary. The conscious entity, whose powers are dependent upon the Supreme Self, performs or abstains from actions of his own accord" (quoted in Bartley, *The Theology of Rāmānuja*, 92).

13. Bartley, *The Theology of Rāmānuja*, 94.

Conclusion

I have only begun to touch on the richness of Rāmānuja's thought, much less on the complexities of panentheism East and West, and there are numerous difficulties that require further reflection and responses. Panentheism is not a "magic pill" either in philosophy or theology. But it is, in my view, an immensely rich model for attempting to conceive Ultimacy. I hope this brief summary will offer a helpful point of orientation for other comparative philosophers as they explore the rich connections between the great metaphysical traditions of the East and West. It is no small thing that distinct philosophical traditions, often treated as discrete and even antagonistic, should converge on an underlying unity of perspective. Indeed, one can hardly fail to note that this unity-in-difference manifests, once again, a panentheistic structure.

In the final analysis, panentheism is far more than a philosophy, however. Just as distinctive forms of spiritual practice are associated with pantheism on the one side and with classical Western theism (God as transcendent of the world, his creation) on the other, so panentheism fosters its own distinctive spirituality as well. From yogic practices to Quaker worship, these spiritualities make their own contribution to the storehouse of the world's spiritual practices. Finally, in an age when humanity is on the verge of decimating the world's ecosystems and bringing about the extinction of many of its species, we must assess metaphysical systems in terms of their ecological potential. Arguably, there is no stronger motivation for valuing and preserving the environment than the affirmation that each organism has its own distinct reality and agency, while at the same time inherent in each is the infinite value of the one overarching and all-encompassing One.[14]

---

14. I gratefully acknowledge the research support of Andrea Stephenson, until recently a doctoral candidate at Claremont Graduate University, which played an important role in preparing this paper. Conversations with Professors Purushottama Bilimoria and Joseph Prabhu have played a significant role in my understanding of panentheism and the Indian philosophical traditions, and I happily express my debt of gratitude to them.

19

"Open Panentheism" and Creation as Kenosis[1]

IN THE PREVIOUS THREE chapters I have advanced a form of Christian panentheism, the belief that the world remains in some sense within the divine, even though God also transcends the world. In the twentieth century at least, panentheism is usually connected with the work of Alfred North Whitehead and his followers, especially Charles Hartshorne. But, in contrast to many process theologians, I find myself compelled also to defend the doctrine of creation *ex nihilo*—the belief that there has not always been a world, and hence that the world is not co-eternal with God. Instead, on this view both the creation of the universe and the details concerning *how* it was created involved free divine decisions. To make these assertions is to endorse the radical contingency of ourselves, of our world—and indeed of the existence of any world whatsoever.

The combination of these two different sources gives rise to an intriguing mediating position, which I shall call *open panentheism*. This theology has a deep affinity with the work of Clark Pinnock and other "open theists" or "free will theists,"[2] though it draws more fully on process resources than most of these theologians do. Open theism is closely linked to process theism in a number of respects.[3] Both conceive of God as involved more deeply in the temporal flow of history than classical theism was willing to countenance; both acknowledge certain limitations on what God can do and know (though, as we will see, for rather different reasons); and both think more

---

1. "'Open Panentheism' and Creation as Kenosis," as found within Clayton, *Adventures in the Spirit: God, World, Divine Action*, 175–84. Reprinted with the kind permission of Fortress.

2. I do not here give an exposition of these schools and presuppose some familiarity with them on the part of readers. "Open theism" is often traced back to Rice, *The Openness of God*. Other works to consult include Boyd, *God of the Possible*; Sanders, *The God Who Risks*; and Basinger, *The Case for Freewill Theism*. I consider Pinnock, *The Openness of God*, to be a particularly significant statement of this view.

3. For examples of a closer dialogue between process and open theism see Stone and Oord, eds., *The Nature and Thy Name Is Love*; and cf. Cobb Jr and Pinnock, eds., *Searching for an Adequate God*.

rigorously than most classical theists did about what is entailed in the use of agency language to describe God and divine action.

Open panentheism seeks to build further on these foundations. It recognizes that deeper ties bind process and open theists than is often acknowledged. On the one hand, process thinkers have formulated urgent problems that open theists must address, problems which may be unanswerable without an increased reliance on process thought. On the other hand, there are resources within classical Christian traditions that can be brought to bear on contemporary challenges to the doctrine of God. Because of these natural linkages, I hope to show, the debate between process and open theism offers some of the most important resources for constructive theology today, especially with regard to the God–world relation. . . .

Open Panentheism

The dialogue with process thought has helped bring to the surface two major challenges to open panentheism. First, one wonders, is the notion of a self-limiting God coherent, and is it sufficient to address to problem of evil? Process theologians have argued that, if God is metaphysically capable of alleviating suffering and does not do so, God is culpable for the results. Second, is the notion of an initial creation "out of nothing" coherent? It turns out that the answers to these two challenges are related and mutually enrich each other. Open panentheism, I will argue, offers the most convincing overall response, in that it draws most effectively on the insights of both process theology and open theism.

All panentheists believe that creaturely agents are located "within" the divine. But how should we conceive this "within"? Clearly it must involve more than just spatial location, since it would be absurd to locate God at some particular point within the universe and make God absent from others. Insights developed in the work of the neo-Whiteheadian thinker Joseph Bracken offer a powerful response to this challenge;[4] they nicely supplement the arguments developed in the previous three chapters. As Bracken has seen, it is easier to conceive that God would create other centers of activity within the divine being if it is God's eternal nature *already* to consist of multiple, non-identical centers of activity. Surprisingly, this natural kinship between panentheism and trinitarian thought is too infrequently acknowledged.

Process panentheists depart from classical panentheists regarding the aseity and immutability of God: the understanding of God as self-sufficient and unchanging. Eastern Orthodox theology is deeply panentheistic, for example, and yet strongly resistant to a temporalized God. As I argued in *The Problem of God*, there is reason to worry that, in trying to meet the "perfection" standards of Greek metaphysics, the

---

4. See especially Bracken, *Society and Spirit*; Bracken, *The Triune Symbol*; Bracken, *The Divine Matrix*; Bracken, *The One in the Many*; and his articles "Process Philosophy and Trinitarian Theology;" and "Energy-Events and Fields," 153–65.

theological tradition has asserted qualities of God that are not appropriate to a biblical theism. Charles Hartshorne saw that theology had been crippled by these Hellenistic assumptions and thereby kept away from its own deeper logic and insights. Whiteheadian process thought for him represented a call for theologians to return to a more appropriate picture of the divine nature.

The God–world relation, Hartshorne rightly saw, is dipolar. For present purposes, dipolarity need mean nothing more than that God is related to the world in two modes: as its eternal Ground, the source of all its possibilities; and as the Infinitely Related One, the One who internalizes and unifies all experiences within the world, bathes them in infinite love, and transmits them back to other experiencers in the form of the divine lure.[5] It is no more difficult to conceive God as both Ground and Responder when God is understood in trinitarian fashion as a community of persons (i.e., person-like fields of force or influence). Creation is free; it manifests God's love. Yet God was not constrained or metaphysically required to create. Advocating such a metaphysical constraint actually *decreases* the free responsiveness and relatedness which its advocates are seeking to safeguard.

As soon as one conceives God as including multiple centers of activity, however, one has introduced a greater disanalogy between human (and other) agents on the one hand and the divine agents on the other than many process theologians (e.g., David Ray Griffin) would allow. As soon as one speaks of the divine as the all-encompassing field of activity, as Bracken does—and especially if one introduces the notion of the *infinite* field of the divine—one has said something different than that God is the "chief exemplification" (*PR* 343) of the same metaphysical principles that pertain to all other agents.

Open theists have consistently maintained some such ontological difference between God and other agents, and I think they have been right to do so. For example, human agents differ from the divine in their nature: finite, not infinite; existing contingently rather than existing in all possible worlds; sometimes placing their own limited interests above the divine rather than being by nature perfectly good. Finite agents need a community (and, indeed, an entire world-system with the consistency of regular laws), whereas the community of divine persons does not intrinsically need a context outside itself. In short, the divine has ontological self-sufficiency that no finite, contingent creature can enjoy. It is sufficient for God to be internally related to godself in order to exist, but no finite creature exists as a result of being internally related.

One can find other ways to express this crucial insight. For example, the divine nature is pre-given; there is (to paraphrase Thomas Nagel) "something it is like to be divine." By contrast, human subjects do not have a pre-given nature. We are "thrown" (Heidegger's *Geworfenheit*); in us "existence precedes essence" (Sartre); we define ourselves in interaction. We are genuinely free, insomuch as we may choose to be like

---

5. See Suchocki, *God, Christ, Church*, chapter 3; Ford, *The Lure of God*.

God and to conform our character to the divine nature, or we may choose to act as if we were *causa sui*. That much, I think, each human being can recognize phenomenologically. Apparently it is essential for the free development of human character that there be a world of other subjects and other things for us to relate to, so that we then "choose this day whom [we] shall serve." Without this fundamental existential choice, it appears, finite agents could not experience the personal and intellectual evolution that we require to become rational, moral agents in the image of the divine. Indeed, one could put the point even more strongly: we are *constituted by* our freedom-in-throwness. But the divine nature is not so constituted; for Whitehead, for example, the primordial divine nature does not change over time. This necessity—that we are constituted by free, finite relatedness whereas God is not—represents perhaps the deepest disanalogy between human and divine nature.

The Kenotic Doctrine of Creation

The doctrine of *creatio ex nihilo*, many process thinkers have argued, stands in some tension with the assertion that God is intrinsically love. Wouldn't God need *always* to be related to some world, as a necessary expression of the unlimited divine love? Moreover, if relatedness is an essential quality of the divine, how could there ever be a time when God was not related to an Other?

Traditionally, theologians have responded to this charge of inconsistency by arguing that God is always *internally related within the divine being*. God has always existed as three persons in divine community.

Although I am drawn to this trinitarian response, I think we must admit that belief in the Trinity is not by itself sufficient to defang the objection. It does make a difference that God's love be expressed *ad extra* at some point. Only if God creates real agents outside of God's self—not automata who acknowledge the deity because they must, but agents who freely love God—only then would it be clear that the divine relatedness is more than self-love. The divine love is most fully manifested in real relatedness to agents who are "other" to God: finite in comparison with the divine infinity, and morally limited in contrast to the One who is essentially good.

So why doesn't this mean that there must always be a world as long as there is God? This is process theology's most pointed question to open theism—one that calls for some serious reflection on the part of advocates of creation *ex nihilo*.[6]

---

6. There are a number of responses to the process objection that *don't* work. First, one might argue that the period of time before creation doesn't really count, since time becomes meaningful only when a world of creatures exists. Hence, the fact that there wasn't always a world doesn't count against the nature of God as loving and as relational. This was (roughly) Augustine's response. When one reflects on it, however, one realizes that it represents a somewhat strange answer. It implicitly admits that all doctrines of creation *ex nihilo* will acknowledge two separate stages: first a stage in the life of God before God was related to a world, and then another stage after creation. Yet, it maintains, the first does not present a problem because it really shouldn't be understood as a *time* (a temporal stage) at all.

For open panentheists, inter-personal relations within God play an essential part in answering this question. The divine essence can be love, even prior to creation, only because the divine exists always as community.[7] Indeed, we understand God's relation to creation, and God's act(s) of creation, *as love* in part by extrapolating from the inner-divine relations. At some point this love was manifested *beyond* the inner-divine relations; at some point the God whose nature is love became internally related to others as well. Like orthodox process theologians, open panentheists affirm that the world is taken up into—indeed, could not exist apart from—the divine being. But, they add, the divine love is manifested just as deeply in that God, not needing to create anything at all, nonetheless created a world of finite beings and processes. The love that is extended from God *ad extra* toward entities who are other than God is even more profound if there was no necessity for God to create *and hence creation was a free act*, than it would be if God was of necessity always accompanied by some world.

Although this particular result is highly reminiscent of the work of open theists, I suggest interpreting it in the context of Bracken's process theology, which we began to consider above. Bracken begins by postulating that God has existed eternally as a trinitarian field of forces, as tri-personal identity. Each aspect of God is personal, or more-than-personal, and together they constitute "a single unbounded field of activity."[8] Open panentheists add that at some point God freely chose to share the divine life, creating finite centers of activity within the space of the divine being. As Bracken writes, "the world of creation is the result of a free decision on the part of the divine persons to share their divine communitarian life with creatures."[9] That is, the divine love manifested, or spilled over, into other centers of activity through an unconstrained divine decision. More strongly than Bracken, though, I would emphasize that finite, created centers of activity, although still contained within the one all-encompassing divine field, differ from God in their essential nature: we are finite, not infinite; we exist contingently, not in all possible worlds; we place our own limited interests above the divine or highest interest, in contrast to the One who is perfectly good by nature (*ens perfectissimum*).[10] Perhaps this is just a difference of emphasis: I stress the difference between finite and infinite (and so also the other divine attributes), whereas Bracken stresses common metaphysical principles that pertain to both types of entities.[11] But even if "difference of emphasis" is the right term, the difference is vital.

But as long as it is possible to distinguish *conceptually* between the two stages, the objection remains unanswered.

7. Zizioulas, *Being as Communion*.

8. I draw here from Bracken, "Creatio ex Nihilo," 246–49.

9. Bracken, "Creatio ex Nihilo," 248f.

10. I do not by contrast assert unlimited omnipotence or believe that God's omniscience extends to the future free decisions of creatures.

11. Thus Bracken writes, "So the issue for me is not so much the contrast between finite and infinite as the dynamic of independence/interdependence among the centers of activity within the

The christological concept of *kenosis* or self-emptying (cf. Phil 2:5–9) offers a particularly powerful means for conceiving this act of creation by a God who until that time was unlimited in power and unconstrained in action. According to a doctrine of "kenotic creation," creation is itself a kenotic, relational act; God freely limited God's infinite power in order to allow for the existence of non-divine agents. This self-limitation is best understood as a self-emptying, insofar as God chose to limit or "empty Godself" of qualities that would otherwise seem to belong to the divine essence, such as omnipotence or the unlimited manifestation of divine glory and agency.[12] We might therefore label the resulting position *open kenotic panentheism*.[13]

Once the world exists, God's experience develops in real interaction with the world. At this point—that is, subsequent to the moment of creation—open panentheists embrace the bulk of what process thought teaches about the God–world relation. God is conceived as combining both an eternal, primordial divine nature and a consequent nature. All possible states of affairs and all "eternal forms" exist primordially in the mind of God. In Michael Lodahl's nice phrase, "the Spirit of God [through Jesus Christ] is identified as the possibility of God that brings the real into emergent being in the world."[14] God offers initial aims to every creature at every moment, and creatures freely choose their responses. God invites creatures to participate in God's own creative activity within the world, resulting in what Lodahl calls *creatio ex creatione* and Paul van Buren describes as *creatio ex amore*. In either case, we become *created co-creators* with God (Philip Hefner).[15] The consequent nature of God then incorporates into the divine experience all the experiences of all beings within the world at every instant. God in relation to the created world manifests love to the highest possible degree because God experiences (i.e., incorporates into the divine experience) all the joys, pains, and sorrows of all created things at all times, and then offers back to them a continual leading "for the common good."

I have argued that this picture is fully compatible with the doctrine of creation out of nothing. But it matters deeply *why* open panentheists assert the *ex nihilo*. In my view, this phrase expresses the deeper insight into the nature of creaturely existence before God. As David Larson notes, it "captures and expresses the almost overwhelming amazement that there is anything at all," the "radical contingency" that characterizes our experience in the world—indeed, that characterizes the existence of our

---

field" (personal communication).

12. On creation as kenosis see, e.g., Polkinghorne, ed., *The Work of Love*, and Dabney, *Die Kenosis des Geistes*. Jürgen Moltmann, who also advocates a kenotic understanding of creation, traces the twentieth-century roots of this concept back as far as Emil Brunner. The Jewish sources he finds in the Kabbalistic notion of *zimzum*; see Moltmann, *God in Creation*.

13. Clayton, "Kenotic Trinitarian Panentheism," 250–55. The present argument is a revision and expansion of my earlier exploration of this topic.

14. Lodahl, "From God to Creation," paper presented to the American Academy of Religion, 2004 Annual Meeting, MS 4.

15. Hefner, *The Human Factor*.

world as a whole.[16] Catherine Keller's recent sortie into the deep provides a powerful picture of the God–world relationship in light of this radical contingency.[17] In the context of mythological language (*bildhaftes Denken*), "chaos" and "ocean" help to express what might have preceded the moment of creation, hence what "material" God might have worked with to produce order out of chaos. But in the more rarified language of metaphysics, creation out of *nothing whatsoever* more powerfully conveys the most radical contingency of created things: they exist out of no necessity of their nature, but only in and through their relationship with the final Ground.

The hypothesis of a kenotic creation out of nothing serves as a crucial component in the mediating position of open panentheism. This view accepts the process insight that a God who is love must exist eternally in relation; yet it locates that relatedness already within the divine nature itself *as a model for* God's subsequent relatedness to all things. God then freely creates space within the divine life for other selves or entities. These others are like God in that they too are centers of activity; hence creation is, as the tradition has held, *imago Dei*. Humans may represent the *imago Dei* in certain distinctive ways; for example, in that we are *conscious* of our relatedness (think of it as a sort of relatedness "second degree"). It would also appear that we freely emulate the divine nature, or freely resist the lure of God, with a much greater range of choice than is available to other animals. Nevertheless we exist contingently and might not have existed at all, just as (according to *ex nihilo*) the universe of which we are parts also might not have existed. The creation of both, being completely free and unconstrained, was a sign of God's grace, that is, of God's eternal character.

---

16. Larson, "Necessarily, Essentially, Neither or Both," paper presented to the American Academy of Religion, 2004 Annual Meeting, MS 4.

17. Keller, *Face of the Deep*. The Hebrew term translated "deep," *tehom*, also means "ocean" and "chaos"; Keller's book offers a rich phenomenology of *tehom* and underscores the significance of this biblical term for an understanding of creation and of human freedom before God.

PART IV

Science & Emergence

20

The Concept of Emergence[1]

From Reduction to Emergence

IT IS WIDELY BUT falsely held that there are only two major ways to interpret the world: in a physicalist or in a dualist fashion. The mistaken belief in this dichotomy has its roots in the confrontation of Newtonian physics with the metaphysical systems that still dominated in the seventeenth century, which were built up out of Greek, Christian, and medieval elements—but we will not worry here about the historical backgrounds to the conflict. It is the thesis of this book that the days of this forced dilemma are past.

The case stands on three legs. Two of these—the revolution in metaphysics brought about by Kant, German idealism, and process thought; and the revolution in the theory of knowledge brought about by non-objectivist epistemologies, contextualist philosophies of science, and inherent limits on knowledge discovered within the sciences themselves—I have explored in other publications and will not reargue here. The present argument against the physicalism–dualism dichotomy is derived from a third source: the revolution brought about by the sciences of evolution. The evolutionary perspective has fatally undercut both sides of the once regnant either/or: physicalism, with its tendency to stress the sufficiency of physics, and dualism, with its tendency to pull mind out of the evolutionary account altogether.

The evolutionary perspective, which is realigning the long-established philosophical frontiers, is the core presupposition of the most successful scientific explanation we have of biological phenomena. More accurately, it is a component in all biological explanations and a label for a large number of specific empirical results.

---

1. "The Rise and Fall of Reductionism"; "The Concept of Emergence"; "The Pre-history of the Emergence Concept"; and "Weak and Strong Emergence," as found within Clayton, *Mind & Emergence*, 1–10. Reprinted with the kind permission of Oxford University Press.

PART IV: Science & Emergence

Now to say that biological evolution directly undercuts physicalism and dualism would be a category mistake. Scientific theories have to be turned into philosophical arguments before they can support or undercut philosophical positions (except, of course, when philosophers make direct errors about empirical facts or scientific theories, as not infrequently occurs). In the following pages I argue that *emergence* is the philosophical position—more accurately, the philosophical elaboration of a series of scientific results—that best expresses the philosophical import of evolutionary theory.

Thus we should say, if the argument turns out to be successful, that it is emergence that undercuts the hegemony of the physicalist–dualism dichotomy. There are now not two but three serious ontological options. And, of the three, emergence is the naturalist position most strongly supported by a synthetic scientific perspective—that is, by the study of natural history across the various levels that it has produced—as well as by philosophical reflection.

The Rise and Fall of Reductionism

The discussion of emergence makes no sense unless one conducts it against the backdrop of reductionism. Emergence theories presuppose that the project of explanatory reduction—explaining all phenomena in the natural world in terms of the objects and laws of physics—is finally impossible. For this reason, the overview of emergence theories in the twentieth century needs to begin by reviewing the difficulties that have come to burden the program of reductionism.

In its simple form, at least, the story of the rise and fall of reductionism is not difficult to tell (I return to the complexities in later pages). Once upon a time there was a century dominated by the ideal of reductionism. It was a century in which some of the deepest dreams of science were fulfilled. Building on Newton's laws, Maxwell's equations, and Einstein's insights, scientists developed a body of theory capable of handling the very small (quantum physics), the very fast (special relativity, for speeds approaching c), and the very heavy (general relativity, or what one might call gravitational dynamics). Chemistry was, for all intents and purposes, completed. Crick and Watson discovered the structure of the biochemical information system that codes for all biological reproduction and heritable mutations, and a short while ago the mapping of the human genome was completed. Breakthroughs in neuroscience promised the eventual explanation of cognition in neurophysiological terms, and evolutionary psychology brought evolutionary biology to bear on human behavior. Each success increased optimism that so-called bridge laws would eventually link together each of the sciences into a single system of law-based explanation with physics as its foundation.

Yet, the story continues, these amazing successes were followed by a series of blows to the reductionist program. Scientists encountered a number of apparently permanent restrictions on what physics can explain, predict, or know: relativity theory introduced the speed of light as the absolute limit for velocity, and thus as the temporal limit for communication and causation in the universe (no knowledge outside our "light cone"); Heisenberg's uncertainty principle placed mathematical limits on the knowability of both the location and momentum of a subatomic particle; the Copenhagen theorists came to the startling conclusion that quantum mechanical indeterminacy was not merely a temporary epistemic problem but reflected an *inherent* indeterminacy of the physical world itself; so-called chaos theory showed that future states of complex systems such as weather systems quickly become uncomputable because of their sensitive dependence on initial conditions (a dependence so sensitive that a finite knower could *never* predict the evolution of the system—a staggering limitation when one notes what percentage of natural systems exhibit chaotic behaviors); Kurt Gödel showed in a well-known proof that mathematics cannot be complete, . . . and the list goes on. . . .

The Concept of Emergence

In a classic definition el-Hani and Pereira identify four features generally associated with the concept of emergence:

1. *Ontological physicalism*: All that exists in the space-time world are the basic particles recognized by physics and their aggregates.

2. *Property emergence*: When aggregates of material particles attain an appropriate level of organizational complexity, genuinely novel properties emerge in these complex systems.

3. *The irreducibility of the emergence*: Emergent properties are irreducible to, and unpredictable from, the lower-level phenomena from which they emerge.

4. *Downward causation*: Higher-level entities causally affect their lower-level constituents.[2]

Each of these four theses requires elaboration; some require modification. The defense of emergence in the following pages refers to a set of claims no weaker than the four theses, but modified as follows.

Concerning 1: ontological physicalism

The first condition is poorly formulated. It does correctly express the anti-dualistic thrust of emergence theories. But the emergence thesis, if correct, undercuts the claim that physics is the fundamental discipline from which all others are derived. Moreover, rather than treating all objects that are not "recognized by physics" as mere aggregates,

---

2. el-Hani and Pereira, "Higher-Level Descriptions: Why Should We Preserve Them?" 133.

it suggests viewing them as emergent entities (in a sense to be defined). Thus, I suggest it is more accurate to begin with the thesis of ontological monism:

1'. *Ontological monism*: Reality is ultimately composed of one basic kind of stuff. Yet the concepts of physics are not sufficient to explain all the forms that this stuff takes—all the ways it comes to be structured, individuated, and causally efficacious. The one "stuff" apparently takes forms for which the explanations of physics, and thus the ontology of physics (or "physicalism" for short) are not adequate. We should not assume that the entities postulated by physics complete the inventory of what exists. Hence emergentists should be monists but not physicalists.

Concerning **2**: *property emergence*

The discovery of genuinely novel properties in nature is indeed a major motivation for emergence. Tim O'Connor has provided a sophisticated account of property emergence. For any emergent property P of some object O, four conditions hold:

i) P supervenes on properties of the parts of O;

ii) P is not had by any of O's parts;

iii) P is distinct from any structural property of O;

iv) P has direct ("downward") determinative influence on the pattern of behavior involving O's parts.[3]

Particular attention should be paid to O'Connor's condition (ii), which he calls the feature of *non-structurality*. It entails three features: "The property's being potentially had only by objects of some complexity, not had by any of the object's parts, [and] distinct from any structural property of the object."[4]

Concerning **3**: *the irreducibility of emergence*

To say that emergent properties are irreducible to lower-level phenomena presupposes that reality is divided into a number of distinct levels or orders. Wimsatt classically expresses the notion: "By level of organization, I will mean here compositional levels—hierarchical divisions of stuff (paradigmatically but not necessarily material stuff) organized by part–whole relations, in which wholes at one level function as parts at the next (and at all higher) levels...."[5] Wimsatt, who begins by contrasting an emergentist ontology with Quine's desert landscapes, insists that "it is possible to be

---

3. O'Connor, "Emergent Properties," 97–98.
4. O'Connor, "Emergent Properties," 97.
5. Wimsatt, "The Ontology of Complex Systems," 222.

a reductionist and a holist too."[6] The reason is that emergentist holism, in contrast to what we might call "New Age holism," is a controlled holism. It consists of two theses: that there are forms of causality that are not reducible to physical causes (on which more in a moment), and that causality should be our primary guide to ontology. As Wimsatt writes, "Ontologically, one could take the primary working matter of the world to be causal relationships, which are connected to one another in a variety of ways—and together make up patterns of causal networks."[7]

It follows that one of the major issues for emergence theory will involve the question of when exactly one should speak of the emergence of a new level within the natural order. Traditionally, "life" and "mind" have been taken to be genuine emergent levels within the world—from which it follows that "mind" cannot be understood dualistically, à la Descartes. But perhaps there are massively more levels, perhaps innumerably more. In a recent book, the Yale biophysicist Harold Morowitz, for example, identifies no fewer than twenty-eight distinct levels of emergence in natural history from the big bang to the present.[8] . . .

Concerning 4: downward causation

Many argue that downward causation is the most distinctive feature of a fully emergentist position—and its greatest challenge. As O'Connor notes, "an emergent's causal influence is irreducible to that of the micro-properties on which it supervenes: it bears its influence in a direct, 'downward' fashion in contrast to the operation of a simple structural macro-property, whose causal influence occurs *via* the activity of the micro-properties that constitute it."[9]

Such a causal influence of an emergent structure or object on its constituent parts would represent a type of causality that diverges from the standard philosophical treatments of causality in modern science. This concept of downward causation, which may be the crux of the emergence theory debate, will occupy us further in the coming chapters. Authors seeking to defend it often criticize the strictures of modern "efficient" causality and seek to expand the understanding of causality, perhaps with reference to Aristotle's four distinct types of causal influence. The trouble is that material causality—the way in which the matter of a thing causes it to be and to act in a particular way—is no less "physicalist" than efficient causality, and final causality—the way in which the goal towards which a thing strives influences its behavior—is associated with vitalist, dualist, and supernaturalist accounts of the world, accounts that

---

6. Wimsatt, "The Ontology of Complex Systems," 225.
7. Wimsatt, "The Ontology of Complex Systems," 220.
8. Wimsatt, "The Ontology of Complex Systems," 222.
9. O'Connor, "Emergent Properties," 97–98. Fundamental for this debate are the works of Campbell, e.g., "'Downward Causation,'" 179–86; and O'Connor, "Levels of Organization, Downward Causation," 1–17.

most emergentists would prefer to avoid. Formal causality—the influence of the form, structure, or function of an object on its activities—is thus probably the most fruitful of these Aristotelian options. Several authors have begun formulating a broader theory of causal influence, although much work remains to be done.

The Pre-history of the Emergence Concept

It is widely conceded that George Henry Lewes first introduced the term "emergence."[10] Precursors to the concept can nonetheless be traced back in the history of Western philosophy at least as far as Aristotle. Aristotle's biological research led him to posit a principle of growth within organisms that was responsible for the qualities or form that would later emerge. Aristotle called this principle the *entelechy*, the internal principle of growth and perfection that directs the organism to actualize the qualities that it contains in a merely potential state. According to his doctrine of "potencies," the adult form of the human or animal emerges out of its youthful form. (Unlike contemporary emergence theories, however, he held that the complete form is already present in the organism from the beginning, like a seed; it just needs to be transformed from its potential state to its actual state.) As noted, Aristotle's explanation of emergence included "formal" causes, which operate through the form internal to the organism, and "final" causes, which pull the organism (so to speak) towards its final telos or "perfection." . . .

A second precursor to emergence theory might be found in the doctrine of *emanation* as first developed by Plotinus in the third century CE and greatly extended by the Neoplatonic thinkers who followed him. Plotinus defended the emergence of the entire hierarchy of being out of the One through a process of emanation. This expansion was balanced by a movement of finite things back up the ladder of derivation to their ultimate source. The Neoplatonic model allowed both for a *downward* movement of differentiation and causality and an *upward* movement of increasing perfection, diminishing distance from the Source, and (in principle) mystical reunification with the One. Unlike static models of the world, emanation models allowed for a gradual process of becoming. Although the Neoplatonic philosophers generally focused on the downward emanation that gave rise to the intellectual, psychological, and physical spheres respectively (*nous*, *psychē*, and *physika* or *kosmos* in Plotinus), their notion of emanation allowed for the emergence of new species as well. In those cases where the emanation was understood in a temporal sense, as with Plotinus, the emanation doctrine provides an important antecedent to doctrines of biological or universal evolution. Finally, process philosophies of the last 150 years are also important contributors to emergence theory; they will be dealt with further below.

---

10. Lewes, *Problems of Life and Mind*, 2 vols.

When science was still natural philosophy, emergence played a productive heuristic role. After about 1850, however, emergence theories were several times imposed unscientifically as a metaphysical framework in a way that blocked empirical work. Key examples include the neo-vitalists (e.g., H. Driesch's theory of entelechies) and neo-idealist theories of the interconnection of all living things (e.g., Bradley's theory of internal relations) around the turn of the century, as well as the speculations of the British Emergentists in the 1920s concerning the origin of mind (on whom more in a moment).

Arguably, the philosopher who should count as the great modern advocate of emergence theory is Hegel. In place of the notion of static being or substance, Hegel offered a temporalized ontology, a philosophy of universal becoming. The first triad in his system moves from Being as the first postulation to Nothing, its negation. If these two stand in blunt opposition, there can be no development in reality. But the opposition between the two is overcome by the category of Becoming. This triad is both the first step in the system and an expression of its fundamental principle. Always, in the universal flow of "Spirit coming to itself," oppositions arise and are overcome by a new level of emergence.

As an idealist, Hegel did not begin with the natural or the physical world; he began with the world of ideas. At some point, ideas gave rise to the natural world, and in Spirit the two are reintegrated. The idealism of Hegel's approach to emergent processes had to be corrected if it was to be fruitful for science, though it would be some eighty years before science began to play a major role in understanding emergence. First it was necessary to find a more materialist starting point, even if it was not yet one driven by the natural sciences. Feuerbach's "inversion" of Hegel represented a start in this direction. For Feuerbach the laws of development were still necessary and triadic (dialectical) in Hegel's sense. But for the author of *The Essence of Christianity*, the development of spiritual ideas began with the human species in its physical and social reality ("species-being"). Karl Marx made the inversion more complete by anchoring the dialectic in the means of production. Now economic history, the study of the development of economic structures, became the fundamental level and ideas were reduced to a "superstructure," representing the ideological aftereffects or *ex-post-facto* justifications of economic structures. . . .

Weak and Strong Emergence

Although the particular labels and formulations vary widely, commentators are widely agreed that twentieth-century emergence theories fall into two broad categories. These are best described as "weak" and "strong" emergence—with the emphatic insistence that these adjectives refer to the degree of emergence and do not prejudge the argumentative quality of the two positions.[11] Strong emergentists maintain that evolution in the cosmos produces new, ontologically distinct levels, which are characterized by their own distinct laws or regularities and causal forces. By contrast, weak emergentists insist that, as new patterns emerge, the fundamental causal processes remain those of physics. As emergentists, these thinkers believe that it may be essential to scientific success to explain causal processes using emergent categories such as protein synthesis, hunger, kin selection, or the desire to be loved. But, although such emergent structures may essentially constrain the behavior of lower-level structures, they should not be viewed as active causal influences in their own right.

Weak emergentists grant that different sorts of causal interactions seem to dominate "higher" levels of reality. They agree with strong emergentists, for example, that evolution forms structures that, as emergent wholes, constrain the motions of their parts. But our inability to recognize in these emerging patterns new manifestations of the same fundamental causal processes is due primarily to our ignorance. For this reason weak emergence is sometimes called "epistemological emergence," in contrast to strong or "ontological" emergence. . . .

It is not difficult to provide a formal definition of emergence in the weak sense: "F is an emergent property of S *if* (a) there is a law to the effect that all systems with this micro-structure have F; but (b) F cannot, even in theory, be deduced from the most complete knowledge of the basic properties of the components $C, \ldots, C$" of the system.[12]

Both weak and strong emergence represent a conceptual break with the reductive physicalist positions to which they are responding. The differences between them are significant and shall concern us more in due course. Weak emergence, because it places a stronger stress on the continuities between physics and subsequent levels, stands closer to the "unity of science" perspective. It has won a number of important advocates in the sciences and in philosophy from the end of the heyday of British Emergentism in the early 1930s until the closing decades of the century. But a number of philosophers have recently disputed its claim to represent a genuine alternative to physicalism. If the charge proves true, as I think it does, weak emergence will leave us saddled with the same old dichotomy between physicalism and dualism, despite its best efforts to the contrary.

---

11. See Bedau, "Weak Emergence," 375–99. Lowe, "The Causal Autonomy of the Mental," 634, claims to be the first to use the terms weak and strong, adapting his usage from John Searle's "emergent1" and "emergent2." Note that "weak" is not used in the literature as a term of derision. Davidson, "Thinking Causes," cites Jaegwon Kim's use of the notion of "weak" supervenience, agreeing with Kim that the term well expresses his (Davidson's) own understanding of mental events. Since my position on mental events is close to Davidson's anomalous monism, I happily follow his terminological suggestion. Weak supervenience, as we will see, corresponds to strong emergence; strong supervenience corresponds to (at most) weak emergence.

12. Beckermann, Flohr, and Kim, eds. *Emergence or Reduction?* 104.

The contrasts between weak and strong theories of emergence—both the issues that motivate them and the arguments they employ—are important. Yet their common opposition to reductive physicalism is a sign of significant common ground between the two positions. Before we enter into a no-holds-barred contest between them, it is crucial to explore their shared history and the numerous lines of connection between them. By attempting a conceptual reconstruction of the history of emergentism in the twentieth century, we will win a clearer picture of the similarities and the oppositions between the two related schools of thought. First the combined resources of the two schools must be marshalled in order to make a decisive case against the metaphysics of physicalism; only then can we turn to the issues that continue to divide them.

21

Defining Emergence[1]

Introduction

THE BATTLE LINES ARE now drawn. In addressing the ontological question about science—the question of what view of the world it supports—one must select among at least three major options: physicalism, emergence, and dualism. Our goal is to see what it means to advocate the emergentist option and why one might choose it over the alternatives.

It is already clear, however, that emergence is no monolithic term. Within the genus of interpretations of the natural world that it includes we have been able to identify two major competing species, commonly referred to as strong and weak emergence. The cumulative argument, I will suggest, favors strong emergence. That is, when the whole spectrum of emergent phenomena has been canvassed—from emergent phenomena in physics, through the study of organisms in their struggle to survive and thrive, and on to the phenomena of brain and mind—it is the perspective that best does justice to the entire range of phenomena. But the battle is hotly contested and, as we will see, some considerations also pull one towards the weak interpretation. The conflict between the two approaches, though often unrecognized, underlies much of the contemporary discussion; inevitably it will set the parameters for the debate as it unfolds in these pages.

The Problem of Definitions

People often ask for a simple definition of emergence. The task proves not to be quite so simple, since in ordinary language the term is not used as a technical term. The

---

1. "Defining Emergence," as found within Clayton, *Mind & Emergence: From Quantum to Consciousness*, 38–47. Reprinted with the kind permission of Oxford University Press.

Defining Emergence

Oxford Universal Dictionary lists thirteen definitions for "emerge/emergence/emergent," of which the one closest to the term's technical meaning within emergence theory is "that which is produced by a combination of causes, but cannot be regarded as the sum of their individual effects." *Webster's Third New International Dictionary* stresses the factor of newness in the last of its fifteen definitions: "appearing as or involving the appearance of something novel in a process of evolution." If forced to give a one-sentence definition, I would say that emergence is *the theory that cosmic evolution repeatedly includes unpredictable, irreducible, and novel appearances.*

But simple definitions fail to satisfy: either they combine features of multiple theories at the cost of superficiality, or they present one particular viewpoint without argument while passing silently over all others. One cannot move on to an examination of the relevant sciences without first pausing to clarify the concept of emergence. But let the reader beware: there are no neutral definitions; every conceptual clarification is actually a plea for the reader to look at the subject in a particular way. The following exposition is no exception—though I will make that case that it is more useful and more accurate than are the opposing approaches to the field.

The authors of one important recent analysis identify six key aspects of emergence: synergism (combined or cooperative effects between objects or systems), novelty, irreducibility, unpredictability, coherence, and historicity. Most generally, emergent properties are those that arise out of some subsystem but are not reducible to that system. Emergence is about *more than but not altogether other than.*

Often one understands the most about a position by understanding what it is opposed to. Generally emergentist positions define themselves against two competitors: *physicalist* positions, which claim that explanations must be given in terms of the constituent parts of some physical system, and *dualist* positions, which claim a causal role for other sorts of things, such as souls or spirits, whose essence could never be derived from the basal physical properties. Tim Crane thus describes the basic two requirements for an emergentist position as "dependence" and "distinctness": "mental properties are properties of physical objects," but "mental properties are distinct from physical properties."[2] That some kind of dependence relationship exists seems hard to deny: destroy enough molecules within a cell and you no longer have a cell; kill enough cells in an organ and the organ ceases to function; watch your discussion partner ingest enough alcohol and his sentences will cease to be coherent.

Emergence means that the world exhibits a recurrent pattern of novelty and irreducibility. In advocating this dual manifesto, emergence theorists tread a narrow path between two precipices. Should higher-order properties in fact be reducible to the underlying micro-physics, then (non-emergent) physicalism is true. But if the properties of life or mind are too novel, too different from the physical world, then emergence theorists are really closet dualists; in that case they might as well come out of the closet and display their true colors. Even if emergence theorists avoid both

---

2. Crane, "The Significance of Emergence," 208.

Scylla and Charybdis, critics argue, they may still fail. For merely to say "not this, not that" doesn't convey very much; the concept of emergence must express a positive thesis. But, the critic continues, *novelty and irreducibility without dualism* may just be a negative specification. At worst the phrase says nothing more than that evolution produces phenomena that are not like what came before, not reducible to it, yet not different enough that they belong to another order of reality altogether.

Five Different Meanings of Emergence

Before proceeding further with the definition question it might be helpful to consider what is the *topic* that emergence addresses. In the broader discussion one finds the term being used in multiple fields, some deeply concerned with scientific topics and others apparently incompatible with science. In fact, one can locate at least five distinct levels on which the term is applied. Care is required to avoid rampant equivocation. As one moves along the continuum between the levels, one observes a transition from very specific scientific domains to increasingly integrative, and hence increasingly philosophical, concepts.

E_1: Theories of Emergence within Specific Scientific Fields

This category refers to occurrences of the term within the context of a specific scientific theory. E_1 thus describes features of a specified physical or biological system of which we have some scientific understanding. The scientists who construct these theories claim that the term, used in a theory-specific sense, is of value to contemporary science as a description of features or patterns of the natural world. Because of this specificity, however, there is no way to establish whether the term is being used analogously across theories, or whether it really means something utterly distinct in each theory in which it appears.

E_2: Levels of Emergence within the Natural World

Used in this sense the term draws attention to broader features of the world that may eventually become part of a unified scientific theory. Emergence in this sense expresses postulated connections or laws that may in the future become the basis for one or more branches of science. One thinks, for example, of the role claimed for emergence in Stuart Kauffman's notion of a new "general biology" or in certain proposed theories of complexity or self-organization.

E_3: Patterns across Scientific Theories

Since it postulates features that are shared by multiple theories within science, E_3 is actually a meta-scientific term. Used in this sense, as it often is in the philosophy of science, the term is not drawn from a particular scientific theory; it is an observation about a significant pattern that allegedly connects a *range* of scientific theories. For example, consider the features that might be common to autocatalysis, complexity, and self-organization. We have some idea of what role each of these three terms plays in at least one branch of science; but it is also possible that they share certain significant features in common. E3 draws attention to these features, whether or not any individual theory within science actually makes scientific use of the term "emergence." It thus serves a heuristic function, helping to highlight common features between theories. Recognizing such broader patterns can help to extend existing theories, to formulate insightful new hypotheses, or to launch new interdisciplinary research programs.

E4: A Theory about the Patterns in the Transitions between Sciences

Emergence in this sense is a broader theory about the evolutionary process. Like E3 it claims that new systems or structures are formed at particular points and that these systems share certain common features. But emergence theories sometimes go beyond the task of describing common features across scientific fields; they sometimes attempt to explain why these patterns should exist. Such theories argue that the similarities and differences across emergent systems are part of a broader pattern in nature—an overall "ladder of emergence," for example. Current work is being done, for example, to understand how chemical structures emerge out of the underlying physics, to reconstruct the biochemical dynamics that underlie the origins of life, and to conceive how complicated neural processes produce cognitive phenomena such as memory, language, rationality, and creativity. E4-type theories attempt to discern the broader pattern that runs across each of these (and other) transition points in nature. As such, they are not themselves scientific theories. A scientific theory that explains how chemical structures are formed is unlikely to explain the origins of life, and neither theory will explain how self-organizing neural nets encode memories. Instead, E4 theories explain why the transition between scientific theories should be as we find them to be in nature.

E5: The Metaphysics of Emergence

Emergence in this sense is a metaphysical theory, in the sense that physicalism and dualism are also metaphysical theories. It claims that the nature of the world is such that it produces, and perhaps must produce, continually more complex realities in a process of ongoing creativity, and it is a thesis about the nature of what is produced. Each of the preceding four types of emergence may serve as evidence for E5, but they alone will not prove it. Metaphysical theories are not limited inferences from the available evidence; they are hypotheses about the nature of reality as a whole. In the final chapter of this work I examine the case for a metaphysics of emergence and the implications that follow from it.

PART IV: Science & Emergence

An Example: Emergence at the Fourth Level

We have seen that emergence can be elaborated as a scientific, a philosophical, a metaphysical, or even a religious thesis. I presuppose that a metaphysical theory of emergence, be it religious or anti-religious, theological or anti-theological, should be guided by the philosophy of science and, ultimately, by a scientific study of the place of emergence in the natural world.

But given that at least three of the types of emergence just summarized (E3–E5) are not directly scientific theories, one wonders what kind of traction the broader theories of emergence really have with the sciences. Can broader theories of emergence be undercut by science? Is the concept of emergence actually helpful for understanding certain trends in recent science? If it is, *which* of the emergentist positions currently on the market best reflects the relevant sciences? One cannot answer these questions, I suggest, without doing some work within the field of the philosophy of science. This field is useful, for example, for locating the *kind* of claim that emergence makes, for specifying how emergence claims might be assessed, and for guiding the process of evaluating them. Philosophers of science have also developed sophisticated theories of emergence, debating questions such as, "Can emergent physical entities exercise causal powers of their own, or does physics cover all the types of causes one needs to introduce?" (I return to this question in a moment.)

As an example, let's consider the case of E4–the type of emergence involving patterns in the transitions between theories. In effect, it represents the suggestion that a specific series of questions be posed to scientists, and that they be considered in a specific order:

1) Is the term "emergence," understood however one wishes to understand it, useful for summarizing current results in one's specific discipline?

2) Which results is it useful for summarizing?

3) When one summarizes these phenomena as emergent, which opposing view is one implicitly rejecting?

4) How strong is the case for emergence in this sense? How important, how useful, is the emergence framework in contrast to the other available frameworks?

Suppose one mentally lines up the collected responses to these questions. The data then lead to an interesting comparative project, for one must now ask:

5) Can one discover any significant similarities in the usages of the term "emergence" as it appears in answer to the first four questions?

An informed answer to this final question allows one to create and test a theory of emergence as a meta-theory about the relationships between scientific disciples and fields. For emergence will be a significant phenomenon in the natural world if we can discover analogies between the *relationships between* various scientific disciplines. This is a second-order enquiry. Let the letters A, B, C, ... stand for the various disciplines: quantum physics, macrophysics, physical chemistry, biochemistry, cell biology, etc. Now focus on the relationships between the particular disciplines: A–B, B–C, C–D, D–E, etc. For convenience, we might label each of these relationships with a number: relation A–B is 1, relation B–C is 2, relation C–D is 3, and so forth. This allows us to pose the question concerning the similarities and differences between the relationships: how are 1, 2, 3, 4, etc., themselves related?

In my view, this may be, in the entire emergence debate, the most important point at which philosophy and science overlap. The question concerns the connection between scientific domains, and raising it may allow one to see something highly significant about the natural world that one would not otherwise have recognized. For example, the results may help scholars to recognize a hierarchy among the fields of science and to reconstruct the principles that give rise to it, whether they involve increasing complexity, or more complex feedback loops, or some other conceptual framework. In the end, talk of hierarchies in nature is theoretically serious only if the principle by which the hierarchy is constructed can be clearly formulated and tested—that is, if it is possible to show that it can be undercut by empirical results, present or future. This method allows in principle for such testing.

Only when this work has been done can one begin to assess the broader philosophical theories about emergence. In formulating the project and beginning to carry it out, the present book attempts to establish a theoretical framework adequate for testing the various claims about emergence being put forward by an increasing number of scientists, philosophers, and theologians. Philosophers ask, for example, how values might supervene on physical states, whether emergence presupposes or undercuts belief in the causal closure of the physical world, whether consciousness exercises its own causal powers or is merely a shorthand way of expressing a certain organization of the physical forces that physics studies, and whether the physical universe is the type of place that supports or undercuts the religious belief that the universe is spiritually significant. But even for those who have no interest in philosophical questions, the methodology proposed here holds promise for assessing the significance of the emergence concept within, and between, the sciences themselves.

Doubts about Emergence

Of course, the positive program just outlined gives rise to a number of questions, doubts, and reservations. Above all, one worries about the gap between scientific and philosophical methods, theories, and assumptions. Philosophy requires theories that are unified, consistent, and as conceptually exact as possible, theories that can be applied without ambiguity across a wide variety of fields. But any attempt to apply such a global philosophical theory to a range of different scientific disciplines immediately raises walls of skepticism. The theoretical contexts are so radically different for any two cases of emergent phenomena in the natural world—say, the emergence of the classical physical world from quantum mechanical states, and the emergence of cell-wide behaviors out of the DNA code—that attempts to apply a unitary philosophical theory may appear as the worst sort of philosophical hegemony. Nor does science fare much better. Almost by definition, scientists cannot convince philosophers that they have a more adequate solution to the problem, since there is no such thing as "a science of emergence." What science offers instead are the particular theories that we already know as the core theories of this or that scientific discipline. Of course, what the scientific theories describe are, at least in some cases, emergent phenomena. But this observation is *meta*-scientific or philosophical rather than directly scientific.

It is not difficult to describe in general terms how emergence might link science and philosophy. Take the particular level we have been considering (E4). One would work to understand the theories and data that describe emergence in the natural world; one would then formulate a philosophical theory stating common features among the various instances of emergence; and one would then test this theory against the scientific examples to determine its adequacy. So far the theory. In actual practice this sort of cooperative venture is rather more difficult. First of all, one has to have some idea of what should count as examples of emergence *before* one begins to examine the various sciences, which means that the philosophy does not just follow the scientific work but also precedes it. Next, philosophers writing on emergence would have to commit themselves to formulating theories that could in fact be supported or undercut by results in the various scientific disciplines; where the results of the tests are ambiguous, philosophers and theologians would have to content themselves with higher doses of agnosticism than is usual in their fields. Agreement to these conditions will not come easily. Further, because the disciplines involved stretch over a wide range from physics to population biology, it is probable that the resulting theory of emergence will provide, at best, a listing of family resemblances across the various disciplines. But family resemblance theories are usually not very attractive to analytic philosophers and traditional philosophers of science, who want more analytically rigorous theories.

To some it will seem strange that one needs to compromise on philosophical rigor in order to achieve genuine traction with science. Are there not a number of cases in the philosophy of physics and philosophy of biology where close partnerships exist between scientific detail and philosophical reconstruction? For example, philosophers have played a major role in the interpretation of quantum mechanics, combining very detailed analytic work with a sophisticated understanding of the quantum physical theories involved.[3] Similar things can be said of the contributions of philosophers such as David Hull and Michael Ruse to discussions of evolutionary biology or of the

---

3. The work of Jeremy Butterfield represents an excellent example of this genre. See Placek and Butterfield, eds. *Non-Locality and Modality*; cf. Butterfield and Pagonis, eds. *From Physics to Philosophy*; also see Butterfield, Hogarth, and Belot, eds. *Spacetime*.

role of game theorists in formulating models of kin selection and reciprocal altruism. But emergence is disanalogous, since a theory in this field will not be successful unless it is derived from more than one scientific discipline. By the nature of the case, emergence is an overarching concept that must pertain to theoretical structures and results in multiple fields. As a consequence it cannot draw too heavily on the details of theories in any particular discipline.

This argument explains my resistance to some of the emergence proposals made recently by Terrence Deacon.[4] Deacon's very clear presentation of three steps of emergent complexity offers a preciseness that one rarely finds elsewhere in the literature; his is perhaps the most sophisticated scientific theory of emergence currently available. Upon closer inspection, however, one realizes that its preciseness comes from a certain predominance of physics in his theory (more particularly, the level of thermodynamic complexity that allows natural selection to operate on the resulting system). This basic physical pattern can manifest itself in more complex forms, say, in cell biology or primate evolution. But on Deacon's view in the cited article, the process itself is not reiterated; stage-three emergence does not become a new starting point for a further process of emergent complexity leading to new emergent wholes. Instead, when the system reaches the point at which there is a self-contained feedback loop upon which the principles of natural selection can operate, the system has achieved all the ontological complexity there is to achieve; beyond this, nature just reiterates the same three-step process in a cycle of increasing physical complexity.

In contrast to this view, I will argue for an iterative model of emergence. As Deacon correctly describes, increasing complexity within a system under certain conditions gives rise to emergent entities or units. These units then become involved in more and more complex relationships until they produce further units which are basic causal agents in their own right, and the process begins again. If this iterative model is correct, it means that no single scientific discipline can express the precise nature of emergence; *emergence is a pattern that runs on a variety of different platforms*. As a consequence, no single scientific theory can provide the precise account of emergence that Deacon seeks.

---

4. Deacon, "The Hierarchic Logic of Emergence."

22

Eight Characteristics of Emergence[1]

It is useful to conclude this analysis of the emergence concept with a summary of the core features of strong emergence as I will be using the term in the remaining chapters. Eight central theses characterize the position:

1. Monism

There is one natural world made, if you will, out of stuff. Some have suggested that everyone who accepts this premise is a materialist. Although the Greek concept of matter (*hylē*) was sufficiently broad to be unobjectional, "materialism" has taken on more limited connotations since the Enlightenment, largely because Descartes and the Cartesians set its cognate, *matter*, in opposition to *mind* in a way the Greeks would never have done. For this reason, I suggest using *monism* as the most neutral word available.

2. Hierarchical complexity

This world appears to be hierarchically structured: more complex units are formed out of more simple parts, and they in turn become the "parts" out of which yet more complex entities are formed. The rapid expansion of solid empirical work in complexity theory now allows us to quantify the increase in complexity, at least in some cases.

---

[1]. "Eight Characteristics of Emergence," as found within Clayton, *Mind & Emergence: From Quantum to Consciousness*, 60–65. Reprinted with the kind permission of Oxford University Press.

3. Temporal or emergentist monism

This process of hierarchical structuring takes place over time: Darwinian evolution (and some forms of cosmological evolution) move from the simple to the more complex. Because new entities emerge in the process, I join with Arthur Peacocke[2] in advocating the label *emergentist monism*.

4. No monolithic law of emergence

Many of the details of the process of emergence—the manner of the emergence of one level from another, the qualities of the emergent level, the degree to which the "lower" controls the "higher," etc.—vary greatly depending on which instance of emergence one is considering. Harold Morowitz, for example, has identified more than two dozen levels, showing how radically different one instance of emergence can be from another. Emergence should thus be viewed as a term of family resemblance.

5. Patterns across levels of emergence

It is possible to recognize and defend certain broad similarities shared in common by most of the various instances of emergence in natural history. I propose five in particular. For any two levels, L1 and L2, where L2 emerges from L1,

> (a) L1 is prior in natural history (b) L2 depends on L1, such that if the states in L1 did not exist, the qualities in L2 would not exist. (c) L2 is the result of a sufficient degree of complexity in L1. In many cases one can even identify a particular level of criticality which, when reached, will cause the system to begin manifesting new emergent properties. (d) One can sometimes predict the emergence of some new or emergent qualities on the basis of what one knows about L1. But using L1 alone, one will not be able to predict (i) the precise nature of these qualities, (ii) the rules that govern their interaction (or their phenomenological patterns), or (iii) the sorts of emergent levels to which they may give rise in due course. (e) L2 is not reducible to L1 in any of the standard senses of "reduction" in the philosophy of science literature: causal, explanatory, metaphysical, or ontological reduction.

6. Downward causation

I have also defended the more controversial thesis of downward causation: in some cases, phenomena at L2 exercise a causal effect on L1 which is not reducible to an L1 causal history. This causal non-reducibility is not just epistemic, in the sense that we

---

2. See Peacocke, "The Sound of Sheer Silence."

can't tell the L1 causal story but (say) God could. It is ontological: the world is such that it produces systems whose emergent properties exercise their own distinct causal influences on each other and on (at least) the next lower level in the hierarchy. If we accept the intuitive principle that ontology should follow agency, then cases of emergent causal agency justify us in speaking of emergent objects (organisms, agents) in natural history. *Emergent properties* are new features of existing objects (e.g., conductivity is a property of electrons assembled under certain conditions); *emergent objects* become centers of agency on their own behalf (cells and organisms may be composed of smaller particles, but they are also the objects of scientific explanation in their own right).

7. Emergentist pluralism

Some argue that 6 (above) entails dualism. I disagree. Downward causation does mean that the position is "pluralist," in so far as it asserts that really distinct levels occur within the one natural world and that objects on various levels can be ontologically primitive (can be entities in their own right) rather than being understood merely as aggregates of lower-level, foundational particles (ontological atomism). But to call this position "dualist" is to privilege one particular emergent level—the emergence of thought out of sufficiently complex neural systems—among what are (if Morowitz is right) at least twenty-eight distinct emergent levels.

8. "Mind" as emergent

The philosophical view I propose is not equivalent to "dual-aspect monism," a view that traditionally implied that there is no causal interaction between mental and physical properties, since they are two different aspects of the one "stuff." By contrast, the present view presupposes that both upward and downward influences are operative.

23

Emergence in Evolution[1]

The Transition to Biology

ILYA PRIGOGINE DID NOT follow the notion of "order out of chaos" up through the entire ladder of biological evolution. But thinkers such as Stuart Kauffman, Brian Goodwin, Christian de Duve, Murray Gell-Mann, and Simon Conway Morris have recently traced the role of the same principles in living systems. Biological processes in general are the result of systems that create and maintain order (stasis) through massive energy input from their environment. In principle, these types of processes could be the object of what Kauffman envisions as "a new general biology," based on sets of still-to-be-determined laws of emergent ordering or self-complexification. Like the biosphere itself, these laws (if they indeed exist) are emergent: they depend on the underlying physical and chemical regularities but are not reducible to them. . . .

Until a science has been developed that formulates and tests physics-like laws at the level of biology, the "new general biology" remains an as-yet-unverified, though intriguing, hypothesis. Nevertheless, recent biology, driven by the genetic revolution on the one side and by the growth of the environmental sciences on the other, has made explosive advances in understanding the role of self-organizing complexity in the biosphere. Four factors in particular play a central role in biological emergence:

1. The role of scaling

As one moves up the ladder of complexity, macrostructures and macromechanisms emerge. In the formation of new structures, one might say, scale matters—or, better

---

1. "Emergence in Biology"; "Emergence in Evolution"; "Toward an Emergentist Philosophy of Biology," as found within Clayton, *Mind & Emergence*, 78–100. Reprinted with the kind permission of Oxford University Press.

put, changes in scale matter. Nature continually evolves new structures and mechanisms as life forms move up the scale from molecules (c. 1 Ångstrom) to neurons (c. 100 micrometers) to the human central nervous system (c. 1 meter). As new structures are developed, new whole–part relations emerge. . . . To recognize the patterns is to make emergence an explicit feature of biological research. As of yet, however, science possesses only a preliminary understanding of the principles underlying this periodicity.

2. The role of feedback loops

Feedback loops, examined above for biochemical processes, play an increasing role from the cellular level upwards. In plant–environment interactions, for example, one can trace the interaction of mechanisms, each of which is the complex result of its own internal autocatalytic processes. Plants receive nutrients, process them, and provide new materials to the environment (e.g., oxygen, pollen). The environment in turn takes up these materials and processes them, so that new resources become available to the plant. . . .

3. The role of local–global interactions

In complex dynamical systems, the interlocked feedback loops can produce an emergent global structure. . . . In these cases, "the global property—[the] emergent behavior—feeds back to influence the behavior of the individuals . . . that produced it."[2] The global structure may have properties the local particles do not have. An ecosystem, for example, will usually evidence a kind of emergent stability that the organisms of which it is constituted lack. Nevertheless, it is impossible to predict the global effects "from below," based on a knowledge of the parts of the system, because of the sensitive dependence on initial conditions (among other factors) minute fluctuations near the bifurcation point are amplified by subsequent states of the system. This form of "downward" feedback process represents another instance of downward causation. . . .

4. The role of nested hierarchies

A final layer of complexity is added in cases where the local–global structure forms a nested hierarchy. Such hierarchies are often represented using nested circles. Nesting is one of the basic forms of combinatorial explosion. Such forms appear extensively in natural biological systems, as Stephen Wolfram has recently sought to show in his massive treatment of the subject. Organisms achieve greater structural complexity, and hence increased chances of survival, as they incorporate discrete subsystems.

---

2. Lewin, *Complexity*.

Similarly, ecosystems complex enough to contain a number of discrete subsystems evidence greater plasticity in responding to destabilizing factors.

Emergence in Evolution

In one sense, emergence in evolution is similar to the sorts of examples we have been considering. As Terrence Deacon notes, it consists of "a collection of highly convoluted processes that produce a remarkably complex kind of combinatorial novelty."[3] In another sense, however, biological evolution adds an importantly new dimension into the productive process that is natural history. Now for the first time causal agents emerge that include an element of "memory," which is isolated by cellular membranes and transmitted, more or less intact, to their offspring via nucleic acids. These new structures make each organism a sort of hypothesis, a guess about what kind of structure might thrive in its particular environment. "The result," comments Deacon, "is that specific historical moments of higher-order regularity or of unique micro-causal configurations can exert *an additional cumulative influence* over the entire causal future of the system."[4] With this new emergent level, natural selection is born.

The title of this section signals a crucial difference in approach between contemporary emergence theory and the British Emergentists of the early twentieth century. By working with the title "emergent evolution," C. Lloyd Morgan and others implicitly claimed to have discovered a new *kind* of evolution. Does "emergent evolution" not hold out the implicit promise that Morgan's theory of emergence will provide the tools to write a more adequate science of evolution? "Emergence *in* evolution" backs away from such claims. Here the assumption is that one must work with the givens of contemporary evolutionary theory, with its data, theories, and methods. If contemporary biology needs to be modified and improved (and even its greatest advocates believe that it does), such changes will come, gradually or rapidly, on the basis of scientific criticisms that reveal areas where its explanations are inadequate—and only as better scientific explanations become available. Standard evolutionary theory will not be shown to be inadequate by the fact that a group dislikes this or that feature of the theories or some implication they seem to have. . . .

In short, "emergence in evolution" suggests that, within the set of theories that we group under the heading of evolutionary biology, particular features can be discovered that are aptly described as "emergent." This approach looks to clarify those features and to show how and why the phenomenon of emergence is significant to an understanding of the biosphere. If this claim is sustained, one is justified in looking for analogies with the emergent features that characterize other phenomena within the natural world.

---

3. Deacon, "The Hierarchical Logic of Emergence," 297.
4. Deacon, "The Hierarchical Logic of Emergence," 297.

PART IV: Science & Emergence

Transformations in Evolutionary Theory

The case for biological emergence is best made not by looking outside biology but by tracing trends in the understanding of evolution, and changes in the study of evolutionary systems, over the last fifty or so years. It is fair to say that the dominant perspective of the "new synthesis" in biology in the mid-twentieth century was mechanistic.

The complicated appearances and behaviors of organisms and ecosystems could ultimately be explained at the biochemical level by gene reproduction and mutation. These processes upwardly determine the structures and functions of cells, organs, and organisms, which are then selected for or against by the environment. . . . Even though the evidence now suggests that this model was overly ambitious in its claims and expectations, it must be said that it remains the (often unspoken) model of many working biologists today.

It is not hard to list the core features of model work within the new synthesis. As noted, it was mechanistic: one looked for the mechanisms that underlie and explain organismic behavior. It was based on the assumption of the possibility of reduction to physical laws, and hence on the centrality of physics for biology. Although one assumed that explanations given in terms of physical laws alone would be far too complex to allow for explaining and predicting biological phenomena, it was assumed that translations of core biological explanatory principles into physical laws was still possible in principle. Above all, it was "bottom-up": systems had to be explained in terms of their constituent parts and the laws governing the parts' behavior; it would be unscientific to try to account for some particular phenomenon in terms of the broader system of which it was a part—unless, of course, that system had in turn been explained in terms of the parts and the laws that produced it. . . .

A new series of suspicions about the dominant program seems to have been unleashed by the theory of punctuated equilibrium of Niles Eldredge and Stephen Jay Gould. The idea that evolution would take place through major jumps, followed by long periods of relative equilibrium and minimal change, is not intrinsically incompatible with the new synthesis. But it does introduce the possibility that there are empirical causal forces at work in evolutionary history that are not captured by genetics plus natural selection. Should broader environmental forces play the major role in determining the overall results of evolution, then the paradigm of upward determination from the level of genes must be incomplete. Additional doubts were raised by what should have been a major victory for the genetic program: the completion of the Human Genome Project (HGP). The hype surrounding the HGP led many to believe that it would unlock the secrets of ontogenetic development. Yet the outcome of the project severely undercut such hopes: with only a few more than 30,000 genes to work with, it is simply impossible for the human genome to program human traits in the level of detail that some had suggested. To the extent, for example, that E. O. Wilson's sociobiology had depended on associating one particular gene with each inherited trait, his program was curtailed by the unexpectedly small number of coding genes.

Thus, it was not a long step to the development of epigenesis. . . . One of the by-products of the renewed focus on epigenesis was a series of new breakthroughs in developmental biology. Gene-governed processes, it was now clear, cannot fully explain the empirical facts of ontogenesis. The development of individual organisms involves the emergence of and interaction between functioning systems at multiple levels. Yet, if genetic causation is only part of the story, why is it that functionally similar adult organisms often develop, despite the fact that vastly different environmental influences may be impacting the ontogenetic process? Old debates between genetic preformation and epigenesis have been replaced by a new "interactionist consensus" regarding development—the view, as Jason Scott Robert puts it, "that neither genes nor environments, neither nature nor nurture, suffices for the production of phenotypes."[5] There is now wide acceptance of the core premises of "the new interactionism": genes and experience together, in their ongoing interaction, are responsible for the structure, functions, and behaviors of living organisms from cells to primates. Gone is the mono-linear causal story presupposed at the middle of the last century. . . .

Even if the new interactionism answers the age-old philosophical problem of *nature versus nurture* with a resounding "both!" it is only the beginning of an immense program of scientific research. Biologically the question is not whether environmental factors influence gene expression—the ability of the environment to switch genes on and off is already well established—but exactly how the process works to produce complex behaviors in organisms. For example, environmental factors play a crucial role in altering transposons, which then influence cellular meiosis and gamete formation by introducing random variations into genetic sequences, producing "genetic drift." . . . Although it is a matter of dispute which (if any) of the philosophers' theories of emergence correctly describe this process, it is clear that the framework of emergence better describes the present theoretical picture than any of the alternatives. . . .

Systems Biology

The interactions between parts and wholes that occur in biological systems mirror the features of emergence that we observed in chemical processes. Yet to the extent that the evolution of organisms and ecosystems evidences a "combinatorial explosion," compounded by factors such as the four just summarized, the causal role of the emergent wholes is greatly strengthened. Natural systems are made up of interacting complex systems and form a multi-levelled network of interdependency, with each level contributing distinct elements to the overall explanation. For this reason the hope of explaining entire living systems in terms of simple laws now appears quixotic.

---

5. Robert, *Embryology, Epigenesis, and Evolution*, 2.

PART IV: Science & Emergence

The new systems approach to biology, the Siamese twin of genetics, has begun to establish the key features of life's "complexity pyramid." Construing cells as networks of genes and proteins, systems biologists distinguish four distinct levels: (1) the base functional organization (genome, transcriptome, proteome, and metabolome); (2) the metabolic pathways built up out of these components; (3) larger functional modules responsible for major cell functions; and (4) the large-scale organization that arises from the nesting of the functional modules. . . .

It is true that the success of systems-biological explanations spells the end of one sort of program: the "bottom-up" derivation of all structures and behaviors from the building blocks of all-determining genes. But systems biology is in fact an *outgrowth* of the revolution in microbiology, not its replacement. Only by understanding the influence of genes on cellular functioning have biologists been able to advance to a systems perspective. It turned out, not surprisingly, that genes activated by biochemical reactions form signaling pathways, which then organize into networks or pathways. An adequate cell biology requires understanding the complex movements both upwards and downwards: not only how the genes set in motion signaling pathways between cells, but also how the dynamics of the pathways and networks of pathways in turn play a causal role in gene expression.

Understanding complex cellular and intercellular behaviors as a product of the *combination* of these upward and downward forces offers, I will suggest, crucial insights into the role of downward causation in nature. The standard physics-based model of the natural world, which serves as the basis for the doctrine known as "physicalism," emphasizes the role of parts in constituting the behaviors of larger objects. Observed macro-patterns are explained as the effect of micro-laws operating on large numbers of parts, and the dynamics of the resulting aggregate are reconstructed as the product of the dynamics of the parts. Systems theory undercuts the downwardly reductionist influence of this physicalist model. . . .

Given this task and the nature of the biosphere, it is natural to think of an organism as a system, which is itself composed of a series of interacting systems, which themselves are composed of systems of systems, and so forth. The biological sciences attempt to reconstruct the dynamics of these interlocking systems and to find the most adequate explanatory tools and concepts for comprehending their evolutionary history and behavior. Because survival and reproduction are the key biological goals, the robustness of systems and organisms becomes a key explanatory category. . . .

Despite the apparent power of this explanatory framework for explaining a wide variety of natural phenomena, one should be somewhat cautious about the initial results. Systems biology is in its infancy; the interconnections are massively complex, requiring interdisciplinary research groups which are expensive to fund; and the complexity of the systems involved makes neat predictions unlikely. . . . Nonetheless, as a theoretical perspective, systems biology offers the most sophisticated understanding of cell and organismic function yet available. As Kitano notes, "a transition is occurring in biology from the molecular level to the system level that promises to revolutionize our understanding of complex biological regulatory systems and to provide major new opportunities for practical application of such knowledge." To understand biology at the system level, Kitano insists, "we must examine the structure and dynamics of cellular and organismal function rather than the characteristics of isolated parts of a cell or organism."

Toward an Emergentist Philosophy of Biology

. . . A successful dialogue between biology and philosophy requires that one begin with the biology, as we have done; only when the facts are on the table can one reflect on their philosophical significance. Thus, for example, whether there is a very large number of distinct levels within the biosphere, with subtle gradations between them, or whether only a smaller number of basic levels exists, is a matter for empirical study. Still, biology raises conceptual or philosophical questions that are not utterly without interest to biologists. The nature of living systems certainly falls into this category.

Systems and entities: the whole–part structure of explanation in biology

It is unfortunate that in recent years the explosion of knowledge in molecular biology has caused all of biology to be painted with a reductionist brush. In explaining the organisms and behaviors that one finds in living systems, the drive to uncover the mechanisms of inheritance is balanced by acute observations concerning the interaction of organisms and their environments. Fully adequate explanations of biological phenomena require the constant interplay of both bottom-up and top-down accounts. Genotypes produce phenotypes, specific organisms, in interaction with the environment; but in the end, it is the fate of the phenotype that determines the fate of the genes.

Organisms exhibit novel individual responses to a wide variety of internal and external stimuli. Behavioral responses can only be described in terms of the interaction of organism and environment. Since these behaviors cannot be defined in physical terms, it is unwarranted to say that they are physically deterministic. . . . Only higher-level studies can explain why damselflies are brightly colored, why viceroy butterflies look like monarchs, why crickets sing, and why acacia trees grow hollow thorns. The mechanism of sexual reproduction exists because the interplay of the environment and phenotypic differences greatly increases the top-down effects of the environment on the evolution of a species. Holistic factors such as appearance, smell, and mate availability, not to mention desires experienced by the organisms, are the driving forces in sexual selection. . . .

Not only are organisms irreducible units in biological explanation; they in turn cannot be treated in abstraction from their environments. The static conception of organisms is actually a fiction; organisms are in continual flux, adapting to environmental stimuli and striving for homeostasis. Ecosystems, for their part, consist of "a set of interlinked, differently scaled processes." Like the most elementary systems in cell biology, ecosystems function as coordinated sets of factors, with interrelationships between variables complex enough that they often need to be treated as qualitative units rather than as aggregates of factors. . . .

Conclusion

In these pages, I have made the case for emergence in the realm of the natural sciences. When the natural process of compounding complex systems leads to irreducibly complex systems, with structures, laws, and causal mechanisms of their own, then one has evidence that reductive physicalist explanations will be inadequate. Cases of emergent systems in the natural world suggest that the resources of micro-physics cannot, even in principle, serve as an adequate explanatory framework for these phenomena.

We found that the scientific examples support both weak and strong emergence. The cases that support strong emergence are those in which it is meaningful to speak of whole-to-part or systemic causation. By contrast, in the cases where laws allow an explanatory reduction of the emergent system to its subvening system (in simulated systems, via algorithms; in natural systems, via "bridge laws") the weak emergence interpretation suffices.

For reasons mentioned at the outset, scientists will prefer weak to strong emergence if the data are neutral between them. The strong view only rises to prominence if there are instances where the data cannot be adequately described by means of the model of passive whole–part constraint as opposed to active causal influence. In these instances, especially where we have reason to think that such lower-level rules are impossible in principle, the strong emergence interpretation is to be preferred. This is the case in at least some of the instances examined here.

I turn next to the examination of mental events and mental properties in their relationship to the biological systems in which they arise. For reasons I will discuss, these cases compel the strong interpretation even more than the biological cases do. Strong emergence—that is, emergence with mental causation—thus represents the most viable response to the mind–body problem. It has the merit of preserving common-sense intuitions about mental causation, thereby corresponding to our everyday experience as agents in the world. Moreover, the evolution of mental events without causal force would represent an unacceptable anomaly within evolutionary history: why expend the organism's valuable resources to produce *qualia* or experiential qualities if they have no causal role to play? Epiphenomenalism makes no evolutionary sense.

The borderline cases in the present chapter should thus be reconsidered on the basis of the outcome of the chapter that follows. This makes the two segments of the overall argument interdependent, and indeed in both directions. The strong emergence of mental causation provides additional impetus to grant the strong interpretation in the case of certain biological phenomena. At the same time, the evolutionary story that I have told in these pages must represent the horizon of interpretation for philosophers of mind. To conclude that both reductive physicalism and dualism are mistaken is to maintain that mind emerges through an evolutionary process. However novel mental events may be, they will never be fully understood apart from the details of this process.

24

Conceptual Foundations of Emergence Theory[1]

THE DISCUSSION OF EMERGENCE has grown out of the successes and the failures of the scientific quest for reduction. Emergence theories presuppose that the once-popular project of complete explanatory reduction—that is, explaining all phenomena in the natural world in terms of the objects and laws of physics—is finally impossible.[2]

In one sense, limitations to the programme of reduction*ism*, understood as a philosophical position about science, do not affect every-day scientific practice. To do science still means to try to explain phenomena in terms of their constituent parts and underlying laws. Thus, endorsing an emergentist philosophy of science is in most cases consistent with business as usual in much of science. In another sense, however, the reduction-*versus*-emergence debate does have deep relevance for one's understanding of scientific method and results, as the following chapters will demonstrate. The "unity of science" movement that dominated the middle of the twentieth century, perhaps the classic expression of reductionist philosophy of science, presupposed a significantly different understanding of natural science—its goals, epistemic status, relation to other areas of study, and final fate—than is entailed by emergence theories of science. Whether the scientist subscribes to one position or the other will inevitably have effects on how she pursues her science and how she views her results. . . .

. . . Defenders of the notion often appeal to Aristotle's four distinct types of causal influence, which include not only efficient causality, the dominant conception of cause in the history of modern science, but also material, formal, and final causality. The trouble is that material causality—the way in which the matter of a thing causes it to be and to act in a particular way—is no less "physicalist" than efficient causality, and

---

1. "Conceptual Foundations of Emergence Theory," as found within Clayton and Davies, eds. *The Re-Emergence of Emergence*, 1–34. Reprinted with the kind permission of Oxford University Press.

2. See, among many others, Clark, *Psychological Models and Neural Mechanism*; Primas, *Chemistry, Quantum Mechanics and Reductionism*; Agazzi, *The Problem of Reductionism in Science*; and Brown and Smith, *Reduction and the Development of Knowledge*. Also helpful is Gillett and Loewer, eds. *Physicalism and Its Discontents*.

final causality—the way in which the goal toward which a thing strives influences its behavior—is associated with vitalist, dualist, and supernaturalist accounts of the world, accounts that most emergentists would prefer to avoid. Formal causality—the influence of the form, structure, or function of an object on its activities—is thus probably the most fruitful of these Aristotelian options. Several authors have begun formulating a broader theory of causal influence, including Terrence Deacon (ch. 5),[3] although much work remains to be done.

The Prehistory of the Emergence Concept

By most accounts, George Henry Lewes was the scholar whose use of the term "emergence" was responsible for the explosion of emergence theories in the early twentieth century.[4] Yet precursors to the concept can be traced back in the history of Western philosophy at least as far as Aristotle. Aristotle's biological research led him to posit a principle of growth within organisms that was responsible for the qualities or form that would later emerge. Aristotle called this principle the *entelechy*, the internal principle of growth and perfection that directed the organism to actualize the qualities that it contained in a merely potential state. According to his doctrine of "potencies," the adult form of the human or animal emerges out of its youthful form. (Unlike contemporary emergence theories, however, he held that the complete form is already present in the organism from the beginning, like a seed; it just needs to be transformed from its potential state to its actual state.) As noted, Aristotle's explanation of emergence included "formal" causes, which operate through the form internal to the organism, and "final" causes, which pull the organism (so to speak) toward its final telos or "perfection."

The influence of Aristotle on the Hellenistic, medieval, and early modern periods cannot be overstated. His conception of change and growth was formative for the development of Islamic thought in the Middle Ages and, especially after being baptized at the hands of Thomas Aquinas, it became foundational for Christian theology as well. In many respects biology was still under the influence of something very much like the Aristotelian paradigm when Darwin began his work.

A second precursor to emergence theory might be found in the doctrine of *emanation* as first developed by Plotinus in the third century CE and then further developed by the Neoplatonic thinkers who followed him. On Plotinus's view, the entire hierarchy of being emerges out of the One through a process of emanation. This expansion was balanced by a movement of (at least some) finite things back up the ladder of derivation toward their ultimate source. The Neoplatonic model thus involved both a *downward* movement of differentiation and causality and an *upward*

---

3. See also Harré and Madden, *Causal Powers*; Dupré, *The Disorder of Things*; and Brandon, "Reductionism versus Wholism versus Mechanism," 179–204.

4. Lewes, *Problems of Life and Mind*, 2 vols.

movement of increasing perfection, diminishing distance from the Source, and (in principle) a final mystical reunification with the One. (The claim that new species or structural forms arise only "top down," as it were, and never in a bottom-up manner represents an important point of contrast with most twentieth-century emergence theories.) Unlike static models of the world, emanation models allowed for a gradual process of becoming. Although the later Neoplatonic traditions generally focused on the downward emanation that gave rise to the intellectual, psychological, and physical spheres (respectively *nous*, *psychē*, and *physika* or *kosmos* in Plotinus), their notion of emanation did allow for the emergence of new species as well. In those cases where the emanation was understood in a temporal sense, as with Plotinus, the emanation doctrine provides an important antecedent to doctrines of biological or universal evolution.[5]

When science was still natural philosophy, emergence played a productive heuristic role. After 1850, however, emergence theories were several times imposed unscientifically as a metaphysical framework in a way that blocked empirical work. Key examples include the neo-vitalists (e.g., H. Driesch's theory of entelechies) and neo-idealist theories of the interconnections of all living things (e.g., Bradley's theory of internal relations) around the turn of the century, as well as the speculations of the British Emergentists in the 1920s concerning the origin of mind, to whom we turn in a moment.

Arguably, the philosopher who should count as the great modern advocate of emergence theory is Hegel. In place of the notion of static being or substance, Hegel offered a temporalized ontology, a philosophy of universal becoming. The first triad in his System moves from Being, as the first postulation, to Nothing, its negation. If these two stand in blunt opposition, there can be no development in reality. But the opposition between the two is overcome by the category of becoming. This triad is both the first step in the System and an expression of its fundamental principle. Always, in the universal flow of "Spirit coming to itself," oppositions arise and are overcome by a new level of emergence.

As an idealist, Hegel did not begin with the natural or the physical world; he began with the world of ideas. According to his system, at some point ideas gave rise to the natural world, and in Spirit the two are re-integrated. His massive *Phenomenology of Spirit* represents an epic of emergence written on a massive scale. The variety of "philosophies of process" that followed Hegel shared his commitment to the "temporalization of ontology," construing reality itself as fundamentally in process. Henri Bergson, William James, and especially Alfred North Whitehead reconstructed the emergence of more and more complex objects, structures, institutions, forms of experience, and cultural ideas. Their work in mathematical physics (Whitehead) and

---

5. Note however that Plotinian emanation entails emergence from the top down, as it were, whereas most contemporary emergence theories speak of higher-order objects emerging out of the lower-level objects and forces that precede them in natural history.

psychology (James) gave their work a more concrete and empirical orientation than one finds in the great German and Anglo-American idealist systems. Whitehead in particular provided a rigorous metaphysical system of "emergent evolution" in his *magnum opus*, *Process and Reality*.[6] Although on Whitehead's view *experience* is present from the beginning and does not emerge at some point in cosmic evolution, nevertheless subjectivity, consciousness, and even the "consequent nature" of God are emergent products of evolution: "For Kant, the world emerges from the subject; for the philosophy of organism, the subject emerges from the world."[7]

Before a close collaboration could arise between science and the conceptual world of emergence, it was necessary that the rationalist and idealist excesses of the Hegelian tradition be corrected. The "inversion" of Hegel by Ludwig Feuerbach and Karl Marx, which replaced Hegel's idealism with a radically materialist starting point, provided the first step. Feuerbach's *Essence of Christianity* traced the development of spiritual ideas beginning with the human species in its concrete physical and social reality ("species-being"). In Marx's early writing the laws of development were still necessary and triadic (dialectical) in Hegel's sense.[8] But Marx eventually completed the inversion by anchoring the dialectic in the means of production. Now economic history, the study of the development of economic structures, became the fundamental level and ideas were reduced to a "superstructure," the ideological after-effects or *ex post facto* justifications of economic structures. . . .

Weak and Strong Emergence

Although the particular labels and formulations vary widely, commentators generally agree that twentieth-century emergence theories fall into two broad categories. These are best described as "weak" and "strong" emergence—with the emphatic insistence that these adjectives refer to the degree of emergence and not to the argumentative quality of the position in question.[9] Strong emergentists maintain that genuinely new causal agents or causal processes come into existence over the course of evolutionary history. By contrast, weak emergentists insist that, as new patterns emerge, the fundamental causal processes remain, ultimately, physical. . . .

Strong emergence: C. D. Broad

We begin with perhaps the best known work in the field, C. D. Broad's *The Mind and Its Place in Nature*. Broad's position is clearly *anti*-dualist; he insists that emergence theory is compatible with a fundamental monism about the physical world. . . .

---

6. Whitehead, *Process and Reality*, 229.
7. Whitehead, *Process and Reality*, 88.
8. Marx, *The Portable Karl Marx*, 87–90.
9. Bedau, "Weak Emergence," 375–99.

Emergence, Broad argues, can be expressed in terms of laws ("trans-ordinal laws") that link the emergent characteristics with the lower-level parts and the structure or patterns that occur at the emergent level. But emergent laws do not meet the deducibility requirements of, for example, Hempel's "covering law" model[10]; they are not metaphysically necessary. Moreover, they have another strange feature: "the only peculiarity of [an emergent law] is that we must wait till we meet with an actual instance of an object of the higher order before we can discover such a law; and . . . we cannot possibly deduce it beforehand from any combination of laws which we have discovered by observing aggregates of a lower order."[11] . . .

Broad concludes *The Mind and Its Place in Nature* by presenting seventeen metaphysical positions concerning the place of mind in nature and boiling them down ultimately to his preference for "emergent materialism" over the other options. It is a materialism, however, far removed from most, if not all, of the materialist and physicalist positions of the second half of the twentieth century. For example, "Idealism is not incompatible with materialism" as he defines it[12]—something that one cannot say of most materialisms today. Broad's (redefined) materialism is also not incompatible, as we have already seen, with theism.

Emergent evolution: C. L. Morgan

Conway Lloyd Morgan became perhaps the most influential of the British Emergentists of the 1920s. I reconstruct the four major tenets of his emergentist philosophy before turning to an initial evaluation of its success.

First, Morgan could not accept what we might call Darwin's *continuity principle*. A gradualist, Darwin was methodologically committed to removing any "jumps" in nature. On Morgan's view, by contrast, emergence is all about the recognition that evolution is "punctuated": even a full reconstruction of evolution would not remove the basic stages or levels that are revealed in the evolutionary process. . . .

Secondly, Morgan sought a philosophy of biology that would grant adequate place to the emergence of radically new life forms and behaviors. Interestingly, after Samuel Alexander, Henri Bergson is one of the most cited authors in *Emergent Evolution*. Morgan resisted Bergson's conclusions ("widely as our conclusions differ from those to which M. Bergson has been led")[13] and for many of the same reasons that he resisted Wallace: Bergson introduced the *élan vital* or vital energy as a force from outside nature.[14] Thus Bergson's *Creative Evolution*, originally published in 1911,

---

10. On the covering law model, see classically Hempel and Oppenheim, "Studies in the Logic of Explanation," 135–75; see also Nagel, *The Structure of Science*.
11. Broad, *The Mind and Its Place in Nature*, 79.
12. Broad, *The Mind and Its Place in Nature*, 654.
13. Lloyd Morgan, *Emergent Evolution*, 116.
14. I thus agree with David Blitz that Morgan's work is more than an English translation of Bergson.

combines a Cartesian view of non-material forces with the pervasively temporal perspective of late nineteenth-century evolutionary theory. . . .

Thirdly, Morgan argued powerfully for the notion of levels of reality. He continually emphasized a study of the natural world that looks for novel properties at the level of a system taken as whole, properties that are not present in the parts of the system. Morgan summarizes his position by arguing that the theory of levels or orders of reality . . . implies (1) that there is increasing complexity in integral systems as new kinds of relatedness are successively supervenient; (2) that reality is, in this sense, in process of development; (3) that there is an ascending scale of what we may speak of as richness in reality; and (4) that the richest reality that we know lies at the apex of the pyramid of emergent evolution up to date.[15]

Finally, Morgan interpreted the emergent objects at these various levels in the sense of strong emergence. As his work makes clear, there are stronger and weaker ways of introducing the idea of levels of reality. His strong interpretation of the levels, according to Blitz, was influenced by a basic philosophy text by Walter Marvin. The text had argued that reality is analyzable into a series of "logical strata," with each new stratum consisting of a smaller number of more specialized types of entities:

> To sum up: The picture of reality just outlined is logically built up of strata. The logical and mathematical are fundamental and universal. The physical comes next and though less extensive is still practically, if not quite, universal. Next come the biological, extensive but vastly less extensive than the chemical. Finally, comes the mental and especially the human and the social. . . .[16]

Emergence is interesting to scientifically minded thinkers only to the extent that it accepts the principle of parsimony, introducing no more metaphysical superstructure than is required by the data themselves. The data, Morgan argued, require the strong interpretation of emergence. . . .

How are we to evaluate Morgan's *Emergent Evolution*? The strategy of arguing for emergent substances clashes with the monism that I defended above, and a fortiori with all physicalist emergence theories. Morgan's strategy is even more regrettable in that it was unnecessary; his own theory of *relations* would actually have done the same work without recourse to the substance notion. He writes, "There is perhaps no topic which is more cardinal to our interpretation . . . than that which centres round what I shall call relatedness."[17] In fact, relation forms the core of his ontology: "It is as an integral whole of relatedness that any individual entity, or any concrete situation, is a bit

---

See Blitz, *Emergent Evolution*.
  15. Lloyd Morgan, *Emergent Evolution*, 203.
  16. See Marvin, *A First Book in Metaphysics*, as quoted by Blitz, *Emergent Evolution*, 90.
  17. Lloyd Morgan, *Emergent Evolution*, 67.

of reality";[18] note the close connection to contemporary interpretations of quantum physics)....

Let's call those theories of emergence "very strong" which not only (a) individuate relational complexes, (b) ascribe reality to them through an ontology of relations, and (c) ascribe causal powers and activity to them, but also (d) treat them as individual substances in their own right. The recent defence of "emergent dualism" by William Hasker in *The Emergent Self* provides an analogous example: "So it is not enough to say that there are emergent properties here; what is needed is an *emergent individual*, a new individual entity which comes into existence as a result of a certain functional configuration of the material constituents of the brain and nervous system."[19]

Strong Emergence since 1970

Emergence theory in general, and strong emergence in particular, began to disappear off the radar screens during the mid 1930s and did not reappear for some decades. Individual philosophers such as Michael Polanyi may still have advocated emergence positions. Generally, however, the criticisms of the British Emergentists—for instance, Stephen Pepper in 1926,[20] W. T. Stace in 1939,[21] and Arthur Pap in 1952[22]—were taken to be sufficient....

In 1973, Pylyshyn noted that a new cognitive paradigm had "recently exploded" into fashion.[23] Whatever one's own particular position on the developments, it's clear that by the end of the century emergence theories were again major topics of discussion in the sciences and philosophy (and the media). Now one must proceed with caution in interpreting more recent philosophy, since histories of the present are inevitably part of what they seek to describe. The authors of the following chapters provide a better picture of the pros and cons of emergence than any single author could. Nonetheless, it's useful to consider the immediate prehistory of strong views in contemporary emergence theory. Two figures in particular played key roles in the re-emergence of interest in strong emergence: Michael Polanyi and Roger Sperry.

Michael Polanyi

Writing in the heyday of the reductionist period, midway between the British Emergentists of the 1920s and the rebirth of the emergence movement in the 1990s, Michael Polanyi was a sort of lone voice crying in the wilderness.... Several aspects of

18. Lloyd Morgan, *Emergent Evolution*, 67.
19 Hasker, *The Emergent Self*, 64.
20. Pepper, "Emergence," 241–45.
21. Stace, "Novelty, Indeterminism, and Emergence," 296–310.
22. Pap, "The Concept of Absolute Emergence," 302–11.
23. Pylyshyn, "What the Mind's Eye Tells the Mind's Brain," 1.

Polanyi's position are reflected in contemporary emergence theories and served to influence the development of the field; I mention just three:

1. Active and passive boundary conditions[24]

Polanyi recognized two types of boundaries: natural processes controlled by boundaries; and machines, which function actively to bring about effects. He characterized his distinction in two different ways: as foreground and background interest, and as active and passive constraint....

2. The "from–at" transition and "focal" attention

Already in the Terry Lectures, Polanyi noticed that the comprehension of meaning involved a movement from "the proximal"—that is, the particulars that are presented—to the "distal," which is their comprehensive meaning.[25] By 1968 he had developed this notion into the notion of "from–at" conceptions. Understanding meaning involves turning our attention from the words to their meaning; "we are looking *from* them *at* their meaning."[26]

3. The theory of structure and information

Like many emergence theorists, Polanyi recognized that structure is an emergent phenomenon. But he also preserved a place for downward causation in the theory of structure, arguing that "the structure and functioning of an organism is determined, like that of a machine, by constructional and operational principles that control boundary conditions left open by physics and chemistry."[27] Structure is not simply a matter of complexity. The structure of a crystal represents a complex order without great informational content;[28] crystals have a maximum of stability that corresponds to a minimum of potential energy. Contrast crystals with DNA. The structure of a DNA molecule represents a high level of chemical improbability, since the nucleotide sequence is not determined by the underlying chemical structure. While the crystal does not function as a code, the DNA molecule can do so because it is very high in informational content relative to the background probabilities of its formation.

At the same time that emergence theory has profited from Polanyi, it has also moved beyond his work in some respects. I briefly indicate two such areas:

---

24. Philip Clayton is grateful to Walter Gulick for his clarifications of Polanyi's position and criticisms of an earlier draft of this argument. See Gulick, "Response to Clayton," 32–47.
25. Polanyi, *The Tacit Dimension*, 34.
26. Polanyi, *Knowing and Being*, 235; emphasis added.
27. Ibid., 219.
28. Ibid., 228.

1) *Polanyi was wrong on morphogenesis.* . . .

2) *Polanyi's sympathy for Aristotle and vitalism clashes with core assumptions of contemporary biology.* . . .

Roger Sperry

In the 1960s, at a time when such views were not only unpopular but even anathema, Roger Sperry began defending an emergentist view of mental properties. As a neuroscientist, Sperry would not be satisfied with any explanation that ignored or underplayed the role of neural processes. At the same time, he realized that consciousness is not a mere epiphenomenon of the brain; instead, conscious thoughts and decisions *do something* in brain functioning. Sperry was willing to countenance neither a dualist, separationist account of mind, nor any account that would dispense with mind altogether. As early as 1964, by his own account, he had formulated the core principles of his view.[29] By 1969, emergence had come to serve as the central orienting concept of his position. . . . Sperry is sometimes interpreted to hold only that mental language is a re-description of brain activity as a whole. But he clearly does assert that mental properties have causal force: "The conscious subjective properties in our present view are interpreted to have causal potency in regulating the course of brain events; that is, the mental forces or properties exert a regulative control influence in brain physiology."[30] . . .

Sperry referred to this position as "emergent interactionism." He also conceded that the term "interaction" is not exactly the appropriate term: "Mental phenomena are described as primarily supervening rather than intervening, in the physiological process. . . . Mind is conceived to move matter in the brain and to govern, rule, and direct neural and chemical events without interacting with the components at the component level, just as an organism may move and govern the time-space course of its atoms and tissues without interacting with them."[31] Sperry is right to avoid the term "interaction" if it is understood to imply a causal story in which higher-level influences are interpreted as specific (efficient) causal activities that push and pull the lower-level components of the system. As Jaegwon Kim has shown, if one conceives downward causation in that manner, it would be simpler to tell the whole story in terms of the efficient causal history of the component parts themselves.[32]

Sperry was not philosophically sophisticated, and he never developed his view in a systematic fashion. But he did effectively chronicle the neuroscientific evidence that

---

29. Sperry, "Mind–Brain Interaction," 196.

30. Sperry, "Mental Phenomena as Causal Determinants," 165. See also Sperry, "Consciousness and Causality," 164–66.

31. Sperry, "Consciousness and Causality," 165.

32. Kim, ed. *Supervenience.*

supports some form of downward or conscious causation, and he dropped hints of the sort of philosophical account that must be given: a theory of downward causation understood as whole–part influence. . . .

Weak emergence: Samuel Alexander

We turn now to what has undoubtedly been the more popular position among twentieth-century philosophers, weak emergence. Recall that weak emergence grants that evolution produces new structures and organizational patterns. We may *speak* of these structures as things in their own right; they may serve as irreducible components of our best explanations; and they may seem to function as causal agents. But the real or ultimate causal work is done at a lower level, presumably that of microphysics. Our inability to recognize in these emerging patterns new manifestations of the same fundamental processes is due primarily to our ignorance and should not be taken as a guide to ontology. The first major advocate of this view, and its classic representative, is Samuel Alexander.

Samuel Alexander's *Space, Time, and Deity* presents a weak emergentist answer to the mind–body problem and then extends his theory into a systematic metaphysical position.[33] Alexander's goal was to develop a philosophical conception in which evolution and history had a real place. He presupposed both as givens: there really are bodies in the universe, and there really exist mental properties or mental experience. The problem is to relate them. Alexander resolutely rejected classical dualism and any idealist view that would make the mental pole primary (e.g., Leibniz, and British idealists such as F. H. Bradley), yet he would not countenance physicalist views that question the existence of mind. Thus, he argued, mind must emerge in some sense from the physical. . . .

In order to generalize this position into a global metaphysical position, Alexander uses "mind" in a much broader sense than as consciousness alone. More generally, the "body" aspect of anything stands for the constituent factors into which it can be analyzed, and the "mind" aspect always represents the new quality manifested by a group of bodies when they function as a whole.[34] This generalization allows him to extend his answer to the mind–body problem to all of nature, producing a metaphysics of emergence. As he defines the concept, "Within the all-embracing stuff of Space-Time, the universe exhibits an emergence in Time of successive levels of finite existence, each with its characteristic empirical quality. The highest of these empirical qualities known to us is mind or consciousness. Deity is the next higher empirical quality to the highest we know."[35] The result is a ladder of emergence of universal

---

33. Alexander, *Space, Time, and Deity*.

34. See Emmet's introduction to *Space, Time, and Deity*, xv. The concept is reminiscent of Whitehead's well-known claim that mind is "the spearhead of novelty."

35. Alexander, *Space, Time, and Deity*, 2:345.

proportions. I reconstruct the steps of this ladder in eight steps, noting the points at which Alexander did not actually differentiate steps but should have done:[36]

1) At the base of the ladder lies Space-Time.

   Time is "mind" and space is "body"; hence time is "the mind of space." Space-Time is composed of "point-instants." Already the early commentators on Alexander found this theory hard to stomach. It has not improved with age.

2) There must be a principle of development, something that drives the whole process, if there is to be an ongoing process of emergence. Thus, Alexander posited that "there is a nisus in Space-Time which, as it has borne its creatures forward through matter and life to mind, will bear them forward to some higher level of existence."[37]

3) Thanks to the nisus, Space-Time becomes differentiated by "motions." Certain organized patterns of motions (today we would call them energies) are bearers of the qualities we can material. So, *contra* Aristotle, matter itself is emergent. (Quantum field theory has since offered some support for this conception. For example, in *Veiled Reality* Bernard d'Espagnat describes atomic particles as products of the quantum field, hence as derivatives of it.[38])

4) Organizations of matter are bearers of macrophysical qualities and chemical properties. This constitutes emergence at the molecular level.

5) When matter reaches a certain level of complexity, molecules become the bearers of life. (This response is consistent with contemporary work on the origins of life, which postulates a gradual transition from complex molecules to living cells.)

6) Alexander didn't adequately cover the evolution of sentience but should have done. Thus, he could have covered the evolution of simple volition (e.g., the choice of where to move), symbiosis (reciprocal systems of organisms), sociality, and primitive brain processing as extensions of the same framework of bodies and their emergent holistic properties, which he called "mind."

7) Some living structures then come to be the bearers of the quality of mind or consciousness proper, "the highest empirical quality known to us."

8) At a certain level mind may be productive of a new emergent quality, which Alexander called "Deity." We know of Deity only that it is the next emergent property, that it is a holistic property composed of parts or "bodies," and that it results from an increased level of complexity.

---

36. Again, see Emmet's excellent introduction to *Space, Time, and Deity*, on which I have drawn in this reconstruction.

37. Alexander, *Space, Time, and Deity*, 2:346.

38. d'Espagnat, *Veiled Reality*.

To be consistent, Alexander had to postulate that Deity is to minds as our mind is to (the parts of) our bodies. It follows that Deity's "body" must be the minds in the universe.... Alexander also ascribed certain moral properties to Deity. But beyond this, one can say nothing more of its nature.... One might have supposed that only a strong emergentist could introduce language of Deity. Yet here we have a case of theological language interpreted in the sense of weak emergence: Alexander introduces this predicate in a manner (largely) consistent with his physicalism. For example, he consistently refuses to talk of the actual existence of a spiritual being, God; all that actually exists is the physical universe....

Alexander's view remains a classic expression of the weak emergentist position. No new entities are postulated; his physicalism remains robust.... Although largely consistent, Alexander's position fails to answer many of the most burning questions one would like to ask of it. If time is the "mind of space," time itself is directional or purposive. But such teleology is rather foreign to the spirit of modern physics and biology. Nor does Alexander's notion of *nisus* relieve the obscurity. Nisus stands for the creative tendency in Space-Time: "There is a nisus in Space-Time which, as it has borne its creatures forward through matter and life to mind, will bear them forward to some higher level of existence."[39] Yet creative advance does not belong to the furniture of physics. If time is "the advance into novelty," then there is an "arrow" to time. But what is the source of this arrow in a purely physical conception? Isn't it more consistent for a physicalist to say that time consists of a (potentially) infinite whole divided into point-instants? . . .

Strong emergentists will add a further reservation: that Alexander does not adequately conceptualize the newness of emergent levels, even though his rhetoric repeatedly stresses the importance of novelty. If life and mind are genuinely emergent, then living things and mental things must play some sort of causal role; they must exercise causal powers of their own, as in the doctrine of downward causation. According to Alexander, a mental response is not separable into parts but is a whole.[40] For the strong emergentist, however, it's not enough to say that mind is the brain taken as a whole; a mental event is the whole composed out of individual neural events and states, *and something more*.

Conclusion

Without a doubt, far more philosophers in the second half of the twentieth century advocated a position similar to Alexander's than to Broad's or Morgan's. . . . The preponderance of the weak emergence position is reflected in the great popularity of the supervenience debate, which flourished in the 1980s and '90s. Standard notions of supervenience accept the causal closure of the world and a nomological (i.e.,

---

39. Alexander, *Space, Time, and Deity*, 2:346.
40. Ibid., 2:129.

law-based), or even necessary, relationship between supervenient and subvenient levels. In its most popular form, non-reductive physicalism, supervenience for a time seemed to preserve both the dependence of mental phenomena on brain states and the non-reducibility of the former to the latter. Yet these are precisely the goals that weak emergence theorists such as Samuel Alexander sought to achieve.[41]...

I think it is important to acknowledge in advance that weak emergence is the starting position for most natural scientists. Many of us may start with intuitions that are in conflict with weak emergence; indeed, the man or woman in the street would find the denial of mental causation highly counter-intuitive. But when one engages the dialogue from the standpoint of contemporary natural science—or contemporary Anglo-American philosophy, for that matter—one enters a playing field on which the physicalists and weak emergentists have the upper hand.

---

41. For standard criticisms of supervenience in the guise of non-reductive physicalism see Kim, *Supervenience and Mind*; Kim, *Mind in a Physical World*; and Kim, ed. *Supervenience*.

25

Emergence from Quantum Physics to Religion[1]

Toward a Constructive Theory of Emergence

THE DIFFERENCES BETWEEN THE authors [in this book] are great enough that one cannot claim that all, or even most, would endorse a single unified theory of emergence—not even a purely naturalistic one, and far less one that makes robust religious claims. This book should therefore be read not as a systematic apologetic for a single theory of emergence, but rather as a sourcebook: it contains the data and theoretical resources necessary for evaluating whether a unified theory of emergence is possible, without actually providing such a theory.

Still, one can't help but wonder whether the scientific developments presented here are of broader philosophical significance. Taken together, do they constitute a sort of cumulative case for an emergence-based understanding of the natural world? Put differently, do insights from recent science and philosophy support a view of natural evolution as producing new levels of reality over time: new types of objects with new forms of causal powers, which therefore require types of explanation unique to each level? If the evidence does support a distinctively emergentist view of the world, what might such a view look like? In what follows I offer a sketch of such a theory—not with the claim that it is the only such theory available, or that all (or even most) of the authors in this volume would endorse it, but as a plausible inference to draw from the data and arguments presented in these pages. *Not* to raise the question of a general theory of emergence at the end of this collection would be to draw back from an obvious possibility when one ought rather to formulate and explore it in a critical and constructive manner.

Unitary theories of emergence come in various types, ranging from those that are emphatically naturalist to those that include a significant role for some transcendent

---

1. "Emergence from Quantum Physics to Religion." As found within Philip Clayton and Paul Davies, eds. *The Re-Emergence of Emergence*, 303–19. Reprinted with the kind permission of Oxford University Press.

dimension. In emergence theories, however, the relationship between the two ends of the spectrum is not fully symmetrical: one can endorse levels of emergence up to a certain point without being required to accept higher and more speculative levels of emergence, yet those who endorse the "higher" levels must acknowledge that these levels remain dependent on the levels that precede them. Thus, although I follow the lines all the way to the religious questions, readers are free to exit the cumulative argument at any point at which they can show that it is more rational to stop than to proceed. . . .

The Philosophy of Emergence

What then of the more philosophical dimensions of emergence theory? Viewed as a claim about the nature of reality, emergentism represents a species of monism; call it *emergentist monism.* Monism rejects multiple kinds of substance, as in Descartes' theory of "thinking stuff" and "extended stuff" (*res cogitans* and *res extensa*), arguing instead that all objects and phenomena in the universe arise out of one basic matter-energy "stuff." Yet a physics-based monism cannot be the last word, since it's equally obvious that the universe produces more and more complex levels of organization. *Emergentist* monism emphasizes continuity through process, the fundamental ontological affinity between all existing things.

Attempting to do justice to the radically new structures and phenomena that arise in universal history, one might however be just as inclined to use the term *emergentist pluralism*, which expresses an ontology of continual becoming. To espouse pluralism is to reject any privileged level of analysis. Combine this emphasis with the previous paragraph, and one obtains the most balanced, and I believe the most justified, view: the universe evidences *both* a downward dependence on the constraints of the lower or earlier levels, *and* an upward dependence of parts on the wholes in relation to which they exist. Hence one should be just as skeptical of the claim, "Well, in the end it's all about physics," as one is of the claim, "The universe exists ultimately in order to produce human consciousness." The emergence of human thought, self-reflection, and consciousness was a surprising and novel occurrence in the history of the universe, but there is no reason to conclude that this level of emergence is ontologically any more fundamental than the emergence of self-reproducing life forms on which the dynamics of natural selection could act. A chauvinism of the highest known level is no less pernicious than a chauvinism of the lowest level currently known to us. . . .

When one looks over the massive literature of the last few decades in the philosophy of mind, one can't help but walk away with the impression that we are really quite uncertain about what to say regarding human consciousness. Some use the strength of the correlations between brain states and first-person experiences as grounds for concluding an identity relationship between them; some use the felt difference of subjective properties to argue for dualist connections; and some use the disanalogies between mental properties and other properties in the natural world as grounds for urging that "folk psychology" be eliminated from our final account of human persons. Distinct from each of the other responses, the emergence programme amounts to the wager that mental phenomena can be understood—without being explained away[2]— by analogy to other emergent relationships in the world. Such an analogy preserves the *differences* between mind and lower-level phenomena while removing the sense that it is "spooky" or ontologically unique in the history of evolution. Instead, emergentists argue, the question of mind can best be addressed by looking for the ways in which mental phenomena emerge from neurological structures and processes, and by studying how these phenomena in turn begin to play a role within broader wholes or contexts (language; culture; social structures and institutions; value judgments; the construction of self-identity), in terms of which alone they can be understood. . . .

Some will complain that the emergence approach makes mental phenomena *too much* like other natural phenomena, and others will complain that it allows them to be *too different*. Some will complain that the emergentist approach does not demand a method of study that is distinct enough from physics and biology, and others will protest because the approach endorses the use of distinctively social scientific and phenomenological methods of inquiry, which diverge too greatly from the natural sciences. But I take the fact that the emergence position can be (and often is) criticized from both sides as sign that it just may have found the right balance between the extremes that tend to dominate the discussion.

Finally, a few words are necessary for those who are made uneasy by the fact that the philosophy of emergence appears metaphysical—those who worry that the empirical grounds for positions of this type are necessarily so minimal as to render them suspect. First, readers are welcome to construe all the unifying language in this proposal in a "regulative" fashion. According to Kant, some usages of language express the drive toward unified understanding that is intrinsic in the human quest to comprehend the world, even while they go beyond the kind of knowledge we have in the ordinary theoretical ("constitutive") use of language.[3] Of course, if you go on to claim to *know* that emergence theories are always only regulative, and hence that one could *never* have any reason to believe they are true, I would be skeptical. Nevertheless, for present purposes it's sufficient if one acknowledges that the human quest to understand and to unify leads us inevitably to appeal to the narrative of emergence across natural history.

Similarly, it is sufficient if the reader acknowledges that *some impetus* toward broader theories of emergence is provided by results within a wide variety of the

---

2. Cf. Dennett, *Consciousness Explained*.

3. I have explored the relationship between regulative and "constitutive" knowledge in chapter 1 of *The Problem of God in Modern Thought* and Kant's application of regulative theories to the question of knowledge of God in chapter 5 of the same work. On regulative language and transcendental arguments see Bieri, Horstmann, and Krüger, eds. *Transcendental Arguments and Science*; and Stern, ed. *Transcendental Arguments*.

natural sciences, as well as data from cognitive psychology, the social sciences, and the philosophy of mind. It may be that the data are suggestive but not conclusive; it may be that at some point the lines emerging from the various sciences get lost in the swirling clouds of metaphysical reflection and disappear from sight, as it were, so that one can't quite claim to have established a comprehensive emergence theory of reality. (Yet how will one know exactly where that point of disappearance is unless one attempts to follow the lines as far as one possibly can?) Nonetheless, it will have been enough if we can establish *the pattern of emergence* that runs (like a second-order derivative) through the domains that are open to sight. More metaphysically minded thinkers will seek to express the pattern as a theory of reality. For the metaphysically more cautious, however, it may suffice to recognize, in light of the contributions to this volume, that considering the connections between the various sciences suggests a pattern of emergence that the individual sciences alone cannot establish—a pattern that sets the mind on a journey of reflection and speculation that cannot be avoided by traditional appeals to empirical criteria or to some supposedly clear "line of demarcation" between science and metaphysics. . . .

Religion and Emergence

. . . In these final paragraphs, I should like to step back from the particular names and essays, in order to reflect for a moment on the religious dimension of emergence and on its potential significance for religious thought. As Gregersen's analysis shows—and his analysis is supported by cross-cultural approaches in contemporary religious studies—it would be difficult to find a view of the world (a metaphysic) that *could not* be seen as having religious significance. As Ursula Goodenough graphically puts it, one may feel the same sense of awe and wonder in observing a transduction cascade as she feels in standing before an ancient Aztec ruin by moonlight: "same rush, same rapture."[4] Hence, any attempt to prove a priori that only certain sorts of views about the world should pass as religious—say, those containing the term "God" or those that postulate a transcendent dimension of reality—are doomed to failure. A fortiori, emergence cannot be a necessary condition for a religious response to the world; nor can one conclude that, because a viewpoint espouses naturalistic emergence, it *cannot* be religious.

This recognition radically changes the nature of the discussion. As soon as the former worries about necessary and sufficient conditions for religiosity have been dispelled, the central question now becomes: what forms might the human religious response take, given the recognition that we are products of emergent evolution within a world of continual process and development? Three major options suggest themselves, depending on whether the religious response focuses on the natural, the

---

4. Goodenough, *The Sacred Depths of Nature*, 46.

emerging and unknown, or the transcendent. The first type, as Gregersen points out, need not depend specifically on emergence. Religious naturalism or "ecstatic naturalism" incorporates the classically religious human responses of awe, wonder, amazement, the appreciation of beauty, and the sense of mystery—all in response to the natural world in the form that the sciences reveal it to us. Only an idiosyncratic definition of religion, say, one that links religion exclusively to belief in God or organized religious communities, could exclude such responses from the realm of the religious.

Religious responses of the second type (responses to the new, novel, surprising, or mysterious) are more diverse. At least three subcategories can be identified, and more could be found as well. The religious response may be evoked by the remarkable, almost mysterious manner in which qualitatively new forms arise out of complex interrelationships of parts-in-systems. Thus, people express amazement that a set of biochemical interactions could produce self-reproducing cells or more complicated life forms, which become agents in a new sort of system, the biological. A similar response may be engendered by the remarkable fact that the amazingly complex organ we call the brain manifests such diverse properties as cognition, awareness, rational decision-making, and a sense of self. Note that this response can have two foci, depending on whether one emphasizes the qualitatively emergent properties themselves or the complexity, regularity, and law-likeness of the underlying structures and processes that give rise to the novel properties. A third religious response in this category arises out of the recognition that the process of emergence is open-ended, that it leads beyond the known and normal toward emergent levels of reality, which may be altogether different from the world that we have known up to this point. A number of religiously oriented texts over the last several decades, and even some new religious movements, depend upon the belief that cultural evolution, and perhaps even cosmic evolution, is producing new and remarkable forms of reality, whether one speaks of the future in terms of the "Age of Aquarius" or the paranormal powers that Michael Murphy chronicles in *The Future of the Body*.[5] The enduring interest in the work of Samuel Alexander (1920) is surely related to the fact that he postulated the most radical possible form of emergence: the emergence of deity. Alexander was a naturalist who believed that only the natural world exists; and yet he argued that, as the universe evolves, it gradually takes on the properties formerly associated with deity (it "deizes" itself).

The final form of religious response to emergence involves the belief that emergent evolution as we perceive it is linked in some way to a transcendent ground, power, or mind. Those who respond in this way have the sense that the law-like order of nature somehow reflects the "mind of God."[6] The theistic worldview expressed in all three of the great Abrahamic traditions reflects the conviction that the amazing fecundity of natural evolution in the end expresses the intentional creative structuring of God. This response to the emerging world is only strengthened if one also holds that

5. Murphy, *The Future of the Body*.
6. Cf. Davies, *The Mind of God*.

God is also being affected by and responding to each new level of emergent reality, as occurs within the various versions of process and temporal theism.... On the Whiteheadian view, the "primordial nature" of God is responsible for providing the range of possibilities for evolution and the creative lure toward ever-greater complexity; the "consequent nature" of God then responds to each occasion of experience, internalizing and valuing all moments of emergent evolution in their distinctness and uniqueness.[7]

The religious response is further intensified for those who hold that the world is somehow located *within the divine*, as is maintained by recent versions of *panentheism*.[8] Panentheists maintain not only that the patterns of emergence are grounded in the divine order and that God continually responds to the evolutionary process, but also that the world is located within the divine presence. Standing closer to the classical metaphysical systems of the East, this view questions the notion of God creating a separate world, set over against the divine, although (in contrast to pantheism) it continues to understand God as also more than the world. Panentheists seek to formulate a single ontological vision rather than sharply separating the becoming of the world from the timelessness and aseity of the divine being. As a result, the emergent processes and features of the world become religiously significant in and of themselves, and not only because of their divine origin or telos.

Given the various compatibilities just sketched, it is obvious that emergentist results in the sciences do not need to exclude all forms of theism. (Of course, if one endorses a completely naturalistic emergence theory, one will have to dispense with all non-naturalistic beings and forces, but in that case it's the naturalism that does the excluding, not the emergence theory as such.) The framework of emergence does however undercut some traditional forms of theism. It undercuts purely atemporal understandings of the God–world relationship, in so far as such views tend to underestimate the importance of time, process, and pervasive change within the natural world. It also at least indirectly undercuts static views of the divine nature, for it would be surprising, though not impossible, that a natural reality characterized by ubiquitous process and interconnection would be the result of a Creator whose nature is essentially non-relational and non-responsive.

It seems to me, finally, that emergence theory tends to undercut dogmatic knowledge claims about the nature of God. Such claims implicitly presuppose that one can have timeless knowledge, a view that implicitly lifts the epistemic agent above and hence out of the flow of history in which she is immersed. If emergence is right, our epistemic situation is constantly changing, in so far as we are products of a pervasive process of biological and cultural evolution. Acknowledging this fact should make one far more suspicious of any knowledge claims that imply, however tacitly, that the

---

7. Cf. Griffin, *Reenchantment Without Supernaturalism*.

8. Cf. Hartshorne, *The Divine Relativity*; and Clayton and Peacocke, eds. *In Whom We Live and Move*.

knower stands above the march of history and has direct and immediate access to timeless truths.[9]

In this final chapter I have sought to draw together some of the lines of reflection introduced in this volume. The book's essays were not intended to defend a single viewpoint, and the discerning reader will find clear and sometimes deep conceptual differences between them. Nonetheless, in presenting arguments for (and sometimes against) emergence across the scientific fields, the various contributions have raised an intriguing and significant possibility: an emergence-based view of the world that links together a wide variety of specific results and patterns. Moving beyond the particular scientific results is not mandated by science, of course, and nothing propels the bench scientist to engage in philosophical reflection of this sort. Yet the more successful emergence-based explanations become in the various particular sciences, the more one wonders what might be their broader significance. This closing chapter has offered one version of a philosophical theory of emergence, albeit certainly not the only possible version. Perhaps it has helped to establish the point that emergence theories, in whatever specific form they may be advanced, are not only of scientific, but also of philosophical and perhaps even religious, interest.

---

9. Obviously, there is much more to be said about the relations between emergence theory and theism in general, and Christian theism in particular. For a fuller statement on the former see Clayton, *The Problem of God in Modern Thought*, chapter 5; on the latter, see my contribution in Murphy and Stoeger, eds. *Emergence*.

26

Why Emergence Matters
A New Paradigm for Relating the Sciences[1]

The Concept of Emergence: A First Approximation

THE CONCEPT OF EMERGENCE is often presented by contrasting it with two alternative (and still widely held) views. According to *reductionist theories*, the phenomena studied by a given discipline are only scientifically (read: truly) understood when they can be expressed using the laws of a lower-level discipline. When scientific reduction is successful, the phenomena become a special case of the more general explanatory framework represented by those laws. If one seeks to reduce any given level to the level beneath it, one must eventually come down to the fundamental laws of physics, the bedrock of all else.

According to *dualist theories*, by contrast, there are gaps in the relations between the various disciplines, such that the reductionist ideal is impossible. Not only can phenomena of *mind or spirit* not be explained in terms of any lower-level laws, but dualists also challenge the claim that mind depends essentially on any of its physical or material substrates. Thus, dualists have classically held that minds are essentially different from bodies and can continue to exist without them. Minds do not rely on the physical energies that sustain bodies and allow them to move; instead they belong to a different ontological order altogether. . . .

---

1. "Why Emergence Matters: A New Paradigm for Relating the Sciences," as found within Philip Clayton, *Adventures in the Spirit: God, World, Divine Action*, 63–74. Reprinted with the kind permission of Fortress.

The Re-emergence of Emergence

... This new perspective goes under multiple names within specific sciences; "emergence" is . . . only an overarching rubric to describe many different research programs in many different sciences. Molecular biologists speak, for instance, of the emergence of a "network perspective," which is necessary for describing how particular types of chemical reactions are catalyzed by evolutionarily related enzymes.[2] The analogue of metabolic networks in the study of cells is *systems biology*, one of the largest growth areas in contemporary biology. Hiroaki Kitano describes its core assumption: "While an understanding of genes and proteins continues to be important, the focus [of systems biology] is on understanding a system's structure and dynamics. Because a system is not just an assembly of genes and proteins, its properties cannot be fully understood merely by drawing diagrams of their interconnections."[3]

In cell biology, what was at first merely a way of expressing reservations about purely gene-driven analyses ("epigenesis" or "epigenetic factors") has become a rigorous study of "system-level insights" in its own right.[4] As Kitano writes, "a transition is occurring in biology from the molecular level to the system level that promises to revolutionize our understanding of complex biological regulatory systems and to provide major new opportunities for practical application of such knowledge."[5] And in an interesting review in *Science*, Kevin Laland baptizes the new approach as "the new interactionism," which describes "how genes are triggered into action by environmental events; how they switch other genes on and off; how they guide neurons to build brains; and how learning operates through gene expression."[6]

The new interactionism goes between the horns of the classical dilemmas, "genes *versus* environment" and "nature *versus* nurture." Indeed, these new perspectives may defuse one further classical dilemma: the dilemma between "upward" and "downward" causation. Reductionists have generally held that all causal influences occur at the level of microphysics; these effects, taking place within highly complex systems, are said to account for the deceptive appearance that distinctively biological or psychological causes exist. In opposition to them, idealists and Cartesian dualists protested that there is a distinct type of cause, mental causes, which are different in kind from physical causes, are not dependent on them, and which exercise their own form of causal agency in the world. But from the systems or interactionist perspective, the entire dichotomy appears to be mistaken. Causality is "circular"; it involves interacting effects between different levels of natural organization, e.g., between the microscopic and the macroscopic. . . .

---

2. Alves, Chaleil and Sternberg, "Evolution of Enzymes in Metabolism," 751–70.
3. See Kitano, "Systems Biology: A Brief Overview," 1662–64.
4. Kitano, "Systems Biology: A Brief Overview," 1664.
5. Ibid.
6. See Laland, "The New Interactionism," 1879–80, drawing on Ridley, *Nature via Nurture*.

PART IV: Science & Emergence

What Makes Emergence Scientific?

It is one thing to speculate about emergence as part of a metaphysical theory, and something else to claim scientific support for the framework of emergence. Although I believe such claims are justified, they bring with them unique challenges.

As long as one continues to do science, one attempts to draw the closest possible connections between the set of phenomena, which one is studying, and the lower-level laws that are available. The scientific study of chemistry is impossible, for example, without its connections to physics; to study the origins of life *means* to try to explain the transition from non-reproducing biochemical molecules to reproducing life forms (and if one could understand life in terms of biochemistry, so much the better); and to understand an animal's behavior scientifically *just is* to explain as much of it as possible in terms of the body's morphology, hormone releases, selective pressures, and the like. The quest to explain phenomena in terms of reconstructible, testable causal systems is so basic to the project of science that we could almost use it as *the* defining characteristic of science.

The phenomenon of emergence makes this project more difficult, but it does not eliminate it. If it had turned out to be possible to explain higher-order phenomena in terms of lower-order laws across the scientific disciplines, then science would be in the position fully to achieve the goal in terms of which it is defined. Even if, as emergence theorists believe, the natural world is such that this downward reduction is often impossible in principle, the goal does not simply disappear, to be replaced by a happy-go-lucky holism. One can still determine the scientific or non-scientific status of a theory about the world by the continued presence of this goal, viz. to connect the phenomena of one level as closely and precisely as possible with the phenomena at the next lower level.

Consider two concrete examples. Walter Elsasser, in his classic *Reflections on a Theory of Organisms*,[7] makes the case for the autonomy of biological explanations. Elsasser believes that the "information stability" of living things cannot be reduced to the physico-chemical stability of molecules. Alongside this emergentist manifesto, however, Elsasser is careful to show how the scientific study of life forms is still possible. He does not argue for the untestability of biological theories, for example, but rather for the necessity of utilizing different kinds of tests. It's just that biological causality "cannot be fully verified by the standard procedure of the physicist or chemist," that is, by "measurement followed by mathematical extrapolation, technically called integration, of the equations of quantum mechanics that govern molecular motion."[8]

Moreover, Elsasser gives very precise, empirical reasons for a certain autonomy of biology, which he defines in a precise and rigorous fashion. Thus, his fourth chapter

---

7. Elsasser, *Reflections on a Theory of Organisms*. Unless otherwise noted, the in-text citations refer to this title.

8. Ibid., 142.

demonstrates how an immense number of molecular configurations are compatible with a given set of physico-chemical constraints. Even if the structure and dynamics of all molecules can be understood by applying quantum mechanical principles, "a cell is much too complex to admit of meaningful analysis in such terms."[9] Because of this "combinatorial explosion" (Harold Morowitz), it is demonstrably impossible to compute cell behavior in quantum-physical terms. Likewise, in a later chapter, Elsasser describes how physicists study stable systems (those in which each mode of motion is stable) and then come to understand what happens when the system is perturbated. All biological systems, by contrast, are massively unstable; they are, in Stuart Kauffman's beautiful expression, always existing "at the edge of chaos."[10] Hence it is not possible to understand them by extrapolation from stable systems and through computation of each perturbation—which is to say: it's impossible to understand them physically. Elsasser states, "Owing to the amplificatory effect, the ultimate changes are no longer predictable."[11] Elsasser concludes that "the morphological future of such [biological] systems [is] unpredictable on the basis of physics and chemistry."[12]

Finally, Elsasser remains committed to the scientific study of biological phenomena, even in light of this unpredictability. He emphasizes that biological results "cannot differ from any known rule of physics and chemistry."[13] He continues to emphasize the importance of structure (morphology) and function as basic to testable biological theories. And he does not advance biological holism as a way of avoiding tests and experiments, but rather as representing a call for a new type of testability: "if the holistic properties are to be verified experimentally, a different type of experiment from that conventionally used by physicists and chemists is required."[14]

Elsasser thus represents a paradigm example of scientific emergence. Under the influence of this example, Morowitz, comments, "emergence requires pruning rules to reduce the transcomputable to the computable; . . . in both Elsasser's approach and [John] Holland's view, biology requires its own laws that are not necessarily derivable from physics, but do not contradict the physical foundations."[15]

Contrast this careful demonstration of how emergence remains a part of the scientific project with the approach to emergence taken by B. C. Goodwin and Rupert Sheldrake. Both thinkers wish to appeal to what they call "morphogenetic fields" and "morphic resonance." Goodwin explicitly refuses to interpret the morphogenetic field in terms of any known forces: "electrical forces can affect it . . . but I would not wish to suggest that [it] is essentially electrical. Chemical substances" can affect it, yet it

9. Elsasser, *Reflections on a Theory of Organisms,* 52.
10. Kauffman develops these ideas in *Investigations* and *At Home in the Universe.*
11. Elsasser, *Reflections on a Theory of Organisms,* 105.
12. Ibid., 142.
13. Ibid., 148.
14. Ibid., 148.
15. Morowitz, "The Emergence of Intermediary Metabolism," 4.

is not "essentially chemical or biochemical in nature." He is nonetheless certain that morphogenetic fields "play a primary role in the developmental process."[16] Similarly, Sheldrake postulates "patterns of oscillatory activity" throughout the world, which he calls morphic resonance.[17] Resonances are strongest, he is sure, with one's own past, somewhat weaker with genetically similar animals, and weaker still with animals from other races. Apparently, though, some resonance still exists between all living things. A genuinely scientific theory of morphic resonances looks unlikely, however, since like Goodwin he is loath to tie them to any known forces. . . .

Unfortunately, this kind of (alleged) testability is not sufficient to make a theory scientific. It's equally crucial that the theories in question specify their connections with the existing body of scientific knowledge. In addition to meeting this condition, a theory of scientific emergence must provide details, given as much as possible in terms of lower-level theories, that show why a given set of phenomena would be irreducible to those theories. When somebody suggests, as Sheldrake does, that there are both energetic and non-energetic fields, it is difficult to see how connections can be drawn with any scientific field theory.

The Logic of Scientific Emergence

Terrence Deacon offers the clearest expression of the logic of scientific emergence available today; it is therefore valuable to consider his recent proposals in some detail. Deacon begins with the empirical evidence that "complex dynamical ensembles can spontaneously assume ordered patterns of behavior that are not prefigured in the properties of their component elements or in their interaction patterns."[18] On his view, only emergence theories can adequately interpret and explain this type of self-organization.

Not all emergences are identical, however. Deacon is the first to have identified three distinct "orders" of emergence. First-order emergence involves the appearance of new properties in the aggregate that are not present in the individual particles. Deacon draws his primary examples from quantum theory and statistical thermodynamics, though he admits that even simpler examples can be adduced, such as how the properties of water molecules produce liquid properties. He writes, "Although the nature of the wave and its detailed underlying dynamical realization in each [particular wave] may differ depending on whether the fluid is water, air, or an electromagnetic field, the ability to propagate a wave is a first-order emergent feature they all share in common."[19] As with the other two "orders" of emergence, Deacon is careful to specify exactly what are the conditions under which this kind of emergence will occur. Thus

---

16. Goodwin, "On Morphogenetic fields," 109–14, cited in Sheldrake, *A New Science of Life*
17. Sheldrake, *A New Science of Life*, 170.
18. Deacon, "The Hierarchic Logic of Emergence," 273–308.
19. Ibid., 290.

he argues, for example, that "it is only when certain of the regularities of molecular interaction relationships add up rather than cancel one another that certain *between-molecule* relationships can produce aggregate behaviors with ascent in scale."[20] In second-order emergence, specific perturbations of a system are amplified, resulting in types of causal effects not seen in the first order. In the formation of snow crystals, for example, the specific temperature and humidity present at each stage of the crystal's descent through the air are "recorded" in the emerging structure of the crystal as it evolves; these features then influence its subsequent structural formation. The structural features emerging at a given point are amplified, in other words, such that they affect all subsequent crystal growth. These "feed-forward circles of cause and effect" are distinctive of this new type of emergent property. Deacon offers detailed examples, drawing from "self-undermining (divergent) chaotic systems, as in turbulent flow, and self-organizing (partially convergent) chaotic systems."[21] Second-order emergence is also found in the so-called autopoietic systems. This type of emergence works not just by aggregating individual components (say, molecules); here systematic features play a causal role. Put differently, forms or structures, and not merely particles, become the operative links in the feed-forward cycle.

Third-order emergence shares this feature from the previous order. Yet now what is passed on is *information or memory*, not merely forms and structures. As a result, Deacon argues, . . . the classic example of third-order emergence is the self-reproducing cell. Cells exhibit features not present in pre-biological physical systems; they contain information—specifically, information sufficient for building other cells like themselves. The information is stored within a boundary (the cell wall), which allows the cell as a whole to function as an entity in its own right on which environmental forces act. Because cells can make copies of themselves in ways that pre-biotic structures cannot, the forces of natural selection can begin to operate for the first time. A cell thus becomes a sort of hypothesis about what informational structure will survive and reproduce most effectively in a given environment. If the cell exists in an environment congenial to its existence, it will make more successful copies of itself than its rivals and come to prosper in its ecosystem. Deacon describes this process as "a sort of self-referential self-organization, an autopoiesis of autopoieses."[22] As a result, cells can only be understood through "a combination of multi-scale, historical, and semiotic analyses. . . . This is why living and cognitive processes require us to introduce concepts such as representation, adaptation, information, and function in order to capture the logic of the most salient emergent phenomena."[23]

Only third-order emergent processes in evolution have the capacity "to progressively embed [other] evolutionary processes within one another via representations

---

20. Deacon, "The Hierarchic Logic of Emergence," 288.
21. Ibid., 295.
22. Ibid., 299.
23. Ibid., 300.

that amplify their information-handling power."[24] Indeed, the process of emergence does not stop with the first self-reproducing cell. Under evolutionary selection pressures, natural systems continue to increase in complexity, discovering ever-new ways of "making a living" (as Stuart Kauffman likes to say) in the world. In Deacon's masterful study, *The Symbolic Species*,[25] for example, he traces the co-evolution of brains and language or culture. Language use, of course, remains dependent on a complex brain and central nervous system, but language can never be reduced to an instinct (Steven Pinker) or a mere byproduct of brain processes; the two evolving phenomena mutually influence one another. The result is a continual growth in complexity of both of them. For example, Deacon argues, language moves from the "iconic" mode of representation to a more complex form of reference involving indexicals, and finally (in *homo sapiens*) to the rich symbolic modes of representation that are the bread and butter of human cultural existence.

In Defense of Strong Emergence

One finds in the literature an ongoing battle between weaker and stronger versions of emergence theory. The more robust version, which I have labeled "strong emergence" and defended in *Mind and Emergence,* makes two claims. First, new *things* emerge in natural history, not just new properties of some fundamental things or stuff; and, second, these emergent things exercise their own types of causal power. Such "downward causation" occurs at many different levels in nature. Strong emergence is a thesis about the nature of natural evolution.

Of course, interpretations of evolution are fraught with controversy. If evolution is really "all about the genes," as Richard Dawkins seeks to convince us, then all evolved structures are nothing more than expressions of this same fundamental dynamic. However rich and staggeringly diverse these manifestations are, they can and should still be understood from a gene-centric perspective. If, on the other hand, the dualists are right, then at some point in the evolutionary process one encounters a radical, ontological break: mind arises. In this sense, dualists remain at heart Cartesians: one can study the entire physical world from atoms to chimpanzees with the same set of mechanistic explanatory tools; but as soon as one turns to man and woman, who alone possess *res cogitans*, a new explanatory tool box is required, one that, they insist, relies instead on the nature of souls and the eternal Laws of Thought.

24. Ibid., 305.

25. Deacon, *The Symbolic Species*. See also Oltvai and Barabási, "Life's Complexity Pyramid," 763–64. Barabási is best known for his popular presentation, *Linked*; for a more technical presentation see Barabási and Albert, "Emergence of Scaling in Random Networks," 509–12. Note that embracing the core principles of network theory does not mean that it will lead to "an accurate mathematical theory of human behavior," as Barabási claims in "Network Theory," 639–41.

In contrast to both views, emergence claims that the story of evolution is one of continuity *and* discontinuity. Continuity first: everything in the natural world is composed of the same "stuff" of matter and energy, and no new substances are added along the way. This means no souls and no personal substances—a difficult entailment for some religious persons. When one pursues the scientific project, one seeks to develop a continuity of understanding to the greatest possible extent. But sharing the scientist's "natural piety" for the world *as it actually expresses itself empirically* also means that one works with whatever explanatory framework best explains the data at present—as long as it is testable and can demonstrate its explanatory superiority over its rivals.

Practicing this natural piety—this commitment to study the world in whatever ways it presents itself to us—means that we are not merely biologists *simplicitur*, much less geneticists only. We are cytologists, systems biologists, botanists, zoologists, primatologists. We are not only molecular biologists and geneticists, but also population biologists and ecosystem theorists. We are interested in the large and complex as much as in the small, in emergent phenomena as well as reducible phenomena. This, I suggest, was the mind set that lay behind Charles Darwin's great breakthroughs....

Conclusion

What Darwin could only envision in 1858 had become scientific reality by the end of the twentieth century. In one sense, discovering complex systems is just "science as usual"; the new systems biology provides causal explanations of natural systems, which are then empirically tested and verified. In another sense, however, emergence represents a new way of doing and understanding science. It is science without reductionism. Now systems of emergent phenomena are understood not only in terms of lower-level laws and processes, but equally in terms of the higher-level systems that constrain their functioning and their outcomes. The science is complicated; there are many more subtleties in the study of emergent phenomena than we have covered here. But enough is on the table for one to see that the results are potentially of revolutionary significance for our understanding of human religion and religious belief....

27

Theological Reflections on Emergence
From Emergent Nature to the Emerging Church[1]

An Emergent Theology in Outline

CHRISTIAN THEOLOGIANS HAVE ALWAYS drawn on the conceptual frameworks or philosophical systems available in their day. True, scripture and traditional affirmations (e.g., the creeds) constrained the answers that were given, and theologians returned again and again to a central set of questions (the questions of Peter Lombard, the major systematic *loci* of Phillip Melanchthon). As the modern era progressed, however, and as new scientific knowledge emerged, many theologians came to believe that the philosophical frameworks that had once guided systematic theologians were no longer adequate.[2] The story of modern theology is the story of finding new answers to the traditional questions in light of things humanity has learned over the last several hundred years.

I agree that there is a core set of topics that a Christian theology is expected to address: Christology, pneumatology, ecclesiology, eschatology, and so forth. But the scaffolding—the organizing framework that one uses to respond to these questions—is not given once and for all; theology is "always reformed, always reforming." It remains valuable to see how the use of new frameworks and organizing principles affects the answers one gives to the classic questions. Hence, I would now like to ask: What would a systematic theology look like if developed out of the context of emergent thinking?

---

1. "Theological Reflections on Emergence: From Emergent Nature to the Emerging Church," as found within Clayton, *Adventures in the Spirit: God, World, Divine Action*, 100–105. Reprinted with the kind permission of Fortress.

2. In *The Problem of God in Modern Thought*, I tried to show why philosophical systems do matter to systematic theology and why modern thinkers were right to search for new ones.

How would one be inclined to respond to the traditional *loci* using the framework of emerging systems?

Consider these responses to nine of the traditional *loci*:

1. *The doctrine of creation*

The doctrine of the created world is the place where the whole range of scientific data concerning emergent systems can be incorporated. It is not the place of a theological doctrine of creation to take the place of science but to acknowledge its findings.[3] Thus, all the scientific detail on emergent systems in evolution found elsewhere in this book and in other publications[4] becomes relevant to a revised doctrine of creation.

Emergent thinking represents a sort of upwardly ascending arrow, since it is hard to avoid the meta-scientific questions that it raises. Is there a further stage of emergence beyond the level of mind, such as spirituality or spirit? Is mind utterly without precedent, or does emerging mind reflect something of the nature of whatever Cause preceded the Big Bang and helped to produce it? If mind is not a strange anomaly in the universe but somehow reflects the nature of its ultimate Source, could it be that the Source also includes other personal qualities—or, at least, that it is not-less-than personal, as I argued in the previous chapter? If so, might that Source, *qua* personal cause, not also have intentions regarding the evolution of the universe, and might it sometimes act in such a way as to further those purposes? The fusion of emergent systems and belief in a Creator God, I have argued, represents the strongest available answer to these questions.

2. *The doctrine of God*

As I will argue in more detail [later in this book], the doctrine of God that best allows belief in divine action to be synthesized with modern science in general, and with the sciences of emergence in particular, is panentheism.[5] Panentheism is frequently defined as the theological view that the world is in some sense contained within God, although God is also more than the world.[6] . . .

---

3. Cf. Pannenberg, *Systematic Theology*, vol. 2, chap. 7.

4. For a summary of the sciences of emergence, see Clayton and Davies, eds., *The Reemergence of Emergence*. Oxford has also recently published Morowitz, *The Emergence of Everything*; and Gregersen, ed., *From Complexity to Life*. The Oxford volumes were preceded by a series of influential books on emergence and science, including Holland's *Emergence: From Chaos to Order*; Lewin's *Complexity*; Barabási's *Linked*; Johnson's *Emergence*; Freeman's *The Emergence of Consciousness*; Taylor's, *The Moment of Complexity;* and especially Deacon's *The Symbolic Species*. I summarize the data in *Mind and Emergence*, chapter 3.

5. See my *God and Contemporary Science* and *The Problem of God in Modern Thought*.

6. I have traced the philosophical foundations of panentheism in *The Problem of God in Modern Thought* and have applied it to the question of divine action in *God and Contemporary Science*. In three

Note that panentheism is consistent with most of the traditional attributes of God. No major modifications need to be made to traditional understandings of divine wisdom, goodness, love, grace, mercy, long-suffering, righteousness, or veracity. The doctrines of divine omnipotence and sovereignty do however need to be modified, insofar as panentheism implies that God has freely chosen to limit God's a priori omnipotence in order to allow other free centers of conscious agency to come into being. Features of the created world that might have been otherwise, such as certain of the laws of nature, represent free divine decisions. But if God is to remain consistent with God's own nature, God is now constrained by those decisions, which means that God's present power is further limited. Even more clearly, the doctrine of God's immutability can no longer be asserted of God unequivocally. The primordial nature of God is indeed unchanging, but the personal responsive side of God is genuinely emergent, in the sense that it comes to encompass new experiences as it enters into new relations with creatures. . . .

3. The God–world relation and divine action

We return to the divine-action debate in more detail [later in this book], but a first sketch of the position is essential here. Several decades of work on the divine action question have resulted in some very clear constraints. Doctrines of creation have always held that, if God exists, God must be viewed in some way as the ultimate source of the natural world. Yet a world that is to provide a stable context for intentional action will need to possess its own integrity and order. On the one hand, if one wishes to preserve the doctrine of providence, one must retain the language of a divine lure. On the other hand, if one moves from that conclusion to affirming a divine manipulation of physical events and human decisions, such that God sometimes directly brings about results in the natural world without the mediation of natural ("secondary") causes, the problem of evil becomes insurmountable . . . for there are innumerable events in the world that a benevolent God would presumably prevent if free and able to do so. Furthermore, as we will see below, if we imagine that God can suspend natural law at will, both the integrity of the natural order and the significance of human action are called into question.

. . . The beauty of panentheism is that, if it is right, the energies at work at the physical level are *already* divine energies, and physical regularities are already expressions of the fundamental constancy of the divine character (as Eastern Orthodox theologians have long taught).[7] Thus, I believe that panentheism brings an indispens-

---

articles in *Dialog* over the last few years I have begun to work out a Christian panentheistic theology: "The Case for Christian Panentheism," 201–8; "A Response to My Critics"; and "Panentheist Internalism," 208–15. Most recently see Peacocke and Clayton, eds., *In Whom We Live*.

7. See the Orthodox contributions to Clayton and Peacocke, *In Whom We Live and Move and Have Our Being*.

able framework to the study of emergent systems, for if the world remains within and is permeated by the divine, then it is possible to speak of divine purposes and goals being expressed even at the stage at which there are no other actually conscious agents. Even the lawful behavior of the natural world can now be an expression or manifestation of the divine character or intentionality....

As organisms evolve and begin to behave in more complex ways, panentheism allows one to speak of a category of divine action that is not merely autonomic—that is, not completely explicable as a mechanical result of God's autonomic agency—but that nevertheless stops short of focal purpose. We can speak of the central features of the biological realm as reflecting the divine character and influence without claiming that kidneys or amoebas themselves possess the goals of functioning as they do. After all, actual purposes can be predicated only of purposive beings; a colony of bacteria functions in a purposive manner without possessing actual purposes. The colony behaves *as if* it really desired to nourish itself and grow, but it does not desire growth in the conscious way that you might now desire a glass of orange juice.

Herein lies the crux of a theological interpretation of the natural world. Like physical regularities, emergent biological regularities reflect the divine character; yet here, because organisms also behave in a purposive manner, there is a place for speaking of divine influence in principle. The influence in question must be intermediate between the conscious influence that is possible in relation to conscious beings and the apparent impossibility of influence (outside of natural law) in physics. If biological organisms are indeed more than machines, and if it is correct to ascribe drives, strivings, and non-conscious goals to them, then there is room for influence on these goals....

4. Christology

Emergent thinking links most naturally with a kenotic Christology, that is, a doctrine of Christ that emphasizes his voluntary self-emptying in the sense of Philippians 2. According to kenotic Christologies, Jesus remains both a revelation of the nature of God and an exemplar for humanity in a no less profound sense than in classical theology. In this Christology, Jesus actualized a potentiality that each human enjoys as one who is made in the image of God, living a life of perfect devotion to God and acknowledging the true relationship of creature to Creator in every thought and action. Panentheists believe that all are located within the divine presence in no less a sense than Jesus was. But gaps remain between what God wills and what we will; this is the core insight of the doctrine of sin. By contrast, according to Christian belief, no such gaps existed in the life of Jesus; he alone perfectly lived a life of perfect union with God.

In the more liberal forms of emergent theology, one finds affirmations of the resurrection of "the Spirit of Christ" but not a physical resurrection of the individual man Jesus. The act of God that produces the resurrection raises the Spirit of Christ, the Spirit or Counselor "whom the Father will send in my name, [who] will teach you all things and will remind you of everything I have said to you" (John 14:26). Because of this act of God, after Jesus' death the "mind of Christ"—Jesus' surrender of his will to the Father's will, for which God "highly exalted him" (Phil 2:9)—remained available to his disciples and later to their followers in the church.

What is attractive about this approach to Christology is that it already incorporates the divine act into Jesus' God-consciousness. It is not as if there is a description of Jesus' will and actions on the one hand and, on the other, a separate metaphysical superstructure of divine intervention added on top of it. Instead, to describe the historical Jesus as I have done *just is* to give an account of divine involvement. In virtue of continually subsuming his will to the divine will, Jesus caused his actions to become *part of* the divine act. There are not two actions, but one: Jesus manifests the divine power by subsuming his will to God's; at the same time (or for the same reason, or in virtue of the same act), God acted through Jesus to manifest God's will and bring about God's intentions.

This fusion of human and divine is what was right about traditional "two natures" Christologies and the traditional doctrine of "incarnation"; it is just that emergent theologians now locate the fusion in *shared action and attitude* rather than in some a priori ontological story. As process theologians describe divine action as "the lure of God" (Lewis Ford), and as traditional theology refuses to separate the act of God and the revelation of God, we too might understand God to be genuinely revealed through human agents who seek to submit themselves to God's will.[8] . . .

5. Pneumatology

The understanding of Spirit is central to emergent theology. Insofar as they accept the emergence of mind and spirit within evolutionary history, these theologies diverge from panpsychist and panexperientialist positions, which make Spirit an inherent element of the world from the beginning. We likewise eschew all dichotomies between Spirit and matter or between Spirit and body, following the lead of emergent theories of human personhood. Even if the divine Spirit precedes all creation, every manifestation of Spirit in the world depends essentially on the evolutionary process.

Nor can the divine Spirit be a timeless entity standing immutably outside the flow of cosmic history. That aspect of the divine being—call it Spirit—that correlates with the spirit of which we have knowledge in ourselves must also be temporal, the emergent result of a long-term process of intimate relationship with beings in the world. On this view, then, Spirit is not a fundamental ontological category but an emergent form of complexity that living things within the world begin to manifest

---

8. As a woman described it to me recently at a Quaker Meeting, "Perhaps God's only act is to make manifest the divine love. Is this not enough?"

at a certain stage in their development. A theological corrective must be made to the "straight emergence" view, however: the Spirit that emerges corresponds to the Spirit who was present from the beginning; and this Spirit's actions—both its initial creation and its continual lure—help bring about the world and its inhabitants as we know them. Insofar as this emergent theology remains panentheistic, it holds that the physical world was already permeated by and contained within the Spirit of God long before cosmic evolution gives rise to life and mind....

6. *Anthropology*

In light of the foregoing points it is clear that the doctrine of anthropology will play a larger role than in many traditional theologies. As we saw above in connection with the knowledge of God, emergent theology begins with an understanding of human beings as bio-cultural agents in the context of evolutionary history. Our bio-cultural existence gives us some initial understanding of the nature of God as agent, though it must then be "corrected" to be appropriate to the role of God as the ground and destiny of all things. In other words, emergent theology (like other forms of dipolar theism) includes two stages: the stage of deriving what can be known of the divine agent through our own experience of agency (the consequent nature), and the stage of modifying that understanding in order that it can be appropriate to the nature of a creator who preceded the universe as a whole (the antecedent nature)....

7. *Ecclesiology*

The church is defined, as formerly, in terms of those who follow Christ and live "in Christ." But the church, like all finite things in general, is an emergent and emerging reality. Thus the original horizon of understanding cannot control all present understandings of the church, its founder, and its role.[9] Because Jesus remains the exemplar of *kenosis*, the reports on and early interpretations of his life and teachings remain crucial....

If the church is an emergent and continually emerging community, it shares a situation and fate with all of humanity. Emergent theologians refuse to separate God from the world in the interest of preserving the divine purity; hence for similar reasons they decline to fundamentally separate the church from the world.... A fitting theology for the emerging church will seek not to be more-than-human, but to be human in light of that toward which humanity is being lured; not to be anti-scientific, but to find through science some intimations of the nature of God; not to be anti-intellectual, but to be more insightfully intellectual; not to eschew human moral reflection

---

9. One will note overtones of the "two horizons" hermeneutics of Gadamer's *Truth and Method*.

and striving, but to incorporate that striving within a theistic framework; not to be world-transcending, but to embrace a world that is in turn embraced by God.

8. Soteriology

An emergent theology will begin not with a specific narrative of fall and redemption, but (as Paul Tillich did) with the structural difference between God and creation, between infinite and finite, between perfect and imperfect. As we saw in considering anthropology, emergent theology embraces the descriptive account of the human being but supplements it with a normative account of how humankind will look when it is true to its nature as *imago Dei*. This structural difference, and not the primordial myth of an original offense and punishment, provides the basis for introducing the concept of sin. The narrative of the fall remains indispensable for its symbolic functions but is not doctrinally foundational. As Tillich also saw, the structural difference between infinite and finite is mirrored in an intense existential experience of sin. Not only with our minds do we conceive the structural difference between God and ourselves, for every human being knows *akrasia* (weakness of will), self-centeredness, and the inability to do as one wishes to do (as potently described by Paul in Rom 7).

An emergent theology cannot endorse an absolute dichotomy between the "old man" and the "new man" of the sort sometimes presupposed in the Pauline doctrine of salvation. Emergence thinking is anti-dualistic, seeking always for the continuities that underlie even the appearance of radical novelty in the world. We no longer need to divide the world into two sharply opposed camps, the reprobate and the redeemed. Rather, the doctrine of salvation now takes on a structure closer to the traditional doctrine of *sanctification*: the new self, the mind of Christ, is continually emerging as individuals align their wills with the will of God. Such an alignment is a matter of *degree*. The process of living more and more of one's life in greater and greater conformity to the will of God is a gradual and never-ending process. . . . I find no place within emergent theology for substitutionary atonement, ransom metaphors, or the focus on the need for a sacrifice to propitiate the wrath of an angry God.

9. Eschatology

According to Wolfhart Pannenberg, the end of history already took place in the death and resurrection of Jesus Christ ("*prolepsis*"), such that the outcome is already certain. Eschatology is not less important for emergent theologians, though they are likely to view precise predictions of the final outcome as rather less certain. We affirm that God set the process of emergence in motion, intending that the creation would take on higher and higher levels of complexity, and hence more subtle and intimate relationships with the divine, thereby allowing more and more of the nature of God to be experienced by the creation. Still, the present understanding of the process of emergence does not provide much information on the ultimate culmination of this historical process, in which God brings all things to Godself.

Nonetheless, were history merely to end with the "heat death" of the universe, it would be rather difficult to conceive what God might have intended by creating these emergent processes at the outset, only to allow them to be condemned in the end to ultimate futility. Why would God engage in relationship with this world—a relationship that on our view affects the very being of God—if the whole process will one day simply evaporate into nothingness? It is the impossibility of resting content with such a response that intensifies the hope of Christians (and others) for a future of the universe in which God becomes "all in all."

Panentheism fits naturally in such an eschatological perspective. John Polkinghorne has argued that only at the end of time can we conceive a state where all things are within God and God is all things.[10] I disagree with his contention that such a panentheistic closeness must be confined to the end of history, but I do concur that panentheism presupposes a telos in which the world conforms more and more fully to the divine character. . . .

According to classic versions of process theology stemming from Whitehead's *Process and Reality*, the only thing one can reasonably hope for is "objective immortality," that is, that all of one's thoughts, feelings, and individual reactions will be preserved eternally in the unchanging and unending experience of God. Marjorie Suchocki has sought to extend Whitehead's thought so that it can include also subjective immortality, the continuing existence of the individual subjective principle.[11] Whether or not Suchocki is successful in integrating the hope for subjective immortality with process eschatology, she has correctly seen that the eschaton must be conceived in such a fashion that it remains relevant to individual agents in the present. . . .

---

10. See Polkinghorne, *The God of Hope and the End of the World*. Tillich also famously held this position (*Systematic Theology*, vol. 3), as have many mystical theologians through the ages.

11. See Suchocki, *The End of Evil*; and Bracken, *World Without End: Christian Eschatology from a Process Perspective* that evaluates and extends Suchocki's process eschatology.

PART V

Science, Spirit, & Divine Action

28

Scientific Causality, Divine Causality[1]

Divine Action in an Age of Science

WE HAVE SEEN THAT the history of theism has developed in two major stages. First came the development of what we have called radical monotheism out of polytheism. Later the question of the relationship of this God to the world had to be thought through again in light of the unmistakable successes of science. Unfortunately, in the process the equation of pantheism with atheism and materialism led to a suspicion of, even hostility toward, all views that drew a close link between God and the world. This suspicion delayed the development of panentheism for several centuries, as evidenced in the overreaction of Western thinkers against the pantheism of Spinoza's metaphysics. In recent years, as we saw, the strengths of panentheism—its ability to satisfy both the biblical revelation and the demands of philosophy have come to the fore.

Along with the question of God's ontological relation to the world comes the question of God's activity in the world. The latter topic, like the debate between classical theism and panentheism, boils down to a fundamental distinction within the theistic camp: that between theism and deism. All agree that it will not be enough for traditional Christian theology if God's only role is to initiate the creation of the world in the beginning but to have no influence on it after that point. Yet many are drawn to (forced to?) deism, the view that God has no further causal influence on the world beyond creation, because of the difficulty of conceiving actual causal incursions ("interventions") of God into the world. As we have seen, not only science but also some theological arguments tell against such a model. Clearly, it is an urgent task for the theologian to provide a clear account of what she means by asserting that God continues to be active in the world....

---

1. "Scientific Causality, Divine Causality," as found within Clayton, *God and Contemporary Science*, 188–219. Reprinted with the kind permission of Eerdmans.

PART V: Science, Spirit, & Divine Action

The changed context for divine action

The present-day crisis in the notion of divine action has resulted as much as anything from a shift in the notion of causation. In pre-mechanistic science, science dominated by the influence of Aristotle, a component of divine causal action or teleology was included in every action. Thus, Thomas Aquinas insisted that every event involved not only the efficient cause (what we would now speak of as the cause of an occurrence), but also the formal and material causes, or the influence of the matter, and the form on the outcome. As a fourth type of causality, Thomas stressed the role of "final causes," that is, the overall purposes of God, which act as one of the causal forces in every event.

It is true that some contemporary theologians have attempted to preserve something like this "final" type of causality. One of the most sophisticated representatives is Wolfhart Pannenberg. In chapter 4 of *Theology and the Kingdom of God*, he adopts something like Aristotelian final causality, speaking of the power of the future as a causal constituent in every event. A similar adaptation or version of final causality is visible in Lewis Ford's "lure of the future," a notion that he adapts from Whitehead. Thomistic overtones can also be heard in theories of divine action that distinguish between primary and secondary causality indirectly in the work of Austin Farrer and more directly in the writings of David Burrell.

Such defenses of "future causality" in one guise or another cannot be quickly dismissed as metaphysical non-starters. Nonetheless, one must still ask whether a primary focus on God's causal activity as emerging from the future can do justice to the changed way of thinking about causality that has dominated scientific theories of the world for the last three hundred years. When a full explanation of a physical event is given in terms of the causal forces that brought it about (efficient causality), this is generally taken as an adequate explanation of the event. . . . That is, we do not take it that, in addition to the explanation of a physical event in terms of physical causes, it is also necessary to explain it in terms of cosmic purposes. One may wish eventually to challenge this widespread tendency, but one can only do so once one has understood how strong its hold is on modern thought.

The shift in thinking just described creates a completely different context for theological reflection on divine action. More precisely, it forces on the theologian a new set of alternatives. It would now appear, at least at first blush, that either God acts as the Divine Architect, who created a finely tuned machine and left it to function in a perfect manner expressive of its Designer, or God becomes the Divine Repairman, whose imperfect building of the machine in the first place requires him, like an inept refrigerator repairman, to return from time to time to fix up errors he made the first time around. Though perhaps not impossible, it is certainly difficult to recreate the pre-scientific framework or to develop an alternative one that allows one, alongside the network of scientific explanations, to speak of another causal system which is equally constitutive of the events in question.

Easy interventions, difficult interventions

It is not difficult to construct a continuum of types of intervention. For Christian theism, the easiest type of divine activity to introduce is creation. Contemporary cosmology allows us to think of some source for the Big Bang. Since that source exists at a moment prior to space and time as we know them, by definition no physical constraints can be placed upon it. (This assumes that the Big Bang is a "singularity," an event that is not an instantiation of any more all-encompassing physical laws.) Thus, it is fully open to theology to speak of a divine cause of all that is. . . . The next easiest type of divine involvement to maintain is "conservation," or God's role in sustaining the universe. Since the notion of sustaining is a metaphysical notion, it does not interfere with any particular natural scientific account. No natural law or natural explanation is changed or challenged when we add, "and making all of these interactions possible is the continual will of God that the universe continue in existence." . . .

The next easiest type of intervention to talk about is a psychological intervention. It is easier to maintain that God "brought" the needy individual to the church service than it is to argue that God fixed the furnace apart from any human agency. The reason for the difference is that we do not possess (at present) laws of human behavior; social scientists can ascertain at most broad patterns of human response, and even these admit an amazing variety of (personal and cultural) exceptions. In the human realm, uniqueness and idiosyncrasy are still the norm. Thus no laws are broken when we speak of an individual action in a non-standard way—indeed, this is almost what we mean by an individual action! . . .

Matters are very different in the natural realm, however. Here we possess an amazing variety of laws and powerful explanations of individual occurrences. We have already seen that it would be metaphysical prejudice to rule out any chance of direct divine action in the natural world; still, the evidence is on the side of regularity. Theological claims for divine action in the natural world are much more difficult to maintain than those that talk about God's influencing the thoughts, wishes, or decisions of an individual person.

The new theological task

To answer this crucial challenge, then, we must enter into the debate that has taken place over the last few years between theologians and scientists. If one is to offer a full theory of divine agency, one must include some account of where the "causal joint" is at which God's action directly impacts on the world. To do this requires one in turn to get one's hands dirty with the actual scientific data and theories, including the basic features of relativity theory, quantum mechanics, and (more recently) chaos theory. Fortunately, we do not need to begin at ground zero, for a number of theologians have been addressing these very questions in a high-profile debate over the last few years. Prominent among the forums has been the ongoing project of the Vatican Observatory and the Berkeley Center for Theology and the Natural Sciences, reflected in a five-volume series of books on the central questions of theology and science. . . .

For the scientist-theologians writing in this area, the most pressing issue is how to avoid de facto deism not merely by calling it unorthodox and expressing their dislike of it, but by actually showing why it is an unnecessary conclusion to draw from contemporary science. Most believe that Christian theologians must be in the position to say what they mean by God's activity in the world and how God's activity can be consistent with the belief that God has created a finite order with a goodness and a perfection of its own.

Finding Genuine Openness in the Physical World

Some of the most important recent approaches to thinking of God's causal activity in the physical world make use of the physics of the smallest particles, quantum mechanics. This is certainly a natural area for scientifically minded theologians to look at since, as the physicist Karl Young notes, "All current bets in physics are on a fundamental theory of the natural world being based essentially on relativity and quantum mechanics."[2] Remember that the question is not how to prove that God is active in the world at particular moments, but rather how to think this possibility in a manner that does not conflict with what we now know of the world. . . .

The answer of quantum mechanics

This is the reason why quantum physics seems to offer such a hopeful arena. For the most widely accepted interpretation of the equations of quantum probabilities holds that the limitations on our knowledge of quantum states are intrinsic to the world itself. It is not that better theories or measuring apparatus will someday allow us to specify the location and momentum of a subatomic particle with exact precision. Rather, there are good physical reasons to think that precise knowledge of this sort will never be possible (the Heisenberg uncertainty principle), in part because the amount of energy necessary for producing this measurement would change or eliminate the very state we were seeking to measure. . . .

There is another feature of the quantum approach that is attractive to the theologian: scientists would not necessarily be able to detect any particular pattern at the

---

2. Quoted in Richardson and Wildman, eds. *Religion and Science*, 239.

microscopic level, even if God were continually guiding the universe by this means. . . .

Other proposals for locating divine intervention within physics

Several other proposals have been made for showing the consonance of divine action and physical theory. Most widely discussed of late is the impact of recent work on "chaos theory," or the physics of dynamic systems far from thermodynamic equilibrium. The physicist John Polkinghorne, for example, has suggested that the phenomenon of chaos, whereby tiny changes in initial conditions have future causal effects that are essentially unpredictable, might represent an "intrinsic indefiniteness" or indeterminism within (at least parts of) the macrophysical world. Clearly, in chaotic systems future states of the universe cannot be predicted from present states, since differences in the initial conditions that are too small for us to detect will lead to vastly different future states of the system. (We see this all the time in weather forecasting, where small differences in the cloud and air masses as they proceed toward a given location lead to vast differences in the actual weather conditions a few days later; differences between, for example, a rainy day or a warm sunshiny one.) If Polkinghorne is right, there might be genuine openness (indeterminacy) not only at the quantum level but also in the "chaotic" parts of the macrophysical world. If so, God might act in these systems to bring about divine intentions without breaking any physical laws ("interventionism"). . . . There seem to be some difficulties with this suggestion, however. For example, are chaotic systems really "indeterminate" or causally open? Most physicists treat them as causally determinate systems. . . .

The default position

Should none of the proposals we are about to consider pan out, the theologian will be left with two major options. On the one hand, she can give up her quest to specify the "causal joint" where divine action occurs and yet still maintain that God is active in the world in some way. Perhaps she would wish to assert that, although God does not carry out any specific actions in the world subsequent to creation, the continued existence of the universe should be understood as a single composite act of God, as Maurice Wiles does in *God's Action in the World*. Or she might speak, following Austin Farrer, of a "primary causality" of God, in and behind every action carried out by every finite agent. This route, similar to the view which Nancy Murphy calls "immanentism" and associates with modern liberal theology, has the advantage of making God causally ubiquitous in the world, though it might also seem that the God who does everything is a God who does nothing. Or she might designate it a matter of pure faith how God brings about his purposes in the world, beyond all grasp of human reason. On the other hand, the theologian might give up altogether on the claim that

God acts in the world. Such a move appears also to move outside of Christian theism, at least in the sense in which the tradition has understood it, siding instead with deism, pantheism, or atheism.

Clearly, then, resolving the "causal joint" debate is not the sine qua non for the survival of Christian theism, although asserting divine action in some sense may be. Nonetheless, it should be clear that it is a high-stakes debate for those who wish to pursue Christian theology in dialogue with the sciences and our general knowledge of the world. . . . A number of solutions to this problem have been attempted. Austin Farrer, followed by Edward H. Henderson, Brian Hebblethwaite, and others, argued for a notion of "double agency." There are two types of causes for any event: a string of finite causes within the world brings it about, and at the same time God is active in bringing about the outcome through a separate type of causality. . . . This view does weaken the sense in which God's causal agency contributes to the actions that humans perform in the world, at least in comparison to many classical views. Nonetheless, it can still be theologically sufficient. Seen in this way, God's role becomes that of one who prepares and persuades, rather than the one who "brings about" human actions. This view is also conceptually much neater than the alternatives, since it attributes basic actions to humans alone. At the same time, it does continue to ascribe a crucial role to God in "luring" humanity and encouraging certain types of actions. Under this model there must be genuine openness in history. . . .

The Contemporary Debate about Divine Causality in Science

One finds in the recent literature a rich variety of positions on science and divine action. The goal of an introductory text must be restricted to examining some representative positions; I will thus limit the discussion in what follows to five of the major approaches that characterize the recent debate. . . .

God's action as "top-down" causality

John Polkinghorne holds the view . . . that all knowledge-claims about the world presuppose certain underlying metaphysical commitments. These commitments, which form the backbone of any view of the world, can in his view be judged only by the pragmatic criterion of their consistency with observed phenomena. When we consider the question of divine agency, we must use this pragmatic standard of evaluation as well. . . . Polkinghorne's alternative to reductionist theories of causation involves a reversal of physics' customary "bottom-up" approach. He suggests that, in addition to traditional reductionist explanations, we should also consider the possibility that a system as a whole could motivate or cause isolated changes in its component parts. Polkinghorne uses the phrase "top-down causality" to signify this type of change. One specific area that Polkinghorne feels may be a likely candidate for "top-down" description is the relation between consciousness and the body. God's action in the world, Polkinghorne speculates, may be similar to the relationship of the soul to the body (though he rejects panentheism)....

A theory of divine action based on quantum indeterminacy

We have already encountered Thomas Tracy's work in the collection he edited, *The God Who Acts*. His extended essay on divine action and the sciences has the advantage of helping theologians step back from and "place" the entire discussion within the theological tradition.... A full doctrine of God requires an open world, one with causal spaces in which God could act. Moreover, these must be such that natural law is not suspended or broken every time God acts, which would make a mockery of the natural order. Finally, it must be the sort of openness that will not be closed up by advances in scientific knowledge, leaving theologians stranded high and dry (again). The history of embarrassment is long enough already.

What kind of "explanatory gaps" would do the trick? They are found "when we are unable to give a complete account of the sufficient conditions for an event," or "when our theories entail that human knowers will not [even] in principle be able to give a sufficient explanation of some of the events that fall within the theory's scope," or when we encounter events that "are not uniquely determined by their antecedents."[3] According to Tracy, gaps in principle are certainly depicted by chaos theory and may be illustrated by quantum theory as well. Of these two cases, up to now only quantum theory has revealed real causal gaps in nature's fabric, since it alone gives evidence of an irreducible indeterminism in nature....

Strengthening the theological requirements

We have already encountered the work of Nancey Murphy above. In *Beyond Liberalism and Fundamentalism,* she attempts to find a via media between "interventionist" theories of divine action and the liberal holistic models that leave no place for specific divine action.... First, Murphy begins with theological criteria rather than describing the scientific results and then developing a theology of divine action to be consistent with them. As she has argued elsewhere, she presupposes that science and theology are epistemically on a par and that both must submit to criticism and correction from the other. It is important to see how different this approach is from most of the authors so far considered. For Murphy, there is no greater initial justification in scientific explanations than in theological ones; in the case of conflict, either may have to give.

---

3. Tracy, "Particular Providence and the God of the Gaps," 290.

As a result, she approaches the divine action question with a robust list of theological requirements[4] and then, given the scientific constraints, tries to make certain common metaphysical assumptions give way. Concretely, this means that theologians should refer to "traditional formulations" of doctrine when evaluating the implications of science: "Only if the formulations of the past turn out to be hopelessly unintelligible should they be rejected or radically changed."[5] She also stresses two necessary conditions for a theory of divine action that is supportive of Christian theory: it must preserve "special divine acts" which allow us "to be able to distinguish between God's acts and the actions of sinful creatures."[6] Additionally, it must allow for "extraordinary divine acts," which Murphy seems to treat in the same way as traditional miracles except that they may not involve the notion of "a violation of the laws of nature."[7] . . . Interestingly, Murphy seems to come to a similar recognition at the end of her piece, recognizing that her position may appear like a "two-language solution"[8] similar to Kant's advocacy of the complementary languages of determinism and free will, each true in its own domain.

4. Murphy, "Divine Action in the Natural Order," 325–57.
5. Ibid., 330.
6. Ibid., 330.
7. Ibid., 331.
8. Ibid., 354.

29

A Panentheistic Theory of Divine Action[1]

No contemporary theologian has come closer to the panentheistic theory of divine action defended in this book than Arthur Peacocke; and of those who hold similar positions, none possesses a superior knowledge of the scientific developments. Peacocke's starting point, like Murphy's, is solidly theological. . . .

But like Philip Hefner's well-known theory of humanity as God's "created co-creator,"[2] Peacocke stresses that there is an ongoing creativity within creation itself: "So we have to see God's action as being in the processes themselves, as they are revealed by the physical and biological sciences, and this means we must stress more than ever before God's immanence in the world."[3] The most adequate way to think of this immanence is to understand the emergence of new forms primitive life, higher organisms, and human self-consciousness as a result of God's immanent creative action in the world. . . .

In this treatment, as in his earlier major publication from which the idea is drawn, Peacocke employs the metaphor of creation as an act of composing and of the created order as a musical composition: Beethoven is "in" the present-day performance of his Seventh Symphony even at the same time that the director and musicians are responsible for their own creative interpretation in a way analogous to the creative role that God continues to play in the creativity of nature and humanity.

How does Peacocke evaluate the various avenues for divine interaction so far discussed? His responses to divine action at the quantum level, to "amplification" by means of chaotic systems, and to "quantum chaos" are uniformly skeptical. Peacocke finds the quantum solution no different than saying that God breaks the laws of classical physics by performing a miracle. For in the sorts of proposals we have been

---

1. "A Panentheistic Theory of Divine Action," from Clayton, *God and Contemporary Science*, 220–31. Reprinted with the kind permission of Eerdmans.

2. Hefner, *The Human Factor*.

3. Peacocke, *Theology for a Scientific Age*, 139.

looking at, God would have to "make some micro-event, subsequently amplified, to be other than it would have been if left to itself to follow its own natural course, without the involvement of divine action." The only difference, he thinks, is that this type of intervention "would always be hidden from us," whereas interventions in a Newtonian universe could be subsequently discovered.[4] I do not think that this response fully recognizes the *tertium quid* nature of, say, the views of Nancey Murphy summarized above. Surely quantum-level theories of divine action involve God's influencing outcomes in the physical world; this is what separates such theories from the Wiles/Kaufman approach, which no longer identifies any particular locus (or loci) of divine action in the world. But precisely a panentheist such as Peacocke should recognize the theological worries associated with God's breaking natural laws. If the world is encompassed by (or, to speak metaphorically, "contained in") God, then its regularities are inner-divine regularities, something like the autonomic functioning of our own bodies. Setting aside such regularities for the sake of focal divine action would amount to a sort of contradiction within the divine being, or at least a contradiction *in actu*. By contrast, God's acting through genuine openings in the fabric of natural law would not raise this problem. Thus, if there is to be focal divine action, the quantum possibility represents a distinct advantage.

Nonetheless, Peacocke's concerns about the scientific details of such an account ought to give one pause; they serve as a good reminder that an opening in the science/theology dialogue is not a conclusive answer. For example, God could act in this way only if we assume "total divine omniscience and prescience about all events";[5] but we may have theological reasons to resist this view. On the scientific side, there is as yet no clear understanding of how, if at all, chaotic systems could amplify individual divine actions on the quantum level such that they made a perceptible difference in the physical world. Moreover, so-called quantum chaos is a highly controversial hypothesis. Peacocke cites Bob Russell's statement: "Whether or not quantum systems do actually display additional statistical behavior beyond that represented by the wave function, that is, whether or not there is a quantum version of classical chaos (called 'quantum chaos'), is still an open question."[6] Finally, the physicist Joseph Ford speaks of the "major battle" being fought over whether such phenomena exist at all; at present, he concludes, "the evidence weighs heavily against quantum chaos," which would represent "an earthquake in the foundations of physics."[7]

How then are we to view a theology of divine action that appeals to quantum indeterminacy? Recall that it is the only area of the physical world presently known

---

4. Peacocke, *Theology for a Scientific Age*, 154. Unless otherwise noted, subsequent parenthetical references in the text are to this work.

5. Ibid., 155.

6. Peacocke, "God's Interaction with the World," 268n11. Unless otherwise noted, subsequent parenthetical references in the text are to this work.

7. Ford, "What is Chaos, That We Should Be Mindful of It?" 366, 370.

to us in which God could bring about effects that would not otherwise have occurred without breaking natural law. Peacocke has urged caution. Our best science tells us that particular quantum phenomena are unpredictable in principle (just as it tells us that near-infinite knowledge of initial conditions would be required to predict outcomes in chaotic systems). If one takes the quantum solution, one attributes a knowledge to God which, although not involving logical contradiction, goes beyond what a finite knower could ever know about the physical world; one also assumes that God can bring about physical effects at the level of an individual electron or photon in a way that is incomprehensible to physics. For some, this will not seem troubling: if God can count the hairs on one's head, why couldn't God know and do things at the microscopic level that no human could? For others, such as Peacocke, the problems with the details of this particular account suggest that theology is better off remaining at the level of general statements about God's purposes in the world. The theologian may note "the new scientific awareness of unpredictability, open-endedness and flexibility and of the inbuilt propensities of natural processes to have particular kinds of outcomes."[8] But she should not go beyond these features of the world to try to specify the "causal joint" through which God brings about his purposes in the world.

According to Peacocke, then, we can never locate a locus of divine action within the interstices of the world and then conceive of it being amplified to affect cosmic history. If God is to act providentially at all, the influence will move not from the part to the whole but from the whole to the part. This he calls, following Donald Campbell and Roger Sperry, "top-down" causation or "whole part constraint."

In scientific contexts, Peacocke admits, what one actually encounters are examples of the influence of "boundary conditions" on the behavior of members of the system: "The set of relationships between the constituent units in the complex whole is a new set of boundary conditions for those units."[9] One example would be the effect on a group of animals of their total environment, an effect reflected in the DNA of those that survive and reproduce most effectively. Another example involves the effect of mental phenomena on brain states . . . . There are also purely physical examples of patterned behavior where the patterns clearly emerge from the system as a whole and are not found in the particles individually. . . . Many of the well-known chaotic phenomena thus fit within this category. While such behaviors are not "emergent" in the strong sense, they go far towards illustrating the important influence of "higher" or emergent levels on lower-level phenomena.

It is my contention that Peacocke's shift to "top-down" causation as the exclusive mode of divine activity in the world importantly transforms the debate about divine agency. Indeed, one might say that it meets the goals of Nancey Murphy's above-mentioned book, *Beyond Liberalism and Fundamentalism*, in a way that is more consistent than her own position on quantum-level causation by God described above. On the

---

8. Peacocke, *Theology for a Scientific Age*, 157.
9. Ibid., 273.

one hand, Peacocke has to give up on direct physical causation by God. It cannot occur in deterministic contexts, since this would involve law-breaking by God, nor, he thinks, does it occur at the quantum level. In one sense, he has to admit, "The word 'causation' is not really appropriate for describing such situations," namely the effect on the parts "of being in the interacting, cooperative network of that particular, whole system."[10] On the other hand, there is still ample space for speaking of God's directing of the world as a whole, hence of divine providence in this sense. This is where panentheism plays its most important role in the theory of divine agency: God, who contains the universe-as-a-whole (though he is much more than it as well) can act directly on the universe as its constraint and overarching context. . . . This holistic influence could operate, then, as a constraining influence on more limited systems within the universe, for instance (eventually) on the biosphere of our planet.

There are of course questions about this approach. On the question of whether whole–part constraint should really be described as causality at all, we have already noted. Another concerns the indirectness of the divine agency here imagined: how significant could God's guidance of the individual be if it comes to her highly mediated? Would Peacocke have to speak of a top-down hierarchy proceeding from the universe-as-a-whole, down through superstrings and galaxies to our individual planet, and then through the history of biological evolution and countless billions of genetic mutations to one person existing today? Such an interpretation is certainly suggested when he writes that "the state of the world as a whole (all-that-is)" is "the field of the exercise of God's influence."[11] But such a model is strangely reminiscent of Aristotle's God, the *nous noetikos*, who transmits motion to the outermost spheres of the heavens (by their emulation of "his" perfection), and from thence down through multiple spheres to the earth and its inhabitants, even without any awareness on their part of what "he" has done—hardly a robust theory of providence! If this will not do, could Peacocke then say that God is "top-downly" active *directly* from the universe-as-a-whole to me? How could such a direct causal influence be specified without the directness and concreteness that worries Peacocke in the quantum-level theological theories discussed above?

Although he denies miracles (breaks in natural law), Peacocke tries to speak of God's activity in the strongest terms available to him. God is present not only to the totality but, as one who is "in, with and under" the universe,[12] he is also present to each individual entity as well.[13] Due to the nature of the panentheistic hypothesis, the creative processes that make up the natural order are likewise "themselves the immanent creative activity of God."[14] Since God is imparting information, we can preserve

---

10. Peacocke, *Theology for a Scientific Age*, 272, N.n22.
11. Ibid., 161.
12. Ibid., 176.
13. Ibid., 162.
14. Ibid., 163.

the doctrines of divine self-communication, revelation, and prayer. Since top-down causation allows us to regard events as manifesting God's overall intentions, general providence plays a role,[15] and even special providence is maintained....

Still, in the final analysis, Peacocke has to admit that his view, like those of Gordon Kaufman and Maurice Wiles discussed above, allows for God's action only "on the world-as-a-whole."[16] Humans may find more divine meaning in some (natural or historical) events than in others, but "God is equally and totally present to all times and places."[17] When one reads that God can influence "any constituent entity or event in the world that God wishes to influence,"[18] or that "Particular events could occur in the world and be what they are because God intends them to be so,"[19] one must therefore interpret the influence as exclusively a holistic, totality-affecting one: God may be intimately present to each entity, but God acts causally on us all only from the (very) top down.

This limitation is perhaps moderately troubling; it becomes more disturbing when one turns to that central Christian concern, the revelation in the person and work of Christ. Consistent with the view just sketched, Peacocke attempts to use recent information theory in order to conceive of a "naturalistic" model of revelation. In opposition to the common separation between revealed knowledge and natural knowledge, he proceeds "by presenting Christology along lines that regard the self-communication of God to humanity as an 'informing' process."[20] The New Testament represents a "development" of seeds of judgment and reflection on Jesus, rather than an "evolution" with mutation. In short, we find in Jesus something like a set of "God-driven" emergent properties, making Jesus a kind of ultimate emergent. Thus he writes, "Might it not be possible for a human being so to reflect God, to be so wholly open to God, that God's presence was clearly unveiled to the rest of humanity in a new, emergent, and unexpected manner?"[21] But emergent properties emerge out of the world and are not imposed on it from outside: "Taking the clue from the Johannine Prologue, we could say that the manifestation of God which Jesus' contemporaries encountered in Him must have been an emanation from within creation, from deep within those events and processes which led to His life, teaching, death, and Resurrection."[22] In this way Peacocke explains that God did not enter an otherwise "closed" world through Jesus, but only made himself known through Jesus, using causal mechanisms fully consistent with the rest of cosmic history.

15. Ibid., 162.
16. Ibid., 163.
17. Ibid., 181.
18. Ibid., 164.
19. Ibid., 159.
20. Peacocke, "The Incarnation of the Informing Self-expressive Word of God," 321.
21. Ibid., 332.
22. Ibid., 331.

PART V: SCIENCE, SPIRIT, & DIVINE ACTION

Now Peacocke wants nonetheless to maintain that Jesus embodied and enacted some highly specific divine intentions. Thus, for instance, God "communicated" through Jesus "an explicit revelation of the significance of personhood in the divine purposes, an insight only partially and incompletely discernible from our reflections on natural being and becoming."[23] Here he must mean more than that Jesus, being the kind of person he was, was lucky enough to come to symbolize God's nature, without God's intending that he do so, since in that case talk of "revelation" would become equivocal. Rather, Peacocke writes as if Jesus' resurrection were a deliberate act of revelation: the resurrection was an event in which "God was able to reveal further the way ahead for Jesus, as 'Jesus the Christ', to draw all humanity after him into a full relation with God."[24] The early witnesses, at least, interpreted Jesus and his fate as "a communication from God, a revelation of God's meanings for humanity," and not just a humanly-authored parable of God's nature and intentions.[25]

Yet without bottom-up causation God's role in the Jesus event can be no more than the limited top-down influence we have already explored.... This position seems to bracket any particular intentions on the part of God, viewing Jesus as someone who happened to activate a spiritual potentiality already built into the created order into his own genetic code through a very long evolutionary process which the eyes of faith can see as having been guided by God.

Many aspects of Peacocke's theory of divine agency are, *en fin de compte*, theologically attractive. Since God's direction involves an "input of information" rather than energy transfers, the old dilemma of how God as non-physical being could bring about physical effects disappears. More importantly, Peacocke's theory of divine action is persuasive rather than coercive. There is no greater respect for free decisions (and preexisting order) than in cases where an agent presents information and allows it to be received and appropriated, or discarded, by other agents—exactly the model he advocates. Theologically, it is appropriate to speak of God's action holistically, at the level of all that is, while still emphasizing God's presence to every individual. Finally, this model avoids that charge that God's actions are intermittent or sporadic; it finds divine providence at the most overarching level while still leaving room for special providence in at least one sense.

Nonetheless, I suggest that we will ultimately need to supplement the top-down theory of divine agency by something more. If the worries are justified that speaking of God's "one act" is too little for Christian theism, as Thomas Tracy has argued, then we have reason also to worry about a God whose agency is top-down only. Given science, "top-down" may well be the best way to conceive general providence, God's overall guidance of the world. But preserving the doctrine of special providence seems to require something more. The theologians working on a theory of quantum-level

---

23. Peacocke, *Theology for a Scientific Age*, 305.
24. Ibid., 308.
25. Ibid., 296.

action (with or without chaos effects) have uncovered a remarkable possibility: that God might act in the world to guide events without breaking natural law or physical regularities. To take their work as settling the matter would be a mistake. But it does represent a possible locus of divine action unparalleled since Newton "laid bare the inner workings of creation." Combining the theories of top-down and bottom-up causation explored in this chapter provides, I think, a viable means of conceiving God's action in the world, one that is acceptable both theologically and scientifically. To complete the theory of divine action, we will need to think more carefully about the fundamental analogy between human and divine action, the task to which the final chapter is devoted.

30

Natural Law and the Problem of Divine Action
Can Contemporary Theologians Still Affirm That God (Literally) Does Anything?[1]

PHYSICAL SCIENCE, IT APPEARS, leaves no place for divine action. To do science is generally to presuppose that the universe is a closed physical system, that interactions are regular and lawlike, that all causal histories can be traced, and that anomalies will ultimately have physical explanations. Unfortunately, the traditional way of asserting that God acts in the world conflicts with all four of these conditions; it presupposes that the universe is open, that God acts from time to time according to particular purposes, that the ultimate source and explanation of these actions is the divine will, and that no earthly account would ever suffice to explain God's intentions.

Moreover, one faces a certain threat of equivocation when one speaks of both God and physical objects as causes. It would at first seem that the meaning of "cause" used of a chemical catalyst and of God's upholding the universe diverges so widely that the same notion shouldn't be used to express both claims. Only if one can provide some broader account of what features chemicals and providence share in common as causes can one make sense of Jewish, Christian, and Muslim claims for divine action in the world.

The problem of divine agency is therefore one of the most pressing challenges theists face in an age of science. Christians and Muslims in particular have traditionally been committed to a robust account of the actions of God or Allah within the natural order. But how can one attribute events to the causal activity of God if science is based on the assumption that any given event is part of a closed system of natural causes? What conceptual framework might allow believers to acknowledge the power

---

1. "Natural Law and the Problem of Divine Action"; "Can Contemporary Theologians Still Affirm That God (Literally) Does Anything?" as found within Clayton, *Adventures in the Spirit*, 185–228. Reprinted with the kind permission of Fortress.

of science without reducing the divine to a "God of the [few remaining] gaps"—or to utter passivity? I assume, because one can hardly deny, that science has been massively successful in explaining events in the natural world. What causes most of the effects we observe in chemistry and physics is not up for grabs, and well-attested scientific explanations are not just "one story among the rest." This is not to deny that scientific conclusions are always preliminary; they remain open to revision, and some will be falsified. Still, the fact that a given theory will possibly be revised in the future does not imply that it stands on the same level as all other accounts of the phenomena on the market today.[2] . . .

Needed: A New Theory of Causation

The challenge I have just sketched requires theologians to do some fundamental rethinking on the topic of divine action. The inherited tools and concepts are no longer adequate, it appears, to make sense of divine action in an age of science. To put it bluntly, the theologian seems to be faced with a uncomfortable choice between two alternatives: either God acts as the Divine Architect only, creating a finely tuned machine and leaving it to function in a consistent manner somehow expressive of its Designer; or God becomes the Divine Repairman, whose imperfect building of the machine in the first place requires him, like a refrigerator repairman, to return from time to time to fix errors he made the first time around. Though not impossible, it is certainly no easy task to develop an alternative perspective that allows one to speak of a "different but epistemically equal" system of divine causes alongside the network of scientific explanations, one that is co-constitutive of physical events in the world.

Many attempts have been made to respond to this challenge. Some have found an opening in quantum indeterminacy. Perhaps, they argue, the physical world is fully lawlike, and even physically closed *in the specific sense that the total amount of energy remains constant*. But quantum physics, at least on the Copenhagen interpretation, reveals a world that is both law-governed and ontologically indeterminate: unobserved subatomic events do not have a precise location and momentum, and probabilistic laws leave some room for chance. How much of an opening does quantum physics create for divine action? It does seem significant that quantum mechanics allows for multiple outcomes given the same initial conditions, insofar as this fact seems to leave room, at least in principle, for top-down influences. . . . Still, "stochastic" or probabilistic laws are still laws. Perhaps they do not determine each individual case, but they do reflect a physical determinism that pertains to the overall system. Also, the laws say nothing about agents, much less free agents; hence they cannot themselves provide the stronger sense of counterfactual free action that theists appear to need to make the case for divine action.

2. Clayton, *God and Contemporary Science*.

PART V: Science, Spirit, & Divine Action

This lack has led some thinkers to set a separate realm of mental causation over against the world of physical causes. Among these non-physical types of causation are the "agent causation" of Richard Taylor[3] and the ubiquitous divine causation ("double agency") of Austin Farrer.[4] On these views, mental or divine causes affect outcomes without introducing new energy into the physical world. Certainly views of this sort leave room for full human and divine agency. Unfortunately, they do not integrate easily with physical science as we now know it, and some versions actually contradict physical descriptions of the world.

What then of human agency? Do humans not enjoy freedom of will: "The stick moves the stone and is moved by the hand, which again is moved by the man."[5] Theists have often argued that as long as humans are free, God could act in the world. After all, if humans can break the chain of physical causality, couldn't God do so all the more? But free will may be less of a trump card than it appears. The dominant view within philosophy has been *compatibilism*, the view that physical determinism is compatible with human agency and moral responsibility.[6] The American legal system, for example, holds individuals responsible if they intend and then carry out an illegal action (say, murder), *even if* the intending was somehow determined by prior causes. According to compatibilists, agents' actions express their character traits; it is irrelevant whether these traits, and consequently the actions themselves, are determined by antecedent causes. Perhaps the "sense of being free" is just mistaken; after all, even a fully determined will could still (falsely) imagine itself to be free. Finally, many scientists argue that neuroscience presupposes (and some would argue that it has already proven) that the only causal agency is physical; aside from brain states and the body's responses, there *is* no "actor" to be found.

Clearly, it is an urgent task for theologians to provide a clear account of what they mean when they assert that God acts as a causal force within the world. *To succeed at this task we need nothing less than a new theory of causation.* This chapter offers a first sketch of such a theory. The argument presupposes that dualism is mistaken and then seeks to show that, nonetheless, *not all causes are physical causes.*

The argument divides into three main parts. I first concede that the threat of equivocation cannot be overcome as long as one's theory of causality includes only physical and divine causes; the gap is just too wide. By contrast, if we find evidence within the natural world of vastly different types of causes, one can perhaps extend the line to include transcendent causal influences as well. And in fact, the study of the

---

3. Taylor, *Action and Purpose*.
4. Farrer, *Finite and Infinite*.
5. Aristotle, *Physica* 256a, 1:427; cf. O'Connor, *Agents, Causes, and Events*.
6. I examine the literature in detail in *In Quest of Freedom*. Indeterminists, of course, deny this claim, arguing instead for "genuine" or counter-factual freedom: you did this action now, but you might have done something different even in identical circumstances. As Sartre (*Being and Nothingness*) puts it in a classic phrase, "the indispensable and fundamental condition of all action is the freedom of the acting being."

natural world *does* reveal vastly different types of causal activity, from classical Newtonian causality to gravity to the influence of quantum fields to the "holistic constraints" found in integrated systems—and on to the pervasive role of mental causes in human life, as in your comprehension of the sentence, "Please stop reading this sentence!"

Of course, the objection naturally arises: are not all natural causal forces ultimately explainable in terms of the laws of the underlying physical reality—unlike divine causes, which are said to issue from a transcendent and free source? In the following sections I marshal the diverse evidence and arguments that point beyond classical notions of physical causality. Taken together, they now encourage us to accept that the genus "cause" includes types of influences other than mechanistic ones.

The final section draws together the results of the earlier sections in support of a systematic theory of divine action. Emergent causal levels, reflecting the hierarchical structure of the natural world, help to elucidate the nature of divine action, though they are not identical to it. The differences that remain between natural and divine causal influences do represent a continuing burden to theists in an age of science. Given an adequately broad theory of causation, however, the burden may be bearable.

This is a high-stakes debate for contemporary theologians. Traditional formulations remain attractive, but they face conceptual objections that some fear are insuperable. Can a scientifically acceptable concept of emergence be developed that will "re-enchant" the world, allowing us to speak of it again as the ongoing handiwork of God? What corresponding changes may be necessary on the side of theology? Can we again find a way to affirm the divine, as Wordsworth once did, in "the light of setting suns, / And the round ocean and the living air, / And the blue sky, and in the mind of man"? . . .

Double Agency and Divine Persuasion

Our argument to this point has important implications for theology. It suggests that divine-action claims are not equally defensible at all levels of the natural world. Claims that there may have been a divine influence in causal histories involving intentional agents must be assessed differently than claims that God has altered a purely physical chain of events. It is more plausible to maintain that God influences human moral intuitions and religious aspirations than to argue that God fixed the broken plumbing system in one's house (unless one *also* calls a plumber to come and do the repairs!). One reason for the difference is that we do not now possess, and may never possess, laws of human behavior. In contrast to natural scientists, social scientists can at most ascertain broad patterns of human response, and even these evidence a virtually unlimited number of personal and cultural exceptions. Within the human realm, it seems, uniqueness and idiosyncracy are the norm. No laws are broken when we speak of an individual action in a non-standard way—indeed, this is almost what we *mean* by an individual action! If human action is indeed non-nomological, divine causal influence on the thought, will, and emotions of individual persons could occur without breaking natural law. If (and only if) downward mental causation is a viable notion, God could bring about changes in individuals' subjective dispositions without negating the laws that we know to hold in physics and biology.[7]

But what kind of causal influence would this be? The great British philosophical theologian Austin Farrer developed a sophisticated account of divine action which he called the "double agency" view.[8] On this view, every action in the world includes a causal role for one or more agents or objects in the world (the "secondary" causes) and a role for God as the "primary" cause of what occurs. . . . Such a view of action implies that God's action in the world should be understood as something more like divine persuasion. . . . The approach I have taken does alter how God's causal agency is said to contribute to human actions in the world, at least in comparison to classical views of divine action. On most classical views, God's decision to bring about an effect in the world was taken to be sufficient for that effect to occur; no concurrence of any finite person or object was required. On this view, by contrast, God must persuade the agent in question to act in a particular way for the event to occur. This, again, implies a special role for mental causes, understood as instances of emergent causality within the natural world that are dependent on the causal laws of biology but not reducible to them. Intentional agents can be convinced or persuaded, whereas (as far as we know) rocks cannot be persuaded to act on their own—no matter how good the arguments. Though it limits the efficacy of the divine will in the world, I nonetheless believe that this position is sufficient to sustain a viable and scientifically acceptable form of theism for today's world.

Consequently, theists do not need to imagine that God brings about human actions or physical events by divine fiat alone. Divine causality is better understood as a form of causal influence that prepares and persuades. On the one hand, this result makes it much more difficult to conceive a divine influence on rocks or other purely physical systems apart from the laws and initial conditions established by God at creation. On the other hand, it does continue to ascribe to God a crucial causal role in "luring" humanity (and, for all we know, perhaps other biological agents as well) and in influencing the interpersonal, moral, intellectual, and aesthetic dimensions of human personhood. The resulting position emphasizes the genuine openness in history. One cannot *know* in advance that God will bring about the ends that God desires to accomplish,[9] although one can know that, if God is God, the final state of affairs will be consistent with God's nature. In all of these respects, there is an obvious affinity of this view with process theology's understanding of the God–world relation.[10] . . .

---

7. Whether there is a God, and whether God in fact carries out these actions, is of course another question, and one that I do not seek to resolve here.

8. Farrer, *Finite and Infinite*; McLain and Richardson, eds., *Human and Divine Agency*.

9. Pannenberg, "Der Gott der Geschichte," 112–28.

10. For example, Griffin, *Reenchantment without Supernaturalism*.

Toward a Theory of Emergent Causality

Let us now attempt to put these various resources together into a single theory of emergent causality. The challenge for this project stems from the fact that explanations in the physical sciences today depend primarily on efficient causation. That is, the success of modern science seems to have been based on its preference for explanations given in terms of traceable and reconstructable causal histories in the natural world. On the inherited view, any talk of form, matter, or purpose becomes causal only when it is reduced to those activating forces that directly or immediately activate change in a physical object. A causal process is a linear chain of events, each of which causes its immediate successor.

The challenge that philosophers and theologians face now is to sketch a new theory of causation. But how is one to reintroduce talk of formal and final causes alongside the efficient causes that are the bread and butter of modern science? The grounds and motivation for the argument must be based on the changes that have occurred as science has moved further and further from the once regnant ideal of universal reduction to physics. Resources for the new approach can be found, *inter alia*, in entanglement phenomena in quantum mechanics, mental causes in psychology, information theory and epigenesis in biology, and the structure of emergence that appears again and again as one climbs the ladder of complexity in the natural world.

Causal relations *up* the emergent hierarchy are uncontroversial, since they rely on efficient causality. The slogan of early modern or "Laplacian" science might be expressed as "causes propagate upward; explanation, and hence ontology, reduces downward." The Laplacian model in scientific explanation involves explaining complex behaviors (or: the behavior of complex bodies) in terms of fundamental forces acting on their constituent parts. It might *look* mysterious that a cell can divide and divide again or the amoeba can engage in what looks like goal-directed behavior. But once one has understood the biochemistry of cell division, the catalytic effect of enzymes, and the basic genetic architecture and functioning of the cell, no unanswerable questions remain. The aggregation of these myriad physical particles and forces tells the complete causal history of cell functioning. With this bottom-up account in place, no other causal story is necessary. Or so it seemed.

But emergence has shown that upward propagation of causes is *not* the whole story. The state of the whole—the whole chemical system within which particles interact, the whole cell, the whole organism, the whole ecosystem, the brain as a whole—affects the behavior of the particles and the causal interactions that they have.

This view is not without its opponents. Thus Carl Gillett argues that no actual downward causal forces are involved; "all individuals are constituted by, or identical to, micro-physical individuals, and all properties are realized by, or identical to, micro-physical properties."[11] Likewise, certain branches of complexity theory, including

---

11. Gillett, "Non-Reductive Realization and Non-Reductive Identity," 28.

complexity theorists such as John Holland[12] who use the word emergence, also allow only upward causation, although they do grant that something new and unpredictable (at least in lower-level terms) emerges. We might speak of these positions as involving at most *weak emergence*, emergence without downward causation. By contrast, I argued [earlier in this book] that the phenomena allow for, and may actually require, the notion of a downwardly propagating causal influence—a view I've called *strong emergence*.

I opened this chapter with the most compelling area, the relationship of the mental to the physical. To make the position as little controversial as possible, I have not posited a separately existing substance called soul or mind, but only the existence of mental predicates. Physicalists construe mental phenomena as properties of a physical object, in this case the brain, whose microphysical causal properties are sufficient to account for the effects that we call mentality. In opposition to the physicalist interpretation, I argued that the explanatory power of mental causation—for example, the ability of our ideas and thoughts to cause bodily movements such as speaking, walking, or raising an arm—is great enough that the limitation of causal forces to the microphysical level is unjustified. The onus is on those who would deny any causal efficacy to the emergent level of mentality.

I then turned to the question of evolution. At first blush it looked like a war to the finish: evolution appears incompatible with theism, and divine providence or action in the world seems incompatible with evolution. Thus, one must ask: what is the rational response to a problem that cannot be solved either from the bottom alone (i.e., through genetics and biochemistry), or from the top alone (i.e., by negating biology and imposing a theological answer)? One looks for a means to bring several different disciplines together to solve the problem—not by making them identical (which is false) or treating them as incompatible (which is inadvisable), but by placing them in a dialectical or systematic relationship. Specifically, the contradiction is overcome if what evolution demands and what theology requires are not contradictory but complementary.

It turns out, I suggest, that the best overall explanation is obtained when one pursues this hypothesis. Contemporary evolutionary theory forbids vital forces or causal influences from outside. Fortunately, theism requires only that the product of the evolutionary process reflect the divine intention to create rational, moral creatures who can be in conscious relationship with the divine. This *might* have occurred by God's initiating a process that God knew in advance would necessarily produce such creatures without the need for any further divine guidance—though the scientific picture today makes complete pre-determination seem unlikely. In the case of evolution, however, it proved possible to find an analog to the downward causation that we experience in conscious volition. According to the analog, God could guide the process of emergence through the introduction of new information (formal causality) and, in

---

12. Holland, *Emergence*.

the case of sufficiently complex organisms, by holding out an ideal or image that could influence development without altering the mechanisms and structures that constrain evolution from the bottom up (final causality).

I close with three limitations to the argument I have sketched. First, science cannot provide unambiguous evidence for final causality; finality language is irreducibly metaphysical or theological. Scientific explanations of biological phenomena must still be sought within the framework of evolutionary biology, and the conclusions and constraints of that discipline are not short-circuited by the broader theory of causality I have defended. Second, the framework of guided emergence is not the same thing as the control of the evolutionary process that traditional theists once defended. Guidance via the informational content of the whole or the goals of conscious agents in the world—agents whose goals may also extend beyond the world as a whole—is not a form of efficient or determining causation; in the end, it is closer to the lure-like nature of final causality in Aristotelian philosophy. But it *is* sufficient to provide an updated version of what was once meant by divine providence, albeit without the omnipotence and predestination claims that often undergirded this doctrine.

Finally, the informational final causes that I have explored do not "prove God," for one can still do adequate science without introducing them. Advocates of "intelligent design"[13] or "irreducible complexity,"[14] by contrast, put forward evidence that they think should convince non-theistic scientists of the inadequacy of their [non-theistic] position. In order to convey the epistemic ambiguity intended by my position, one might better say that there is a "quasi-purposiveness" in nature. In chapter 5 of the *Adventures . . .* text, I called this, following Kant, *purposiveness without purpose*. The Kantian parallel suggests viewing such assertions as having an "as if"-status: the biological world develops *as if* it were being guided by a divine hand. Of course, one might believe something more theologically and argue for more metaphysically. But for purposes of the discussion with science, all one needs to show is that scientific conclusions do not require one to speak of this guidance as a mere fiction, and this, I believe, the argument has accomplished.

---

13. Dembski, *The Design Revolution*.
14. Behe, *Darwin's Black Box*.

31

Rethinking Divine Action[1]

THEISM IS DOUBLY HARD to conceive in the contemporary context. First, in the face of science's strong push towards immanent explanations one must make the case that language about a transcendent being or dimension is meaningful. Although I have argued that the rejection of transcendence is unnecessary, clearly the move to transcendent mind is one that many resist. Once it is made, a second challenge arises: the task of making some sense of the idea of divine causal activity in the world.

The second step is more difficult than the first: it is easier to hold that there is a ground of all things than to maintain that this ground also actively influences the world in some way. For example, a creation of all things "before the foundation of the world" does not interfere in any way with scientific explanation, whereas a God who would be doing things within the cosmos subsequent to the big bang would be encroaching on the territory for which the sciences are responsible. The possibility of direct conflicts is very real. Moreover, making this claim is metaphysically more difficult or, as one might say, more "expensive." A God who carries out actions has to be conceived not just as a ground or force but also as an agent, which means that the divine must be somehow analogous to human agents. Modern philosophy, at least until the middle of the nineteenth century, represents a sustained struggle with the difficulties of this notion.

Part of the problem is that we are no longer sure what to make of the notions of mind or spirit. The metaphysical resources of the Western tradition—the conceptual worlds of *ruach, pneuma, spiritus, Geist*—are difficult to reconcile with the attitude and results of contemporary science. One can of course still assert that "God is Spirit, infinite and perfect in his being and perfections," as the Westminster Confession has it; one can affirm that humans are made "in the image of God" (*imago Dei*); and one

---

1. "Trading Mind-body Dualism for Theological Dualism; Rethinking Divine Action," as found within Clayton, *Mind & Emergence: From Quantum to Consciousness*, 185–99. Reprinted with the kind permission of Oxford University Press.

can conclude that each human therefore possesses a God-like spirit or soul, as the Pope recently reaffirmed in his statement on evolution. But whereas this view once accorded nicely with the natural science (natural philosophy) of a previous era, it stands in deep tension with the approaches and the results of the science of our own.

That is where the emergence argument comes in. If successful, this argument represents a *tertium quid* between physicalist treatments of mind, which leave no place for talk of spirit, and dualist treatments, which simply assume (in my view, too easily) the continuing validity and usefulness of such language. Having followed the argument for strong emergence through the opening four chapters, and having traced the theory of mind that it supports, one now wants to know: how does it realign traditional views of the God–world relationship? If there is divine agency, how should it be reconceived in light of our new understanding of human agency?

Though the fact has not always been admitted, the relationship between understanding human agents and understanding the divine agent has always been a two-way street. Not infrequently, theories of the divine agent (theologies) have strongly influenced how human persons were conceived (the *imago Dei* argument). But just as clearly, ideas about what humankind is—variously influenced by art, religion, philosophy, societal and political structures, and cultural practices—have provided models for how God is to be conceived. In an age of absolute monarchy and male dominance, God was naturally conceived as the King of Kings; in an age of deterministic physics, God was known as the divine watchmaker, the Ground of order and lawfulness; and in an age of dualism, God became pure spirit, pure mind (*nous noetikos*), independent of all things physical. In an age of emergence, how should the divine agent be conceived? In this context, what sense can be made of the idea of divine influence on the world? Or is that an idea that is simply no longer credible?

The dilemma that faces the theist is not difficult to state. The theist can construe human and divine agency as similar by seeing human mental activity as involving the introduction of a new, non-physical energy into the universe, in which case one ends up with a strongly dualistic picture of the mind–body relation; or one can preserve the continuity between mind and body, say by seeing the energy of mind as a sort of "transduction" of biochemical energy (Christian de Duve),[2] in which case one ends up with a more dualistic picture of the God–world relation. In the latter case, human agents are conceived as existing in much greater continuity with other natural processes and energies and hence as being ontologically more distant from the divine agent. As a result, however, it becomes more difficult to conceive the relation between the "bottom-up" effects expressed as the operation of physical laws and the "top-down" or focally intended divine actions through which God is imagined to communicate with human minds. I have advocated accepting the second horn of the

---

2. See de Duve, *Life Evolving*, 208–26, esp. 223–24. De Duve's solution allows for mental causation in a manner that clearly is not dualist, and yet it preserves a fully bidirectional interaction between body and mind.

dilemma, interpreting mind as in continuity with the natural world—in part because it preserves the possibility of neuroscience, and in part out of the conviction that, if one has to countenance some measure of dualism, the relation between an infinite God and a finite world is the right place to locate it. After all, as soon as one affirms the existence of a God who does not depend upon the existence of the physical world, has one not already advocated a position that is, at least in this respect, irreducibly dualistic?

Rethinking Divine Action

The various pieces are now in place for addressing the question of divine action. I have made the case for strong emergence in physics and biology; I have defended an understanding of mind that allows for mental causation without depending on a dualism that would obviate neuroscientific study; and I have explored a view of the God–world relation that radicalizes the immanence of God. What response to the problem of divine action is suggested by the resulting position?

It does not seem possible to defend physical miracles in a way that does not conflict with the approach, methods, and results of contemporary science. Now there may be one conceivable type of divine causal activity within the realm of physics that would circumvent the conflict, namely if one postulated that God affected the world at the quantum level (assuming that quantum events are indeed ontologically indeterminate), influencing this or that wave function collapse in one direction or another while still maintaining the overall probability distributions that are basic to quantum physics.

In this case, no laws would be broken. The trouble, of course, is that we do not now and never could in the future possess any evidence that a God in fact influences the world at this level. Nor can we tell any convincing story of how God might amplify even billions and billions of such quantum-level interventions so as to convince (say) the hostage-taker not to kill the children who are under his control. The quantum approach encounters a further difficulty: if the level of the mental is anomalous (not governed by laws), then God could not, even in principle, determine the outcome of someone's thought through this mechanism, though in principle God could make one thought or another more probable. It remains important, for any assertion of actual divine influence on the world, that the physical world be an indeterminate system, since otherwise the physics would not leave room for the spontaneity of animal behavior or the effects of downwards mental causation; and with these gone, the idea of divine influence on outcomes would become vacuous. Still, it is, I suggest, impossible to solve the problem of divine action at the quantum level alone. . . .

But matters are not the same when it comes to human action. (In principle, and *mutatis mutandis*, these arguments would apply to animals as well, though I do not explore that possibility here.) In the case of human thought and the actions that stem from it, no laws determine the decision-making process. Of course, given the structure of a brain, a given life history, and a specific set of environmental inputs, one result may be much more likely than others. But no natural laws are broken if, on the basis of a process of reflection, you do something different from what it was probable that you would do. I have argued that strong emergence is consistent both with the constraining effects of the relevant physical and biological systems and with the data on human behavior, including introspective phenomena, whereas its competitors are not. Weak emergence does not do justice to the reality of mental causal agency. Dualism postulates the addition of qualitatively different energies by a qualitatively different kind of cause, reflecting the agency of an altogether different kind of substance. In addition to being unnecessary, the dualist response makes a mockery of the neurosciences, understood as the scientific study of the correlations between states of the central nervous system and the experienced phenomena of consciousness. If brain states are the result of inputs from a purely mental kind of energy that is unrelated to the electrochemical causal powers in the brain, then no knowledge of the interaction is possible; one would face a lawlike system that on a regular basis acts in a completely un-lawlike manner. By contrast, if conscious causes are emergent properties of the neurological systems that compose the brain, then some understanding of their operation is possible, even if they are not in the end controlled by overarching covering laws.

What then of divine influence on mental processes? Certainly it is not ruled out by the present conception. On this view, although thought is a natural phenomenon it is not determined by physical laws and is upwardly open to higher types of causality. It is permissible to construe divine causality as one of these higher levels of causality. Since human actions are already unpredictable on the basis of prior brain states and environmental conditions no determining conditions are broken when (if) a divine influence leads to a different outcome.

But how similar are these putative divine causes to mental causes understood as emergent? Here the theist faces a dilemma. The resources of emergence theory can help her introduce and defend divine action, but only if she construes the divine as the next emergent level in the cosmic evolutionary process. Earlier we considered theorists such as Samuel Alexander who were willing to make this move. For Alexander God was not a pre-existing being but a new type of property, "deity," that comes to characterize the world at a certain point in its complexification. Obviously, this sort of theory, although it may offer a naturalized framework for speaking of the influence of deity, will not yield divine action in anything like its traditional form. Most forms of theism are (rightly) highly reticent to construe God as merely an emergent feature of the world.

Assuming then that one resists a fully emergentist theology, the resources of emergence will be of only limited assistance in formulating a theory of divine influence on human thought. The energy of divine causality, whatever it is, is not adapted or modified from energies elsewhere in the universe, because divine causes are not the product of the same natural system. Hence the principles that have been so fruitful in explaining human thought will not be able to do the same for divine influences. Consequently, divine causes will not be knowable in the same fashion, for the standard ways we come to know the processes of emergent systems and their products will not be available in this case....

Of course, the fact that bottom-up divine action would be forever undetectable does not make it impossible. But I should think that one would want *some* reason for advancing the idea that God is causally active right at the heart of physics, lest the claim appear meaningless.... Indeed, there is even a sense in which reference to transcendent or divine influences is a natural next step in one hierarchy: the hierarchy of meaning. When basic physical, emotional, and social needs are met, humans invariably raise questions of the "ultimate meaning of it all." In the quest to understand what reality is ultimately, and what is our place in it, humans often turn to the language of transcendence. This fact serves as reason to preserve a type of discourse that allows broader theoretical proposals to be formulated and perhaps even tested. Questions of this sort are not amenable to empirical resolution, since by their very nature they go beyond what empirical theories could ever establish; they could thus never become subsets of scientific theorizing....

Integrating Personhood and Divine Action

What happens when one tries to work out the specifics of divine action? What sort of account can be defended? Remember that the guiding challenge is compatibility or plausibility, not proof. The goal is not to demonstrate that specific divine actions have occurred, but to find out whether divine action would necessarily contradict natural law. Of course, it is always possible for believers to jettison all laws and regularities or to imagine them superseded by dramatic divine interventions. Thus, one can imagine that, through a very large number of small miraculous interventions, God could create precisely those differentiated waves in the air that, upon striking the ear, the believer would hear as distinct words "spoken" by God. For many, however, such bold physical miracles no longer offer a credible picture of divine agency in the world.

One treads a delicate line here. The more vague the allusions to divine influences on the world, and the more they are based on a pure appeal to mystery, the less convincing they become for those who are skeptical in principle about the reasonableness of claims for divine action. Conversely, the more compatible such claims turn out to be with acceptable natural accounts of human agency, the more credible they become. Yet if the resulting account is *identical* to the natural accounts in everything it predicts, there is no reason to interpret it as an instance of divine action.

The most adequate account must lie somewhere between these extremes. On the one hand, it will locate some area or areas within nature that could in principle be upwardly open to divine influence. Macro-world physics, the physics of Newton's laws, represents the least plausible realm of all: we have strong reason to think that these physical processes are deterministic, and the theoretical framework that comprehends them leaves no place for talk of persons, intentions, meanings, or purposes. On the other hand, the concepts one uses to identify and describe the area of potential divine influence must be such that whatever influences take place could plausibly influence other parts of the natural world. As we have seen, a soul would meet the first criterion but fail at the second; a brain, or perhaps even the neural correlate of a specific idea, would meet the second but fail at the first. Therein lies the difficulty of the problem....

Given these factors, it is easy to see what was wrong with divine action understood as God producing or helping to produce a specific idea formed within the brain of a specific person at some time. It appears that talk of producing thoughts in a bottom-up manner by manipulating brain states is not the right level of analysis for approaching the question of divine action. There is a way to conceive divine agency at the appropriate level of complexity and with the appropriate concepts, but only if one introduces the idea of the emergent level of "the person as such" or "the person as a whole." We might define it as *that level that emerges when an integrated state is established between a person and her body, her environment, other persons, and her overall mental state, including her interpretation of her social, cultural, historical, and religious context.* States of the person as such might include happiness, contentment, conflict, or fulfillment. Thus, the person in this sense might experience *anomie*, in Emile Durkheim's sense of the term, or she might experience that sense of meaningfulness which Peter Berger connects with the idea of a "sacred canopy."

It is not necessary to commit oneself to a particular understanding of the ontological status of the person in order to speak of her causal role.... Nonetheless, it was possible to accept an irreducible causal role for mental causes in so far as one cannot make sense of human behavior without them. A similar epistemic caution is warranted in the present case. It is justified to postulate that the person as such plays a causal role in those various behaviors that we speak of as personal actions. As long as the integrated level presupposed in the idea of personal action plays this vital explanatory, causal role, we do not need to dismiss it as a mere fiction. But accepting the reality of personal action also, and in my view rightly, demands a more complex account of the relations between individual mental causes and the broader (explanatory and causal) concept of personal intentions. Mental causes are more tightly correlated with particular brain states, though they are not identical to them. Likewise, the intentions of a person as such are dependent on individual mental causes, though again without being identical to them. The layered nature of these relationships makes it more difficult to formulate explanations that jump over multiple levels. It is hard to draw direct correlations, for example, between person-level intentions and specific brain states. Such intentions invariably involve not just the relation between a particular idea and a particular brain state but reference outwards to many different ideas, to other persons, to culture and history, and perhaps to the divine. . . .

But humans also experience higher-order affective responses of much greater complexity, such as the sense of harmoniousness or well-being or dissonance. Once one has accepted mental causality, it becomes gratuitous to equate all such higher-order affective responses with releases of hormones and neurotransmitters. Ironically, it is this reductionism of the emotional realm which undergirds a seemingly very different response, the Platonic ascent to disembodied thought discussed above. Emotions, seen as primitive and undifferentiated, must be left behind if the highest levels of human cognition are to appear in their pure form. In contrast to both views, human existence in the world suggests that the conscious life—experiencing our most complex interrelationships, solving the most complex sorts of problems, synthesizing diverse dimensions into an integrated response or attitude—is accompanied by a higher-order affective state that is just as differentiated, as general, and as efficacious as the corresponding mental processes. . . .

I have argued that the human person, understood as integrated self or psychophysical agent-in-community, offers the appropriate level on which to introduce the possibility of divine agency. Here, and perhaps here alone, a divine agency could be operative that could exercise downward causal influence without being reduced to a manipulator of physical particles or psychotropic neurotransmitters. Only an influence that worked at the level of the person as such could influence the kinds of dimensions that are religiously significant without falling to the level of magic: a person's sense of her relations with others, her higher-order affective states, her ethical striving, and her sense of the meaningfulness of her existence in relation to the world around her.

By the nature of the case, one cannot give a very precise account of how the agency of an integrated person might be related to neurophysiological processes; reconstructing this type of agency requires the tools of the human sciences (psychology, sociology, and anthropology, but also history, the arts, ethics, etc.). It cannot be a direct relationship between an idea and a brain state but must involve the broader social and cultural context as well—which gives us reason, once again, to conclude that the human sciences are unlikely ever to be reduced to neurophysiology. As persons, and as social scientists, we nevertheless have good reason to think that persons do in fact do things qua persons in the world.

The situation for theists is similar, albeit one step further removed. The theist will be unable to explain in human-scientific terms how it is that God affects the person as such. We do know—or at least it is a core postulation of science—that all natural influences on the affective or mental state of persons are mediated through some sort of physical inputs to the person: spoken words, gestures, texts, artistic creations. By the nature of the case, the divine influence posited by theists would not be mediated in this fashion. This makes divine influence disanalogous to all other influences on human persons, again reflecting the dualistic moment in any account of divine action. Nevertheless, we have found a way to construe that influence that does not require negating or setting aside what is known scientifically about mind and emergence. The model I have employed—an influence at the level of integrated persons, which in turn influences specific mental, affective, and physical processes—avoids the implausibilities of the competing models of divine action.

32

On Divine and Human Agency
Reflections of a Co-laborer[1]

> Religion is the vision of something which stands beyond, behind, and within, the passing flux of immediate things; something which is real, and yet waiting to be realized; something which is a remote possibility, and yet the greatest of present facts; something that gives meaning to all that passes, and yet eludes apprehension; something whose possession is the final good, and yet is beyond all reach; something which is the ultimate ideal, and the hopeless quest.
>
> Alfred North Whitehead[2]

> Religion will not regain its old power until it can face change in the same spirit as does science. Its principles may be eternal, but the expression of those principles requires continual development.
>
> Alfred North Whitehead[3]

A SET OF BRILLIANTLY interconnected insights underlies Arthur Peacocke's work. The core motivation for his naturalism is the recognition that science stands in tension with many traditional views of divine action. If one accepts a picture of the world consistent with scientific practice and results, then one cannot imagine that God regularly intervenes in the natural order in a miraculous way, setting aside the patterns of nature and directly bringing about particular physical or chemical changes independent of the causal antecedents for these particular events. Peacocke insists, however, that preserving the integrity of the natural order is not inconsistent with Christian faith.

---

1. "On Divine and Human Agency: Reflections of a Co-laborer," as found within *Arthur Peacocke*, ed. by Clayton, *All That Is*, 163–75. Reprinted with the kind permission of Fortress.

2. Whitehead, *Science and the Modern World*, 275.

3. Ibid., 270.

The world can still be created by God and sustained in its existence at every moment by the divine will. Moreover, the world can be located within God, as panentheists maintain, such that God is "in, with, and under" all things, present to them in the most intimate way possible. The result is a notion of divine influence strong enough to undergird many, if not most, of the traditional Christian doctrines. This, at any rate, is my understanding of the program of Arthur Peacocke.

It is always difficult to write a response to the work of one's teacher. In younger years one tends merely to restate the teacher's own views. Then comes a phase when, in order to prove one's own independence, one criticizes overly harshly, hence often unfairly. With age, however, comes a new freedom to recognize the ongoing influence, to acknowledge one's debts with gratitude, and to express misgivings without onus.

The development of my own work in the field of science-religion discourse is intricately linked to the research program of Arthur Peacocke. Reading his work and engaging in intensive, multiyear conversations with him has significantly influenced not only my focus on panentheism and emergence, but also the particular form that these theories have taken in my writing. My debt is deep and lifelong, as is my gratitude. The critical concerns that surface in the following pages do not diminish but rather grow out of that relationship of influence.

Varieties of Naturalism

As his Essay shows, Peacocke is interested in a "naturalistic Christian faith" and is thus engaged in the project of "naturalizing" Christianity. But to what degree? Upon reflection, one realizes that there are many different ways to "naturalize" a faith tradition. Of course, both the process and the product vary widely depending on which tradition one has in mind; naturalizing Judaism or Hinduism has different requirements from naturalizing Christianity. It would turn out, I predict, that formulating a fully naturalized Hinduism, Buddhism, or Judaism is less difficult than fully naturalizing Christianity.

But even within a single tradition, such as Christianity, the project of naturalizing is not monolithic. One discovers a number of different ways that one might approach the task—an impression strengthened, incidentally, by the various responses contained in this volume. Consider these four approaches to naturalizing Christianity. First, one might view Christianity as a whole, its truth claims as well as its normative beliefs, as being of only historical or aesthetic interest, somewhat in the way that stories about the Greek gods still intrigue us today. Second, one might treat Christianity as still having ethical (or moral or political) interest, even though its system of beliefs is false. Although in this case one would not expect people to believe its specific truth claims, one would nonetheless maintain that the Christian tradition expresses certain values that continue to be crucial for living well and for rightly ordering human interactions. Within this group some affirm that other religions express these values in an equally effective fashion, whereas others insist that the Christian story represents a particularly powerful expression of these fundamental values.

A third kind of Christian naturalist retains some truth claims from her tradition, but only those that are fully consistent with science. Miracle claims have to go, she notes, along with all claims for a more-than-natural status for Jesus Christ. In fact, once one has begun to de-supernaturalize, she insists, the project must be carried out to the bitter end, on pain of inconsistency. Thus, for example, if "God" means a supernatural entity, the Creator and Sustainer of the universe, then language about God must either be eliminated altogether or thoroughly naturalized, such that the term now refers only to natural features and functions.

Modern theology is chock full of methods for naturalizing theistic language in this way. One thinks immediately of Ludwig Feuerbach, who understood the real referent of theological language to be the unlimited potential of human "species being." Or perhaps language about God might be preserved for the sake of its useful functions, as long as one does not thereby intend actually to refer to any existing divine being or beings. In whichever version, the functionalist strategy has been common within the social sciences from their founding figures until the present, from Emile Durkheim through Karl Marx through Sigmund Freud and on to Pascal Boyer and Scott Atran today.

On this third view, "God" might also be interpreted in the Kantian sense as an idea that is indispensable for practical reasoning, without thereby entailing the claim that a divine being actually exists. (Kantians reinterpret the notions of freedom and immortality in a similar fashion.) Neo-Kantians in the nineteenth century further extended the strategy of treating God as a "regulative" concept: one may speak "as if" there were a god yet without committing oneself to the assertion that some specific being of this type actually exists. The same move is often made with regard to divine action, of course; many use the language of divine action without claiming that any God-initiated events actually occur. All such language may be symbolic, for example—a way of describing how *we* view events in the world, rather than an account of any actual causal influence.

Fourth and finally, the "naturalizer" might preserve language of a Ground or Source of all things yet without asserting that this Ground or Source makes any direct interventions into the natural order. This fourth distinct approach to naturalizing Christianity seems to come closest to what Peacocke has in mind, and in the following pages I will examine it in some detail. It's important to note at the outset that this fourth category actually serves as the heading for at least two rather distinct methods, which we might label the "no influence" and the "no intervention" views. The "no influence" view, usually called *deism*, argues that the Ground or Source cannot have any causal impact at all on the natural world. Advocates include Baruch Spinoza and present-day "Ground of being" theists. The "no intervention" view, which Peacocke holds along with many other scholars in our field, allows in principle for an influence of God on the world, while insisting that the influence is exercised without breaking or setting aside natural laws.

As far as I can tell, no understanding of divine action that is stronger than the "no intervention" view would still count as a naturalized Christianity in any serious sense. Assume, for example, that God intervenes in the natural order in ways that set aside the natural patterns which we call the laws of nature. In this case the resulting outcomes will have to be explained, at least in part, by reference to this supernatural agent, God, and what God has done, *rather than* through the context of natural causes alone. It is the appositive "rather than" which, I take it, the naturalizing project seeks to overcome.

In short, the phrase "naturalistic Christian faith" serves as the rubric for at least four radically different programs, running from Christian atheism on the one side to personal theism with a real (though non-interventionist) sense of divine action on the other. Recognizing the broad spectrum of *degrees* of naturalizing, and the fact that Peacocke stands at the milder end of the continuum of naturalisms, helps one to understand the proposal that he has advanced here. More radical programs of naturalizing allow God-language, if at all, only in the domains of what David Hume famously called the "Before" and "After." Proponents of more radical naturalization do in fact sometimes say that "it's as if" the entire natural order were surrounded by, upheld by, or dependent on "God," but they passionately reject any real assertions of divine influence and often insist on the purely metaphorical (hence, non-metaphysical) character of all God-language.[4] By contrast, as long as one continues to speak of "special divine action," as Peacocke does—that is, as long as one imagines an influence of God on some particular natural event E, such that the full explanation of E must include some reference to that divine activity—one has accepted a partially rather than fully naturalized Christian faith.

The challenge of divine action

We've now located Peacocke's proposal with reference to other projects that might also fall under the rubric of a "naturalistic Christian faith." The task now is to evaluate it on its own terms.

The goal of Peacocke's project is to identify and defend a middle space between two positions on divine action that he believes are untenable: traditional miracle claims on the one hand, and the denial of all special divine action on the other. Thomas Aquinas provided what has become the classic definition of miracles. He distinguished three "degrees" of miracles, noting that "the highest degree in miracles" involves "those works wherein something is done by God that nature can never do. For instance, that two bodies occupy the same place, that the sun recede or stand still, that the sea be divided and make way to passers by. . . . The greater the work done

---

4. See for example Kauffman, "Beyond Reductionism," 808–28.

by God, and the further it is removed from the capability of nature, the greater the miracle."[5] Some 700 years later, C. S. Lewis defended another version of third-degree miracles in his famous book on divine action: "Nature (at any rate the surface of our own planet) is perforated or pock-marked all over by little orifices at each of which something of a different kind from herself—namely reason—can do things to her." He added, "If God annihilates or creates or deflects a unit of matter He has created a new situation. . . . Immediately all Nature domiciles this new situation, makes it at home in her realm, adapts all other events to it."[6]

This is the sort of divine action that Peacocke's naturalizing project seeks to dispense with, and he studiously avoids affirming any specific miraculous events of this kind. At the same time, he resists the conclusion that *no* special divine action occurs. Contrast his view with that of Maurice Wiles, who defends one of the more radically naturalized versions of Christianity. Wiles retains the notion of God but clearly refuses to make God the explanation of any particular event—which is presumably why advocates of special divine action have so consistently directed their fire in his direction. Wiles does not believe that God carries out intentional acts in the world; hence he denies that "we can properly speak of God being more creative in one place than in another."[7] Yet he still wishes to speak of "the living God, the source of all life and the source of the authentic life which his worshipers seek to realize in grateful awareness of his all-pervasive and sustaining presence."[8] That is, the only act that God actually performs is the universal act of creating and sustaining the world. Humans are nevertheless free to *see* individual events *as* acts of God, and thus to speak of special divine action in this (regulative, symbolic, or fictive) sense. The reason for this strategy is clear. As Gordon Kaufman argues elsewhere, contemporary science presupposes that the natural world is a tightly interconnected web of events; each part of the web is a causal consequence of other parts (perhaps with the addition of some randomness), rather than a self-initiating agent of its own. Kaufman therefore concludes that particular divine actions are "not merely improbable or difficult to believe: they are literally inconceivable."[9]

Clearly Peacocke does not wish to argue for a complete absence of intentional or "special" divine influence, as Wiles and Kaufman do. It turns out, however, that the middle domain between absence and intervention is rather difficult to specify. Many theologians have the intuition that some such *tertium quid* must exist, but it has turned out to be difficult to specify it in a conceptually rigorous manner. Think, for example, of the mediating proposal developed by James Kellenberger, who writes:

5. Aquinas, *Summa contra Gentiles*, III, Q. 103.
6. Lewis, *Miracles*.
7. See Wiles, "Religious Authority and Divine Action," 186.
8. See Wiles, *God's Action in the World*, 108.
9. See Kaufman, "On the Meaning of Act of God," 175–201. For a helpful presentation of these authors see Saunders, *Divine Action*, chapter 2.

> Natural miracles occur through God's agency; they are not instances of God's direct action. There is no intervention by God, but God, as creator, is deemed thinkable for establishing the ground of natural events.[10]

As Nicholas Saunders notes:

> There appears to be no real distinction on this account between a "natural" event and one of God's actions.... By again shifting the emphasis away from causal questions Kellenberger feels able to assert that someone who identifies and believes that a particular event is a natural miracle will be thankful to God for its existence, while if the event is seen as only natural this element of thankfulness will be missing.[11]

Saunders' challenge is clear enough. Yet Peacocke has seen, as Saunders did not, that developing an adequate account of *human* agency in the world—one that is deeply naturalistic while still preserving the distinctive features of personal causality—may be an indispensable step toward formulating a credible theory of divine agency in the world. No theory of human agency is by itself sufficient to prove divine action, of course. But for those who hope to offer a "theology for a scientific age," the detour through human agency may well be necessary.

The problem of personal agency

In a variety of publications, Peacocke has described the scientific picture of the world as involving a network of embedded systems. Parts constitute wholes, which themselves become parts within greater wholes, and so forth, until one reaches the entire cosmos as a single interrelated natural system. The scientific evidence in favor of this account is strong enough that it needs no further defense here.

Let's assume that Peacocke has met the first objective of a naturalistic Christian theology, namely to show the compatibility between *at least some form of* Christian faith and this particular scientific picture of the world. A science of embedded causal networks does not need to negate or undercut belief in the existence of God, divine creation, divine sustenance of the world, or divine omnipresence in the strongest possible sense. That God may have had intentions in creating the world, and may continue to have intentions in sustaining it, and that God can be present both to the whole and to every one of its parts, are both perfectly acceptable within this framework. Given these two premises, it is also unproblematic to speak of *the creation of the world as a whole* as a divine act.

So far so good. But Peacocke also wants to say more. In *God and Science* he adds:

---

10. See Kellenberger, "Miracles," 157.
11. Saunders, *Divine Action*, 51.

> In thus speaking of God's interaction with the world, it has not been possible to avoid speaking of God's single "intentions," of God having purposes, thereby using the language of personal agency. For these ideas of whole–part constraint by God cannot be expounded without relating them to the concept of God as, in some sense, an agent, least misleadingly described as personal.[12]

Surely this is right: what distinguishes theists from deists (and others) is their continuing desire to speak of God's intentions and purposes in the world after the moment of creation. It therefore becomes urgent for us to ask: does Peacocke's framework allow him to speak in this fashion? As we will see, there is at least some reason to worry that it does not.

The core notion that Peacocke uses to describe relations among the different embedded systems or levels of reality from a scientific perspective is *whole–part constraint*. Wholes formed out of parts within nature in turn constrain the behaviors of those parts. (Note his emphasis elsewhere that "'whole–part' is synonymous with 'system–constituent.'"[13]) When Peacocke turns to the questions of personal agency and the God–world relation, he begins by appealing to this notion. What is worrisome about this strategy, however, is that whole–part constraint is not a form of agency, at least not in anything like the normal, intuitive sense of this term. Wholes constrain the behavior of their parts in a passive sense, whereas personal agents are actors who are the active authors of their own actions. Two chemicals may react differently when they are held together by a test tube than they would if the molecules were floating freely in a large body of liquid, but we would not normally say that the test tube is an "agent" in the chemical process. The architecture of the motherboard within your computer constrains the electronic processes that occur, but your motherboard's architecture as such is not an agent. Imagine that it turns out (an assumption I take to be false) that all there is to human thought are the neuronal signals and the electro-chemical interactions at the synaptic junctures. Clearly the aggregate that we call the brain as a whole—that is, the sum total of neurons and neural connections for a given individual—constrains the outcome of the neural processes within it. But we would not therefore conclude that the brain as a whole is an agent; rather, we would say that the structural features of the brain affect the behavior of its parts in certain ways. In short, whole–part constraint is not sufficient for agential or intentional language.

Sometimes Peacocke seems to feel the force of this problem. Over the course of his career he has vacillated between speaking of "whole–part constraint" and "top-down causation." Where he speaks of top-down causation, he invariably offers a conceptual framework robust enough to support mental causation and personal agency. At other times—disappointingly—he either treats the two different concepts as interchangeable or seeks to subsume the latter under the former. Thus he writes, for

---

12. Peacocke, *God and Science*, 19.
13. See Peacocke, "Emergence, Mind, and Divine Action," 267n10.

example, "Hence the term *whole-part influence* will be used to represent the net effect of *all* those ways in which a system-as-a-whole, operating from its 'higher' level, is a determining factor in what happens to its constituent parts, the 'lower' level."[14] Now recall Peacocke's view that "whole–part" is synonymous with "system–constituent." Also, let's omit the phrase "operating from its higher level" for the moment, since it's not yet clear in what sense wholes are "operators." Doing so yields the thesis statement, "Hence the term *system–constituent influence* will be used to represent the net effect of all those ways in which a system-as-a-whole . . . is a determining factor in what happens to its constituent parts, the 'lower' level."

But systems as "determining factors" in this sense are not of intentional agents; hence such language is not sufficient to give a (non-reductive) account of intentional agency. Recall the example of the brain and its neurons above. Peacocke seems to recognize the difficulty when he proceeds to assert, "One should perhaps better speak of '*determinative influences*' rather than of 'causation.'"[15] For here's the problem: doesn't the generic term "determinative influence" obscure a crucial distinction—the distinction between the types of "influence" that are sufficient for intentional agency and causality, and the types that are not? If this *is* the crucial distinction, as I think, what are the conditions that must be fulfilled for an instance of "determinative influence" to count as intentional agency?

Three approaches to personal agency

In two recent articles, both appearing in collections from Oxford University Press, Peacocke offers a sophisticated response to this problem, which represents one of the most intriguing proposals available in our field today. The first article, already cited above, offers a brilliant analysis of three different approaches for conceiving the notion of mental causation. The first approach—"Levels H are states of the brain; levels L are individual neuronal event"[16]—is clearly meant to exclude mental causation as such; the causation to which it refers must be neuronal, and perhaps ultimately microphysical.

The second approach at least does not dismiss mental causation altogether: "Levels H are mental-with-brain states; levels L are individual neuronal events."[17] As Peacocke comments (I omit his references to his diagrams), "This is to postulate that the higher-level now mental-with-brain states have a determinative influence, *jointly* with the lower-level neural states, on the succession of mental-with-brain states . . . ."[18] This approach seeks to make room for the insight that the level of the mental is genuinely emergent; it is not reducible to the neuronal or microphysical level. After all, if mental

---

14. Peacocke, "Emergence, Mind, and Divine Action," 265, emphasis added.
15. Ibid., 264.
16. Ibid., 269.
17. Peacocke, "Emergence, Mind, and Divine Action," 270.
18. Ibid., 271.

phenomena *are* non-reducible, they must have some effect (assuming, as we must, that "to be real is to do something").

Unfortunately, however, this second approach is not yet able to explain what *is* this more-than-physical causation that produces these new kinds of effects. It must clearly involve more than the "two levels of description" approach that John Searle advocated in 1984, since Peacocke himself criticizes that view.[19] Yet if we are told merely that two dimensions or levels conjointly bring about some effect, we have not yet been given an actual theory of mental causation—apart from the initial claim that something called "the mental" plays *some* role here. Surely, when faced with such an elliptical claim, the principle of parsimony will suffice to direct one's attention toward the type of causality that is better understood—the efficient causality of physical forces. In order to take the "both-and" in this position seriously, one would need to know exactly what it is that "the mental" is supposed to be doing. But those who advocate the second approach do not yet take on this task.

Thus, one must turn to Peacocke's third interpretation of mental causation for an account of intentional agency. This account holds that "Levels *H* are mental states; levels *L* are brain states," and "mental activity—the content of our consciousness describable in first-person language—is a real emergent *from* brain activity."[20] For "this mental emergence is a distinctive reality which has its own determinant efficacy."[21] Peacocke brings powerful arguments in defense of this third option; together they provide strong support for the conclusion that intentional agency requires mental causal activity. If one rejects mental causation in this third sense, one should conclude that language of intentional agency is illusory, since the kind of causation that it requires does not occur. Only if first-person mental activity is treated as a real emergent, "Could [it] be causally effective on successive brain states.... Mental events, such as intentions—whatever they are ontologically—have determinative ('causal') efficacy in the physical world."[22]

Divine agency and the imago Dei correlation

Let us use the term *imago Dei correlation* to convey the formal connection that almost inevitably exists between one's understanding of God and humanity.[23] The correlation may exist between views of human personhood and divine personhood, or between human and divine agency, or between God's relation to the world on the one hand and the relation of an individual's thought and consciousness to her body on the other. For

---

19. Ibid., 267n11.
20. Ibid., 271.
21. Ibid., 272.
22. Ibid., 271, 273.
23. I examine the correlation in chap. 6 of *In Quest of Freedom*.

panentheists, for example, it takes the form of what I have called "the panentheistic analogy."[24]

It is thus not surprising that each of Peacocke's three approaches to human consciousness and mentality would produce a separate understanding of the God–world relation and divine action. The first approach does not exclude the existence of God, but it makes any direct influence of God-as-agent on human thought impossible, since it rules out mental or spiritual causation.[25] Nonetheless, as we saw above, there might still be symbolic and figurative uses of Christian language that could be built on top of this ontological platform, as it were. One thinks of the sometimes rich uses of Christian language that one finds among leading deists through the centuries.

The same is true for the second approach. I believe that all the Christological and sacramental language that Peacocke employs in his Essay, above, and most of what occurs in his other publications, *could* still be retained under this interpretation. Although talk of divine effects and mental causes could no longer be given a direct or literal interpretation, symbolic re-interpretations might take up the slack. On this approach the constraining effects of the world-as-a-whole could not literally represent an intentional guidance by God; at least the model provides one with no grounds for making such a claim. Nonetheless, one could always reply, "I picture God to myself as something like an intentional agent who is able to exercise mental (or perhaps better, spiritual) agency. And my model allows me to say that 'the universe as a whole' constrains all of its parts. Thus I shall speak of this highest whole-part constraint *as if* it were the expression of an underlying divine intention." One would have to admit that the language of direct intentional causation is not actually supported by the model, but it's not *inconsistent* with the model either. Advocates of this second view claim that a naturalistic theory of human persons warrants nothing stronger than whole–part constraint, and then, perhaps for religious reasons, they supplement that conclusion with what can only be understood as metaphorical theological language of divine intentional agency at the level of the universe-as-a-whole.

Of course, once one has chosen to define the divine-human relation in this way, one could extend a similar status to much of traditional Christian language. Having assumed that "God" is intending whatever effects follow from universal whole–part constraint, one might then naturally speak of those effects as an influx of divinely-intended information into the system. Since whole–part constraints can in some way influence every part within the system, one could imagine this divine influence as extending also to every individual person. This move might open the door to yet further extensions of theological metaphors. For example, one could imagine that the (divinely intended) informational content from the universe-as-a-whole also applies to oneself, *treating* it *as*

---

24. See Clayton, *God and Contemporary Science*, chapter 8.

25. An indirect influence might still be possible. For example, God might bring about direct changes at the micro-physical level, which might then be augmented by some mechanism until they induced changes in human thought.

a personal communication from *deus pro nobis*, "God for us." Christological and sacramental language could then be added as further metaphorical extensions of the content of this "divine communication." At the same time, by emphasizing that one has drawn one's model from the natural sciences, one might well claim that one's talk of divinely intended content is consistent with the scientific worldview.

Such a use of theological metaphors may not be explicitly ruled out by contemporary science in the way that strong miracles language is. The trouble, however, is that, even if the language of divine agency is not strictly speaking contradicted by science, it is utterly unsupported by any analog in the natural world. Earlier we saw that whole–part constraint by the brain, in the sense of Peacocke's second approach, is not sufficient to count as intentional agency. On what grounds, then, could whole–part constraint justify one in treating the universe-as-a-whole as exhibiting intentional personal agency? The apparent arbitrariness of this move should lead one to give marked preference to the final of Peacocke's three approaches to personal agency—or else to abandon talk of divine action in any sense stronger than what Wiles and Kaufman have advocated.

Personal divine agency

Although the third approach implicitly underlies virtually all of Peacocke's theological treatments of the God–world relation, it is worked out explicitly in the two recent papers mentioned above.[26] Peacocke clearly understands God to be a constraining influence on all that exists. It seems obvious that the Ground of all things would be related to the-world-as-a-whole *at least* as strongly as the way in which a system is related to its constituents. But Peacocke decisively supplements this minimal condition by adding the framework of panentheism, that is, the view that the world is contained within the divine, although God is also more than the world. Panentheism offers a way to personalize the divine "whole–part constraint" without falling into pantheism, i.e., the complete identification of God and world.[27]

Peacocke recognizes that his theory of whole–part influence "depend[s] on an analogy only with complex natural systems in general and on the way whole–part influence operates in them."[28] Yet, as we have seen, that particular analogy can't do all the work in the case of the God–world relation, at least not if theism is also to involve the notion of divine personal agency. Thus Peacocke adds, "There is little doubt that [my model] needs to be rendered more cogent by the recognition that, among natural systems, the instance *par excellence* of whole–part influence in a complex system is that of personal agency."[29] . . .

26. Peacocke, "Emergence, Mind, and Divine Action," and "Emergent Realities with Causal Efficacy."
27. See Clayton and Peacocke, eds., *In Whom We Live.*
28. See Peacocke, *Paths from Science Towards God*, 114.
29. Ibid., 114.

The burning question is whether talk of this new kind of causality, the causality of personal agency, can be justified. On the third approach to mental causation given above, it clearly is; under the first two approaches, I have argued, it is not. If this argument is sound, Peacocke's options become very clear. Only if he is willing to endorse mental causation in the third, stronger sense, as I also am—and assuming that our arguments in defense of the third option hold up—could he be warranted in speaking of divine personal influence on the world. (Again, remember that we are discussing a necessary but not sufficient condition for a theory of divine action.) Only if mental causation is viable[30] can one make sense of theological statements of the sorts he makes in [his essay within this book]. . . . Divine influence of this sort cannot be merely an instance of whole–part constraint. Rather, it manifests *distinctively personal causation on God's part, causation that makes a difference within the world.*

. . . I have argued, however, that as long as Peacocke wishes to defend some form of personal theism, he is obligated to supplement whole–part constraint with a theory of personal causation. One must first defend some form of mental causation: "Persons as such experience themselves as *inter alia* determinative agents with respect to their own bodies and the surrounding world (including other persons), so that the exercise of personal *agency* by individuals transpires to be a paradigm case and supreme exemplar of whole-part influence."[31] Only then can one extend the analogy to argue that

> God could cause particular events and patterns of events to occur which express God's intentions. These would then be the result of "divine action," as distinct from the divine holding in existence of all-that-is, and would not otherwise have happened had God not so intended.[32]

Conclusion

We have found no inherent impossibility to the "naturalistic Christian faith" that Peacocke espouses in this book and elsewhere. Now conservatives sometimes argue that there is no way to preserve Christian language without a "higher" view of divine action. But if their claim is that there is no coherent, consistent way to use Christian language without (say) physical miracles, the claim is not true: Arthur Peacocke's overall program, at least in the form defended here, offers one such way. (Indeed, assuming

---

30. This "only if" phrase demands one qualification. Throughout this response I assume—as I think Peacocke does also—that one needs to give some sort of an account of what one means by divine action language. This claim may be, and often is, disputed by authors on this topic. Thus some have argued that no conceptual account is necessary because all language about God is symbolic, apophatic, regulative, pragmatically useful, or "internal to the practice of faith." Any one of these approaches might allow one to speak of divine "acts" in the world (the scare quotes now become crucial!) or to label various events as "expressions of divine grace."

31. Peacocke, "Emergence, Mind, and Divine Action," 273–74.

32. Peacocke, "Emergent Realities with Causal Efficacy."

that even more radical forms of naturalized Christianity than Peacocke's are possible, there may be multiple consistent models. This would mean that internally consistent reinterpretations of the Christian tradition can be found across the spectrum from fundamentalism to Christian atheism—which is not to say that all of these reinterpretations are equally plausible or desirable).

In particular, it turns out to be possible to use Christian theological language with some level of coherence on *any* of the three approaches to mental causation that Peacocke outlines. One need not doubt that a deep religious and devotional attitude, serious moral commitment, and transformative religious experience can occur within each of the three models. The task is therefore not merely to determine whether Christian language *can* be used consistently within a vastly more naturalized context than the worldviews that dominated during most of the history of Christian thought (although Peacocke sometimes writes as if that were the main task facing a "theology for a scientific age"). The harder task is to evaluate what is the best overall balance of naturalism and theism—a burning question for our day that I have only begun to address here.

We did begin the process of evaluation, however. Among the myriad methods for evaluating theological proposals we focused on the issue of coherence, and specifically on the quest for a deeper coherence between one's view of personal agency and one's theory of divine agency, or what I called the "*imago Dei* correlation." Of the three theories of mental causation that Peacocke analyzes, we found that only the third—"mental events, such as intentions . . . have determinative ('causal') efficacy in the physical world"[33]—could do justice to the notion of divine personal agency. It is indeed true that personal agency represents the "paradigm case and supreme exemplar of whole–part influence."[34] This third type of approach must therefore undergird any adequate theory of agency, both in the case of personal agents and in the case of divine agency.[35]

---

33. Peacocke, "Emergent Realities with Causal Efficacy."

34. Ibid., 273–74.

35. Many aspects of the interpretation and constructive position presented here were developed in multiyear correspondence and conversations with Steven Knapp, whom I also thank for detailed criticisms of an early draft of this essay.

PART VI

Progressive Theology

33

Things have Changed, or "Toto, we're not in Kansas Anymore"[1]

OVER THE LAST YEARS all of us have watched the geography of the American church undergo a radical transformation. It's almost as if there has been a major earthquake—or, more accurately, a series of major earthquakes—realigning the entire landscape in which we live. It reminds me of pictures of the San Andreas Fault in California. On the west side of the fault line you can see an outcropping of rocks coming down the hill. On the east side of the line you see the rock ridge continuing on its way back up the other hill. The trouble is, the ridge on the east side is about a hundred yards further south from the one on the west—the entire land mass has rearranged itself. That's what many of us see as we look around American society today.

Religion in America Fifty Years Ago

I wasn't an adult in the 1950s, so I can't speak from experience about the church in the post-war, Eisenhower era. But I can point you to a fantastic description of American religious life in the 1950s in the classic study by Will Herberg, *Protestant, Catholic, Jew*. In the vast majority of the communities that Herberg studied, people's Christian or Jewish identity was one of the very top items on their identity checklist. It stood up there with their patriotic identity as Americans (in fact, as in our day, the two were frequently confused with each other!). Especially if you lived in a smaller town, you would very likely have attended the same church that your parents had attended. Probably you would have been baptized and married in the same church, and you expected your funeral service to take place there in due course.

---

1. "Things have Changed, or 'Toto, we're not in Kansas Anymore,'" as found within Clayton, *Transforming Christian Theology,* 11–16 Reprinted with the kind permission of Fortress.

PART VI: PROGRESSIVE THEOLOGY

Not only that, but you would have shared most of your fundamental values in common with the others in your congregation. Since the vast majority of Americans were either Protestant, Roman Catholic, or Jewish there was a remarkable degree of consensus, and thus a relatively small range of choice. Your church or synagogue taught and reinforced your core values about faith, sex, family, politics—you name it. It was also the center of your social world. Two or three times a week Christians came to church to be together with other church people. Church social events stood at the center of your social life, and your life partner (for that's what marriages were expected to produce in those days) was very likely drawn from your broader church community.

Thus Herberg could write in 1955 that, "Almost everybody in the United States today locates himself in one of the three great religious communities. Asked to identify themselves in terms of religious 'preferences,' 95 per cent of the American people, according to a recent public opinion survey, declared themselves to be either Protestants, Catholics, or Jews." It was not a great decade for free thinkers. . . .

Herberg's data showed that church membership was growing twice as fast as the American population was. It was the Golden Age for the American church. But it was not to last long.

The '60s and '70s

We know the 1960s as a time of radical change, when huge transformations in beliefs and values began to take place. What is interesting about the early 1960s, however, is that, although values did begin to change, Christian and Jewish communities continued to provide the primary point of orientation for most people. It was a time of revolutionary (and often confusing) transition within American culture, and yet for a long time people continued their high levels of involvement in churches and synagogues. It was well into the 1970s, or even later, before the cultural changes produced gaps between the people and their congregations, so that they gradually began identifying less with their traditional religious communities.

By the late 1960s and early 1970s, however—the period when I came of age religiously—there was a wide, almost disorienting range of religious options. My own story was perhaps not untypical for the time: I could continue to attend the mainline Presbyterian church that had been my church home since elementary school. I could attend an evangelical Bible study group associated with one of the evangelical churches in my area. I could attend a charismatic prayer meeting once a week, affiliated with a Pentecostal church. I could actually start attending the Assemblies of God church. Or I could make a community of "Jesus People" my Christian home, becoming a part of what would later be called the non-denominational or independent church movement. (In fact, over time I tried *all* these options—as many others were also doing.)

Having all these options to decide from was way more confusing than if I had been living in Ames, Iowa, or Bakersfield, California, in the 1950s! Still, note one feature of this choice: *all of these options were options in organized religion.* The option, "spiritual but not religious," was just beginning to appear on the map of American religious choice, but it involved at that time only a small percentage of the American public. In the early 1970s most of our real religious options were still "institutional" options.

American Religion in the Early Twenty-first Century

Now fast-forward to today. Surveys funded by the Pew Charitable Trust indicate an ever-increasing number of Americans are stepping outside of institutional religion altogether. You are probably already familiar with the steady decrease in membership in mainline churches. But did you know that, according to a recent U.S. Religious Landscape Survey, "the United States is on the verge of becoming a minority Protestant country"? According to the Pew Forum on Religion and Public Life, only 51 percent of Americans still report that they are members of Protestant denominations. Evangelical Protestant churches, together with historically black Protestant churches, make up 33.2 percent of the overall adult population, whereas mainline Protestant churches now represent only 18.1 percent of that population. Moreover, the "graying" of the mainline continues; roughly half the members of mainline churches are age fifty and older. The 2008 Pew report also points out a new pattern: "the proportion of the population that is Protestant has declined markedly in recent decades while the proportion of the population *that is not affiliated with any particular religion* has increased significantly" (emphasis added). Throughout the period of the '70s and '80s, a constant 60 to 65 percent of respondents identified themselves as Protestant. The early '90s began a period of steady decline. By 2006, both the Pew survey and the General Social Surveys (GSS) found Protestant affiliation down to roughly 50 percent. Most of the overall decline is due to the rapid membership drop in the mainline churches. The Pew report notes, "What scholars who have analyzed the GSS data have found is that the proportion of the population identifying with the large mainline Protestant denominations has declined significantly in recent decades, while the proportion of Protestants identifying with the large evangelical denominations has increased."

But the evangelical churches haven't been shielded from losses either. The publishing arm of the Southern Baptist Convention, LifeWay Christian Resources, reported recently that in 2007 "the number of people baptized in Southern Baptist churches fell for the third straight year," reaching "the denomination's lowest level since 1987," and "total membership dropped by nearly 40,000." In 2007 alone baptisms dropped nearly 5.5 percent. Similar losses in other evangelical denominations are viewed with serious concern among leaders. The grounds for these declines will occupy us throughout the coming pages. One obvious reason is that the range of religious options and identities has exploded for Americans today. Most of us know friends, colleagues, or acquaintances who are Christian, Jewish, Muslim; Buddhist, Hindu, Taoist; atheist, agnostic, "doubting believers"; pantheist, panentheist, neo-pagan; Mormon, Jehovah's Witness, Church of God; Baháʼí, Zoroastrian, perennialist—the list goes on and on. Faced with such a confusing array of options, more and more Americans are choosing not to choose. They develop "serial religious personalities," progressing gradually (or not so gradually) through a huge range of religious options, influenced by age, friends, geographic location, newspapers, or the most recent books they find in the Metaphysics section of their local bookstore. I think a lot of Americans feel like the six-year-old who finally convinces her parents to take her to Baskin-Robbins: it's so overwhelming to encounter that huge range of flavors that you just can't decide which one to try. Some try them all; others stop coming.

This bewildering multiplicity of religious (and non-religious) options is only the start for Christianity's new context. What it means to be church today, and what it will mean over the coming two to three decades, is affected just as strongly by the explosion of new technologies and the radically new forms of social networking that they create. Who could have imagined just ten years ago that millions of people would find their primary social home on a website? That we would spend more time on Facebook than on the phone? That millions of us would find our life partners through eHarmony.com? That the future of Iran would be significantly influenced by Twitter.com? That a president would be elected in no small part because of personal appeals posted on YouTube? First emailing, then texting, now tweeting and other new options are fundamentally transforming our social world. Religious identities by 2020—just a few short years away—will be determined by technologies that we can't even begin to imagine today.

Consider the role of Beliefnet.com. This amazing website and social networking center is now the go-to place for millions of Americans when they want to learn about religion, post personal thoughts and responses, or find religious community. Pastors and religious authorities no longer interpret the religious options for most Americans today, whether or not they still attend a church or synagogue; websites do. We can learn anything—and proclaim anything—directly on the Internet. If you are unsure about your religious identity, for example, just try the "Belief-O-Matic" function at Beliefnet.com. As the opening blurb proclaims:

> Even if YOU don't know what faith you are, Belief-O-Matic™ knows. Answer 20 questions about your concept of God, the afterlife, human nature, and more, and Belief-O-Matic™ will tell you what religion (if any) you practice . . . or ought to consider practicing . . . (Warning: Belief-O-Matic™ assumes no legal liability for the ultimate fate of your soul.)

Things have Changed, or "Toto, we're not in Kansas Anymore"

No wonder people feel a little strange participating in a social arrangement called the "local congregation," a structure designed for the world of the eighteenth century, before there were cars or even light bulbs!

34

Why the Answers Must be Theological[1]

EVERY CHRISTIAN HAS A theology. For that matter, so does every Jew or Muslim or Hindu. A theology, in the broadest sense, just means what you believe about God (*theos*). Tragically, theology somehow got turned into a professional sport—a move that produced many of the negative tendencies that we already know from professional sports in America (except for the high salaries).

The invention of "theologians" as the professional authorities on Christian belief may turn out to be one of the really damaging things that have occurred in the history of the church. This invention doesn't get as much press as the invention of clergy—which has tended to undercut the "priesthood of all believers"—but it's right up there in importance. As long as there are professional theologians, those who *don't* carry this honorific title begin to assume that they can't do theology or aren't allowed to. The result was almost inevitable: intelligent, thinking people tend to sit in pews and wait for someone else to tell them what they should believe. If what they hear from the pulpit or from other sources of theological authority matches what they happen to believe, then they feel confirmed in their sense that they are right (and others must be wrong). If what the theological authorities are saying does *not* match what they believe, their recourse is to leave the church, convinced that they have no place there. Or, they may stay, but with a vague feeling of unsettledness or even guilt, worrying that their own religious intuitions and experiences don't quite fit in. Some become rebels, with no recourse but to protest against the church establishment from outside. Others just give up their own beliefs, bow to authority, and begin trying to believe what the professional theologians tell them they *ought* to believe.

None of these solutions is good. The professionalization of theology has taken it out of the hands (and heads) of those to whom it really belongs: every believing person, and every person who would like to believe. The results have been not only

---

[1]. "Why the Answers Must be Theological," as found within Clayton, *Transforming Christian Theology*, 19–26. Reprinted with the kind permission of Fortress.

unproductive but also damaging for the spiritual lives of many who are Christians or who would like to know more about this Way.

Of course, churches have tried out a variety of means to address people's confusion about what they really believe. Some years ago, people began to define a subgroup of church-attendees as "seekers." Making room for seekers allows people to participate in the religious community as fully as they wish, yet without having to pretend that they believe things that they don't believe. I sometimes wish that whole churches would describe themselves as seekers—Christian communities where every attendee brings what he or she knows and has experienced of God, yet where no one claims to have God fully figured out. But there's also a downside to this term. Its very meaning contrasts "seekers" with "possessors." So it tends to imply that the rest of the people in the community already *have it*, whereas the seekers are the second-class citizens who are merely trying to *find it*. This then tends to create yet another two-tiered system, another version of the "haves" and the "have-nots." It's obvious such thinking doesn't fit for "a people on the Way." The real contrast is not seekers versus possessors, but seeking and finding—and seeking some more. Since the moments of finding, we believe, never occur without the participation of God, pride and possessiveness are not exactly the right responses.

So what's the first step in returning theology to the people?

A Theology is a World-and-Life-View

The quickest way to understand why the dichotomy between professional theologians and the rest of us won't work is to talk about worldviews. A worldview is just what it sounds like: your overall view of the world, the cosmos, and everything in it. Until you think about it, much of your worldview is probably subconscious. *Others* can often describe what we really believe by watching how we live, but we may be unaware of it. Since worldviews also include many beliefs about how one should live, I prefer to call them *world-and-life-views*, or WLVs for short.

Every person has a WLV, a set of beliefs about what exists and what is most valuable. Some WLVs include beliefs about ultimate reality; some of *those* affirm that God is the ultimate reality; and some of *those* are Christian WLVs. So you see that a theology is only one kind of a WLV, and a Christian theology is only one form of theology. Jewish, Muslim, and Hindu practices all presuppose WLVs that are theological. Existentialism, materialism, and the "scientism" of a person like Richard Dawkins are non-theological WLVs. In the end, *every person who carries out conscious actions in the world possesses a WLV*, whether or not he or she is aware of it.

One of my early jobs was teaching philosophy in a university in California. My first semester I was assigned to teach four sections of critical thinking, and every semester after that for some years I taught one or two additional sections of that same class. You probably already know that classes like critical thinking and freshman comp are pretty far down the popularity charts. I didn't realize until I walked into the class the first day, however, that most students viewed my class as one of the most onerous requirements of their entire freshman year. I either had to find a way to make critical thinking fun, or my teaching career was quickly going to become hell on earth. Gradually I found a model that worked—so well, in fact, that teaching critical thinking became one of the great joys of my teaching career. The secret is WLVs. Every freshman student had to do what I'm now asking you to do. Each of them had to bring to awareness the beliefs, attitudes, and values that he or she held at the subconscious level. Concrete beliefs and values came first, since they're easier to access. Then gradually the students moved to more and more abstract beliefs and values. By the end of the class, students could identify their WLVs and show how these beliefs (implicitly or explicitly) guide their actions. For the final exam I gave them hard moral and ethical and political dilemmas, and they had to compose answers to them by appealing to their own WLV. The class became famous; students would say, "Yeah, for Clayton's final you have to write out your whole worldview!"

Implicitly, I was teaching that philosophy, like theology, is an amateur sport. Every human being who knows that he or she will someday die naturally engages in philosophy. Hence, I used to argue, there should be no such thing as a "professional philosopher." It was fascinating to explore with students what their WLVs really were and then to track the complex ways that their WLVs supported (or undercut) their actions. Now people under thirty may have an easier time surfacing what they really believe. But if they can do it, why can't every adult? Is it that we're afraid that what we really believe is not what our parents taught us or what our churches say we should believe—and perhaps not even what *we* thought we believed before we started thinking about the subject.

The same thing is true of theology. *Theology is just the shape your WLV takes if you believe in God.* For this reason, theology is—or at least *ought* to be—an amateur sport. Everyone who believes in God is, by that very fact, a theologian, and everyone who believes that God is somehow revealed in the one called Jesus Christ is, to that extent, a Christian theologian. If so many of us are theologians, then the idea of a "professional theologian" is a misnomer. It's a dangerous concept that can easily disenfranchise ordinary believers as they struggle to get clear on where they really stand.

In fact, as we've already seen, the situation today is much worse. Professional theologians (whether they intend it or not) often end up training believers in what they are *supposed* to believe, producing the sorts of negative consequences I mentioned in the Introduction. I want to suggest a radically different model. If some people are to be paid for being theologians, then they should view themselves as coaches, not just as conveyers of true propositions. Just as a good soccer coach runs drills that help players develop skills and improve their game by building on their own strengths, so theologians should teach in such a way that helps believers get better at recognizing and formulating their own beliefs.

Of course, along the way there's content to learn as well. We must continue to teach what's in the Christian scriptures, since they are the primary texts about Jesus. We also need to teach how these texts have been interpreted throughout history. But do we really need to be doctrinaire and exclusivist in how we do this? What if we start teaching what have been the core Christian questions and answers over the last two thousand years, and then asking the men and women in our classes to develop their own personal affirmations (testimonies) on the central topics of the Christian faith? I'll come back to this idea shortly and describe how this might be done.

Imagine letting theology classes be more like the critical thinking classes I used to teach. Future ministers might be asked to write out their Christian world-and-life view, to learn to debate openly (and well!) about what they believe, and then to become proficient at applying it to real-life situations in their lives, in congregations, and in the world today. Imagine how such training would change preaching and ministry and church leadership! Now imagine what would happen if local churches and other Christian groups started doing the same thing with *every person* who is trying to understand what it means to live life with a Christian WLV. Imagine groups of us struggling together to apply our Christian WLVs to the burning questions in our local communities and to the global challenges facing humanity—and then putting our conclusions and resolutions into action. A lot of honest and much-needed conversations would start to happen. And the results, I suggest, could well be revolutionary. That, in a nutshell, is the *transforming Christian theology* vision I hope you'll begin to share.

Sources for Christian World-and-Life-Views

It should be unnecessary to say, but treating theology as a WLV is not to demean it, to lower it in stature, or to rob it of all authority. Indeed, isn't the opposite true? I believe that a theology that's merely a list of propositions that one is supposed to believe is far *less* significant. Jesus said that the man or woman who wants to follow him must love his Way even more than his or her own life (Luke 14:26). Once it's acknowledged that each of us has a WLV, we can start to ask questions about what role God really plays in this view. Christian discipleship is not about a bunch of oughts that you don't really believe; it's about the life-view by which you really live. As a result, theology as WLV requires a level of honesty from each person that a lot of Christians are just not used to bringing to their week-to-week church practices.

Some people have told me, "I don't need theology. Theology is abstract and overly intellectual. I just want to follow Jesus." If I thought the idea of WLVs replaced or distracted from following Jesus, I wouldn't put it forward; in fact, I wouldn't have written this book in the first place. But the assumption is wrong; there is no conflict *and can be no conflict* between the two. To follow Jesus well is going to take a bit of thought. Who is he? What were the key themes of his ministry? How do we speak and live those themes powerfully in today's context? How and where does God speak today? If you don't bring your underlying beliefs on these topics to the surface, how do you know how to live? Perhaps you're being guided by some faulty assumptions, such as, "I can have inner, infallible certainty of what is the right thing for the church as a whole to do if it's to be genuinely Christian," or "Except for my pastor, no one else has any knowledge, experience, or expertise that I need in order to follow Jesus well." We're often tempted to take a shortcut from our own inner feelings of conviction to action in the world. It's far wiser to let inner leadings be mediated through the broader sense of who God is and what we need—in short, through a WLV.

It's therefore crucial to pause for a moment and to ask: What are some of the important sources for doing theology as a world-and-life-view? Well, the sources for a given WLV will vary a bit depending on the view. The Bible is the primary formative source for a Christian WLV, just as the Qur'an is formative for Muslims and the Vedas and Upanishads are formative for Hindus. (Of course, not only religious people have formative texts; the books of Karl Marx play the major role for Marxists, and the works of Jean-Paul Sartre and Albert Camus are central for existentialists.) I like to use something called the Wesleyan Quadrilateral in describing the sources of theology: scripture, tradition, experience, and reason.

Scripture

A Christian WLV is going to have a lot to do with Jesus, whether as symbol, moral exemplar, great prophet, living Lord, or all of the above. The central sources on the life and teachings of Jesus are the New Testament documents, which themselves grow out of the canonical texts of the Hebrew Bible. Thus, these documents are going to be authoritative for Christians in one way or another. Exactly in what *way* they are authoritative has been a matter of deep disagreement among many Christians, and wars (certainly symbolic wars, and sometimes worse) have been and continue to be fought over this question. For Christians today, I suggest, the key thing is not to get your doctrine of scripture exactly right before you start; rather, it is to use scripture—deeply, intelligently, and constantly—as you seek to address the difficult questions of our day in your thoughts and actions.

Tradition

Because of my position, at least once a month some person sends me an essay or book in which he claims to have found the "true meaning" of the scriptures. Invariably, these readings are completely individual and make no reference to the work that any scholar (or, for that matter, any other Christian) has ever done to interpret the scriptural texts. Apparently the authors believe that their intimate connection to the Holy Spirit is so flawless that no errors or prejudices could possibly creep in and mar their ability to hear what the Spirit is telling them about the texts. If you are like me, you greet such claims with a healthy dose of skepticism. Each of us is deeply enough influenced by his or her own presumptions, culture, historical period, and ego that we really need the corrective influence of others who are attempting to read the texts insightfully and accurately. This is the function of tradition. I do not view tradition as a compilation of infallible facts about the true meaning of the Bible to be accepted without question. Instead, I view it as the resource of many generations and many centuries of readers who have struggled with what God could be saying in and through the scriptural reports on the Hebrew tradition, on Jesus' life, and on the early church.

Experience

Experience is everyone's favorite source, and well it should be. If someone tells you to believe something that conflicts totally with what you've experienced, sooner or later you're likely to abandon it. As we'll see later, experience is a great starting point for folks who are unsure exactly of their own WLV. However, we live in a culture and age where private, individual experience often trumps all other sources. Only honest judgment will reveal whether you are one who has not explored your own experience deeply enough to know what you really believe or one who has allowed private experience to overshadow the other sources.

Reason

The flip side of living in the "age of experience" is a suspicion of reason. In evangelical, progressive, and liberal churches today, reason is the most under-utilized of the four sources. Presentations of scientific results are relatively rare, despite the crucial role of science in our world today, and attention to philosophical reflection comes infrequently if at all. Nor do those who have left the churches altogether—the seekers and those who are "spiritual but not religious"—manage in general to find a better balance between inner experience on the one side and careful reflection and study on the other. I am immensely encouraged, however, to see younger Christians, often in emerging churches and other non-traditional forms of Christian community, thinking very deeply about the core questions of their faith. Perhaps we are heading into an age when people will find it easier than in the late twentieth century to balance the four sources.

These four sources are not meant to be exclusive. Other theological sources are sometimes listed separately, including contemporary culture, science, other world religions, prayer, spiritual practices, and the experience of the oppressed. Although I think most of these can be fit into the preceding list, I agree that it's sometimes valuable to emphasize these other sources as well—as long as one doesn't ignore the

Part VI: Progressive Theology

primary four. The point is not to construct an exclusive list but to provide a sense of the areas you can turn to as you work to figure out your own WLV.

35

Postmodern Believing[1]

OUTSIDE OF THE WORLD of conservative evangelicals, many American Christians seem to have some pretty serious problems saying what it is that they believe with all their heart, soul, strength, and mind.

We act as though we're really unsure what sorts of things (outside of science and common sense) we're allowed to have deep, life-changing beliefs about—beliefs that we take seriously as probably true. Why has believing become so hard?

Three Last Gasps of Late Modernity

1. *Scientism*. "Scientism" still dominates the academic world and many segments of our society. Scientism is the belief (dogma) that, in a science-dominated world, one should only have beliefs about matters that have been empirically settled. We can believe that the speed of light is 299,792,458 meters per second, or that light is both wave and particle. But when it comes to things like a sunset, the beauty of the world, or the sense that life is valuable or meaningful, we are only supposed to have *experiences*. After all, we are told, these are not the sorts of things that anyone *can* hold true or false beliefs about—with the exception, again, of the scientific, empirically accessible aspects of experience. Regarding the great questions that humanity has continually posed to itself—the questions with which philosophers have wrestled and on which religious persons have differed—one is supposed to say, "We will just never know." One then presumably returns to her everyday life and pours her energies into things that matter more, where she can "really make a difference" in the world.

---

1. "Postmodern Believing," as found within Clayton, *Transforming Christian Theology*, 35–42. Reprinted with the kind permission of Fortress.

2. *Return to the Pre-modern.* Scientism is one late modern answer to the question of what we may believe. It still dominates in Europe and North America, as it does in much of Japan and China. The next answer is just as unattractive. This one thumbs its nose at the entire modern worldview and returns to what is essentially a pre-modern mindset. *All* the modern concern with religious plurality, and all attempts to integrate one's faith with developments in modern science and philosophy, are left by the wayside. Moving back to a pre-modern worldview, we are told, is the only way to preserve all the claims of scripture, and hence the only way to be authentically Christian in today's world. The irony should be obvious: these people retain authenticity precisely by *not* engaging with today's world, substituting a first-century context for a twenty-first-century one. Of course it's easy to be a Christian if you adjust your beliefs about history, science, and culture to first-century standards. But it's hardly an incarnational approach, since it doesn't engage the world that actually surrounds us.

3. *Fundamentalism.* Fundamentalism in religion represents the last gasp of religion in the *modern* context. Religion, conceived under the modern paradigm, always fights to define its exact boundaries. Thus modern religion, at least in its most extreme forms, attempts to exactly specify the propositions that it affirms. Exact boundaries can be drawn, for example, by arguing that the Bible is dictated by God (the "plenary" doctrine of inspiration) and thus is utterly without error, including in all matters of history and science. The doctrine that the Qur'an was literally dictated by Allah makes the same claim. Or one can try to delineate a complete list of the central Christian propositions, as Carl F. H. Henry attempted to do in his theology, and as the authors of the list of "Christian fundamentals" did in the 1880s. From there, in classical modern fashion, one then deduces exactly what are the ethical demands of Christianity. Moderns like this. It allows them to know, *independent of all cultural or historical contexts* (including the contextual leading of the Holy Spirit, I fear), exactly what is *the* Christian thing to do in any given situation. Many modern theologians have then fought tooth and nail to defend their list of true propositions from scientists, philosophers, and advocates of other religious traditions.

Perhaps these three strategies sound familiar to you. What's encouraging is that they set the stage for some much-needed new ways of believing. Postmodern believing is not less deep and powerful than modern believing. But it encourages some very different (and, I think, refreshing) attitudes toward certainty and doubt.

Doubt Is Not Sin

Soon after my conversion I was asked to be a "counselor" at a Billy Graham Crusade. I served in this role many times, which I suppose means that I have "won many people for Christ." The biggest crusade I participated in took place in a large sports stadium. When the evangelist called for people to convert to Christ and the organ started to play "Just as I Am, without One Plea," counselors like me would gradually stand up all over the stadium and make our way to the altar that had been set up in front. (They never told us this, but obviously this huge group of people that was popping up all over and walking to the altar would give the audience the impression that about a third of the people who had come to the meeting were converting to Christ. You'd almost feel left out if you *didn't* go forward!) We could all recognize each other by a particular sign, so we could tell who had actually come forward to get converted, and we each picked a convert to counsel by standing on his or her right side. After we explained Billy Graham's Four Spiritual Laws to our convert-candidates, we prayed the Sinner's Prayer with them, and they were saved. We had to make sure that they were safe from any doubts that Satan might bring to them the next day (like, "Was that for real?"). So we would have them memorize a simple jingle to help them hold out against the devil's temptations. It went: "God says it in His Word. I believe it in my heart. That settles it forever."

The trouble is, not only for new converts but also for a very large number of committed Christians and seekers, that *doesn't* settle it forever. Each of us encounters some doctrines, or some points in our lives, where believing is not quite so easy, where the doubts refuse to depart. Some questions and concerns are relatively trivial, and some remain amorphous, but a few are much more serious and much more precise. As an example of the first, relatively trivial kind, I well remember being a teenager and thinking, "I know every word in the Bible is supposed to be true. But somehow I just have trouble believing that women should have to cover their heads in church 'because of the angels' (1 Cor 11:10)." Apparently (according to some scholars) Paul thought that if the women in church left their heads uncovered and the angels saw their long hair, it would cause the angels to lust, that is, feel sexual attraction toward them. "Are angels really the kind of beings that struggle with lust when they see a woman's long hair in church?" I wondered. Paul's main reason was different: "A man ought not to have his head veiled, since he is the image and reflection of God; but woman is the reflection of man" (v. 7). I didn't find this reason convincing either. I discovered, however, that my conservative friends and pastors didn't appreciate questions like these.

Other doubts reflect more fundamental concerns. Some of these are profound, such as the lifelong struggle with the problem of evil and suffering. A few years ago a woman sat in my office and described how her sister had slowly and painfully died of bone cancer. She had big doubts: "Let's suppose that God can and does answer our little prayers, like helping us find a date or a parking spot. If God is able to do supernatural things like that at any time, then why did he do nothing while my sister slowly died? He must have had some particular reason to make her suffer and die like this. But what could that reason have been? Was she somehow more wicked than the people who *don't* die of cancer?" In the end, she told me, "After watching what my sister went through, I just can't believe in this God anymore."

Return to a Thinking Faith

Often, the way the debate is set up confronts thinking Christians (and non-Christians also) with an impossible choice. Those on our right seem to be saying, "Believe, or shut up," while those on our left argue, "*All* religious believing is absurd. Humans just can't know anything about matters of ultimate reality or ultimate value." According to them, religious belief only leads to dissent, to distraction, and ultimately to religious wars and fundamentalism. It's better simply to trash the whole thing, or at best, allow religion to add a little warm, pastel coloring to the admittedly rather cold and indifferent universe that science offers us. "Still," they add, "it's fine if you want to send your kids to Sunday school (or have them bar or bat mitzvahed, if you're Jewish), since a little exposure to religion might help make them more moral people. Just don't let them take the stuff too seriously." Many in our society today experience this dichotomy as a complete stalemate. Both sides are unattractive, we feel. And yet we wonder whether there can even be a third option.

I believe that this dichotomy is simply false. There *is* a third option. In fact, a whole rich world of options lies between scientific reductionism on the one hand and an uncompromising belief-without-doubts on the other. Two relatively minor adjustments open up this space for postmodern believing. One of them involves reordering believing and belonging; I return to it in the next section. The other involves giving up the assumption that doubts should be viewed as sin. Having questions about inherited beliefs is not a sign of a willful spirit, spiritual immaturity, or moral turpitude. It is simply the way that mature human minds work as they struggle to integrate the various facets of their experience into a coherent whole.

This is such a simple step, and yet it is at the same time immensely liberating. Many of us have unconsciously imbibed the principle that doubting always means sinning, without ever realizing what we have swallowed. I remember gradually recognizing this fact after reading Gary Gutting's book, *Religious Belief and Religious Scepticism*. There Gutting affirms that religious belief requires "a total commitment to its implications for action that is incompatible with continuing reflection on its truth." According to Gutting, it is "simply foolish" to "[give] up everything for a belief that I think requires further discussion and evaluation." But I'm just not convinced that the commitment needed for action is incompatible with continuing reflection. Why can't I continue to be a disciple of Jesus in my actions, while sometimes encountering doubts in my thought? Can't I be faithful to Jesus' Way even while I am struggling with many of the doctrinal claims from within the theological tradition? . . .

The amazing thing about allowing ourselves to acknowledge doubts, I have found, is that over the long haul it does not *increase* doubting but actually helps to *decrease* its frequency and severity. It's like other areas in life: when we attempt to sweep things under the table or hide them in the closet, they somehow start festering; their influence increases and gradually they begin to dominate in a very negative fashion. They just won't stay hidden. By contrast, when we bring our fears out into the open and examine them by the light of day, we often find that they are rather less intractable. After all, during the light of day we can consult with friends, teachers, and pastors; we can read books on the subject; and we can bring the whole powers of our own mature reflection to bear on the problems. When we're in the closet, we just can't see clearly enough to do these things!

If we are allowed to bring the full range of our adult problem-solving capacities to bear on our doubts, we can often find some constructive ways through our difficulties. After all, many of the questions that people ask us, and that we ask ourselves, involve serious issues that deserve careful attention. The net result is often that we can distinguish then what lies at the heart of our own religious life from the issues that lie more at the periphery, with the result that the doubting becomes less destructive that we had thought. One result of responding in this way is that we become much more able to listen to the doubts of others and to respond intelligently to their questions than we would have before.

Belonging, Behaving, Believing

That brings me to the second major feature of postmodern believing. I first learned this from Phyllis Tickle's fantastic book, *The Great Emergence* (Baker, 2008), but it is now so widely cited on the Web that most people have forgotten where it comes from. Like many other people, I was taught that the only route to being a disciple of Jesus—and indeed, the only route to *any* serious Christian identity—was *believe, behave, belong.* Many of us have been told from the very beginning to build our lives around the verse, "If you confess with your mouth, 'Jesus is Lord,' and believe in your heart that God raised him from the dead, you will be saved" (Rom 10:9, NIV). So we first sit down and try to *believe* the Christian propositions that people tell us we should believe. (In more conservative Christian circles, this means that you have to believe that scripture is the inerrant Word of God. Once you believe that, you are committed to believing a very large number of propositions indeed!) Then we try to *behave* in line with all these propositions. Generally we are told that obedience is always "by the grace of God." Still, we know that if we mess up, it sure isn't *God's* fault! Finally, only when things are going well with the believing and behaving can we really *belong*, that is, be a member of the Christian community in good standing. When things aren't going that well, we feel that we really shouldn't be there.

Like many others, I have found these marching orders to be the cause of rather continuous guilt. We know that we want to live the "Spirit-filled life"; we want to "live by grace" and to enjoy a "victorious Christian walk with God." But then we encounter some rather steep demands among the items on the list of what we're supposed to believe and do. I, for one, kept stumbling over the phrase in the Sermon on the Mount, "Be perfect, therefore, as your heavenly Father is perfect" (Matt 5:48). You've got to admit that sets a pretty high standard for the *believe, behave, belong* game. When, for whatever reason, we begin to worry that we aren't quite living up to the standard, we start to ask whether we really belong in the body of God's Chosen. If they let us in at all, we'd better seat ourselves in the very back row of the church, preserving the forward rows for the holier members of the congregation. (Indeed, some of us fear that the Moral Patrol may show up at any instant to remove us from the sanctuary, since we don't really belong there in the first place!)

A postmodern understanding of religious believing in general, and of Christian discipleship in particular, reverses the order. I don't perfectly understand all the details of Jesus' Way, and I *know* that I don't perfectly follow what I do understand. But for cultural, historical, and personal reasons, it is the way that I have seen God. There is no other way that is a live option for me, and dispensing with the attempt to seek and to know God through Christ is somehow just not a live option. As Simon Peter said to Jesus at one point, more in perplexity than as a resounding statement of faith, "Lord, to whom [else] can we go? You have the words of eternal life" (John 6:68). One can even repeat those words in times of despair. As Martin Luther said, perhaps also with more perplexity than bravado, "Here I stand; I can do no other. God help me. Amen!"

And here is the liberating insight: in that I find myself on this Way, *I already belong.* I may not be certain about many of the beliefs, and I may find myself continually falling short. I may have troubles with the institutional church. But I can't help belonging to that group of people who are associated with this Way, just as I belong to the One who somehow first found me. The life given through grace by One who transcends me is not driven by the motor of my believing; its fuel is not the quality of my behaving. Nor is it primarily about the particular denominational membership that I may use to identify myself. With all our warts and uncertainties, some of us just find ourselves with an attraction to this figure Jesus, or with powerful religious experiences associated with him, or with moral and political convictions in which his teachings play an irreducible role. That belonging comes first. We want to be his disciples. It doesn't matter that we doubt, wander, wonder, and frequently knit our brows in confusion and despair. We are where we are. Perhaps we, like Martin Luther, can "do no other."

Years ago, a wise Presbyterian pastor named Blair Moffett tried to convince me of this point. I was a graduate student in religion and philosophy at Yale University and struggling with doubts. I told him I wasn't sure I could become a member of his church, because I wasn't sure that I could really affirm all the sentences new members were supposed to say out loud when they joined. It makes me smile to think of it now, but I even wrote out detailed philosophical critiques of those few short sentences in the Presbyterian hymnal. Blair tried to convince me that it wasn't about getting all the details right up front. We join others who find themselves on the Way, and then, as we walk together, we struggle to clarify our beliefs and to get clearer on our calling and on the nature of the One who calls us. In the end, as it turned out, Blair was right.

Always Already on the Way

I don't think this point really sunk in for me until some years later, when I found myself standing in front of a large group of young Muslim students in Yogyakarta. I had traveled to Indonesia to speak to an interfaith conference. On the second afternoon I was to be "the Christian speaker" who, along with two Muslims and a Jew, would address the topic of the nature of the human person. As one would expect from any good young theology professor, I had carefully researched my topic and had prepared a brainy and rather abstract talk on the major tenets of Christian theological anthropology. But as I looked out over the faces of the three hundred eager and intelligent Muslim students, it finally dawned on me. Whatever doubts and worries I might have about my own believing and behaving (and I had many), however problematic "Christian identity" might seem to me, in their young eyes I was indisputably a representative of Christianity. Suddenly I realized that the niceties didn't really matter. They knew me as one of the followers of Jesus, whom people call "Christians," and they would judge me in that light. I also knew that I wanted to be numbered among his followers. It would be downright dishonest to duck out of this role into some safe place of neutrality and agnosticism in order to nurse my philosophical worries.

At that moment I finally got it: the belonging, the identification with Jesus' Way, comes first, not last. Many of us realize that we are somehow *already there* as soon as we stop to think about it. "Here I am; I can do no other." We know the behaving matters, but it doesn't come first; it's not the precondition for belonging. I belong because of grace. Grace is *immer schon da*, as the German theologians say—it's "always already there."

The concern with behaving always comes second. I knew I had to try to act in a Jesus-like way with this group of impressionable young students; the details of my believing would have to sort themselves out later. (Or not.) For the moment, my task was to offer a more positive portrait of a Jesus-follower than they had encountered before. My Christian predecessors had done horrendous things to Muslims over centuries and centuries of our common history. The first step of behaving, I suddenly knew, was to admit how wrong these crusades were from the standpoint of the Jesus-Way. I threw away my prepared text and stepped up to the microphone to express my sorrow over what *we Christian believers* had done, and continue to do, to Muslim believers. As one identified with this Way, I had to start my talk on human nature by acknowledging *our* wrongs and expressing my sorrow about them.

That, in short, is the lesson of postmodern Jesus-discipleship: *belong, behave, believe*. It's not as neat and pretty as the account I was taught when young: "get your

PART VI: Progressive Theology

beliefs right, then get your life in order, and then you can join us." But then again, human existence is rarely as black and white, as neat and pretty, as we were taught when we were young.

36

A Theology of Self-Emptying for the Church[1]

THEOLOGIES ALWAYS INVOLVE THE weaving together of God's story and one or more human stories. In Christian theologies, Jesus' life and teaching play a central role in the resulting narrative. We've explored in more general terms what theologies are and aren't. It's time now to consider a very specific example of how a theology is discovered, constructed, and applied. Given all I've said, I have no choice but to keep it personal. The theology you're about to read is also my theology.

The idea is simple: we have been talking about the Seven Core Christian Questions. These are the questions to which, in one form or another, the Christian church has come back again and again. When I ask future pastors to prepare their Credos, their statements of faith, I ask them to give sophisticated responses to each of these seven questions:

- Who is God, and how is God related to the world? (the doctrine of God and the God–world relation)

- Who is Jesus Christ? What was his life, teaching, and mission? (Christology)

- Who is the Holy Spirit? How is the Spirit related to the Father and to the Son (the question of the Trinity)? (pneumatology)

- What is humanity, man and woman? How are we like the other animals, and what is the "image of God" that distinguishes us from other animals? (anthropology)

- What and why is sin? What is salvation? What is Jesus' role in bringing it about, and what is our role? How is salvation linked to discipleship and sanctification? (soteriology)

- What is the church? (ecclesiology) (It's only a four-word question, but there is much, much to be said here.)

---

1. "A Theology of Self-Emptying for the Church," as found within Clayton, *Transforming Christian Theology*, 94–114. Reprinted with the kind permission of Fortress.

- What is the Christian hope? What occurs after death, and what is heaven? And what is the role of Jesus Christ in this all? (eschatology)

One must also pay attention to the roles played by all four of the different *sources* of theology in answering each of these questions for him- or herself:

- What does scripture teach? How does it help us to answer each question?
- What has the Christian tradition held? What must be retained and what may have been mistaken in the traditional answers that were given to these questions?
- What role does reason play? (This might include science, philosophy, other academic disciplines, and other world religious traditions.)
- What role does experience play—both individual experience and the corporate experience of the church—in answering each question?

There is no briefer, clearer account of the emerging theologies of our day than Doug Pagitt's *The Emerging Church and Embodied Theology*. In fact, Doug's assumptions about theology are so insightful that I repeat them here, as a sort of test for the reflections that you'll be reading in a moment. Among his guidelines are:

- Theology is meant to be temporary
- Theology is meant to be profession
- Theology is always contextual
- Theology is to be particular
- Theology is a Spirit-led practice
- Our theology is taking place in an age of tremendous change
- Theology is for unity, not uniformity
- Theology is to be participatory
- Christendom is not the goal

One caution: this experiment will only really work if you read it side by side with other theologies. If you take my example as the *only* framework for a genuinely transforming theology today, it would invalidate the entire message of this book. Ideally I would write a chapter each on four or five *different* practical theologies for our day, in order to encourage you to develop your own Credo, your own statement of belief. There's not enough space to do that here. But the least I can do is to encourage you to read some of the other great new theologies that are being written. Read a post-conservative theologian like Roger Olson. Read a clear process theologian like John Cobb, or Marjorie Suchocki's *God, Christ, Church*. Read the theological reflections of an emergent thinker like Brian McLaren. Read Scot McKnight's *A Community Called Atonement*, where Scot (in the final part) interprets atonement as a form of *praxis*, as something we actually do in the world. In his account, atonement as "missional praxis" takes on many forms: fellowship, justice, baptism, Eucharist, and prayer, to name a few.

When I work with church groups and with future pastors, I caution them that theology is never done from some abstract place. A theology is never "a view from nowhere." Thus they must begin as concretely as possible. I begin with the ancient Christian hymn, quoted by Paul in Philippians 2, as my starting point, but I expect and urge others to begin in different places. Begin from where you live. If you are called to ministry with youth, or with Twelve-Step programs, or with migrant workers, or with mixed-race congregations, or with the aging, you *should* bring the context and concerns of your ministry to your emerging theology. If you are nursing a sick relative, or had a parent die, or have gone through a divorce, or lost your job, that context should play a role in how you answer the Seven Core Christian Questions. If you are a professional scientist, you will have different concerns from those of a business woman, a school teacher, a denominational administrator, or a church musician.

One final thought: people often say that you cannot tell part of the Christian story unless you tell the whole Christian story. I agree that the church as a whole needs to make known the entire Christian proclamation, but I do not agree that every Christian who struggles to find his or her own distinctive voice must always tell the whole story every time. That's a recipe for silence (which is in fact what has happened!). The reason is that, to meet this standard, you'd have to take *yourself* out of the equation. If you speak from the heart about your particular Christian location, then you will inevitably emphasize the things that *you* have known and understood and experienced. There is an honesty and authenticity about such first-person experience that, in my experience, speaks volumes. So let the reader beware: there is much more to Christian proclamation than my story, as there is more to Paul than Philippians, more to Philippians than the passage about Jesus' self-emptying, and more even to this specific passage than the verses on which I focus.

The Christ Hymn in Philippians 2

"Have this mind among yourselves, which you have in Christ Jesus . . ." (Phil 2:5, RSV). What you're about to read is, from a Christian perspective, *the* central narrative in God's relationship with the world God created. The particular contribution of Christian voices within the dialogue of world religions is to talk about this narrative. We believe that the values embodied here offer a crucial window onto the divine nature and purposes. In fact, for us it is *the central window*.

Thus, it's all the more interesting that Paul begins the passage by calling us not to hold the narrative at arm's length. It must not be placed up in the heavens, out there somewhere, or shoved away onto a distant holy altar, or left to rest somewhere in ancient history. He wants it to represent the "mind" that we have about Christianity. The Greek word is *phroneisthō*, which means "be minded in this way." It's interesting that the root for this word is *phronesis*, which is the word that the Greek philosopher Aristotle uses for practical wisdom—that down-to-earth sort of wisdom people live by when they are good at dealing with things and people in the actual world. Paul also emphasizes that this is not just a story about the eternal deity, but it reflects the very practical way of thinking that Jesus manifested in his earthly life. And it is that mindset that Jesus lived that we are to have in our own daily living.

"*. . . who, though he was in the form of God, did not count equality with God a thing to be grasped*" (v. 6). Here Paul gives the background to what Christians call the incarnation, the becoming human of God. The Jesus whose "mind" we are to emulate was, before his birth, in the very form of God and enjoyed "equality with God." Although Paul does not engage here in any lofty speculations as to how this could be, this is the position that the church later came to describe in the doctrine of the Trinity—the belief that the one divine Godhead is actually constituted by three "persons" (or aspects—*hypostases*).

Now I must admit that, when I am working to interweave my story with God's story, I do not pause for long to speculate on how there could be a pre-incarnate logos or what it means in technical terms for Jesus Christ to be God, the second person of the Trinity. I fear we theologians may have overemphasized these questions, forcing them on others too early and without enough sensitivity. Telling my story does not require me to legislate these doctrines for the church community as a whole. My story is so small and humble that it can get by with far less nuanced observations. This Jesus, whose "mind" I am being called to emulate, was no ordinary mortal. His life was tied up in some mysterious way with the very life of God. Whatever "equality with God" may mean, it certainly means that this is an extremely authoritative story for those of us who interpret our lives in terms of it. The text tells me that there must be something distinctive about Jesus' life, if he was "in the form of God."

Finally, the shocking phrase, "did not count equality with God *something to be grasped*," deserves special attention. It suggests a distinction between those who "grasp" at equality with God, and those who, like Christ Jesus, do not grasp at (or for) this equality. It has never crossed my mind to grasp at equality with God; my grasping is of a much more petty nature: grasping for power or prestige or honor. Still, the verse tells me that my theology will have to include some crucial categories that caution me about grasping. And it will have to mention the sorts of things that I and those around me tend to grasp at: money and wealth; power and prestige; influence; control over others; and the like.

"*. . . but emptied himself . . .*" (v. 7). Here the Greek verb is *ekenōsen* from the noun *kenosis*, for self-emptying. Theologians thus call this the "kenotic" hymn, and the technical name for the theology I am putting forward is *kenotic theology*.

In this notion of self-emptying we encounter what is for me the central Christian teaching about Jesus' "mind," about God's self-revelation—and indeed about God's own eternal nature. When I ask what it means for me to try to love as God loves, the answer must always begin with self-emptying. What Christ emptied himself of was having the *highest conceivable* glory, the glory of equality with God's eternal nature. I suspect that for most of us the temptations are rather more humble. Still, the text forewarns me to pay attention to the temptations that I am inclined to grasp at and not let go.

I expect that these will include possessions, lifestyles, social relationships, privileges, longings and lusts, pride, and matters of belief. That is, I expect to find that the grasping will involve holding onto private prejudices, assumptions, or inherited systems of belief, *including my religious beliefs, my beliefs about God and ultimate values.*

If a theology and the lifestyle that goes with it are to be Christ-like, they will be pervaded by this self-emptying. They will involve letting go of the security and neatness of systems of belief that produce pride. I must be careful not to hold things or beliefs as if they were my right or the ground of my personal security, safety, and identity. From the text I expect to find this need for self-emptying lying at the very core of my being, beliefs, and desires—there where it matters most, and there where I find it hardest to recognize.

"*. . . taking the form of a servant, being born in the likeness of men . . .*" (v. 7). This ancient Christian hymn, which we believe is the oldest Christian hymn found in the New Testament (not including the baptismal formula in Matt 28:18–20), cites two examples of what Christ empties himself to become: "a servant," and "the likeness of men." Clearly, for God to become a human being was a huge form of humbling; we are, after all, rather tiny and limited creatures. You don't even need the notion of God in order to recognize how limited we are. Imagine what humanity and this planet would be like if every human had the genius of Einstein, or the spiritual vision of Ghandi. Now imagine that every human being, or even a significant number of us, had even twice Einstein's intelligence. Instead of being so short-sighted, for example, I imagine that we'd be voting for policies that ensured the long-term good of our species, other species, and our planet as a whole. Now imagine that many of us had ten times that intelligence—just think of what we could do! And yet none of this is even a ripple on the chart of divine intelligence, for God's intelligence must be *infinitely* greater than that of an Einstein. Given the contrast, the enormity of Christ's self-emptying begins to sink in.

But Jesus' self-emptying lay not just in becoming human. Of all the types of human he could have become: king, emperor, Mozart, Einstein—he took on the "form of a servant." When I read these words, I hear resonances and echoes of much of the New Testament. I hear the words, "Whoever wants to be first must be the last of all and the servant of all" (Mark 9:35). I hear the powerful words of Jesus' action just prior to his final supper with his disciples: "Jesus, knowing that the Father had given all things into his hands, and that he had come from God and was going to God, got up from the table, took off his outer robe, and tied a towel around himself. Then he poured water into a basin and began to wash the disciples' feet and to wipe them with the towel that was tied around him" (John 13:3–5).

"*And being found in human form he humbled himself and became obedient unto death, even death on a cross*" (v. 8). Well before we are adults, we know what death is. We recognize it as the end of all of our projects—that line in the sand after which we no longer lead and decide. It is also the frightful and frightening mystery of the apparent end of all that we have become. . . .

Living the Christ Hymn

That, in short, is the narrative of the Christ. Christians believe that it is at the same time God's story. What does it mean for it to become *my* narrative as well? In some ways that is the central question of this entire book. So I challenge you to try to tell your story, in all the rich and personal detail of an autobiography, *inside of* this story of Jesus' self-emptying. You can meditate directly on the text, as I have done here. You can read it in the broader context of Paul's letter to the Philippians, or the Pauline epistles, or the New Testament, or the Bible as a whole. Indeed, you can stretch your horizons even wider (after all, when the topic is God, nothing that exists really falls completely outside the narrative). Thus, you can even read this Christological hymn in light of the whole of human history, or the whole history of our earth, or even the whole history of the universe as science is now revealing it to us. You can include other religions or philosophies, or art and literature, or personal experience and psychology. In short, the sky's the limit. *Anything and everything you say as you carry out this exercise is theology.*

But remember: the results must continue to have something to do with your own life. They have to involve how you follow this Way that Jesus taught and lived. The only way for me to remain true to this insight in what follows is to write from my own perspective. It's not that my perspective is particularly interesting or notable. But, for obvious reasons, it's the only story that *I* can tell in an authentic manner. (I cannot take credit for your virtues or feel penance for your vices, but I can do so for mine.) If reading about the demands that Christ's self-emptying make on me inspires you to think about what they might mean for you, and thus to begin to do theology in your own right, these next few pages will have served their function. . . .

Self-Emptying Theologies

I've keenly felt the dilemma raised by these last pages. Self-emptying is not the sole Christian message, nor is it a message that all Christians need to hear. Yet it was crucial that I model the start of an answer to the Seven Core Christian Questions that draws from scripture, tradition, reason, and experience—and one that is personal and honest at the same time. The goal is not that you will leave the theological labors to me (or to anyone else), merely internalizing the results of someone else's work. The hope instead is that you will read these last pages so deeply that you'll be able to begin identifying your own theology, letting it emerge out of your own situation and then drawing from it the insights you need in order to grow into deeper discipleship in your own personal and communal context.

Still, your theology is not *reduced* to your situation and context. For Christians there must always be something authoritative in Christ's self-emptying. Moreover, the vast majority of us in Europe and North America enjoy positions of unimaginable power, comfort, and luxury compared to the Two-Thirds world. It doesn't take much travel in the Third World to realize that, if Jesus' sentence "they have received their reward" (Matt 6:16) is true of anyone in the world today, it must be true of us. I thus suspect that the call to emulate the One who "humbled himself" may be particularly relevant to the theologies, and to the discipleship, of a large number of us.

There's one last reason for stressing this particular example. It has to do with the turn to postmodern believing that we explored earlier. For many men and women today, the claims to certainty made by "modern" Christians come across as the very opposite of self-emptying. Whatever the *intent* of those who proclaim that they have the full truth, or the perfect interpretation of scripture, or the only path for the church to follow in today's world, the results are painful. To the ears of many of us in this postmodern world, a Christianity shorn of the condemnation of all other groups and individuals better conveys the spirit and message of the One whom we follow. As radical as it sounds, I suggest that we need to apply the attitude of self-emptying *even to our own Christian theologies.*

This new postmodern spirit—the quest to find common ground with others, even as we voice the distinctive features of our own faith—also promises to make us much more effective as we turn our attention from the needs of the church to the needs of our surrounding society. That, at any rate, is the argument I will be making in the few chapters that remain.

37

Toward a Progressive Theology for Christian Activism[1]

Now you know *how* to do it. What do the results look like? How do progressive theologies actually function? What are they based on, and what do they affirm? What can they accomplish? We will close with concrete examples of how a progressive theology can be grounded in scripture and how it can speak powerfully and prophetically to today's world.

Why Is It Controversial for Christians to be Boldly Progressive?

There are two different senses of the word *progressive*. The broader sense of the term— changing, improving, making things better—should be uncontroversial. How could a theology not to be progressive in this sense? Our theological understanding is always evolving under the guidance of the Holy Spirit and in response to new events in human history. The sixteenth-century Reformers said that theology is *semper reformanda*, always reforming. No matter how "high" your doctrine of the Bible, it cannot mean that theology becomes static. Theologies express our ongoing attempt to interpret scripture, our attempt to say what it means here and now—in *this* world, reacting to *these* new ideas, in conversation with *these* people, in dialogue with *this or that* world religion or philosophy. Theologies are never the absolute revelation of God, for they always includes a human dimension—the perspective of their authors.

But progressive theologies have a concrete side as well. In actual practice they always imply specific social, political, and even moral positions. Progressive theologies in this sense tend to emphasize social justice issues as strongly as they emphasize questions of individual responsibility and morality. The term is typically used of mainline Christians and "progressive evangelicals" rather than of conservatives. One would use it of President Obama but not of President Bush. One finds a broad range of

---

1. "Toward a Progressive Theology for Christian Activism," as found within Clayton, *Transforming Christian Theology*, 146–60. Reprinted with the kind permission of Fortress.

organizations dedicated to supporting progressive Christianity, including many helpful web-based resources.

Why has there been resistance to progressive theologies? Weren't Jesus' life and ministry boldly progressive, even revolutionary? Jesus spoke to centers of political power and took on the religious authorities of his day. He challenged the rich and powerful, placing himself consistently on the side of the poor and oppressed. He even associated the kingdom of God, which stood at the center of his teaching, with this transformation: "Blessed are you who are poor, for yours in the kingdom of God" (Luke 6:20).

One reason for the resistance, I assume, is that people read "progressive" as a code word for supporting homosexual marriages or ordaining gay clergy. At the Transforming Theology denominational summit, several denominational leaders expressed their fears that the term *progressive* has become divisive in a time when they need to be expansive. In 2009, heads of denominations—such as Katharine Jefferts Schori of the Episcopal Church of America, Mark Hanson of the Evangelical Lutheran Church of America, and Mary Hulse of the American Baptist Church—are working to prevent schism within their communions. If they identify themselves as progressive *in the narrow sense of the term*, that will be seen as a declaration of war on conservatives. By this black-and-white logic, the word *conservative* would be reduced to the sole meaning of *opposed to homosexuality*—a narrowing that should cause conservative Christians to feel equally uncomfortable.

This narrowing of Jesus' entire kingdom message to sexual ethics, and to one particular sexual issue, is immensely damaging to the gospel and the church. It is divisive to the church, distracts from her message, and is destructive to how the church is perceived in our broader society outside the church. Single-issue theologies will not transform society. Yet both sides in this damaging cultural debate are complicit in narrowing their theologies to (or toward) a single issue, at the expense of Jesus' broader message and mission.

Brian McLaren recently blogged about four major crises: the crisis of the planet, the crisis of poverty, the crisis of peace, and the crisis of purpose. By this last he meant "a dysfunctional spirituality system that fails to provide a framing story capable of healing the previous crises."[2] Here are issues worthy of deep Christian attention and powerful action. When your personal reflections, and the discussions within your community, start to be obsessed with these four crises, then you know that you're devoting yourselves to issues as weighty as the ones that stood at the center of Jesus' ministry. If they *don't* preoccupy you, you're probably being distracted by the small stuff or by battles over single issues.

---

2. McLaren, "Everything Must Change."

PART VI: Progressive Theology

Social Transformation in Luke 4, Luke 6, and Matthew 25

As you pursue the "Conversations Worth Having" (see part 4), I hope you will engage in studies of Jesus' progressive message that include the entire Hebrew Bible and New Testament, the entire history of Christian thought, and the whole range of contemporary progressive theologies. . . .

What startling words for the Son of Man to choose in order to begin his ministry! Clearly he was identifying with the Messiah, the Redeemer. But the recipients, the beneficiaries, were not what one (then or now) would expect: the poor, the prisoners, the blind, the oppressed. . . .

Again we have a key moment in Jesus' ministry. Here, more clearly than at Nazareth, Jesus preached an upside-down gospel, a gospel of reversal. The kingdom of God he came to proclaim is a kingdom of complete social transformation. The rich and well-fed have nothing in this kingdom. Its blessings come to the poor and hungry, those who weep and are despised (as the Son of Man will eventually be also). . . .

We do not have to fight over the more general issues: When does Jesus "come in glory"? Is hell literal or figurative? This parable, coming at the end of Jesus' teaching ministry and couched in terms of ultimate judgment, could not be more emphatic. The one who "sits on his throne in heavenly glory" does not just identify with, relate to, or love the needy. He claims to *be* the needy: "I was hungry . . . I was thirsty . . . I was a stranger . . . I was sick . . . I was in prison." Equating himself with the lowest of the low, Jesus offered his most-radical-ever statement about what the kingdom of God is and requires. The only moment in the New Testament that's more radical is the crucifixion—the steps toward which begin, according to Matthew, immediately after Jesus told this parable.

This central New Testament text begs to be thought through theologically. Its essential structure is echoed in the earliest Christian hymn, the narrative of Christ's self-emptying (Philippians 2) that we examined earlier.

In both texts the One who is exalted as the highest *actually becomes* the lowest. What is the Christ? He is the one who, humbling himself, identifies with those who have the least. He lives and acts *for them*—indeed, so radically that he becomes indistinguishable from them. "Whatever you did for one of the least of these brothers of mine, you did for me." I challenge you to begin to think through the implications of this act of complete identification for *each* of the Seven Core Christian Questions: not only for the doctrines of God, Christ, and Spirit, but also for your understanding of humanity, salvation, the church, and the nature of the Christian hope for the future. What you'll find, I suggest, is the basis for a powerful, biblically based, world-transforming, progressive theology.

Working with God for the Salvation of the World

Many of us grew up in a world where you talked about *either* salvation *or* social justice. The problem is "sin, not skin"—or so I was taught at a mostly black, conservative church I attended during college. Well, here's what the new progressives are saying: *you no longer have to choose.* The problem is *both* sin *and* skin (racism). And the full Christian answer involves *both* salvation *and* social justice. (Brian McLaren and Chuck Gutenson work out this both/and beautifully in a rich online discussion of the gospel and social justice.) Why did we ever think that we faced a forced choice between them?

Here's a case in point: the heading for this section comes from one of the leading progressive theologians in the country, John Cobb, addressing one of the most liberal denominations, the United Church of Christ (UCC). This talk, given only a few weeks ago (and now available online), powerfully conveys progressive theology without liber*alism*. There is no more fitting capstone for this book. With John's permission, I have generalized his references to the UCC to the church as a whole. This prophetic call opens with the words:

> My challenge can be put very simply. I am proposing that the church take as its mission working with God for the salvation of the world. The proposal makes many assumptions. First, it assumes that the world needs saving. . . . A second assumption is that God cares about the salvation of the world. This is an assumption that is made implicitly by all who pray the Lord's prayer. We ask that God's will be done on earth. Having learned to pray this way from Jesus, it is hardly possible to think that God's will for the world is immense destruction and suffering. . . . A third assumption is that God is already working in and through creatures, and especially human beings, toward the salvation of the world.

It's not that "salvation" means *less* than it once did; we now realize that it means *more*. Sin continually separates us from God; we fall short of God's call to us; without God's grace in Christ, the church affirms, we are unable to heed the call to love. But the human destruction of the natural world now means that we must work (with God) to save nature as well—just as we must work to right the injustices that have been built into our social structures, the injustices that directly produce unspeakable suffering for other human beings.

Cobb affirms that God is already working in and through creatures. But he does not affirm "supernatural interpretations of historical events, or . . . that any part of the biblical record is necessarily inerrant, or . . . that there are no other sources of wisdom."[3] He strives for a theology that is consistent with science and not dismissive of other religions and philosophies. Yet the resulting theology is robust enough to

---

3. John B. Cobb's challenge to the church was given in an address to several of the Western annual conferences of the United Church of Christ in 2008.

speak unapologetically of working for the salvation of the world. It's also ready to affirm the unique value of Christianity:

> Of the world's religions, Christianity has the tradition that points most strongly to efforts to save the world. . . . Christians and post-Christian secularists have been the most important actors on the world scene in recent centuries, and just for this reason we Christians have special responsibility for dealing positively with the world's problems. Also, historical consciousness is crucial for wise direction of efforts today, and this has been honed most among us.[4]

In recent years Christian churches have been losing the battle of significance. For many people, it seems less and less important to meet together with other Christians. Pastors have built mega-churches by offering people what they already want: the promise of financial success, of friends and community, of feeling good. But mainline churches are not convincing society, or even their own members, that when Jesus' followers are involved with others in missional living, they're dealing with the most significant thing in their entire life. . . .

Imagine what would happen if people became convinced that the biggest, most important vision for the future of humanity and the planet was the one that they found in progressive groups and churches, and that nothing else in their lives was as important. Imagine what would happen if they felt that the values that exceeded all others in importance were taught and lived paradigmatically in these Christian communities. Imagine that governments, universities, and social organizations paled in comparison. Would we not see a flow of committed people, bringing their best energy and effort to learning, preparing, and acting on behalf of this vision? . . .

But this *is* the Christian vision. It's a vision of people finding reconciliation with God and with each other; people not afraid to bring this vision into dialogue with the best of the world's science, philosophy, and religion; people whose calling it is to work (with God) for the salvation of this planet and all its inhabitants. It's Jesus' vision of the kingdom of God. . . .

A moment's reflection, and a touch of humility, reminds us of how deeply we are the products of our background and culture. My vision for a both/and form of Christian theology and proclamation would not have seen the light of day without years of immersion in evangelical schools, followed by years of work among progressive Christians.

But all of us are children of our age as well. This book was born during the last months of Barack Obama's historic campaign for president. Some of the most heartfelt passages were written through a blur of tears as I watched this inspiring leader first accepting the election results and then being inaugurated as our nation's first black president. My call to a critical, reflective faith echoes Obama's moving call at the 2004 Democratic Convention in Boston, as he proclaimed that "religious commitment did

---

4. Ibid.

not require me to suspend critical thinking, disengage from the battle for economic and social justice, or otherwise retreat from the world that I knew and loved." Obama's progressive vision rocked the nation in 2008, exactly forty years after an equally gifted black leader, Martin Luther King Jr., presented a prophetic Christian vision for change that transformed American society forever.

Yet these pages are finally being published not in the months of great vision and hope—yes we can, yes we can—but in a season of rapidly hardening realism, if not outright cynicism. If there's one place on earth that eats up idealism and spits out cynicism, it's Washington DC. One by one, the president's agendas for change, which expressed the dreams of millions of Americans, are being ground to dust. Compromise after compromise follows, leading gradually to death by a thousand qualifications. Obama's conservative opponents openly and proudly admit that their primary goal is to destroy him. With Langston Hughes we ask, "What happens to a dream deferred? Does it dry up like a raisin in the sun?"

In this season of disappointment, readers may ask, "Is it also so with the dreams for the church? Will our vision of 'rekindling theological imagination' die as quickly as the dream of a Washington in which the spirit of collaboration and change triumph over 'business as usual'?" The question is fair. Clearly, as much is at stake for the mainline church today as is at stake for America under this administration. We hover on the edge of a great "tipping point," after which the sustaining institutions of mainline Christianity will begin to close and massive numbers of congregations will be no more. Is it our fate, too, to dry up like a raisin in the sun?

But the situation is *not* the same. An administration lasts for four short years. It can be brought to a standstill by voter apathy and selfishness, by the media's spin, and by an opposing party bent only on destruction. But God is from everlasting to everlasting. The great vision we have been exploring—the vision for the salvation of the world—will not go away in four years. As long as there are human beings, there will be some who refuse to be ruled by selfishness and short-sightedness, some who put the kingdom of God ahead of all other goals. Cynicism may arise like a virus among the middle aged, but there will always be some who are ready to give their lives for Jesus' Great Reversal: "Your sons and your daughters shall prophesy, your old men shall dream dreams, and your young men shall see visions" (Joel 2:28).

For many of us, this is a time of great optimism. Complacency is the church's greatest enemy, and few people who have their eyes open today are complacent. At no time since Augustine and the Fall of Rome in the fifth century has the church stood before such revolutionary change. Many well-worn practices will be abandoned, and many beloved congregations will close. But the Spirit of God will continue to move upon the face of the waters.

So I call the courageous and faithful back to theology—to give an account of their deepest Christian commitments and their relevance for our day. No narrow theologizing will do. It's not enough just to justify existing practices, to make one's own in-group comfortable at the expense of all the rest. This new theology, genuinely transformative theology, calls for deep personal involvement, openness to criticism and new information, engagement with the world as it really is and with other persons as they really are. It calls for the courage to be unsure, to question, to know when to say, "I don't know." Above all, it calls for the most comprehensive and transforming vision that your mind can contain and your heart can dream—the vision of the coming kingdom of God. Would anything less be worthy of the One who calls us, the One who emptied himself, even Jesus of Nazareth?

38

Introducing Organic Marxism[1]

MANY PEOPLE IN DEVELOPED nations believe—we think wrongly—that they have nothing to learn from Karl Marx. Their governments and their media have told them that it's impossible to implement socialist principles in political and economic systems. The collapse of East Germany and the USSR, the decreased role of Communist parties in the European nations, the difficulties faced by socialist governments and parties in Latin America and elsewhere—these are the developments that critics point to in arguing that Marxism has failed as a socio-economic system. Even in the People's Republic of China, where Marxism is enshrined in the national constitution, one hears skepticism about the continuing relevance of Marxist analyses.

In practice, most of global economics now functions according to the principles of the so-called free market economy—with disastrous consequences for the planet and much of its population. The domination of capitalist principles has been so thorough that Francis Fukuyama proclaimed "the end of history" in 1992, arguing that humanity has finally attained its highest and ultimate form of government, Western-style capital-based democracy.[2] Many commentators, especially in the United States, appealed to Fukuyama (inaccurately, as it turned out) to support their belief that free market principles had won a final and decisive victory over every other form of economic system.

The advocates of Fukuyama's thesis in the early 1990s would have been surprised to hear that, just two decades later, the public outcry against unrestrained capitalism, and against the government policies that support it, has grown in volume and influence. Of all the factors causing this change, none has served to highlight the limits of the capitalist system more than the global environmental crisis.

---

1. "Introducing Organic Marxism," as found within Clayton and Justin Heinzekehr, *Organic Marxism: An Alternative to Capitalism and Ecological Catastrophe*, 3–14. Reprinted with the kind permission of Process Century Press.

2. Fukuyama, *The End of History and the Last Man*.

PART VI: Progressive Theology

Global capitalism has created the greatest ecological and humanitarian catastrophe in the history of human civilization. The unrestrained pursuit of wealth on the part of those with economic power has left approximately half the world's population—over three billion people—living on less than $2.50 a day.[3] At least 80 percent of humanity lives on less than $10 a day.[4] Whereas forty years ago the gap between the richest 20 percent and the poorest 20 percent on the planet stood at 50 to 1, today the disparity in wealth has risen to 80 to 1. The evidence is overwhelming that the wealthiest nations have designed the world economic system to bring maximum gains to themselves. Under the present system, it is virtually impossible for the poor nations to catch up. Multinational corporations are able to utilize tax loopholes, cheap raw materials, inexpensive labor, "free trade" agreements, and lax enforcement of existing treaties in order to continually produce the highest possible profits for their shareholders. Unfortunately, the United States is a leader in allowing unequal conditions at home and in supporting unequal conditions abroad.

As if the human consequences of capitalism were not enough, the planet itself now moans under the unbearable burden of these practices. No pillaging army in its drive for conquest has had as devastating an effect upon global ecosystems as international corporations have in their drive for profit. Wealthy individuals and companies continue to use their positions of dominance to rack up short-term gains at the long-term expense of the planet.

Now that the Intergovernmental Panel on Climate Change (IPCC) has brought the conclusions of climate science to public attention, no one can claim *not* to know the consequences for the planet, and for human civilization, if we continue to produce carbon emissions at present levels. Yet, unfortunately, our present capital-based economic system requires continually expanding markets. The science is clear: "growth economics" has run up against the absolute limits to its growth—planetary limits. It has been approximately three million years since the earth experienced atmospheric carbon levels of the present magnitude (over 400 parts per million). These "greenhouse gases" have turned our planet into a hothouse—or better put, a pressure cooker.

Because of these global developments, support has been growing for a radical shift of the political and economic models that we use to structure human civilization. Central to such a paradigm shift are the society-based economic principles derived from Marx and the history of Marxism. The time is ideal for a return to the enduring insights of Marxist analyses for a very simple reason: unrestrained capitalism is now threatening civilization as we know it. Diminishing resources, global climate disruption, weakening economies in both the developed and developing nations—these are present-day realities. As humanity draws nearer and nearer to the edge of the cliff,

---

3. <http://www.globalissues.org/article/26/poverty-facts-and-stats#src1>.

4. Shaohua Chen and Martin Ravallion, "The developing world is poorer than we thought, but no less successful in the fight against poverty," World Bank, August 2008, <http://www.globalissues.org/article/26/poverty-facts-and-stats#src1>.

massive social unrest and political disruptions will push human societies ever more quickly over the edge.

The severity of our planetary situation is a present and urgent reason for forward-looking thinkers to seek solutions beyond the status quo. *Nothing less than a shift in the global economic paradigm* will allow human nations, cultures, and civilizations to survive in anything like the forms in which we have known them heretofore. If you see that your car is heading off the road and toward a brick wall, you do not keep your foot on the accelerator. The vehicle of the capitalist growth economy has left the old, safe road and will soon hit its wall. The consequences forecast by scientists are almost incomprehensible: melting ice caps, rising sea levels, lack of food and drinking water for hundreds of millions of people, mass starvation, and the extinction of 30 to 40 percent of the planet's species. If this situation is not sufficient reason for nations to begin instituting new socioeconomic practices, it is hard to say what *would be* a sufficient reason.

Marxist Socioeconomic Policies after "Industrial Marxism"

At the same time that unrestrained capitalism threatens to destroy the planet, its major alternative, Marxism, has come under increasing criticism. Many theorists in the West seek to give the impression that it has been largely discredited. In light of this situation, it is not sufficient merely to point out the false promises of capitalism. One must also engage in a careful process of sorting through the legacy of Karl Marx's work in order to establish what a viable Marxism will mean in the twenty-first century. The program of Organic Marxism calls for a number of important revisions and updates of classical Marxist thought and practice:

1) *Marxism is not a universal predictive science.* The dream of social determinism was one of the many myths of European modernism that must now be left behind. We may not be able to list the objective factors that will predict a global revolution of the proletariat and the advent of a purely utopian socialist society. It follows that no national economy can be managed and controlled by central planning alone. Human ideals and philosophies, and even human religions, play crucial roles in motivating personal and social behaviors across cultures and nations. Marxists today do not dismiss ideas as a mere "superstructure," and we do not believe that the forces of production are the only real causal factors in history.

2) *Marxists do not need to insist only on state ownership, state-run businesses, and the abolition of all market forces.* Most actual socioeconomic systems are "mixed" or "hybrid" systems and are in this sense "impure." The push by wealthy individuals and businesses to increase their profits must be constrained and restrained by social policies and institutions at the government level; hence central planning and government restraints must play some role. But twenty-first-century Marxists

also make room for a limited role for market forces at the local, national, and international levels. Governments that strive for just social and economic conditions for all their citizens do not have to eliminate competition and private ownership.

Marx wrote in the context of early industrialization in the West. The solutions he proposed addressed exploitation of workers in the industries of his day—the kind of exploitation that continues today, for example in the garment industry in developing nations such as Bangladesh. Other parts of the global economy are post-industrial. Marxist analyses still reveal truths about these economic systems (such as global financial markets and the service sector), even though the solutions may not be identical to those that Marx proposed.

3) *Marxism was never meant to be a purely theoretical dispute among university professors.* The European debate over Marxist theory, long dominated by modernist assumptions, has in recent decades splintered into literally dozens of competing schools. Scholars engaged in increasingly abstract debates concerning the minutiae of their various competing theories, often with little obvious relevance to the realities of governing cities and countries. Theories divided into sub-theories and schools into sub-schools until in the end (some critics say) each scholar has become the chief advocate of a school consisting of himself or herself alone. When major Marxist figures and movements did arise—the Frankfurt School, Althusser, Habermas—whose insights began to influence public policy, their followers inevitably began to quarrel amongst themselves, decreasing the practical influence of their teachers. Too few Marxist authors have submitted their theories to rigorous testing in the fires of *realpolitik*, and those who have tried to do so in recent years—in Europe, Asia, and Latin America—have tended to work within the assumptions of the present-day global economic system. Only a radical blending of theory and practice in the study and implementation of Marxism will correct the imbalances of the past.

4) *Critics are wrong in their claim that Marxism has become a meaningless label for whatever random practices a socially-oriented government chooses to impose.* A "Marxism without real content" will not help human civilization through the crisis that it now faces. Not only will its capitalist opponents quickly realize that it is empty of content; the intellectuals, the students, the businessmen, and eventually even the bureaucrats of a nation will recognize it as well. It is all too easy to recognize when Marx's terms are used in a rote fashion and do not actually provide a substantive guiding framework for government policies and initiatives. When one fails to draw clear lines that lead from theory and practice, others begin to wonder whether the language is being used only to maintain the status quo. By contrast, updated Marxist analyses of the dynamics of wealth and power can help leaders to modify unjust systems and to implement wise policies.

One can welcome positive features in the traditions stemming from Marx's work, while still insisting that many of the classic forms of Marxism need updating, including German, Soviet, and early Chinese theories and practices. From this it by no means follows that Marxism as such has been superseded or that its core principles no longer have any significant meaning. As the coming chapters will show, the central Marxist insights remain as vital as ever—in fact, given the global situation today, perhaps more so.

5) *A vibrant, living Marxism cannot be "one size fits all."* According to modernist European assumptions, only a universal theory—a theory that is applicable everywhere and at all times—can be a true theory. As constructive postmodernism has shown, however, theories grow in, through, and out of their particular contexts, just as a plant grows in a particular soil and ecosystem.[5] The only useful Marxism for our time will be a *postmodern* Marxism, which means that it will exist only as adapted to a particular time and place: this nation, this culture, this language and history, these particular needs of these particular people. In these pages we defend a *culturally embedded Marxism*: a set of core commitments that take different forms as they are applied in different political and economic contexts.

Organic Marxism and "Ecological Civilization"

> [People] make their own history, but they do not make it just as they please; they do not make it under circumstances chosen by themselves, but under circumstances directly encountered, given, and transmitted from the past. The tradition of all the dead generations weighs like a nightmare on the brain of the living.[6]

In the second decade of the twenty-first century, we find ourselves in a new world, facing challenges that humanity has never faced before. Many around us ignore the writing on the wall, others turn inward to their own private pleasures and gains, and the most dangerous spend their careers promising that the problems are not really there because science and technology will make them magically disappear. Avoiding planetary disaster will take men and women of courage who think change, advocate for change, and work sacrificially to bring about change.

The leaders of the new ecological civilization will need conceptual resources adequate to this daunting task. For their overarching framework, they require a social, economic, and political philosophy that places *the common good*—of humanity, and of the planet—above all else.

---

5. Griffin, ed., *The Reenchantment of Science*; Griffin and Falk, eds. *Postmodern Politics for a Planet in Crisis*.

6. Cowling and Martin, eds., *Marx's Eighteenth Brumaire*, 19.

Given this goal, it becomes a top priority to diagnose and deconstruct those assumptions of European modernism that history has shown to be inadequate. Unfortunately, Marx uncritically accepted many of these assumptions. If his work is to speak to the needs of our postmodern world, it will need a bold reformulation that draws on newly available conceptual resources. Fortunately, the natural alliance between Marxism and environmental philosophy has long been recognized. Already in the 1960s Ernst Bloch was linking Marxism to the ecological movement, using the expression, "transcending without transcendence."[7]. . .

Conclusion: New Resources

The good news is that new conceptual resources are now available for constructing a significantly revised form of Marxism. In these pages we will explore the developments in the sciences and in the philosophy of science that support this emerging postmodern, organic paradigm. Among them, ecosystem studies and ecological philosophies play a particularly important role. We have also drawn from cultural studies, which traces the different ways that cultural beliefs, norms, and practices are embedded and embodied in different societies. Too often Marxism has been taught and implemented as if it were "one size fits all." Without sensitivity to cultural dynamics and divergences, neither this nor any other political philosophy can be successfully applied.

The final resource that appears in these pages is process philosophy. To our knowledge, this is the first book on Marxism written from a process perspective. Some Chinese Marxists are already interpreting process philosophy as a new school within contemporary Western Marxism. As process philosophy begins to play a larger and larger role in China, it is important to think carefully about the ways that it leads to a deeper understanding of Marxist principles. For example, it is highly significant that process thinking appears in many places in traditional Chinese philosophy, in Confucian and Daoist thinkers, and even in the most ancient text in the Chinese philosophical tradition, the *I Jing*.

In the end, the work of all political and economic theories will be judged by the fruits of their application. No one denies that radical changes are necessary; indeed, it's increasingly clear that they must come quickly. Even non-Marxists know the most famous sentence Karl Marx ever wrote: "The philosophers have only interpreted the world, in various ways: the point, however, is to change it."[8] We dedicate this book to all those men and women around the world, young and old, who are dedicated to building a sustainable ecological civilization in our time.

---

7. See Bloch, *Atheismus im Christentum*.

8. Marx, "Theses on Feuerbach" (first published in 1843), in Marx, *The German Ideology*. Marx's "Theses on Feuerbach" are also available online, <http://www.marxists.org/archive/marx/works/1845/theses/>.

39

The Ecology and Praxis of Organic Marxism[1]

The Manifesto of Organic Marxism

AT THE HEART OF the Manifesto stand three central claims: capitalist justice is not just; the "free market" is not free; and the costs of global climate disruption will be most severe among the poor. Recognizing these truths, we call on global leaders to reorganize human civilization according to ecological and socialist principles.

1) Capitalist justice is not just. Justice is conceived very differently in capitalist and Marxist theory. Marx writes, *"From each according to his ability, to each according to his need."* This famous phrase reflects Marx's society-based understanding of what is just. By contrast, the capitalist theory of justice says, "From each according to his wishes, to each according to the market." That is, each person decides which part of the market to invest his time and money in, and how hard to work. Whatever the market then pays him—or doesn't pay—counts as just.

As Organic Marxists, we blame this capitalist view of justice both for worker inequities and for the growing environmental catastrophe. We now know that the planet itself cannot sustain the payouts that the capitalist system provides to the world's wealthiest 1 percent, nor the lifestyle of consumption and waste that they buy with their wealth. With Marx, we advocate a system that brings the distribution of resources into harmony with *what people actually need to survive, not with their unlimited desires*. All the evidence shows that, within capitalist systems, the wealthy do not freely redistribute their wealth to the poor. Across virtually every culture, when the wealthiest are able to pocket high profits and decide how to spend their money, they choose luxurious lifestyles and high personal consumption. Only a postmodern socialist order will limit these excesses.

---

1. "The Ecology and Praxis of Organic Marxism," as found within Clayton and Justin Heinzekehr, *Organic Marxism: An Alternative to Capitalism and Ecological Catastrophe*, 193–228. Reprinted with the kind permission of Process Century Press.

2) *The "free market" is not free.* The "father of capitalism," Adam Smith, believed that markets are the most rational and moral way to regulate human interactions. According to *laissez-faire* capitalism, governments are required not to intervene in the markets in any way. Smith even used the metaphor of God: markets are so good at rewarding the virtuous and punishing the lazy that it is *as if* an "invisible hand" were guiding capitalist society.

Ironically, Adam Smith's doctrine came to be known as the "free market" doctrine. As a result, generations of people have confused the "freedom" of human rights and basic human liberties—a freedom that humans care much about—with the alleged freedom of the wealthy to accumulate as much wealth as they can.

Anyone who looks at the world in 2014 with open eyes will recognize that Adam Smith was wrong. Capitalism has created a massive underclass of people whose work is not rewarded with wealth and comfort. The unrestrained pursuit of wealth on the part of those with economic power has left approximately half the world's population— *over three billion people*—living on less than $2.50 a day.[2] The richest four hundred families in America possess more wealth than the bottom 155 million Americans combined.[3] The evidence is overwhelming that the wealthiest nations have designed the world economic system to bring maximum gains to themselves. This is not a "free" market; it is a market of virtual slavery for the increasingly impoverished classes around the globe. It is time for us to rise up and require markets to play the role of servant, not of master. Henceforth we expect markets to serve a subordinate role, fostering the goal of the "common good" for the planet as a whole.

3) *The costs of global climate disruption will be most severe among the poor.* Unless we intervene, climate change will wreak untold suffering on the world's poorest citizens and on a third to a half of animal species.

In the *Communist Manifesto*, Karl Marx writes that workers "have nothing to lose but their chains" and calls them to "Unite!"[4] Marx's call to action has not been without response, as the history of socialism over the last 165 years shows. But Marx's call by itself has until now been insufficient. People in power have enjoyed their physical comfort and the toys that technology provides. By contrast, those stuck in poverty, despite their numbers, have not had the power or the education to overthrow unjust economic and social systems. Multinational corporations have been able to unduly influence governments and world leaders, blocking reforms. Unless something significant changes on this planet, it's unlikely that the deadly grasp of global capitalism will be loosened.

---

2. <http://www.globalissues.org/article/26/poverty-facts-and-stats#src1>.

3. Liu, "How America is Rigged for the Rich," <http://www.cnn.com/2014/04/09/opinion/liu-income-inequality/>.

4. Marx, *Manifesto of the Communist Party* (1848), chapter 4, online at <https://www.marxists.org/archive/marx/works/1848/communist-manifesto/ch04.htm>.

But significant changes *are* taking place on this planet. Scientists agree that the effects of climate disruption are becoming increasingly severe. Social and economic systems as we know them are coming under increasing pressure. Many will collapse, along with the governments that are based upon them. The future will not be "business as usual."

Much can be done. To choose the common good over a wealth-driven economy means implementing the socialist principles that are implied by Organic Marxism. It's time for governments to rule for the people, rather than for the wealthy. It's time for transnational agreements to limit the power of multinational corporations, allowing the people to rebuild our societies on the basis of sustainable "steady state" economics.[5]

Humanity has two choices. We can begin now to turn away from the myth that it is best for the planet is to let wealthy people rule in their own interest. Or we can wait until the collapse of capital-based civilization in order to initiate structures that serve the common good. Now, not later, is the time to act.

---

5. See the materials of the Center for the Advancement of the Steady State Economy: <www.steadystate.org>.

40

The Many Faces of Integration
Liberal Faith between Church, Academy, and World[1]

AT THE END OF our journey, one wants to know: what will the actual mode of religious life look like when it lives out this form of theology as adventure? It takes courage to actively seek out the scientific and philosophical results that offer the greatest challenges to theism in general and to Christian belief in particular. In this new mode of religious life, doubts and uncertainties are no longer shoved away, or suppressed as sinful. Just as pursuing differences and concerns in personal relationships often leads to growth and intimacy, so wrestling with the tough challenges of our age leads to a stronger and more enduring form of faith.

The red thread that runs through these chapters is *integration*. At every point I have resisted calls to circle the wagons in order to protect inherited Christian beliefs from outside examination and criticism. Yet, like many, I find deep value in much that the Christian tradition has handed down. There is no integration if one sees contemporary culture and science as enemies from which one need to protect her faith on every front. Nor is there integration if one retains nothing from the tradition *with which* to engage as she dialogues with science, philosophy, and other religious traditions. This drive to integrate is an ethical and a deeply religious commitment that I believe lies at the very core of Christian identity in today's world.

Among all the theological traditions, there is one that has stressed the project of integration above all others. Liberal theology after Schleiermacher inherited the sixteenth-century motto, *Ecclesia reformata, semper reformanda!* (the church reformed and always reforming) and moved the call to continually new forms of integration into its very self-definition. It may well be that in the eyes of many liberal theology

---

1. "The Many Faces of Integration: Liberal Faith between Church, Academy, and World," as found within Clayton, *Adventures in the Spirit: God, World, Divine Action*, 255–67. Reprinted with the kind permission of Fortress.

has come to mean the gleeful overturning of the entire theological tradition. But de(con)struction of the tradition itself was not the brief of the modern theologies of integration. In this closing chapter, I wish to reclaim that great integrative project—with its wide-ranging conceptual, ethical, political, and personal dimensions—as the core commitment of a new liberal theology for our day.[2] The project that we have been pursuing through these pages defines a challenge, calls for a new set of methods, and, I believe, also signals a set of vibrant new answers.

The task of integration to which I am calling not only theologians but Christians in general is undertaken today in the context of what is now widely known as "the crisis of liberalism." This crisis—and the opportunities it brings—involve liberals of all stripes. A few decades ago the liberal church could give powerful and (relatively) unified expression to its identity. People knew and admired the values the mainline churches brought to the contemporary world. Not only that, but these theologians were also able to give powerful descriptions of the *conceptual foundations* for their action. They could speak a vibrant liberal theology. Today the foundations have become obscure:

> Turning and turning in the widening gyre
> The falcon cannot hear the falconer;
> Things fall apart; the center cannot hold;
> Mere anarchy is loosed upon the world,
> The blood-dimmed tide is loosed, and everywhere
> The ceremony of innocence is drowned;
> The best lack all conviction, while the worst
> Are full of passionate intensity.[3]

The best of us seem to lack conviction, while the worst are full of passionate intensity. Where are our "public theologians" today? Jay Adams puts the charge in harsh terms: "If I had to choose between putting a saloon or a liberal church on a corner, I'd choose the saloon every time. People who drink up the pay check in the saloon are less likely to become Pharisees, thinking that they don't need the Great Physician, than those who weekly swill the soporific doctrine of man's goodness."[4]

What has happened to liberalism? Where are the days when every intellectual American was reading that new book by Paul Tillich or one of the Niebuhr brothers? Where can one find theologians who seek for a finely honed balance between inherited tradition and contemporary world in the ways that Friedrich Schleiermacher, Paul Tillich, and Karl Rahner once did? It is a potent heritage, which in the past has

---

2. Note that in speaking of a new liberal theology, I do not identify with neo-liberalism in economic theory, a policy advocated by Milton Friedman with disastrous consequences for international economics and U.S. foreign policy.

3. Yeats, "The Second Coming."

4. See <http://www.monergism.com/thethreshold/articles/topic/liberaltheology.html>, visited February 2005.

had a transformative influence on society and the church as a whole: powerful convictions, powerful arguments, and powerful leaders in the church, the academy, and society. Today, one worries, the mainline churches seem to be suffering from a sort of liberal laryngitis.

The Crisis of Liberalism

Recall one of those powerful liberal voices: William Sloane Coffin, chaplain at Yale from 1958 to 1975. James Carroll describes one scene from this time: Coffin approached the podium

> with corduroy jacket and work boots for vestments. . . . [In his talk] there was the trademark pithiness, the rhetorical sophistication, the erudite citations, and . . . the Scriptures as a native language. [There was] the unbridled passion with which Coffin announced his gospel. . . . And what a gospel it was. The world he described was upside-down: the church on the side of the poor; the powerful at risk for losing everything; the disenfranchised as sole custodians of moral legitimacy. Coffin . . . was perhaps the first person from whom [I] heard that defining question: Whose side are you on? [My] answer would be the nearly ten years in coming that it took for [me] to go to jail [following a Washington protest] . . . .[5]

Few liberal Christian leaders today play the role Coffin once played, and few have his impact. Clearly, the *pieces* are still there, and many—pastors, bishops, scholars, church members—still speak with resounding voices, moving and motivating those who hear them. But the liberal theology that could move mountains, that could turn a world upside down, is less obvious. Not only outsiders, but even liberal theologians themselves are struggling to say how we are different from the world. Ours is an age when the social and intellectual dividing line between church and non-church is no longer as firm and fixed as it once was. That fundamental social *and worldview* identity people once had as church people, which was so clear to previous generations, is absent for many today.

Contrast this struggle for identity with the "loud and clear" identity enjoyed within conservative churches. One unimpeachable source describes the roots of American fundamentalism at the Niagara Bible Conference in 1878. About thirty years later the General Assembly of the Presbyterian Church into a series of tenets that came to be known as the five fundamentals: "the inerrancy of the Scriptures; the virgin birth [and deity] of Jesus; the doctrine of substitutionary atonement; the bodily resurrection of Jesus; and the miracles . . . of Jesus Christ," along with his second coming.[6]

---

5. Foreword to Coffin, *Credo*, xi.

6. Cited from *Wikipedia*, an online encyclopedia; see <http://en.wikipedia.org/wiki/Fundamentalist_Christianity>, visited June 2018.

In the confusing world we live in, conservative evangelicals today have a passionate commitment to the truth of a number of propositions; and they believe there is a clear moral imperative behind most of their actions. Evangelicals can also tell a clear narrative about modern thought and culture, using terms like "secular humanism" and "back to the Bible!" In its most extreme form, as in Hal Lindsey's *The Late Great Planet Earth*, this narrative describes how the world is moving into the "last days" and how only God's direct intervention can save it now.

The contrast is at its harshest when liberals describe their religious beliefs using terms like "lifestyle choice." This language suggests that what we as liberal Christians do in the world is "what we're into"; but—the world assumes—it's perfectly fine to be "into" other things as well (meditation, driving one's sports car, learning Italian). "Lifestyle choice" and "lifestyle preference," I fear, are not by themselves enough to motivate Christian identity. Talk of "my personal political convictions" is not enough. Even talk of "my spiritual journey" is not enough to ground a powerful liberal voice. Set free from our heritage, the word "spiritual" filters down to the lowest common denominator. As we saw in the previous chapter, if doing sacred dance makes me feel fully human and fully alive, then engaging in such activities must *ipso facto* make me a spiritual being. In a time when the mainline churches are seeking to rediscover their heritage and identity, when they are uncertain how to speak powerfully to the academy and the world, how can theologians provide leadership in the process?

Liberal Christians are not accustomed to speaking in ringing tones today. Why should this be? Theology since Schleiermacher has a clear and powerful heritage, albeit one that does not separate black from white as clearly as conservatives do. Our heritage, I have suggested, is the quest for a full and powerful integration. It's possible today to regain a sense of that tradition, which I call *the quest for a new integration*. I shall first try to express the core theological commitment of this integrative Christian theology, and then restate that commitment as a vision for Christians both in the academy and outside.

The Root Meaning of Integration

What is this new quest for integration? And why choose integration as *the* heritage and *the* defining characteristic of a new liberal Christianity? Listen for a moment to the words of a powerful Christian voice, a man whose main battle was for integration, so that (as he said) freedom might ring from every mountainside. Dr. Martin Luther King Jr. was asked, "When will you be satisfied" in your quest for integration? He answered,

> We can never be satisfied as long as the Negro is the victim of the unspeakable horrors of police brutality. We can never be satisfied as long as our bodies, heavy with the fatigue of travel, cannot gain lodging in the motels of the

highways and the hotels of the cities. We cannot be satisfied as long as a Negro in Mississippi cannot vote and a Negro in New York believes he has nothing for which to vote. No, no, we are not satisfied, and we will not be satisfied until "justice rolls down like waters, and righteousness like a mighty stream." (Amos 5:24)[7]

King's was a vision of integration and of justice. Dr. King's words on the steps of the Lincoln Memorial, at the culmination of that massive march from Birmingham, remain especially prescient:

> I have a dream that one day, down in Alabama, with its vicious racists, with its governor having his lips dripping with the words of "interposition" and "nullification"—one day right there in Alabama little black boys and black girls will be able to join hands with little white boys and white girls as sisters and brothers.... I have a dream that one day every valley shall be exalted, and every hill and mountain shall be made low, the rough places will be made plain, and the crooked places will be made straight; "and the glory of the Lord shall be revealed and all flesh shall see it together."[8] (Isaiah 40:4-5)

That's the voice and highest calling of an integrative Christianity. These words resonate with the famous song by Holly Near, "It Could Have Been Me," written to honor the four students at Kent State who were shot to death during an anti-war rally: "It could have been me, but instead it was you; and I'll keep doing the things that you were doing until we are through...."

The New Integration

The priorities and tasks of classical liberal thought remain equally vital today; its core goals have not been achieved. To achieve them, liberals need to return to and to study afresh the classic texts of our heritage, those of Schleiermacher and Ritschl and Troeltsch, of Rauschenbusch and Bonhoeffer and Tillich. At the same time, there are also *new* forms of integration that demand our attention today; the need for integration at the beginning of the twenty-first century is greater than ever. Consider the fertile fields for integration in our present context:

- multiple religious traditions;
- diverse cultural traditions;
- science and religion;
- complicated ethical questions, from bioethics to new forms of human relationship;

---

7. Breidlid et al., eds., *American Culture*, 86. The speech is also widely available online. I quote it from: <http://www.americanrhetoric.com/speeches/mlkihaveadream.htm>, verified April 7, 2008.

8. Ibid., 86.

- the continuing struggle to integrate faith and politics;
- the new opportunities for constructive dialogue between liberals and evangelicals within the one church catholic;
- and the "lived integration" of one's corporate beliefs with one's corporate practice.

As Peter Berger writes, "The old agenda of liberal theology was the contestation with modernity. . . . The much more pressing agenda today is the contestation with the fullness of human religious possibilities."[9] Those who practice Christianity today practice it against a rich tapestry of variegated religious options in a way that wasn't true for most Americans a few decades ago.

The task for liberals today, Peter Berger argues, is to learn to "hold convictions without either dissolving them in utter relativity or encasing them in the false absolutes of fanaticism."[10] American religion too often contents itself with one of two escape routes: the embrace of a false certainty, happily marketed by various orthodoxies, or the certainty that there *is* no access to truth, resulting in nihilism and utter relativism.[11] As we confront the pluralism of modern societies, Berger argues, we must "steer a course between a limitless tolerance which passively and yet progressively' reads the signs of the current age but surrenders to it with 'nothing to say,' on the one hand, and, on the other hand, a conservative fanaticism that denies the current age by writing about it 'without having ever listened' to it."[12]

The Core Commitment

If one is to pursue new forms of integration, one must be able to formulate the distinctive content and the distinctive methods that once characterized liberal Christianity. A major influence on Dr. King was Reinhold Niebuhr's *Moral Man, Immoral Society*, which "tempered King's faith in humanity with an analysis of the corrupting influence of organizations over individuals."[13] Niebuhr opened King's eyes to the "big picture" approach to the gospel. He writes in *Love and Justice*:

> The gospel cannot be preached with truth and power if it does not challenge the pretensions and pride, not only of individuals, but of nations, cultures, civilizations, economic, and political systems. The good fortune of America and its power place it under the most grievous temptations to self-adulation. If there is no power and grace in the Christian church "to bring down every high

---

9. Berger, *The Heretical Imperative,* 183.
10. Ibid., 183.
11. Ibid., 18–19. I here modify a formulation from Tino Garcia.
12. Tino Garcia, personal communication, modified, quoting Berger, *A Far Glory*, 15–16.
13. See <http://www.sparknotes.com/biography/mlk/terms.html>, visited March 2005.

thing which exalteth itself against the knowledge of God," the church becomes not merely useless but dangerous.[14]

But one cannot consistently point at the influence of institutions on individual belief and action without at the same time granting their influence on *one's own belief* as well. To paraphrase the Sermon on the Mount (Matt 7:4) "How can you say to your sister, 'Let me remove the speck of institutional bias out of your eye,' when the log of cultural locatedness is in your own eye?" Integration is a radical notion, for it becomes necessary to recognize that one's own beliefs and practices, one's very definitions of "insider" and "outsider," are also products of cultural construction.

Perhaps one can conceive the new integrative theology as a form of radical Wesleyanism. Radical Wesleyans endorse a more radical sense of what has come to be known as "the Wesleyan quadrilateral." Scripture and tradition take on new meanings when integrated with present-day reason and experience. H. Richard Niebuhr beautifully formulates this vision:

> [Theology must] try to develop a method applicable not to all religions but to the particular faith to which its historical point of view is relevant. Such theology in the Christian church cannot, it is evident, be an offensive or defensive enterprise which undertakes to prove the superiority of Christian faith to all other faiths; but it can be a confessional theology which carries on the work of self-criticism and self-knowledge in the church.[15]

As Niebuhr says later, "we try to understand, not how features in our past are repeated in our present, but how our present grows out of our past into our future."[16] For "revelation is a moving thing, . . . its meaning is realized only by being brought to bear upon the interpretation and reconstruction of ever-new human situations in an enduring movement, a single drama of divine and human action."[17]

Three Examples of Integration in Action

Let me begin with an example from the recent discussions between science and theology. In the sciences today, most religious truth claims are seen as suspect; one encounters a fair degree of skepticism when one enters into this discussion as a Christian. The reason is that when religious conservatives have addressed science, they have repeatedly and vocally proclaimed a break with science wherever scientific results seem to conflict with traditional Christian beliefs. Some argue that science's methodological naturalism is unacceptable to Christians, who must always insist on a supernatural

---

14. Niebuhr, *Love and Justice*, 97.

15. Niebuhr, *The Meaning of Revelation*, 18. I am grateful to Zach Simpson for assistance on the Niebuhr research.

16. Ibid., 128.

17. Ibid., 136.

worldview. Others argue that explaining complex phenomena like consciousness or prayer in terms of repeatable experiments and underlying causal mechanisms is antithetical to Christianity, which must therefore oppose it. One way or another, conservatives say, walls must be built to protect Christianity from the encroachment of science.

Contrast the approach of an integrative Christian theology. It is our calling and our right to enter fully into the scientific project, either as scientists or in dialogue with scientists. As a scholar in this field, I need have no fear of any success in science; I share the excitement of each new advance in explanation. I know that it is *possible* that key beliefs I hold will in the end be accounted for by purely naturalistic mechanisms. Perhaps consciousness is not a causal force; perhaps values are a product of the "selfish gene" in its struggle to survive the evolutionary process; perhaps religious beliefs will in the end be better explained by cultural and biological forces. In the end, I will accept whatever turns out to be the most successful explanation. But I *think* that purely naturalistic and value-free accounts will *not* succeed in the end, and at this point the evidence seems to support this conclusion. Across its various fields, science raises questions that cannot be answered within the natural sciences—metaphysical questions that lead right into the heart of theology. Out of physics emerge the self-replicating organisms of biology; out of biology emerge beings with advanced cognitive capacities and cultures; out of human existence emerge questions of the ultimate meaning of the universe and of life after death. Studying the psycho-social-physical beings that we are, one hears clear "intimations of transcendence." We need persons with the courage and the expertise to trace these lines of transcendence from their scientific origins to their ultimate theological source.

A new breed of liberal theologians, I suggest, is in an ideal position to integrate science and religion in this fashion. Because the drive toward integration is essential to our faith, because our faith is not only a given but also a quest, we do not need to build walls—indeed, we *may* not build walls—to immunize our beliefs from possible falsification. Such liberal thinkers vehemently reject a pseudo-science that is custom-designed to support supernaturalism, just as we resist a religion that is stripped of all its convictions and reduced to its purely naturalistic functions. Our quest is for nothing less than the full integration of science and religion, the full harmony between the two without the reduction of the one to the other.

Integrative theologians, students, and professors also do not need to be afraid of the social scientific study of religion. . . . We know that there is a psychology of religious conversion; we know that there are distinct sociological patterns within distinct denominations; and we acknowledge the cultural influences on specific religious practices and beliefs. Yet we *advocate* the social scientific study of religion, for we believe it will reveal in the long run the genuinely transcendent element in religious belief. Close study will not eliminate religion but will open insights into the God-directed aspects of human existence.

PART VI: Progressive Theology

A final example: liberal Christians generally defend a social ethics that draws from political theory and the analysis of American society today. The liberal religious voice is not defined in opposition to secular culture and all political involvement. It takes the real complexes of society as given, and *then* draws on the values of the Christian scriptures and traditions to challenge structures of injustice, suppression, oppression and prejudice.

A Radically Incarnational Theology

This vision for a new liberal theology[18] represents a powerful calling. It takes some courage; it takes a prophetic voice; it takes a hatred of the trivial; it takes a willingness to be hard-nosed; it takes a constant refusal to become self-absorbed. At the heart of this vision lies the contention that liberal approaches to theology, by their very nature, work continually to integrate what humanity knows—our history, our science, our highest moral values, our involvement with political institutions—with the tradition handed down through the centuries.

This is a radically incarnational theology. The new integration means integrating the best of contemporary experience and contemporary reason with the inherited resources of Christian scriptures and traditions. We each seek to wed the resources of our tradition with the unanswered problems of our own day. To be a liberal *Christian* is to return continually to the scriptures and traditions in the attempt to understand what are genuinely Christ-like responses. But to be a *liberal* Christian is not to take the inherited traditions as complete in themselves. This is the famous hermeneutical moment: only when the "horizon" of the text and tradition is fused with the horizon of our contemporary world is the Christian voice complete.

This means that scripture and tradition do not in themselves complete revelation. To claim that revelation does not end with scripture and tradition is a radical and perhaps frightening notion. It's also a powerful theological truth. Fundamentally, it's the insight of incarnation. If Jesus is fully God and fully human, that is, one who is incomplete until both dimensions are included, why would one expect that the church, the *Body* of Christ, would be complete without a similar need for ongoing incarnation? If God once integrated with humanity, is it not our continual calling to integrate with ever-new contexts of knowledge, ever-new social contexts, ever-new contexts of ministry? Sadly, there is a strong inclination to over-emphasize one end or the other of "Wesleyan quadrilateral"—either scripture/tradition or experience/reason. Either one so valorizes the past that the present has no genuine input, or one so overemphasizes the present context that the past becomes mere allegory, myth, or story, contributing nothing essential. An incarnational theology means a calling to *continual integration*.

---

18. Niebuhr, *The Meaning of Revelation*, 136.

The core question behind the new integration, then, is this: what *today* are the new incarnations of scripture and tradition with reason and experience? What tomorrow will be the new fruits of their union? Integration is not the most famous feature of the conservative mind, but it has traditionally been a defining feature of liberal Christianity. The new liberal approach connotes an adventure of open inquiry, of genuine grappling with the world we live in, of honest acknowledgment of difficulties. In such grappling, integrative theologians proclaim, revelation continues to happen today. H. Richard Niebuhr gave a powerful description of this revelation:

> We climb the mountain of revelation that we may gain a view of the shadowed valley in which we dwell and from the valley we look up again to the mountain. Each arduous journey brings new understanding, but also new wonder and surprise. *This mountain is not one we climbed once upon a time; it is a well-known peak we never wholly know, which needs to be climbed again in every generation, on every new day.* There is no time or place in human history, there is no moment in the church's past, nor is there any set of doctrines, any philosophy or theology of which we might say, "Here the knowledge possible through revelation and the knowledge of revelation is fully set forth." *Revelation is not only progressive but it requires of those to whom it has come that they begin the never-ending pilgrim's progress of the reasoning Christian heart.*[19]

Consider one brief example, the integration of belief and scholarship. Widespread in the church today is the sense of a dichotomy between its mission and the striving for academic excellence. By contrast, the new liberal vision involves intellectual rigor and academic excellence as forms of service to the church, which then become part and parcel of her mission. We believe that both traditional theology and contemporary scholarship can assist in such a revisioning, both within the church and without.[20]

Some critics worry that scholarship raises too many questions and allows for too much doubt. But it is surely possible to combine critical inquiry with passionate faith. I share Peter Berger's conviction that such an approach "embodies *precisely* the balance between skepsis and affirmation that . . . defines the only acceptable way of being a Christian without emigrating from modernity."[21] This combination of openness and affirmation is, I believe, the new liberalism's greatest strength. If we were committed only to fighting for the purity of the "truth once received" or for the continuation of particular structures or a particular understanding of the church, we would have less

---

19. Niebuhr, *The Meaning of Revelation*, 137 (italics added).

20. My thesis is simple, thought the details aren't: it has always been the fundamental nature of liberal Christianity to speak a voice that is both revisionary and yet in continuity with the Christian tradition. Put differently, the prophetic voice of liberal Christians has been to bring the resources of the Christian faith to bear on contemporary society in a way that transforms *both* the society *and* the Christian faith itself.

21. Berger, *Questions of Faith*, viii, emphasis added.

to offer. But if liberal believers are willing to listen as well as to proclaim, to adapt what we have in order to be more effective at being who we are, we can be powerful agents of understanding and change.

A Prophetic Role for Theology

There are many ways to serve the church. The church is served by those who seek to preserve it in its current form against new challenges, and it is served by those who seek to keep its traditions fresh and alive. It is also served by those who exercise the prophetic function. Prophets are those who challenge existing structures, who call others back to what is essential. Because they ask people to look at things in a new way, to respond differently than they have responded in the past, prophets make people uncomfortable. Nevertheless, we need prophets among us. For successful communities exist not in pristine isolation but in deep integration with their surroundings. As Majorie Suchocki writes in *God, Christ, Church*,

> On a social level, human communities are a complex bonding oriented toward the perpetuation of the community. The boundaries of the community are more or less fluid, since communities are sustained not only by their members, but by their interaction with wider societies and environment.[22]

In general, liberal education exercises three distinct functions: it teaches the great intellectual traditions; it helps students to adapt them to the intellectual challenges of their day; and it offers fruitful new solutions to burning social and political problems. New forms of liberal theological education must perform three similar functions: continue to train students in the great theological traditions of the past, though not uncritically; help them to adapt these theologies to contemporary challenges; and exercise a prophetic function within the church and society.

Theology must retain this prophetic function as well. Recall the motto with which this chapter opened: *Ecclesia reformata, semper reformanda*: always reformed, always reforming. To grasp the core principles of the Christian proclamation, to encounter the kerygma associated with Jesus, is to encounter a message of resounding power, a leaven that should transform everything it comes in contact with.

What would a prophetic theology look like today? It must retain the four dimensions mentioned above. In it *scripture* exercises a prophetic function, because it calls theology to look for the word of God in it; *tradition* has a prophetic function, because it reveals the restless activity of the Holy Spirit, always bringing new insights and new ways of thinking and acting; *experience* is prophetic, because in the heart of the individual burn experiences and insights that cannot be exactly fit into any pre-existing structure, insights with the power to transform and to create anew. And *reason*? Prophetic reason gives us words to match our convictions, clear thinking to

22. Berger, *Questions of Faith*, viii, emphasis added.

challenge obscurities of the past, skepticism to question what may be false, a probing mind to quest for the truth wherever it lies, and arguments to persuade others of what we have found. As the famous bumper sticker reads, "If you think education is expensive, try ignorance."

Paul Tillich once wrote that prophecy "is the message of the shaking of the foundations, and not those of their enemies, but rather those of their own country. For the prophetic spirit has not disappeared from the earth."[23] Prophets, like students, are those who dream a future that may be better than the present. One reads in Joel, "Your sons and your daughters shall prophesy, your old men shall dream dreams, your young men shall see visions" (2:28); and the Proverb adds, "Where there is no vision, the people perish" (28:19). The church desperately needs institutions within it where those dreams can still be dreamed, the hard questions asked, the visions developed and nurtured for a lifetime.

The question is, Will theologians foster and support the radical work of integration? Or will they follow that pattern that Max Weber called "the institutionalization of charisma"? Will they quench the spirit of experimentation and integration, of perplexity and prophecy, that I have taken as the defining feature of a truly integrative Christianity?

Conclusion

Some, perhaps many, will disagree with the new liberal program I have outlined in this book. I close with a plea to those who do disagree: please don't tell us that only he or she serves the church who accepts it, relates to it, and seeks to perpetuate it in her current form. Please don't exclude from our midst those who would see differently: those who would invite into our congregations not only immigrant peoples but also their immigrant customs and ways of doing things; those who would exercise loving, long-term relationships in different forms and combinations than have traditionally been sanctioned; those who would challenge existing structures of power, whether within the church or outside it and who would build new structures in their place; those who would use means to share their faith—rap or rock or street drama or the new liturgies of the emerging church—that make us uncomfortable because they are too loud or rude or ugly.

I think in closing of my former colleague Mario Savio, whom history has credited with founding the free-speech movement at Berkeley in the mid-1960s. I frequently picture Mario standing on the roof of the police car to which he had been handcuffed, and saying, "Sometimes you have to throw yourself on the gears to stop the machine." Mario had prophetic courage, motivated in part (he told me at one point) by his own Catholic heritage. Listen to Mario Savio's exact words:

---

23. Tillich, *The Shaking of the Foundations*, 7–8.

PART VI: Progressive Theology

> There is a time when the operation of the machine becomes so odious, makes you so sick at heart, that you can't take part; you can't even passively take part, and you've got to put your bodies upon the gears and upon the wheels, upon the levers, upon all the apparatus, and you've got to make it stop. And you've got to indicate to the people who run it, to the people who own it, that unless you're free, the machine will be prevented from working at all!

Integration is a messy business. If there were a formula for it, it wouldn't be integration. Peter Berger sees this clearly:

> If relativity is a stormy sea of uncertainties, [our] faith does not magically make the waters recede so that we can march through them on a dry path. What it does do is give us the courage to set sail on our little boat, with the hope that, by God's grace, we will reach the other shore without drowning.[24]

A genuinely integrative theology is a high calling, and we should pursue it with pride and conviction. Let us be avant garde, think new thoughts, dream new dreams, and imagine a future that no one has imagined before. For this, I believe, is our particular vocation and our distinctive contribution.

---

24. Ibid., 7–8.

Select Bibliography

Agazzi, Evandro. *The Problem of Reductionism in Science*. Episteme 18. Dordrecht: Kluwer Academic, 1991.

Alexander, Samuel. *Space, Time, and Deity*. The Gifford Lectures for 1916–18. 2 vols. London: Macmillan, 1920.

Allison, Henry. "Spinoza and the Philosophy of Immanence: Reflections in Yovel's *The Adventures of Immanence*." *Inquiry* 35 (1992) 55–67.

Alves, Rui Raphael, A. G. Chaleil, and Michael J. E. Sternberg. "Evolution of Enzymes in Metabolism: A Network Perspective." *Journal of Molecular Biology* 320 (2002) 751–70.

Armstrong, Karen. *The History of God*. New York: Random House, 1993.

Barabasi, Albert-László. *Linked: The New Science of Networks*. Cambridge: Perseus, 2002.

———. "Network Theory—The Emergence of the Creative Enterprise." *Science* 308 (2005) 629–41.

Barabasi, Albert-László, and Reka Albert. "Emergence of Scaling in Random Networks." *Science* 286 (1999) 504–12.

Barbour, Ian. *Myths, Models and Paradigms: A Comparative Study in Science and Religion*. New York: Harper & Row, 1974.

Barrow, John D., and Frank J. Tipler. *The Anthropic Cosmological Principle*. Oxford: Oxford University Press, 1988.

Bartley, C. J. *The Theology of Rāmānuja: Realism and Religion*. London: Routledge Curzon, 2002.

Basinger, David. *The Case for Freewill Theism*. Downers Grove: InterVarsity, 1996.

Beckermann, Ansgar, Hans Flohr, and Jaegwon Kim, eds. *Emergence or Reduction? Essays on the Prospects of Nonreductive Physicalism*. New York: de Gruyter, 1992.

Beckers, H. *Schelling's Geistesentwicklung in ihrem inneren Zusammenhang*. München: Bergmann, 1875.

Bedau, Mark. "Weak Emergence." In *Philosophical Perspectives XI: Mind, Causation, and World*, 375–99. Atascadero, CA: Ridgeview, 1997.

Behe, Michael. *Darwin's Black Box: The Biochemical Challenge to Evolution*. New York: Free Press, 1998.

Bennett, Jonathan. *A Study of Spinoza's Ethics*. Indianapolis: Hackett, 1984.

Berger, Peter. *A Far Glory: The Quest for Faith in an Age of Credulity*. New York: MacMillan, 1992.

———. *The Heretical Imperative: Contemporary Possibilities of Religious Affirmation*. Garden City: Anchor/Doubleday, 1979.

———. *Questions of Faith: A Skeptical Affirmation of Christianity*. Malden, MA: Blackwell, 2004.

Bergson, Henri. *Creative Evolution*. Translated by Arthur Mitchell. Lanham University Press of America, 1983.

Bieri, Peter, Rolf P. Horstmann, and Lorenz Krüger, eds. *Transcendental Arguments and Science: Essays in Epistemology*. Dordrecht: Reidel, 1979.

Blitz, David. *Emergent Evolution: Qualitative Novelty and the Levels of Reality*. Episteme 19. Dordrecht: Kluwer Academic, 1992.

Bloch, Ernst. *Atheismus im Christentum: zur Religion des Exodus und des Reichs*. Frankfurt am Main: Suhrkamp, 1968.

Bohm, David. *Causality and Chance in Modern Physics*. Philadelphia: University of Pennsylvania Press, 1961.

Boyd, Gregory. *God of the Possible*. Grand Rapids: Baker, 2000.

Boyer, Pascal. *Religion Explained: The Evolutionary Origins of Religious Thought*. New York: Basic, 2001.

Bracken, Joseph. "*Creatio ex Nihilo*: A Field-Oriented Approach." *Dialog* 44 (2005) 236–49.

———. *The Divine Matrix: Creativity as Link between East and West*. Maryknoll: Orbis, 1995.

———. "Energy-Events and Fields." *Process Studies* 18, no. 3 (1989) 153–65.

———. *The One in the Many: A Contemporary Reconstruction of the God-world Relationship*. Grand Rapids: Eerdmans, 2001.

———. "Process Philosophy and Trinitarian Theology." Parts I and II, *Process Studies* 8, no. 4 (1978) 217–30 and 11, no. 2 (1981) 83–96.

———. *Society and Spirit: A Trinitarian Cosmology*. London: Associated University Presses, 1991.

———. *The Triune Symbol: Persons, Process and Community*. Lanham: University Press of America, 1985.

Brandon, Robert N. "Reductionism versus Wholism versus Mechanism." In *Concepts and Methods in Evolutionary Biology*, edited by Robert N. Brandon, 179–204. Cambridge: Cambridge University Press, 1996.

Breidlid, Anders, et al., eds. *American Culture: An Anthology of Civilization Texts*. New York: Routledge, 1996.

Broad, C. D. *The Mind and Its Place in Nature*. London: Routledge and Kegan Paul, 1925.

Brierley, Michael. "Naming a Quiet Revolution: The Panentheistic Turn in Modern Theology." In *In Whom We Live and Move and Have Our Being: Panentheistic Reflections on God's Presence in a Scientific World*, edited by Philip Clayton and Arthur Peacocke, 1–15. Grand Rapids: Eerdmans, 2006.

Brown, Robert. *The Later Philosophy of Schelling: The Influence of Boehme on the Works of 1809–1815*. Plainsboro: Associated University Press, 1977.

Brown, Terrance, and Leslie Smith. *Reduction and the Development of Knowledge*. Mahwah, NJ: Erlbaum, 2003.

Bucheim, Thomas. "Die reine Abscheidung Gottes: Eine Vergleichbarheit im Grundgedanken von Fichtes und Schellings Spätphilosophie." *Zeitschrift für philosophische Forschung* 42 (1988) 95–106.

Butterfield, Jeremy, and Constantine Pagonis, eds. *From Physics to Philosophy*. Cambridge: Cambridge University Press, 1999.

Butterfield, Jeremy, Mark Hogarth, and Gordon Belot, eds. *Spacetime*. Brookfield: Dartmouth University Press, 1996.

Campbell, Donald. "'Downward Causation' in Hierarchically Organized Biological Systems." In *Studies in the Philosophy of Biology*, edited by Francisco J. Ayala and T. H. Dobzhansky, 179–86. Berkeley: University of California Press, 1974.

———. "Levels of Organization, Downward Causation, and the Selection-Theory Approach to Evolutionary Epistemology." In *Theories of the Evolution of Knowing*, edited by G. Greenberg and E. Tobach, 1–17. Hillsdale: Erlbaum, 1990.

Carman, John Braisted. *The Theology of Rāmānuja: An Essay in Interreligious Understanding*. New Haven: Yale University Press, 1974.

Charlton, William. "Spinoza's Monism." *The Philosophical Review* 90, no. 4 (1981) 503–29.

Clark, Austen. *Psychological Models and Neural Mechanisms: An Examination of Reductionism in Psychology*. Oxford: Clarendon, 1980.

Clayton, Philip. *Adventures in the Spirit: God, World, Divine Action*. Minneapolis: Fortress, 2008.

———. "Biology and Purpose: Altruism, Morality, and Human Nature in Evolutionary Perspectives." In *Evolution and Ethics: Human Morality in Biological and Religious Perspective*, edited by Philip Clayton and Jeffrey Schloss, 121–34. Grand Rapids: Eerdmans, 2004.

———. "The Case for Christian Panentheism." *Dialog* 37 (Summer 1998) 201–8.

———. "Conceptual Foundations of Emergence Theory." In *The Re-Emergence of Emergence: The Emergentist Hypothesis from Science to Religion*, edited by Philip Clayton and Paul Davies, 1–34. Oxford: Oxford University Press, 2008.

———. "The Ecology and Praxis of Organic Marxism." In *Organic Marxism: An Alternative to Capitalism and Ecological Catastrophe*, edited by Philip Clayton and Justin Heinzekehr, 193–228. Toward Ecological Civilization Book 3. Claremont: Process Century, 2014.

———. "Emergence from Quantum Physics to Religion." In *The Re-Emergence of Emergence: The Emergentist Hypothesis from Science to Religion*, edited by Philip Clayton and Paul Davies, 303–20. Oxford: Oxford University Press, 2008.

———. *Explanation from Physics to Theology: An Essay in Rationality and Religion*. New Haven: Yale University Press, 1989.

———. *God and Contemporary Science*. Edinburgh Studies in Constructive Theology. Grand Rapids: Eerdmans, 1997.

———. "In Defense of Christian Panentheism." *Dialog* 37 (1998) 201–8.

———. *In Quest of Freedom: The Emergence of Spirit*. Frankfurt Templeton Lectures 2006, edited by Michael G. Parker and Thomas M. Schmidt, 112–32. Göttingen: Vandenhoeck & Ruprecht, 2009.

———. "Introducing Organic Marxism." In *Organic Marxism: An Alternative to Capitalism and Ecological Catastrophe*, edited by Philip Clayton and Justin Heinzekehr, 3–14. Toward Ecological Civilization Book 3. Claremont: Process Century, 2014.

———. *In Quest of Freedom: The Emergence of Spirit in the Natural World*. Göttingen: Vandenhoeck & Ruprecht, 2008.

———. "Kenotic Trinitarian Panentheism." *Dialog* 44 (2005) 250–55.

———. *Mind & Emergence: From Quantum to Consciousness*. Oxford: Oxford University Press, 2004.

———. "On Divine and Human Agency: Reflections of a Co-laborer." In *All That Is: A Naturalistic Faith for the Twenty-First Century*, by Arthur Peacocke, edited by Philip Clayton, 163–75. Theology and the Sciences. Minneapolis: Fortress, 2007.

———. "Panentheism Today: A Constructive Systematic Evaluation." In *In Whom We Live and Move and Have Our Being: Panentheistic Reflections on God's Presence in a Scientific World*, edited by Philip Clayton and Arthur Peacocke, 249–64. Grand Rapids: Eerdmans, 2006.

———. "Panentheism in Metaphysical and Scientific Perspective." In *In Whom We Live and Move and Have Our Being: Panentheistic Reflections on God's Presence in a Scientific World*, edited by Philip Clayton and Arthur Peacocke, 73–94. Grand Rapids: Eerdmans, 2006.

———. "Panentheisms East and West." *Sophia* 49, no. 2 (2010) 183–91.

———. *The Problem of God in Modern Thought*. Grand Rapids: Eerdmans, 2000.

———. *Religion and Science: The Basics*. London: Routledge, 2011.

———. *Transforming Christian Theology: For Church And Society*. Minneapolis: Fortress, 2010.

———. "Religious Truth and Scientific Truth." In *Phenomenology of the Truth Proper to Religion: An Anthology*, edited by Daniel Guerrière, 43–59. Albany: SUNY, 1990.

Clayton, Philip, and Steven Knapp, eds. *The Predicament of Belief: Science, Philosophy, and Faith*. Oxford: Oxford University Press, 2011.

Clayton, Philip, and Arthur Peacocke, eds. *In Whom We Live and Move and Have Our Being: Panentheistic Reflections on God's Presence in a Scientific World*. Grand Rapids: Eerdmans, 2004.

Cobb, John B. Jr., and Clark H. Pinnock. *Searching for an Adequate God: A Dialogue between Process and Free Will Theists*. Grand Rapids: Eerdmans, 2000.

Coffin, William Sloane. *Credo*. Louisville: Westminster John Knox Press, 2004.

Collins, C. John. *The God of Miracles: An Exegetical Examination of God's Action in the World*. Wheaton, IL: Crossway, 2000.

Cook, Francis H. "Just This: Buddhist Ultimate Reality." *Buddhist-Christian Studies* 9 (1989) 127–42.

Cowling, Mark, and James Martin, eds. *Marx's Eighteenth Brumaire: (Post)modern Interpretations*. London: Pluto, 2002.

Crane, Tim. "The Significance of Emergence." In *Physicalism and its Discontents*, edited by Carl Gillett and Barry Loewer, 207–24. Cambridge: Cambridge University Press, 2001.

d'Espagnat, Bernard. *Veiled Reality: An Analysis of Present-day Quantum Mechanical Concepts* Reading: Addison-Wesley, 1995.

Dabney, D. Lyle. *Die Kenosis des Geistes: Kontinuität zwischen Schöpfung und Erlösung im Werk des Heiligen Geistes*. Neukirchen-Vluyn: Neukirchener, 1997.

Davidson, Donald. "Thinking Causes." In *Mental Causation*, edited by John Heil and Alfred Mele, 3–17. Oxford: Clarendon, 1995.

Davies, Paul. *God and the New Physics*. New York: Simon & Schuster, 1984.

———. *The Mind of God*. New York: Simon & Schuster, 1992.

Dawkins, Richard. *The Blind Watchmaker: Why the Evidence for Evolution Reveals without Design*. London: Penguin, 1987.

———. *The God Delusion*. Boston: Bantam, 2006.

———. *Unweaving the Rainbow: Science, Delusion, and the Appetite for Wonder*. Boston: Mariner, 1998.

Deacon, Terrence. "The Hierarchic Logic of Emergence: Untangling the Interdependence of Evolution and Self Organization." In *Evolution and Learning: The Baldwin Effect*

Reconsidered, edited by Bruce H. Weber and David J. Depew, 273–308. Cambridge: MIT Press, 2003.

———. *The Symbolic Species: The Co-Evolution of Language and the Brain*. New York: Norton, 1997.

de Dijn, Hermann. "The Articulation of Nature, or the Relation God-Modes in Spinoza." *G. Crit. Filosofia Italia* 8 (1977) 337–44.

de Duve, Christian. *Life Evolving: Molecules, Mind, Meaning*. New York: Oxford University Press, 2002.

Dembski, William A. *The Design Revolution: Answering the Toughest Questions about Intelligent Design*. Downers Grove: InterVarsity, 2004.

Dennett, Daniel C. *Consciousness Explained*. Boston: Little, Brown, 1991.

Donagan, Alan. *Spinoza*. New York: Harvester-Wheatsheaf, 1988.

Drees, Willem. *Religion, Science, and Naturalism*. Cambridge: Cambridge University Press, 1996.

Dupré, John. *The Disorder of Things: Metaphysical Foundations of the Disunity of Science*. Cambridge: Harvard University Press, 1993.

el-Hani, Charbel Nino, and Antonio Marcos Pereira. "Higher-Level Descriptions: Why Should We Preserve Them?" In *Downward Causation: Minds, Bodies and Matter*, edited by Peter Bøgh Andersen, Claus Emmeche, Niels Ole Finnemann, and Peder Voetmann Christiansen, 118–42. Aarhus: Aarhus University Press, 2000.

Elsasser, Walter. *Reflections on a Theory of Organisms*. Quebec: Editions ORBIS, 1987.

Farrer, Austin. *Finite and Infinite*, 2nd ed. London: Dacre, 1959.

Flew, Anthony. *God: A Critical Inquiry*. La Salle: Open Court, 1984.

Ford, Joseph. "What Is Chaos, That We Should Be Mindful of It?" In *The New Physics*, edited by Paul Davies, 346–70. Cambridge: Cambridge University Press, 1989.

Ford, Lewis. *The Lure of God: A Biblical Background for Process Theism*. Philadelphia: Fortress, 1978.

Fowler, Jeaneane. *Perspectives of Reality: An Introduction to the Philosophy of Hinduism*. Portland: Sussex Academic, 2002.

Freeman, Anthony. *The Emergence of Consciousness*. Charlottesville: Imprint Academic, 2001.

Friedman, Joel. "How the Finite Follows from the Infinite in Spinoza's Metaphysical System." *Synthese* 69, no. 3 (1986) 371–407.

Fukuyama, Francis. *The End of History and the Last Man*. New York: Free Press, 2006.

Gadamer, Hans-Georg. *Truth and Method*. Edited and translated by Garrett Barden and John Cumming. New York: Crossroad, 1975.

Gehlen, Arnold. *Man: His Nature and Place in the World*. New York: Columbia University Press, 1988.

Gilead, Amihud. "Spinoza's *Principium individuationis* and Personal Identity." *International Studies in Philosophy* 15 (1983) 41–57.

Gilkey, Langdon. *Naming the Whirlwind: The Renewal of God-Language*. Indianapolis: Bobbs-Merrill, 1969.

Gillett, Carl, and Barry Loewer, eds. *Physicalism and Its Discontents*. New York: Cambridge University Press, 2001.

Gillett, Carl. "Non-Reductive Realization and Non-Reductive Identity: What Physicalism Does Not Entail." In *Physicalism and Mental Causation*, edited by Sven Walter and Heinz-Deiter Heckmann, 19–28. Charlottesville: Imprint Academic, 2003.

Goodenough, Ursula. *The Sacred Depths of Nature*. New York: Oxford University Press, 1997.

Goodwin, Brian C. "On Morphogenetic fields." *Theoria to Theory* 13 (1979) 107–14.

Gregersen, Niels, ed. *From Complexity to Life: On the Emergence of Life and Meaning*. New York: Oxford University Press, 2003.

Griffin, David Ray. *The Reenchantment of Science: Postmodern Proposals*. Albany, NY: SUNY Press, 1988.

———. *Reenchantment without Supernaturalism*. Ithaca, NY: Cornell University Press, 2001.

———. *Whitehead's Radically Different Postmodern Philosophy: An Argument for Its Contemporary Relevance*. Albany, NY: SUNY Press, 2007.

Griffin, David Ray, and Richard Falk, eds. *Postmodern Politics for a Planet in Crisis: Policy, Process, and Presidential Vision*. Albany: State University of New York Press, 1993.

Guessoum, Nidhal. *Islam's Quantum Question: Reconciling Muslim Tradition and Modern Science*. London: I. B. Tauris, 2010.

Gulick, Walter. "Response to Clayton: Taxonomy of the Types and Orders of Emergence." *Tradition and Discovery: The Polanyi Society Periodical* 29, no. 3 (2003) 32–47.

Harré, Rom, and E. H. Madden. *Causal Powers: A Theory of Natural Necessity*. Oxford: Blackwell, 1975.

Harris, Sam. *The Moral Landscape: How Science Can Determine Human Values*. New York: Free Press, 2010.

Harrison, Edward. *Masks of the Universe*. New York: Macmillan, 1985.

Hartshorne, Charles. *The Divine Relativity: A Social Conception of God*. New Haven: Yale University Press, 1948.

Hasker, William. *The Emergent Self*. Ithaca: Cornell University Press, 1999.

Hempel, Carl, and Paul Oppenheim. "Studies in the Logic of Explanation." *Philosophy of Science* 15 (1948) 135–75.

Hefner, Philip. *The Human Factor: Evolution, Culture, and Religion*. Minneapolis: Fortress, 1993.

Hick, John. *An Interpretation of Religion*. New Haven: Yale University Press, 1989.

Hitchens, Christopher. *God Is Not Great: How Religion Poisons Everything*. New York: Twelve. 2007.

Holland, John. *Emergence: From Chaos to Order*. Cambridge: Perseus, 1998.

Johnson, Steven. *Emergence: The Connected Lives of Ants, Brains, Cities, and Software*. New York: Touchstone, 2001.

Kant, Immanuel. *The Groundwork of the Metaphysics of Morals*. Translated by Allen Wood. New Haven: Yale University Press, 2002.

Kaufman, Gordon. "On the Meaning of Act of God." *Harvard Theological Review* 61 (1968) 175–201.

———. *The Problem of God*. Cambridge: Harvard University Press, 1981.

Kauffman, Stuart A. *At Home in the Universe: The Search for the Laws of Self-Organization and Complexity*. New York: Oxford University Press, 1995.

———. "Beyond Reductionism: Reinventing the Sacred." *Zygon: Journal of Religion and Science* 49, no. 4 (2007) 808–28.

———. *Investigations*. New York: Oxford University Press, 2002.

Kellenberger, James. "Miracles." *International Journal for the Philosophy of Religion* 10 (1979) 145–62.

Keller, Catherine. *Face of the Deep: A Theology of Becoming.* London: Routledge, 2003.
Kennington, Richard, ed. *The Philosophy of Baruch Spinoza.* Washington: Catholic University of America Press, 1980.
Kim, Jaegwon. *Mind in a Physical World: An Essay on the Mind-Body Problem and Mental Causation.* Cambridge: MIT Press, 2000.
———, ed. *Supervenience.* Aldershot, UK: Ashgate, 2002.
———. *Supervenience and Mind: Selected Philosophical Essays.* Cambridge: Cambridge University Press, 1993.
Kirkpatrick, Frank G. "Understanding an Act of God." In *God's Activity in the World: The Contemporary Problem*, edited by Owen Thomas, 110–28. Chico: Scholars, 1983.
Kitano, Hiroaki. "Systems Biology: A Brief Overview." *Science* 295 (2002) 1660–64.
Kuhn, Thomas. *The Essential Tension: Selected Studies is Scientific Tradition and Change.* Chicago: University of Chicago Press, 1977.
Lakatos, Imre. "The Methodology of Scientific Research Programs." In *Trinity in Process: A Relational Theology of God*, edited by Joseph A. Bracken and Marjorie Hewitt Suchocki, 133–62. New York: Continuum, 1997.
Laland, Kevin. "The New Interactionism." *Science* 300 (2003) 1877–80.
Larson, David R. "Necessarily, Essentially, Neither or Both: How Does God Love the Universe?" Paper presented to the American Academy of Religion Annual Meeting, 2004.
Laudan, Larry. *Progress and its Problems.* Berkeley: University of California Press, 1977.
Lawrence, David. "The Dialectic of Transcendence and Immanence in Contemporary Western and Indian Theories of God." In *Transcendence and Immanence: Comparative and Multi-Dimensional Perspectives*, edited by Liu Shu-hsien et al., 347–63. Hong Kong: New Asia College, 2001.
———. "Siva's Self-Recognition and the Problem of Interpretation." *Philosophy East & West* 48 (1998) 197–231.
Levine, Michael P. *Pantheism: A Non-Theistic Concept of Deity.* London: Routledge, 1994.
Lewes, G. H. *Problems of Life and Mind.* 2 vols. London: Kegan Paul, 1875.
Lewin, Roger. *Complexity: Life at the Edge of Chaos.* Chicago: University of Chicago Press, 1992.
Lewis, C. S. *Miracles: A Preliminary Study.* New York: Macmillan, 1977.
Lindbeck, George. *The Nature of Doctrine: Religion and Theology in a Postliberal Age.* Philadelphia: Westminster John Knox, 1984.
Lipton, Peter. *Inference to the Best Explanation.* London: Routledge and Kegan Paul, 1991.
Lodahl, Michael. "From God to Creation: Pursuing the Trinitarian Reflections of Gregory of Nyssa as a Critique of *Creatio ex Nihilo*." Paper presented to the American Academy of Religion Annual Meeting, 2004.
Loptson, Peter. "Spinozist Monism." *Philosophia* 18 (1988) 19–38.
Lowe, E. J. "The Causal Autonomy of the Mental." *Mind*, 102 (1993) 629–44.
Lucash, Frank. "On the Finite and Infinite in Spinoza." *Southern Journal of Philosophy* 20 (1982) 61–73.
MacQuarrie, John. *Thinking about God.* London: SCM, 1975.
Marion, Jean-Luc. *God without Being: Hors-texte.* Translated by Thomas Carlson. Chicago: University of Chicago Press, 1991.
Marvin, Walter. *A First Book in Metaphysics.* New York: MacMillan, 1912.
Marx, Karl. *The Portable Karl Marx.* Edited by Eugene Kamenka. New York: Penguin, 1983.

Mason, Richard V. "Spinoza on the Causality of Individuals." *Journal of the History of Philosophy* 24 (1986) 197–210.

McFague, Sallie. *Metaphorical Theology*. Philadelphia: Fortress, 1982.

McLain, F. Michael, and W. Mark Richardson, eds. *Human and Divine Agency: Anglican, Catholic, and Lutheran Perspectives*. Lanham: University Press of America, 1999.

McLaren, Brian. "Everything Must Change: Jesus, Global Crisis, and a Revolution of Hope." September 2, 2007. https://brianmclaren.net/everything-must-change-jesus-global-crisis-and-a-revolution-of-hope/.

Moltmann, Jürgen. *God in Creation: A New Theology of Creation and the Spirit of God*. Minneapolis: Fortress, 1993.

Moreau, Joseph. "Spinoza Est-il Monist?" *Revue de Théologie et de Philosophie* 115 (1983) 23–35.

Morgan, C. Lloyd. *Emergent Evolution*. The 1922 Gifford Lectures. New York: Henry Holt, 1931.

Morowitz, Harold. *The Emergence of Everything: How the World Became Complex*. New York: Oxford University Press, 2002.

Morris, Thomas V., ed. *Divine and Human Action: Essays in the Metaphysics of Theism*. Ithaca: Cornell University Press, 1988.

Murphy, Michael. *The Future of the Body: Explorations into the Further Evolution of Human Nature*. Los Angeles: Tarcher, 1992.

Murphy, Nancey. "Divine Action in the Natural Order: Buridan's Ass and Schrödinger's Cat." In *Chaos and Complexity: Scientific Perspectives on Divine Action*, edited by Robert Russell, Nancey Murphy, and Arthur Peacocke, 325–57. Vatican City State: Vatican Observatory, 1995.

———, ed. *Emergence: From Physics to Theology*. Oxford: Oxford University Press, 2010.

Murphy, Nancey, and William R. Stoeger, SJ, eds. *Evolution and Emergence: Systems, Organisms*. Oxford: Oxford University Press, 2007.

Nagel, Ernst. *The Structure of Science: Problems in the Logic of Scientific Explanation*. London: Routledge and Kegan Paul, 1961.

Nesteruk, Alexei V. *Light from the East: Theology, Science, and the Eastern Orthodox Tradition*. Minneapolis: Fortress, 2003.

Nicolescu, Basarab, and Magda Stavinschi, eds. *Science and Orthodoxy: A Necessary Dialogue*. Bucharest: Curtea Veche, 2006.

Niebuhr, H. Richard. *Love and Justice: Selections from the Shorter Writings of Reinhold Niebuhr*. Edited by D. B. Robertson. Louisville: Westminster/John Knox, 1957.

———. *The Meaning of Revelation*. New York: MacMillan, 1960.

Nielsen, Kai. *God, Scepticism and Modernity*. Ottawa: University of Ottawa Press, 1989.

Nygren, Anders. *Meaning and Method*. Philadelphia: Fortress, 1972.

O'Connor, Timothy. *Agents, Causes, and Events: Essays on Indeterminism and Free Will*. New York: Oxford University Press, 1995.

———. "Emergent Properties." *American Philosophical Quarterly* 31 (1994) 83–98.

Oltvai, Zoltán N., and Albert-László Barabasi. "Life's Complexity Pyramid." *Science* 298 (2002) 750–64.

Pannenberg, Wolfhart. "Der Gott der Geschichte." In *Grundfragen systematischer Theologie: Gesammelte Aufsätze*, vol. 2, 112–28. Göttingen: Vandenhoeck und Ruprecht, 1980.

———. *Systematic Theology*. 3 vols. Translated by Geoffrey W. Bromiley. Grand Rapids: Eerdmans, 1991–98.

Pap, Arthur. "The Concept of Absolute Emergence." *The British Journal for the Philosophy of Science* 2 (1952) 302–11.

Peacocke, Arthur. *All That Is: A Naturalistic Faith for the 21st Century.* Edited by Philip Clayton. Minneapolis: Fortress, 2007.

———. "Emergence, Mind, and Divine Action: The Hierarchy of the Sciences in Relation to the Human Mind-Brain-Body." In *The Re-Emergence of Emergence*, edited by Philip Clayton and Paul Davies, 243–68. Oxford: Oxford University Press, 2006.

———. *God and Science: A Quest for Christian Credibility.* London: SCM, 1996.

———. *Paths from Science towards God: The End of All Our Exploring.* Oxford: One World, 2001.

———. "The Sound of Sheer Silence." In *Neuroscience and the Person*, edited by Robert J. Russell et al., 126–42. Vatican City: Vatican Observatory, 1999.

———. *Theology for a Scientific Age: Being and Becoming Natural, Divine, and Human.* Minneapolis: Fortress, 1993.

Pepper, Stephen. "Emergence." *Journal of Philosophy* 23 (1926) 241–45.

Peters, Ted. "On Creating the Cosmos." Blog Series. https://biologos.org/blogs/archive/series/on-creating-the-cosmos-by-ted-peters.

Pinnock, Clark. *The Openness of God: A Biblical Challenge to the Traditional Understanding of God.* Downers Grove: InterVarsity, 1994.

Placek, Tomasz, and Jeremy Butterfield, eds. *Non-Locality and Modality.* Dordrecht: Kluwer Academic, 2002.

Plato, *The Republic.* Translated by Benjamin Jowett. Hoboken: Capstone, 2012.

Polanyi, Michael. *Knowing and Being: Essays.* Edited by Marjorie Grene. London: Routledge and Kegan Paul, 1969.

———. *The Tacit Dimension.* Garden City: Doubleday Anchor, 1967.

Polkinghorne, John. *The God of Hope and the End of the World.* New Haven: Yale University Press, 2002.

———. *Science and Providence: God's Interaction with the World.* Boston, Kluwer, 1996.

———, ed. *The Work of Love: Creation as Kenosis.* Grand Rapids: Eerdmans, 2001.

Pols, Edward. "Power and Agency." *International Philosophy Quarterly* 11 (1971) 293–313.

Primas, Hans. *Chemistry, Quantum Mechanics and Reductionism: Perspectives in Theoretical Chemistry.* 2nd ed. Berlin: Springer-Verlag, 1983.

Putnam, Hilary. *Reason, Truth, and History.* Cambridge: Harvard University Press, 1981.

Pylyshyn, Z. W. "What the Mind's Eye Tells the Mind's Brain: A Critique of Mental Imagery." *Psychological Bulletin* 80 (1973) 1–24.

Rice, Richard. *The Openness of God: The Relationship between Divine Foreknowledge and Human Free Will.* Minneapolis: Bethany, 1985.

Richardson, Mark, and Wesley Wildman, eds. *Religion and Science: History, Method, Dialogue.* New York: Routledge, 1996.

Ricoeur, Paul. *Conflict of Interpretations: Essays in Hermeneutics.* Edited by Don Ihde. Evanston: Northwestern University Press, 1974.

Ridley, Matt. *Nature via Nurture: Genes, Experience, and What Makes Us Human.* New York: HarperCollins, 2003.

Robert, Jason Scott. *Embryology, Epigenesis, and Evolution: Taking Development Seriously.* Cambridge: Cambridge University Press, 2004.

Rorty, Amélie Oksenberg. "The Two Faces of Spinoza." *Review of Metaphysics* 41 (1987) 299–316;

Russell, Robert J., Nancey Murphy, and Arthur Peacocke, eds. *Chaos and Complexity: Scientific Perspectives on Divine Action*. Vatican City State: Vatican Observatory, 1995.

Sanders, John. *The God Who Risks*. Downers Grove: InterVarsity, 1998.

Sartre, Jean-Paul. *Being and Nothingness*. Translated by Hazel E. Barnes. New York: Citadel, 1956.

Saunders, Nicholas. *Divine Action and Modern Science*. Cambridge: Cambridge University Press, 2002.

Schacht, Richard. "Adventures of Immanence Revisited." *Inquiry* 35 (1992) 69–80.

Schelling, Friedrich Wilhelm Joseph von. *Schellings sämmtliche Werke*. 14 vols. Stuttgart: Augsburg, 1856–61. Vol. 7, 1859.

Schleiermacher, Friedrich. *On Religion: Speeches to its Cultured Despisers*. Translated by Richard Crouter. Cambridge: Cambridge University Press, 1988.

———. *Soliloquies*. Translated by Horace Leland Friess. Chicago: University of Chicago Press, 1926.

———. *Über die Religion*. Philosophische Bibliothek Vol. 139b. Leipzig: Otto Braun edition, 1911.

Schwarz, Hans. *The Search for God*. Philadelphia: Augsburg, 1975.

Searle, John. *The Rediscovery of the Mind*. Cambridge: MIT Press, 1992.

Sheldrake, Rupert. *A New Science of Life: The Hypothesis of Morphic Resonance*. Rochester: Park Street, 1995.

Shirley, Samuel. *Spinoza's Ethics*. Indianapolis: Hackett, 1982.

Soskice, Janet Martin. *Metaphor and Religious Language*. Oxford: Clarendon, 1985.

Sperry, Roger. "Consciousness and Causality." In *The Oxford Companion to the Mind*, edited by R. L. Gregory, 152–66. Oxford: Oxford University Press, 1987.

———. "Mental Phenomena as Causal Determinants in Brain Function." In *Consciousness and the Brain: A Scientific and Philosophical Inquiry*, edited by Gordon G. Globus, Grover Maxwell, and Irwin Savodnik, 161–78. New York: Plenum, 1976.

———. "Mind-Brain Interaction: Mentalism, Yes; Dualism, No." *Neuroscience* 5 (1980) 195–206.

Spinoza, Benedict. *Ethics*. Translated by Samuel Shirley. Indianapolis: Hackett, 1982.

Stace, W. T. "Novelty, Indeterminism, and Emergence." *The Philosophical Review* 48 (1939) 296–310.

Stamm, Erna. *Der Begriff des Geistes bei Schelling*. Göttingen: Franz Rehbock, 1930.

Stern, Robert, ed. *Transcendental Arguments: Problems and Prospects*. New York: Oxford University Press, 1999.

Stone, Bryan P., and Thomas Jay Oord, eds. *The Nature and Thy Name Is Love: Wesleyan and Process Theologies in Dialogue*. Nashville: Kingswood, 2001.

Suchocki, Marjorie Hewitt. *God, Christ, Church: A Practical Guide to Process Theology*. New York: Crossroad, 1989.

———. *The End of Evil: Process Eschatology in Historical Context*. New York: SUNY Press, 1988.

Taylor, Charles. *Sources of the Self: The Making of the Modern Identity*. Cambridge: Harvard University Press, 1989.

Taylor, Mark. *The Moment of Complexity: Emerging Network Culture*. Chicago: University of Chicago Press, 2001.

Taylor, Richard. *Action and Purpose*. Atlantic Highlands: Humanities, 1973.

Tilby, Angela. *Science and the Soul: New Cosmology, the Self, and God*. London: SPCK, 1992.

Select Bibliography

Tillich, Paul. *The Shaking of the Foundations*. New York: Scribner's Sons, 1948.

———. *Systematische Theologie I und II*. Berlin: de Gruyter, 1987.

Tipler, Frank J. *The Physics of Immortality: Modern Cosmology, God and the Resurrection of the Dead*. New York: Anchor, 1997.

Tracy, David. *Blessed Rage for Order*. New York: Seabury, 1975.

Tracy, Thomas. "Particular Providence and the God of the Gaps." In *Chaos and Complexity: Scientific Perspectives on Divine Action*, edited by Robert John Russell, Nancey Murphy, and Arthur Peacocke, 289–324. Vatican City State: Vatican Observatory, 1995.

Wartofsky, Marx W. "Nature, Number and Individuals: Motive and Method in Spinoza's Philosophy." *Inquiry* 20 (1977) 457–79.

Weinberg, Steven. *Dreams of a Final Theory: The Scientist's Search for the Ultimate Laws of Nature*. London: Vintage, 1994.

Wesson, Robert. *Cosmos and Metacosmos*. Chicago: Open Court, 1989.

Westermann, Claus. *Creation*. Translated by John Scullion, SJ. Philadelphia: Fortress, 1974.

Whitehead, Alfred North. *Process and Reality: An Essay in Cosmology*. Corrected edition. Edited by David Ray Griffin and Donald W. Sherburne. New York: Free Press, 1978.

———. *Science and the Modern World*. Lowell Lectures 1925. New York: Macmillan, 1925.

Wiles, Maurice. "Religious Authority and Divine Action." In *God's Activity in the World: The Contemporary Problem*, edited by Owen C. Thomas, 174–92. Chico: Scholars, 1983.

Williams, Bernard. *Ethics and the Limits of Philosophy*. Cambridge: Harvard University Press, 1985.

Wilson, David Sloan. *Darwin's Cathedral: Evolution, Religion, and the Nature of Society*. Chicago: University of Chicago Press, 2002.

Wilson, Edward O. *Consilience: The Unity of Knowledge*. New York: Vintage, 1998.

Wimsatt, William C. "The Ontology of Complex Systems: Levels of Organization, Perspectives, and Causal Thickets." *Canadian Journal of Philosophy*, Supplementary vol. 20 (1994) 192–224.

Yeats, W. B. "The Second Coming." In W. B. Yeats, *The Poems*. New York: Macmillan, 1983.

Yijie, Tang. "The Enlightenment and Its Difficult Journey in China." Translated by Franklin J. Woo, *Process Perspectives* 34, no. 2 (2012) 1–34. <http://www.ctr4process.org/publications/ProcessPerspectives/archive/PP-34.2-Spring2012.pdf>.

Yovel, Virmiyahu, ed. *God and Nature: Spinoza's Metaphysics*. Leiden: Brill, 1991.

———. "Spinoza and Other Heretics: Reply to Critics." *Inquiry* 35 (1992) 81–112.

———. *Spinoza and Other Heretics*. 2 vols. Princeton: Princeton University Press, 1989.

Zizioulas, John D. *Being as Communion: Studies in Personhood and the Church*. Crestwood: St. Vladimir's Seminary Press, 1985.

Books Written by Philip Clayton

The New Socialism: Sacred and Secular Roots of a Transformative Politics Coauthored with Justin Heinzekehr (in preparation).

Now What? Rebuilding the Sacred from the Rubble of God. Coauthored with Claudia Pearce (in preparation).

What Is Ecological Civilization? . . . And Why It May Be the Most Important Idea for the Future of the Planet. Coauthored with Andrew Schwartz. Anoka, MI: Process Century, 2018.

God and Gravity: A Philip Clayton Reader on Science and Theology. Edited by Bradford McCall. Eugene: Cascade, 2018.

Organic Marxism: An Alternative to Capitalism and Ecological Catastrophe. Coauthored with Justin Heinzekehr. Claremont: Process Century, 2014.

= Chinese translation, trans. Xian Meng, Guifeng Yu, and Lixia Zhang (Beijing: The People's Press, 2015): [美]菲利普克莱顿贾斯廷海因泽克著；孟献丽于桂凤张丽霞译：《有机马克思主义——生态灾难与资本主义的替代选择》，北京：人民出版社，2015年。

= Spanish translation by Gorgias Romero García: *Marxismo Orgánico: Una alternativa al capitalismo y a la catástrofe ecológica*. Claremont: Process Century, 2016.

Confronting the Predicament of Belief: The Quest for God in Radical Uncertainty. Edited by James W. Walters, Philip Clayton, and Steven Knapp. Edmond: Crowdscribed, 2014.

The Predicament of Belief: Science, Philosophy, Faith. Coauthored with Steven Knapp. Oxford: Oxford University Press, 2011.

Religion and Science: The Basics. London: Routledge, 2011. Second edition, 2018. Swedish translation, forthcoming.

Transforming Christian Theology: For Church and Society. Minneapolis: Fortress, 2009. Danish translation, 2011. Korean translation, 2012.

In Quest of Freedom: The Emergence of Spirit in the Natural World. Göttingen: Vandenhoeck & Ruprecht, 2009. German translation: *Die Frage nach der Freiheit. Biologie, Kultur und die Emergenz des Geistes*. Vandenhoeck & Ruprecht, 2009. French translation: *Les origines de la liberté. L'Émergence de l'esprit dans le monde naturel*. Translated by Allesia Weil. Paris: Éditions Salvator, 2012.

Adventures in the Spirit: God, World, Divine Action. Minneapolis: Fortress, 2008. Chinese translation, underway.

Mind and Emergence: From Quantum to Consciousness. Oxford: Oxford University Press, 2004. German translation: *Emergenz und Bewusstsein. Evolutionärer Prozess und die Grenzen des Naturalismus*. Göttingen: Vandenhoeck & Ruprecht, 2008.

Romanian translation, 2008. Spanish translation, 2011. Chinese translation, 2015. Korean translation, in process.

The Problem of God in Modern Thought. Grand Rapids: Eerdmans, 2000.

Books Written by Philip Clayton

God and Contemporary Science. Edinburgh: Edinburgh University Press, 1998.

Das Gottesproblem, vol. 1: *Gott und Unendlichkeit in der neuzeitlichen Philosophie*. Paderborn: Ferdinand Schöningh Verlag, 1996.

Explanation from Physics to Theology: An Essay in Rationality and Religion. New Haven: Yale University Press, 1989. German translation: *Rationalität und Religion. Erklärung in Naturwissenschaft und Theologie*. Translated by Martin Laube. Paderborn: Ferdinand Schöningh, 1992.

Books Edited by Philip Clayton

Thought at the Edge of Collapse: Reception and Response in the work of Philip Clayton. Festschrift edited by Zachary Simpson (in preparation).

Narrowing the Freedom Gap: Genetics, Neurology, and Faith. Coedited with Jim Walters (in preparation).

How I Found God in Everyone and Everywhere: An Anthology of Spiritual Memoirs. Coedited with Andrew M. Davis. New York: Monkfish, 2018.

Socialism in Process. Coedited with Justin Heinzekehr. Anoka, MI: Process Century, 2017.

Panentheism across the World's Traditions. Coedited with Loriliai Biernacki. New York: Oxford University Press, 2013.

All That Is: A Naturalistic Faith for the Twenty-First Century. Essays in honor of Arthur Peacocke. Minneapolis: Fortress, 2007.

Practicing Science, Living Faith: Interviews with Twelve Leading Scientists. Coedited with Jim Schaal. New York: Columbia University Press, 2007.

The Oxford Handbook of Religion and Science. With associate editor Zachary Simpson. Oxford: Oxford University Press, 2006. Arabic translation, 2014.

The Re-Emergence of Emergence: The Emergentist Hypothesis from Science to Religion. Coedited with Paul Davies. Oxford: Oxford University Press, 2006.

Evolution and Ethics: Human Morality in Biological and Religious Perspective. Coedited with Jeffrey Schloss. Grand Rapids: Eerdmans, 2004.

Science and Beyond: Cosmology, Consciousness and Technology in the Indic Traditions. Coedited with Roddam Narasimha, B. V. Sreekantan, and Sangeetha Menon. Bangalore: NIAS, 2004.

In Whom We Live and Move and Have Our Being: Panentheistic Reflections on God's Presence in a Scientific World. Coedited with Arthur Peacocke. Grand Rapids: Eerdmans, 2004.

Quantum Mechanics. Vol. 5 of *Scientific Perspectives on Divine Action,* coedited with Robert J. Russell, John Polkinghorne, and Kirk Wegter-McNelly. Vatican City: Vatican Observatory, and Berkeley: Center for Theology and the Natural Sciences, 2002.

Science and the Spiritual Quest: New Essays by Leading Scientists. Coedited with Mark Richardson *et al*. London: Routledge, 2002.

The Theology of Wolfhart Pannenberg: Twelve American Critiques. Coedited with Carl Braaten. Minneapolis: Augsburg, 1988.

Index

Abrahamic traditions, 82, 95, 193
Agape, 94-95,
Agnostic, 31, 35, 84, 87-88, 162,
Alexander, Samuel, 131, 80, 185-88, 193, 241
Allah, 41, 230, 274
Altruism, 74-75, 80-81, 163
Anonymous Christians, 319
Anthropic Principle, 18
Antinomian, 30
Apologetics, 83, 88
Apophatic, 30, 257
Aquinas, Thomas, 61, 171, 216, 249
Aristotle, 4, 9, 40, 151-52, 176-77, 184, 186, 216, 226, 284
Assemblies of God, 262
Atheism, 21, 60, 105, 113, 116, 118, 215, 220, 249, 258, 300
Augustine, 23, 111, 141, 293

Barth, Karl, 10
Beliefs, 3-7, 12, 17, 20, 31, 33-35, 39, 43-46, 50, 53-54, 69, 74-77, 82-84, 88, 96-100, 118, 247, 262, 266-68, 270, 273-74, 276, 278-80, 285, 300, 304, 307-11
Bergson, Henri, 178, 180
Bible, 34, 38-39, 46, 51, 115, 178, 262, 270-71, 274-75, 286, 288, 290, 306-307
Big Bang, 14, 16, 151 178, 205, 217, 238
Biochemistry, 161, 198, 235-36
Biology, 21, 28, 39, 41, 43, 74-76, 79, 81, 118, 121, 148, 158, 161-63, 167, 169-73, 177, 180, 184, 187, 191, 197-99, 203, 234-37, 240, 311
Bracken, Joseph, 123, 130, 139-42, 178
Brahman, 42-43, 129, 135-36
British Emergentists, 153, 169, 178, 180, 182,
Broad, C. D., 179
Buddhism, 5, 18, 35, 44-46, 53, 247

Capitalism, 295-97, 301-02
Catholicism, 46, 261-62, 309, 315

Causality
 Divine, 116, 215, 220, 234, 241
 Emergent, 234-235
 Final, 151-52, 176-77, 216, 235, 237. *See also* Teleology
 Mental, 92, 124, 154, 174-75, 179, 188, 197, 232-36, 239-41, 243-44, 252-55, 257-58
 Scientific, 215-22
Charismatic, 48, 262
Christianity, 10-11, 37, 39-40, 44, 46, 49, 75, 81, 83, 85, 87, 99, 153, 179, 247-50, 258, 264, 274, 279, 283, 287, 289, 292-93, 306-11, 313, 315
Christology, 129, 131, 204, 207-08, 227, 281
Church, 46, 48, 140, 204, 208-09, 217, 261-71, 275, 278, 281-84, 287, 289-93, 304-907, 309, 310-315
Classical philosophical theism, 70-71, 118, 128, 261
Classical Western theism, 110, 113-14, 116, 137
Cobb, John B., 138, 282, 291
Compatibilism, 232
Complexity, 44, 78-79, 108, 125, 132, 149-50, 158-161, 163-65, 167-68, 171, 181, 183, 186, 193-94, 202, 205, 208, 210, 235-37, 243-44
Contingency, 78, 138, 143-44
Cosmology, 14-19, 21-24, 35, 39, 66, 217
Cosmos, 16-19, 23-24, 129, 154, 267
Creatio ex Nihilo, 114, 138, 141-44
Culture, 10, 12, 14, 25-27, 30, 34, 49, 51-54, 79, 81-83, 90, 121, 191, 202, 244, 262, 271, 274, 292, 297, 299, 301, 304, 307-12

Death, 49, 54, 86-87, 99-100, 106, 109, 114, 136, 208, 210-11, 282, 286, 293, 308, 311
Dipolar theism, 123, 209
Diversity, 10, 20, 31, 46, 108, 129-30
Darwinism, 28, 41, 45, 74-75, 81, 165, 177, 180, 203

333

Index

Davies, Paul, 18, 22, 124, 130, 176, 189, 193, 205
Dawkins, Richard, 28–29, 47—48, 74–75, 202, 267
Deacon, Terrence, 163, 1609, 177, 200-02, 205
Dennett, Daniel, 47, 191
Descartes, René, 68, 103, 121–22, 151, 164, 190
Divine action, 34, 70, 99, 116, 118–19, 123–25, 131–32, 138–39, 196, 204-08, 215–25, 228–34, 238–53, 256–57, 304
DNA, 162, 183, 225
Doubt, 60, 82–87, 96, 97–98, 161, 179, 185, 187, 256, 258, 264, 274–279, 304, 313
Downward causation, 149, 151, 165–66, 168, 172, 183–84, 187, 197, 202, 236
Drees, Willem, 21–22
Dualism, 42, 114–15, 147–48, 154, 156, 158–59, 166, 175, 182, 185, 232, 238–41

Eastern Orthodoxy, 139, 296
Ecclesiology, 131, 204, 209, 281
Ecosystem, 43, 53–54, 79, 113, 125, 137, 168–71, 174, 201, 203, 235, 296, 299, 300
Einstein, Albert, 148, 285
Élan vital, 180
Embodiedness, 77
Emergence
    Strong, 147, 153–54, 156, 164, 174–75, 179, 181–82, 202, 236, 239–41
    Weak, 154-156, 174, 179, 185–88, 236, 241
Emergentist monism, 165, 190
Epigenesis, 171, 197, 235
Epiphenomenalism, 174
Eschatology, 24, 131, 204, 210–11, 282
Ethics, 14, 19,30, 39, 54, 61, 64, 73–76, 81, 107–08, 119, 244, 289, 308, 312,
Evil, 48, 85, 115, 119, 139, 206, 211, 275
Evolution, 14, 21, 23, 35, 37–45, 50, 69, 74–76, 81, 90–91, 121, 141, 147–50, 154, 156–58, 163–67, 169–75, 178–82, 185–86, 189, 191–94, 197, 201–205, 208–09, 226–28, 236–37, 239, 241, 262, 269, 289, 293, 297, 311
Experience, 4–8, 13, 26–32, 34, 41–45, 47, 59–61, 64–66, 69, 72, 77–81, 88, 90–95, 98-9, 122, 124, 130–31, 140–43, 171–74, 178–79, 185, 190, 194, 203, 206, 209–11, 236, 241, 243–44, 257–58, 261, 266–67, 270–72, 273, 276, 278, 282–83, 286, 296, 310–14
Explanandum, 3–4, 8
Explanans, 3-4, 8
Explanation, 3–8, 12–14, 21, 32, 43, 60–62, 72, 74–76, 80, 85, 89–90, 93, 105, 108, 116, 124, 147–48, 150, 152, 157, 166, 169–74, 180,184–85, 189, 195, 198, 203, 216–17, 220–21, 230–32, 235–38, 243, 249–50, 311

Fallibilism, 99
Falsification, 14, 61, 311
Feedback loops, 161, 168
Freedom, 25, 61, 67–68, 71–72, 80–81, 83, 115, 134, 136, 141, 144, 232, 247–48, 254, 302, 307
Ford, Lewis, 208, 216
Freud, Sigmund, 14, 26, 104–05, 248
Fundamentalism, 30, 221, 225, 258, 274, 276, 306

Genotypes, 173
German idealism, 106, 118, 147,
God-world relation, 119–22, 131, 139–40, 143–44, 194, 206, 234, 236, 239–40, 255–56, 281
Goodness, 23, 94, 206, 218, 236, 305
Goodwin, Brian C., 167, 19–200
Gould, Stephen Jay, 170
Grace, 39, 100, 128, 130, 135, 144, 206, 257, 277–79, 291, 309, 316
Gregersen, Niels Henrik, 128, 192–93, 205
Griffin, David Ray, 127, 131, 140, 194, 234, 299

Harris, Sam, 21–22, 51
Hartshorne, Charles, 123, 133, 138, 140, 194
Heaven, 19, 27, 38, 87, 114, 226, 278, 282–83, 290
Hefner, Philip, 143, 223
Heidegger, Martin, 64, 72, 105, 140
Heisenberg, Werner, 20, 149, 218
Hermeneutics, 62, 209
Hick, John, 30
Hierarchies, 125, 161, 168
Hinduism, 42–43, 247
History, 9–10, 14, 30, 33, 38, 41, 45, 59, 61–63, 69, 77–78, 81–82, 86, 92, 97, 99, 104, 106, 110, 115, 121–22, 131, 134, 137, 148, 151–55, 165–66, 169–72, 174, 177–79, 184–85, 190–91, 194–95, 202, 208–11, 220–21, 225–27, 234–35, 241, 244, 258, 266, 269, 274, 279, 283, 286, 288, 290, 295–302, 312–13, 315
Hitchens, Christopher, 49
Holism, 20, 49, 151, 167, 198–99
Homeostasis, 174
Homo sapiens, 33, 72, 202
Hope, 43, 48, 50, 66, 77, 88, 96–97, 99, 100, 105–06, 110, 132, 137, 139, 170–71, 21,

218, 222, 246, 251, 269, 282, 287, 290, 293, 316
Human genome project, 19, 148, 170
Hume, David, 60, 63, 94, 249

Imago Dei, 144, 210, 238-39, 254, 258
Immanence, 65, 103-09, 124-25, 223, 240
Infinity, 65, 70-71, 108, 115, 122, 141
Intersubjective, 5-8, 69
Irreducibility, 26, 149-50, 157-58
Islam, 37, 40-42, 44, 46, 50, 52, 177

James, William, 178-79
Jesus Christ, 37, 99, 143, 210, 248, 268, 281-82, 284, 306
Judaism, 10, 37-39, 49, 86, 247

Kant, Immanuel, 9, 20-21, 31, 60, 63-64, 103-06, 108, 122, 147, 179, 191, 222, 237, 248
Kaufman, Gordon, 59, 224, 227, 250, 256
Kauffman, Stuart, 158, 167, 199, 202, 249
Keller, Catherine, 144
Kenosis, 94, 138, 143, 209, 284. *See also* Self-emptying
Kierkegaard, Soren, 5
Knapp, Steven, 82, 89, 96, 132, 258

Leibniz, Gottfried Wilhelm, 94, 103, 185
Lewes, George Henry, 152, 177
Long-suffering, 206
Love, 27, 34, 48, 52, 67, 73, 78, 80-81, 94-95, 99-100, 125, 138, 140-44, 154, 206, 208, 284, 290-91, 293, 309

Materialism, 13, 16, 34, 40, 46, 164, 180, 215, 267
Marx, Karl, 28, 51, 104-05, 153, 179, 248, 270, 295-303
McKnight, Scot, 282
Melanchthon, Philip, 204
Metacosmos, 16-17
Metaphysics, 14, 17, 20-22, 30, 40, 59, 61-65, 72, 77, 103, 105, 107-08, 119-22, 131, 139, 155, 159, 144, 147, 181, 185, 192, 215, 264
Micro-physics, 157, 174
Middle ages, 9, 177
Mind, 11-13, 26, 28-30, 33-34, 37, 42, 45-46, 70, 73, 78, 84-85, 90-95, 100, 107, 114-16, 124, 128-29, 120, 131-32, 136, 143, 147, 151-53, 156-57, 164, 166-67, 174, 175, 177-88, 191-93, 196, 202-03, 205, 208-10, 218, 224, 233, 236, 238-40,

147-48, 152, 253, 256-57, 261, 273-74, 276, 283-84, 292, 294, 313, 315
Modernity, 83, 273, 309, 313
Mohammed, 41
Moltmann, Jürgen, 111, 130, 143
Morality, 21, 74-76, 80-81, 288
Morgan, C. Lloyd, 169, 180-82, 187
Mormon, 264
Morris, Simon Conway, 167
Multiverse, 34, 91-94
Murphy, Nancey, 10, 132, 193, 195, 219, 221-25

Nagel, Thomas, 140, 180
Natural theology, 6-7, 10, 22
Naturalism, 13, 21-22, 25, 34-35, 40, 46, 60-61, 85, 193-94, 234, 246-47, 249, 258, 310-11
Nature, 5-6, 9, 12, 14, 17-18, 20-24, 26-27, 29, 31-32, 34, 40-43, 46, 49, 52-53, 62-63, 66, 68-74, 76, 78, 80-81, 83, 87, 90, 92, 94, 99, 103, 105-08, 112, 115, 117, 120, 122-26, 129, 131, 135, 138-44, 150, 159, 161, 163, 165, 168, 171-73, 179-80, 185, 187, 190-95, 197, 200, 202, 204-10, 221-24, 226, 228, 233-34, 237, 242-46, 249-50, 252, 264, 279, 283-85, 290-91, 312-13
Neo-pagan, 264
New Testament, 9, 99, 115, 227, 270, 285-86, 290,
Newton, Isaac, 20, 23, 147-48, 224, 229, 233, 243
Nisus, 186-87
Novelty, 77, 94, 157-58, 169, 182, 185, 187, 210,

Ontological, 112, 115-17, 123-24, 136, 140, 148-52, 154, 156, 163, 165-66, 190-91, 194, 202, 205, 215,
Ontotheology, 9, 21, 72, 231, 239-40, 243, 254-55
Oord, Thomas Jay, 81, 130, 138, 174
Organic Marxism, 295-303
Organisms, 14, 113, 125, 152, 156, 166, 168, 170-74, 177, 186, 198-99, 207, 223, 237, 311

Panentheistic analogy, 116-17, 121, 124, 255
Panentheism
　Emergentist, 125, 127
　Eschatological, 127
　General, 16, 32, 65, 67-68, 70-72, 103, 110-16, 105-07, 109-31, 133-35, 137-44, 205-07, 211, 194, 215, 221, 226, 247, 256

Panentheism *(continued)*
  Neo, 127
  Open, 138–39, 141–44
  Pansacramental, 127
  Pansynthetic, 127
  Participatory, 127, 282
  Sapiential, 127
  Trinitarian, 127, 143
Pannenberg, Wolfhart, 69, 205, 210, 216, 234
Pantheism, 21, 105–12, 117, 122, 128, 137, 194, 215, 220, 256
Peacocke, Arthur, 27, 70, 118, 125–27, 132, 165, 194, 206, 223–28, 246, 248–58
Peirce, Charles Sanders, 123
Pentecostal, 48, 262
Persuasion, 233–34
Peters, Ted, 19
Phenomenology, 45, 65, 144, 178
Phenotype, 171, 173
Philosophers, 25, 40, 48–52, 61, 63, 68, 93–94, 97, 108, 120, 131, 134, 137, 152, 154, 160, 161–62, 173, 182, 185, 187, 235, 273–74. *See also* Philosophy
Philosophy, 6–7, 9–10, 14, 19, 29, 40–42, 49, 52, 61, 65, 67–69, 72, 76, 80, 82, 105–06, 108–10, 118, 120, 123, 125, 134, 136–37, 139, 152–54, 158, 60–62, 165, 168, 173, 176–88, 188, 192, 215, 232, 237–39, 268, 274, 278, 282, 288, 292, 299–300, 304. *See also* Philosophers
Physicalism, 34, 147–50, 154–59, 172, 175–76, 187–88
Physics, 11, 14, 17–22, 32, 61, 72, 79, 111, 116, 118, 147–50, 154, 156–57, 161, 163, 167, 170, 172, 174, 178, 181–82, 187–90, 198–99, 207, 218–21, 223–25, 231, 239–43, 264, 311
Plasticity, 169
Plotinus, 61, 152, 177–78
Pluralism, 13, 17, 61–62, 108, 122, 166, 190, 309
Plurality, 62–63, 85–86, 274
Pneumatology, 131, 204, 208, 281. *See also* Spirit
Polanyi, Michael, 182–84
Polkinghorne, John C., 127, 143, 211, 219–21
Popper, Karl, 51, 60
Postmodernism, 9–13, 83, 104, 273–279, 287, 299–301
Pre-modern, 83, 274
Primordial, 93, 141, 143, 194, 206, 210
Process philosophy, 118, 139, 211, 234, 300
Providential, 34, 93, 225

Qualitative, 112, 116, 124, 131, 174, 193, 241

Qur'an, 6, 34, 40–41, 46, 52, 270, 274

Rahner, Karl, 305
Rāmānuja, 127, 134–37
Rationality, 5, 7–8, 60, 65, 72, 88, 96, 159
Reductionism, 13, 18, 40, 44, 147–48, 176–77, 203, 244, 249, 276. *See also* Reductionistic
Regulatory systems, 173, 197
Religion, 1–14, 18–22, 24–42, 44–46, 48–55, 69, 72, 74–75, 77, 83, 86–87, 93–94, 104, 117, 143–44, , 189, 192–93, 203, 218, 239, 246–47, 261–65, 271, 274, 276, 278, 283, 286, 288, 291–92, 297, 308–11
Reproduction, 148, 170, 172–73
Resurrection, 37, 86, 100, 207–10, 227–28, 306
Righteousness, 34, 206, 308
Romanticism, 26, 32
Rorty, Richard, 104–06, 109

Salvation, 5, 104, 210, 281, 290–93
Saunders, Nicholas, 250–51
Schleiermacher, Friedrich, 25–27, 32, 117, 304–05, 307–08
Scientia, 14
Scientism, 28, 267, 273–74
Scientists, 12, 19–20, 25–26, 29, 35, 39, 42–45, 49–53, 61, 85, 148, 158, 160–62, 174, 188, 217, 228, 232–33, 237, 244, 274, 297, 303, 311
Scripture, 6, 10, 34, 43, 50, 135–36, 204, 269–70, 274, 277, 282, 286–88, 306, 310, 312–14
Self-emptying, 143, 207, 281–87, 290. *See also* Kenosis
Skepticism, 17, 19, 59–62, 65, 103, 162, 271, 295, 310, 315
Socialism, 302
Sociality, 79, 186
Sociology, 14, 121, 244
Soteriology, 131, 210, 281
Southern Baptist Convention, 263
Space-time, 149, 185–87
Spinoza, Benedict, 67, 73, 103–09, 122–23, 129, 215, 248
Spirit, 5, 14, 17, 20, 22, 25–27, 30, 39, 41–43, 46–47, 49–50, 69, 86, 100, 108, 113–15, 120, 132, 134, 136–39, 143, 153, 157, 161, 178–79, 187, 196, 204–05, 207–09, 228, 238–39, 246, 255, 263, 267, 270–71, 274–75, 277, 281–82, 285, 287–90, 293, 304, 307, 314–15. *See also* Pneumatology
Suchocki, Marjorie, 211, 282, 314
Supernaturalism, 194, 234, 311
Survival, 38, 81, 168, 172, 220

Index

Systematic Theology, 9–16, 69–71, 118, 204–05, 211
Systems Biology, 171–72, 197, 203

Taoism, 18
Teleology, 17, 40, 187, 216. *See also* Causality, Final
Temporality, 77
Theologians, 5, 8, 10–11, 14, 16–24, 30, 50, 59, 63–66, 111, 115–17, 119–25, 131, 136, 138–42, 161–62, 204, 206–11, 216–18, 221–22, 228, 230–35, 250, 266–268, 279, 284, 291, 305–07, 311, 313, 315
Tillich, Paul, 71–72, 93, 114, 210–11, 305, 308, 315
Tracy, Thomas F., 221, 228
Tradition, 5–14, 20–22, 27, 30, 33–35, 37–47, 49–55, 60–61, 63–65, 69–71, 77, 81–88, 91, 93, 95–96, 99, 104–05, 111–12, 117–21, 125–26, 130–34, 137, 139–41, 144, 151, 162, 166, 178–79, 192–94, 204–10, 215, 220–22, 230, 233, 237–41, 246–49, 255, 258, 262, 270–71, 274, 282, 286, 292, 299–300, 304–08, 311–15
Transcendence, 20, 32, 64–65, 72, 95, 103–04, 106–07, 124–25, 238, 242, 300, 311
Transcendentalism, 69
Trinity, 10, 69, 115, 141, 281, 284

Truth, 5, 7–8, 10–12, 15, 19, 22, 26, 29–31, 40, 51, 55, 59, 61–63, 72, 75, 77, 83–84, 118, 123, 195, 209, 247–48, 276, 287, 298, 301, 307, 309–10, 312–13, 315

Ultimacy, 63, 82, 84, 88, 113, 137
Ultimate Reality, 34, 42, 46, 84–85, 87, 89–95, 133–34, 267, 276

van Huyssteen, Wentzel, 10
Veracity, 206
von Schelling, Friedrich Wilhelm Joseph, 67–73, 93, 107, 131

Wesleyan Quadrilateral, 270, 310–12
Wesleyans, 270, 310, 312
Whitehead, Alfred North, 93, 123, 131–32, 138–41, 178–79, 187, 194, 211, 216, 246
Whole-part Influence, 168, 173–74, 185, 226, 252–58
Wiles, Maurice, 219, 224, 227, 250, 256
Wilson, David Sloan, 28, 75
Wilson, E. O., 30, 170
Wisdom, 40, 206, 284, 291
Wissenschaft, 14

Yovel, Yirmiyahu, 104–08.

www.ingramcontent.com/pod-product-compliance
Lightning Source LLC
Chambersburg PA
CBHW060454300426
44113CB00016B/2582